S0-BLE-577

From Models to Modules:

Studies in Cognitive Science from the McGill Workshops

Edited by

Irwin Gopnik
Myrna Gopnik

McGill University

THEORETICAL ISSUES IN COGNITIVE SCIENCE
ZENON W. PYLYSHYN, Series Editor

ABLEX PUBLISHING CORPORATION
NORWOOD, NEW JERSEY

Printed in the United States of America.

Library of Congress Cataloging-in-Publication Data
Main entry under title.

From models to modules.

(Theoretical issues in cognitive science)
Bibliography: p.
Includes index.
1. Cognition. 2. Psycholinguistics. I. Gopnik, I. (Irwin) II. Gopnik, Myrna.
BF311.F75 1986 153 85-20952
ISBN 0-89391-355-3

Ablex Publishing Corporation
355 Chestnut Street
Norwood, New Jersey 07648

Contents

Preface

The 15 papers in this volume are the result of a series of Cognitive Science Workshops held at McGill University during 1982 and 1983. The workshops were organized by members of the McGill Cognitive Sciences Group under the chairmanship of Myrna Gopnik and Carl Frederiksen, and were funded by a grant from the Alfred P. Sloan Foundation.

There were seven Workshops, each organized around one of the following topics: language acquisition and development; text and text processing; computer chess; grammars, parsers, and language comprehension; scientific reasoning and problem solving; language and the brain; and semantics. There were about 40 presenters and commentators in all, and a large, varied, but overlapping, audience made up predominantly of linguists, psychologists, philosophers, computer scientists, and neurologists.

It would be foolishly utopian to expect an overall theoretical framework for the cognitive sciences to emerge from such an interchange. What does emerge, however, are a number of suggestions, tentative though they may be, for constructing isomorphisms between various forms and levels of cognition, and a few shrewd guesses about where isomorphisms are likely, or unlikely, to be found. These positive and hopeful results led the organizers of the Workshops to feel that it would be worthwhile to share a gleaning of the available papers with their fellow cognitivists.

The Editors wish to acknowledge the invaluable organizational assistance of Mike Dillinger and the secretarial assistance of Anna Dillinger. A special word of thanks must also go to the Sloan Foundation whose generosity made the Workshops possible and to Gordon A. Maclachlan, Vice-Principal Research and Dean of the Faculty of Graduate Studies, for his moral and financial support.

Introduction

A convenient way to characterize Cognitive Science is by partitioning it into three hierarchical levels:

1. philosophical analysis
2. functional processes
3. physical instantiations

These levels correspond roughly to the major disciplines which have come together to trade insights and paradigms:

1. philosophy
2. linguistics and psychology
3. neuro-science

The appropriate activity for level 1 is ordinarily abstract, theoretical, argumentative, i.e., nonempirical—although it often constructs its theses around the empirical findings from the other two levels. Level 2 is ordinarily empirical, i.e., observational and experimental, but most often in a "black-box" style of examining inputs and outputs rather than directly accessing mechanisms. Even aphasia and other neuro-linguistic and neuro-psychological research seems to fall primarily in this category. Level 3 is simply neurophysiology at whatever level of generality it is available. Unfortunately, it is rarely available in a form that can provide models for the two levels above it. Note that computer science has not been included as a distinct element in this scheme. Although it pervades Cognitive Science, it seems much more to provide a source of models and metaphors for the other levels than a constitutive level of its own.

The papers in this volume all fall within levels 1 and 2, although many make reference to level 3 in a more or less speculative way. And many of the papers are pervaded by the vocabulary of computation, although none of them actually compute. The clearest example of level 1 is perhaps the paper of Belnap, which provides a semantic analysis of questions in natural language within the logic of a Montague grammar. Although there is no observation or experimentation as such, there is the rich source of introspective data available to a native speaker. Bunge's paper is also philosophical, but in a very different sense. Rather than arguing for a specific analysis, it argues for a general orientation to linguistic research which would bring it into neurology on one side and sociology on the other. Buckingham's paper similarly deals with "framework" issues, providing a review of the issues and metaphors which relate neurology, psychology, and linguistics. Schnitzer's proposal for a "neutral monism" also provides a review of the mind–body problem as affected by such things as aphasia research and stratificational grammar. It is an effort, echoed by some of the other papers, to transform the mind–body problem from the philosophical, strictly speaking, to the empirical, loosely speaking. A brief summary review of these issues is provided by Paradis.

The papers which are most explicitly "linguistic" are perhaps those of Grimes, Olson, and Torrance, and of Hall and Nagy. However, it is noteworthy that they all situate the linguistic data in the broader framework of speech act theory and metacognition rather than in a more narrowly technical grammatical approach. The most typically "psychological" of the papers are two which forward the modularity of mind hypothesis: Seidenberg and Tanenhaus's and Frazier's. The former concentrates on lexical processing, while the latter focuses on the module by module translation of competence into performance.

Finally, there are the papers which depend most heavily on the approaches of Computer Science and Artificial Intelligence, although each paper displays an approach distinctly different from the others. For example, Bruce uses the concept of "robot" to model "mutual belief" in human discourse, whereas Arbib uses computational models to describe mechanisms in the perception and production of language. MacWhinney and Anderson, on the other hand, explain that they are using computational simulation of syntax and lexical structure purely for the goal of attaining maximum explicitness. For Soloway and Ehrlich, it is programming itself which provides the data for exploring problem solving, rather than the other way around, as it is in the other papers. This is similar to the way Bordage uses medical diagnosis as a source of data for understanding problem solving. Both of these papers also give promise of some sort of practical applications to improve human problem solving of a fairly pragmatic and direct kind.

To conclude this brief tour of the papers which follow, just a brief word about the Table of Contents. The Editors believe that all of these papers are contributions to a fully *integrated* Cognitive Science which has not yet come into existence. Rather than impose an artificial, and premature, unity by some ad hoc means of classification, we have presented them largely but not precisely in the same order and grouping as in the original Workshops which were the occasion, presumably, for their first appearance.

PART I

LANGUAGE ACQUISITION AND DEVELOPMENT

Chapter 1

The Acquisition of Grammar*

Brian MacWhinney
John Anderson
Carnegie-Mellon University

1. INTRODUCTION

In this paper, we give a brief sketch of a model that gives a reasonably explicit account of the shape of the fundamental principles underlying language acquisition. We believe that, unless solid bridges are built between child language research and cognitive science in general, there is a real danger that many of the advances made in the area of child language research will be lost. Roger Brown (1977) explains our worries:

> Developmental psycholinguistics has enjoyed an enormous growth in research popularity...which, strange to say, may come to nothing. There have been greater research enthusiasms than this in psychology: Clark Hull's principles of behavior, the study of the Authoritarian personality, and, of course, Dissonance theory. And in all these cases, very little advance in knowledge took place....A danger in great research activity which we have not yet surmounted, but which we may surmount, is that a large quantity of frequently conflicting theory and data can become cognitively ugly and so repellent as to be swiftly deserted, its issues unresolved.

Brown's warning should not go unheeded. In order to avoid the fate of becoming "ugly," child language research must become more firmly grounded on general principles deriving from cognitive psychology and linguistic analysis. There is continuing research aimed at grounding language acquisition theory on principles of generative grammar (Wexler & Culicover, 1980). Such work is typically well-grounded in linguistic theory, but often fails to pay attention to the overall architecture of human cognition. Our own approach is to work within the constraints of both linguistic theory and cogni-

* Thanks to Joseph Stemberger for providing us with examples of speech error types. Thanks to Pat Langley for providing criticisms on an earlier draft of this chapter.

tive theory. Unlike Chomsky (1980), we assume that human cognition is unitary and that language is not a special "organ" of mind. We believe that language is special in the sense that it, more than any other system, has utilized virtually every major aspect of the general cognitive system (excepting perhaps aspects of visual processing). Because language has commandeered so much of the mind, its structure is quite complex. Despite this complexity, the pervasive utilization of old cognitive structures by the linguistic function means that language processing is governed by basic principles of cognitive processing and that the acquisition of language can be explained in terms of general learning principles. The overall framework we will adopt is that of production system theory (Newell & Simon, 1972). The particular instantiation of production system theory we support is that proposed by Anderson (1983) as ACT*.

Our approach constitutes a merger of two major lines of research on the acquisition of language by the young child. The first is John Anderson's (1977, 1981, 1983) LAS model of the acquisition of the rules of syntax. The second is Brian MacWhinney's (1975, 1978, 1982, in press) dialectic model of the acquisition of lexical structure. These two lines of research have made remarkably similar assumptions about the nature of the learning process and the overall cognitive system, while focusing on largely separate aspects of the language acquisition. Both of us have found that neither of these problems can really be addressed independently of the other. Issues of segmentation and the control of grammatical morphemes have played an important role in Anderson's formulation of LAS, whereas problems in affix order and case are centrally involved in MacWhinney's attempts to account for the develoment of morphology. It is clear that, from the viewpoint of the theory of language development, the formulation of a model that deals adequately with both syntax and word formation would be a major advance.

The model developed by MacWhinney for lexical processing is a parallel interactive activation system. Anderson, in developing a model of syntactic processing, emphasized the use of goals to impose a sequential structure on the application of productions. However, we have discovered that these two models are really quite alike. MacWhinney also requires a sequential discipline to organize the sequencing of phonemes and to permit orderly access to the lexicon. Moreover, the pattern-matcher for ACT*'s production system is a parallel interactive system, with many properties in common with MacWhinney's. By making a few significant changes in the architecture of ACT*, a single system can account for both syntactic and lexical processing. This merged model will enable us to better understand the way in which lexical processing interfaces with syntactic processing.

We believe that computational simulation is the most appropriate format for the building of the needed bridges between child language research and cognitive science in general. A computational model is being utilized in this research not as a replica of the human being, but as a means of attaining explicitness in psycholinguistic research. The authors are well-aware of the problems inherent in the artificial intelligence approach to cognition (Chandrasekaran & Reeker, 1974; Dresher & Hornstein, 1976). No one should misconstrue the ontological or phenomenological (Wittgenstein, 1953) status of computer simulations. In particular, no one should attempt to view the computer as a brain. Simulation on present-day machines cannot duplicate mental processes (Hinton & Anderson, 1981), it can only mimic them Anderson, 1978). However, even this mimetic function allows us to compare alternative models by measuring their relative goodnesses-of-fit to a set of data. In this sense, current computational models are best viewed as devices for the evaluation of theoretical claims.

Our own research program builds upon an increasingly active current of research in the formal representation of language acquisition. Much of this research has focused on topics in grammatical inference and induction defined rather strictly within automata theory (Biermann & Feldman, 1972; Blum & Blum, 1975; Feldman, 1972; Gold, 1967; Horning, 1969; Pao, 1969). We take this work as representing the basic logical framework against which models of language acquisition must eventually be represented. There have also been formal demonstrations of learnability (Anderson, 1976; Baker, 1977; Culicover & Wexler, 1977; Hamburger & Wexler, 1973, 1975; Pinker, 1982; Wexler & Culicover, 1980; Wexler, Culicover, & Hamburger, 1975; Wexler & Hamburger, 1973) articulated within the framework of particular models of language structure and processing. Of equal importance is the tradition that has focused on the nature of learning heuristics (Block, Moulton, & Robinson, 1975; Braine, 1971; Harris, 1977; Kelley, 1967; Kiss, 1973; Klein & Kuppin, 1970; Langley, 1982; Levelt, 1975; MacWhinney, 1978; Miller, 1967; Reeker, 1976; Siklossy, 1972), often with a particular eye toward simulating data from child language acquisition. These various currents and their results are fully reviewed in MacWhinney (1978), Pinker (1979), and McMaster, Sampson, and King (1976). Unfortunately, we do not have space here to detail our indebtedness to each of these authors.

The following five sections summarize our model of language use and acquisition. The five topics that organize the presentation are as follows:

1. *General Architecture:* Here we review the general architecture of the ACT* system with a special focus on the parallel interactive processes underlying pattern matching.
2. *Lexical Activation:* We show how the various modes of lexical processing (rote, analogy, combination) can be understood within the single framework of a theory of parallel activation.
3. *Syntactic Processing:* We argue that the ordering of elements in sentence production is controlled by a serial goal-based syntactic process.
4. *Monitoring:* We show how the system operates in four modes to detect errors in comprehension and production.

5. *Acquisition:* Finally, we explain the development of new abilities in both lexical and syntactic processing in terms of a set of nine modes of acquisition.

2. GENERAL ARCHITECTURE

In ACT* behavior is characterized as being under the control of production rules which are condition-action pairs. For purposes of exposition let us consider the following production rules:

P1: IF the goal is to communicate: {[+obj][+anim][+fur][+canine]}
THEN set as subgoals to:
1. generate /d/ in onset position
2. generate /aw/ in nucleus position
3. generate /g/ in coda position

P2: If the goal is to communicate: [+obj],[+anim],[+fur],[+feline]
THEN set as subgoals
1. generate /k/ in a onset position
2. generate /ae/ in nucleus position
3. generate /t/ in coda position

For short-hand we will denote these rules as:

P1: [+obj][+anim][+fur][+canine]----->/d/ /aw/ /g/

P2: [+obj][+anim][+fur][+feline]----->/k/ /ae/ /t/

The semantic features given above are somewhat fanciful, but our argument does not depend on particulars of semantic analysis. The critical observation is simply that there will be partial overlap among the features underlying *dog* and *cat.*

Let us suppose the child's goal is to communicate the features [+obj], [+fur], [+anim], and [+feline]. Then there would be a partial match to the conditions of the two productions above. In ACT*, these features would be activated, and activation would spread from them to the two productions. Each production would be activated to the degree its conditions were matched by active features. In this example, P2 would be more activated. We believe that there is an inhibitory competition among productions like these which overlap in their conditions. Because of this, P2 would inhibit P1 and the spekaer would product /k/-/ae/-/t/ rather than /d/-/aw/-/g/.

In the theory developed in Anderson (1983), the productions would wait until a clear winner was determined in the inhibitory competition. Then the winning production would fire, and its action would be executed. The evidence from speech errors (Garrett, 1980; Stemberger, 1982) indicates that this architectural principle is wrong. Rather, the actions of the productions should be activated to the degree their production is active. By allowing for relative degrees of activations of actions, we can account for blends such as /d/-/ae/-/t/, where the /d/ comes from *dog* and the /ae-t/ comes from *cat*. Thus, rather than having productions fire in an all-or-none manner as in Anderson (1983), we now allow that productions be allowed to fire to varying intensities. This introduction of relative degree of production activation is a significant augmentation to the production system architecture. Other standard assumptions that go along with the notion of varying levels of activation are: (a) that, at any time, any cognitive unit or element has a nonnegative level of activation associated with it; (b) that each unit has a resting level or strength; (c) that elements that reach a certain threshold of activation become "working memory" elements and continue to provide activation for a certain time; and (d) that spread of activation occurs in parallel both top-down and bottom-up.

The following factors determine the activation of various production rules:

1. *Strength of rules:* The strength of rules reflects the frequency and recency of their successful firing. Stronger rules receive more activation. To illustrate this, note that common irregulars like *went* tend to resist overregularization more than less common irregulars like *mend* (MacWhinney, 1978).
2. *Specificity:* The matcher rewards rules for having features matched. Thus, in word recognition, *cat* is better than *at* as a match to /k/-/ae/-/t/, since it matches three segments and *at* only matches two. A special case of this is the superiority of portmanteau forms to their analytic counterparts. In French, both *du* and *de + le* compete for the masculine partitive. However, because *du* is more specific, it gets more activation. Without support from "specificity," the less frequent form *du* might never win out over *de + le*. But, because of specificity, it is generally the case that rote forms dominate over combinatorial forms (MacWhinney, 1978, 1982).
3. *Accuracy:* The matcher penalizes rules for having too many features, i.e., for having features that are not active in working memory. Thus, when matching to /k/-/ae/-/t/, the item *bat* will be penalized for the failure to match a /b/.
4. *Data refractoriness:* The pattern matcher attempts to assign each active element in working memory to a single rule. This means that, if a particular element matches more than one rule (e.g., [+fur] matches P1 and P2), there will be an inhibitory relationship set up among these elements. This is what prevents multiple competing rules from applying to the same goal. As McClelland and Rumelhart (1981) note, this inhibitory relationship makes "the rich get richer and the poor get poorer" in that good guesses are supported and poor guesses eliminated.

5. *Top-down support:* If there is considerable activation of a particular action element, that activation will also support the production patterns that led to it. As we will see, such support can lead to the phenonema of haplology, malapropism, and analogy.

3. LEXICAL ACTIVATION

In the 1978 version of the dialectic model, MacWhinney proposed that lexical items could be generated by either *rote, analogy,* or *combination.* We will refer to the general process of lexical generation as *spellout.* In addition to these three basic processes, the process of *selection* works when two mutually exclusive alternatives have been activated. In this section, we will see how rote, analogy, combination, and allomorphic selection can be put into the framework of an interactive activation system such as the one described above. In effect, these modes of activation fall out as consequences of the principles governing pattern matching in ACT*.

One very important aspect of our current approach is the way in which we understand the interface between serial and parallel processes. We are hypothesizing that lexical activation occurs in parallel, and that much of syntactic processing is controlled by a serial mechanism. To interface these processes, we allow syntax to activate a data structure that controls phonological generation. No serial control is enforced while activation is taking place within an arena. Once units have been activated to confidence level, the data is then read out into articulation.

A great deal of child language theory has been based on the analysis of lexical errors made by children. In this section we will refer to errors made by children and errors made by adults. Later we will discuss these various error types as important phenomena that any model of natural language acquisition and processing most be able to explain. Our examples of speech error types are all taken from Stemberger (1982) and, in many places, our analysis closely parallels that of Stemberger (1982).

3.1 Rote

Rote application occurs when all the output segments of a given form are activated by a single production. For example, when lexicalization converts the meanings underlying *dog* to /dawg/ it must do so by rote, since the morpheme *dog* is an unanalysable unit. Productions P1 and P2 from the previous section instantiated rote rules for *dog* and *cat.* MacWhinney (1978, 1982) has surveyed a variety of developmental phenomena that indicate that higher-level forms such as complex words and phrases are often used in a rote fashion. Examples of these phenemona include:

1. Children often use words in phrases before they use them independently. Thus, *I could easily do that* can occur before *could,* and *can't* can occur before *can.*

2. It often happens that children start to make overgeneralizations for forms that they earlier produced without error. Thus, at first, children say *went* and *jumped;* later they say **goed* and *jumped.* This suggests that *jumped* is being controlled first by rote and then by combination.
3. Children often use both words and longer phrases without superfluous markings. Thus, *say bye-bye* may mean "bye-bye", *hat on gone now* may mean "hat gone now", and "brush your teeth" may mean "toothbrush".
4. Failing to analyse phrases may also lead children to use pronouns incorrectly, as in *I carry you* instead of *you carry me.*
5. Children may use affixes and other operators in contradictory ways, as in *shoes on off.*
6. Sometimes, children may produce whole sentences far in advance of their usual productions, as in *No, Mommy, I don't want to go to bed* produced by MacWhinney's son Ross during the two-word-stage.
7. In both children and adults, frequent words are less subject to overregularization than infrequent words. Thus, *went* resists **goed* better than *thrust* resists **thrusted.*
8. Related items have an intonational/clitic integration. For example, *want to* and *let me* have become *wanna* and *lemme.*
9. The semantic class of an item may not be coded at first. This can lead to *rices* for "rice grains", or *many lions,* then **many lion,* and then *many lions* again.
10. Correct wholes may precede their analysed pieces. For example, *drop* may be used causatively before the appearance of *I made it fall* or *I felled it.*
11. At first, polysemy may not be detected in compounds. Thus, MacWhinney's son Ross confused his friend Matt with the doormat and the button of a shirt with the button on a television.

3.2 *Analogy*

In a system with interactive activation within a given arena, analogy can occur when one or more rhyming items obtain enough top-down support to activate output segments that would not otherwise be activated. For example, the production of the /z/ of /p/-/l/-/u/-/g/-/z/ may arise from top-down support for /r/-/u/-/g/-/z/, /b/-/u/-/g/-/z/, and so on. These forms also receive activation from [+pl], giving them enough total activation to then activate the post-code segment /s/ which is not competing with any other segment. In this way, P3, P4, and P5 can work in concert to produce the output /p/-/l/-/u/-/g/-/z/.

P3: [+obj][+round][+blocks]-----> /p/-/l/-/u/-/g/

P4: [+obj][+soft][+covers][+pl]-----> /r/-/u/-/g/-/z/

P5: [+obj][+anim][+small][+crawls]-----> /b/-/u/-/g/-/z/

Note that both the partial semantic match and top-down feedback from the /u/ and /g/ in P3 contribute to the activation of P4 and P5. The more productions like P4 and P5 that get activated, the stronger the analogy.

3.3 *Combination*

In ACT*, combination occurs when the input causes two or more rules to fire. If we look at the activation of a form like "dogs," we see that it can be produced by either rote or combination. In fact, for regular forms, the two modes of processing converge on the same solution. The rules below would implement the combination route to pluralization:

P6: [+obj][+canine][+furry]----->/d/-/aw/-/g/

P7: [+pl]----->/z/,/s/,/i/-/z/

P7 is actually an abbreviation for the following series of productions:

P7 ′: [+pl]----->/z/

P7 ′ ′: [+pl]----->/s/

P7 ′ ′ ′: [+pl]----->/iz/

Of course, since P7 ′, P7 ′ ′, and P7 ′ ′ ′ differ in strength, the elements on the right-hand side of the abbreviated rule P7 also differ in strength.

3.4 *Selections*

Within this same interactive production framework, we can also illustrate the operation of rules governing the selection between alternative segments of morphophonemes. Following Hooper (1976) and Hudson (1980), allomorphic variation is viewed as based on morphophonemic alteration. In the current model, selections on a given level are bound to items on that level. Thus, morphophonological selections are bound to morphemes, phonological selections are bound to segments, and syntactic selections are bound to relational features. Morphophonological selections serve to boost the activation of one of the alternatives in a morphophoneme. Consider the rule for the /f/-/v/ alternation in English plurals. here P10 converts the /f/ to /v/:

P8: [+human][+female][+married]----->/w/-/al/- coda/f/, coda/v/

P9: [+pl]----->/-s/ or /-z/ or /-iz/

P10: coda/f/, coda/v/+[+pl]----->/coda/v/

In P8, coda/f/ receives stronger activation than coda/v/, so that it would normally be the winner. However, P10 gives /v/ additional activation to overcome the activation of the /f/. Rules like P10 can be stated with a variety of levels of generality by conditioning them on (a) segments, (b) competitions between segments, and (c) morphemes. In languages like Hungarian, rules such as P10 can be bound to a whole series of alternative affixes and alternative stems, thereby demonstrating a certain limited productivity. Even in English, P10 applies not only to *wife,* but also to *knife, life, leaf,* and so on.

Phonological selections operate much like morphophonological selections, except that they are conditioned on segments rather than morphemes. For example, the change of an /n/ to a /m/ in Hungarian *honve:d---> homve:d* can be controlled by P13 in conjunction with P11 and P12.

P11: coda/n/--->coda[+dental] coda[+voiced] coda[+continuant] coda[+nasal]

P12: onset/v/--->onset[+labiodental] onset[+voiced] onset[+cont.] onset[+fric.]

P13: coda[+dental]+onset[labiodental---->coda[+labial]+onset[+labiodental]

3.5 *Cooperation and Competition*

It is worth noting that the four modes of activation—rote, combination, analogy, and selection—can cooperate or compete. For example, rote, analogy, and combination can each cooperate to activate the plural form /p/-/l/-/u/-/g/-/z/. In cases like this, where all of the rules agree on the items being activated, we do not expect to see any errors. In fact, rules may disagree and we will still see no error, if the strongest rules are also the correct rules. Far more interesting are the cases where disagreement leads to error, since these tell us something about competition processes that are usually masked by correct performance. Three types of errors can be traced directly to competition between lexical items. These include *head-on blends,* a sub-type of blending we call *insertion,* and *semantic extension.*

3.5.1 Head-on Blends. When two competing items fail to suppress each other, they end up activating their respective segments. The problem of resolving the competition then falls on the shoulders of phonological activation. In such cases of fight-to-the-finish, head-on, competition, some segments may come from one morpheme and some from another. Consider this example:

P14: [+gustatory][+property]...----->f l a v o r

P15: [+gustatory][+property]...----->t a s t e

If these two rules are approximately equally active, we can get a mixture of their two actions such as *flaste.* In the current model, each of the segments in these productions is actually being given a full autosegmental positional characterization. Thus, both the /fl/ of *flavor* and the /t/ of *taste* are defined as onsets of the first syllable. Thus, these two segments are competing with each other. Similarly, the /st/ of *taste* is competing with the /v/ of *flavor.* The /r/ of *flavor* is competing with an empty second syllable in *taste*. For brevity, these syllable/position/slot characterizations of segments are being omitted.

Blends occur when two items are competing for the same slot and neither can achieve dominance. Children make blends just as adults do (MacWhinney, 1974; Leopold, 1937–1949), indicating that head-on competition between content words is fairly basic to the system. Examples of blends from Stemberger (1982) include: Stiff—stuck—stuff it in this box. (stick/stuff); it removes the dirst. (dirt/dust); Look at him proon himself. (groom/preen).

3.5.2 ***Insertion.*** Competition can also lead to the insertion of a whole morpheme into a position where it is not directly competing with other morphemes. In general, this means that closed-class morphemes can intrude themselves in this way, whereas competition between open-class morphemes, which function as the nuclei for lexical arenas, leads to head-on blending. Adult errors of this type, with the insertions marked by parentheses, include *ingredients(es), seven-day-(year)-old baby, landed(ed), you needed (a) bilateral damage, we just put it in (with) the cage,* and *I've been (keep) thinking that.* Children do a lot of this too. English examples include *foots(es), sevens(es), mommy get (it) ladder,* and *me and Ross (and I).* Some Hungarian examples are *pingvink(ek)* and *ram(om)(ra).* A French example is *mon (mien de) chapeau (a moi).* In general, insertions occur when the competing units are able to open up structures that are not competing for the same positional slot. When competing structures are targeted for the same position, we will find blends rather than insertions.

3.5.3 ***Semantic Extension.*** Sometimes, the wrong lexical item can be retrieved on the basis of a partial match. For instance, consider the following overlapping rules:

P16: [+covering][+poss-animal][+strands]-----> hair

P17: [+covering][+poss-animal][+barbs]-----> feather

P18: [+covering][+head-loc][+strands]-----> hair

Rules P16 and P18 are two rules for *hair,* one for animals in general and one for the top of human heads while P17 is a rule for feather. One might assume that, if one's goal was to describe feathers on the head, P16 and P18 might in combination overrule P17 and lead to the production of *hair.* If this happens, it would be a *semantic extension.* Semantic extensions include case errors, antonym substitutions; within-class errors, errors based on perceptual similarity, functional errors, and so on. Although semantic extensions are not rare in adults, a truly huge number of semantic extensions have been reported from children. In deliberate attempts to elicit extensions, researchers have found up to 40% extensions. Even in free-speech corpora, very high levels have been reported from some children.

3.6 Top-down Support

In comprehension, top-down support is spread from the meanings being activated back down to the morphemes matching those meanings. In generation, activation spreads from the sound segments being activated back up to the morphemes matching the output. Thus, the equivalent of top-down support in generation is "bottom-back" support. Three types of speech errors indicate that items that are activated for production feed activation back up to the morphemic and semantic levels. These three types are: semantic extensions within idioms, malapropisms, and haplologies.

3.6.1 Semantic Extensions Within Idioms. For semantic extensions to occur within idioms, there must be some top-down support. This is because, in the context of the idiom, the word being replaced does not have its usual meaning. Examples of such errors are *I'm in the store for a parakeet* for *I'm in the market for a parakeet* and *It was skinnily disguised as...* for *It was thinly disguised as...* The idiom can be represented by a rule like P19:

P19: [+state][+description][+desire][+purchase]--->"be" "in" "the" "market" "for"

Here the words in quotes are taken to be concepts or prepackagings of semantic material. The item "market" reactivates its component pieces by P20:

P20: "market"--->[+public[+place][+purchasing]

These features then give top-down support for "store" which replaces "market" in the output. Semantic extensions within idioms have never been reported for children.

3.6.2 Malapropisms. Further evidence for top-down support comes from klang-associations or malapropisms such as *excavator* for *executor.* For further examples see the footnote. Examples from Stemberger (1982) include *you used coupons* for *you used croutons, Rape! Murder! Plunge!* for *Rape! Murder! Pillage!, There was a meeting in Toyota* for *There was a meeting in Kyoto,* and *of getting 'em sick to test their reproductive sickness* for *of getting 'em sick to test their reproductive success.* There are very few reports of true malapropisms in children. It is true that children make errors like *Judas Asparagus* for *Judas Iscariot,* but in children such errors are usually due to misperception of some new word.

3.6.3 Haplology. Consider the following set of rules:

P21: [+desire]...----->/n/-/i/-/d/

P22: [+past]----->/t/, /d/, or /i/-/d/

Acting directly, P21 and P22 would lead to the correct form *needed.* However, in cases where P22 failed to fire in time or with sufficient strength, the principle of top-down support would allow the /d/ in /n/-/i/-/d/ to be matched to the /d/ in P22. This would then "use up" the past feature, according to the principle of data refractoriness, and block additional application of P22. The output in this case would be *need,* rather than *needed.* Both adults and children produce many haplologies of this sort and languages have developed a variety of specific ways of dealing with this pervasive tendency to haplology (Menn & MacWhinney, 1984).

4. SYNTACTIC PROCESSING

What was described in the previous section was a model of how lexical items are generated and how lexical errors arise in children and adults. This account based on the work of MacWhinney. A recent detailed update of that work is given in MacWhinney (in press). What we will describe in this section is Anderson's theory of syntactic control of sentence production. We can think of syntax as a hierarchical control system that sequentially orders the lexicalization of individual lexical items. The architectural principles are identical to those we used for the lexical component. Anderson's theory is given a fairly thorough exposition in Chapter 7 of Anderson (1983). Here we will just present an overview of its main points.

4.1 Free and Bound Rules

As with the lexical component, there are a set of rules which decompose higher level goals into lower-level goals. Although the principles governing rule structure are similar, syntactic rules make far more extensive use of hierarchical control than do lexical or morphological rules. Consider this rule:

P23: IF the goal is to describe a proposition involving a relation between an agent and an object
THEN set as subgoals to:
1. lexicalize the agent,
2. lexicalize the relation,
3. lexicalize the object.

This rule underlies the canonical subject-verb-object order of active English sentences. Such a rule sets subgoals corresponding to the phrase structure of language. Basically, phrase structure is the goal structure produced by syntactic productions. General rules like P23 make use of conditions based on semantic features such as [+agent] and [+object]. Rules of this type are what MacWhinney (1982) has called "lexically-free" syntactic rules.

Many rules make mention of particular lexical items. MacWhinney (1982) treats these as "lexically bound." Examples of such rules include:

P24: IF the goal is to lexicalize a constituent and the listener has heard the constituent mentioned,
THEN set as subgoals to:
1. activate "the"
2. lexicalize the constituent

P25: IF the goal is to lexicalize an item and the item is a unitary concept
THEN set as subgoals to:
1. activate the sound of the item

P26: IF the goal is to describe a relation and it is an ongoing action and the action is currently happening
THEN set as subgoals to:
1. activate "is"
2. lexicalize the action
3. activate "ing"

Rules like P25 above provide the bridge between the syntactic component and the lexical component by achieving lexical look-up. This provides the index to lexical productions like P1 and P2. Together these rules can generate a sentence like *The dog is chasing the cat.* Note that rules like P26 provide for control of discontinuous elements by goal embedding. Interfacing such productions with a parallel mechanism requires the marking of places in syntactic rules where "pushes" are made to separate lexical arenas. When processing is complete in a given lexical arena, a "pop" occurs, and the material in that arena is then sent back to the matrix production for compilation.

4.2 Transformations

Transformations can be understood as operations on goal trees such as the one formed by the firing of P23-P26. First, planning productions operate to produce a goal structure, and then transformations reorganize them. The following is an example of the planning production that would underlie the generation of the question *Is the dog chasing cat?*

P27: IF the goal is to question the truth of a proposition
THEN set as subgoals to:
1. plan the communication of the proposition
2. move the element coding tense to the beginning
3. execute the plan

This production would plan the generation of the declarative sentence, then transform it to question form, and then actually produce the transformed sentence. Thus, ACT*s planning and transformation processes underlie the transformational component of English.

We realize that this formulation of transformations is much different from that in recent versions of standard theory, where a single transformation is allowed to move anything and where filters and constraints limit the varieties of derived structures. We agree with the emphasis on stating constraints on the grammar. (In fact, the rule types we allow are limited to lexical mapping rules like P1, selection or allomorphy rules like P10, and three types of syntactic rules: lexically-bound rules, free rules, and class rules.) However, transformations occupy a somewhat different role within our psycholinguistic approach, since we see transformations are operating in a "metaprocedural" fashion upon the basic output of the grammar (as in subgoal 1 of P 27).

4.3 *Compilations of Transformations*

For even fairly complex structures, speakers are able to generate output directly from phrase structure without utilizing explicit on-line transformations (Bresnan, 1982). In both the dialectic model and ACT* this occurs as the result of a compilation process which can "compile out" the explicit planning and transformation. Compilation of one version of the question transformation would produce a rule of the form:

P28: IF the goal is to question the truth of a proposition between an agent and an object and the relation describes an ongoing action and the action is currently happening

THEN set as subgoals

1. To activate "is"
2. To lexicalize the agent
3. To activate the name for the relation
4. To activate "ing"
5. To lexicalize the object.

In this case, information controlling the activation of the verb auxiliary "is" has migrated to the main generation production. The previous production had planned a sentence, transformed it, and then executed it; the current production directly generates the question. Such a compiled production makes possible more automatic and less resource-demanding sentence generation. Forming such compiled productions is one of the nine acquisitional modes we will discuss later.

4.4 *Syntactic Errors*

Anderson (1983) ignored the impact of interactive activation in his exposition of the structure of the syntactic component. Without considering interactive effects, it is difficult to account for certain types of speech errors in which whole morphemes are either lost or misplaced. However, the current formulations of production action and competition can be used to explain both morpheme loss and morpheme misplacement. In both children and adults, closed-class items are lost far more frequently than open-class items, despite the fact that closed-class items are more frequent and hence inherently stronger. We view the loss of closed-class items as a result of the binding problem that arises during the transfer from serial to parallel control.

Morpheme misplacements include transpositions, anticipations, and perseverations. The mechanism underlying each of these types is the same. If there are two simultaneous goals to activate two lexical terms, it is possible to have the description of one be invoked through partial matching in the context for the other. This will produce transpositions with affix stranding, as in these examples from Stemberger (1982): *he doesn't have any closets in his skeleton* for *he doesn't have any skeletons in his closet,* or without stranding, as in *there's a beard hanging from your hair* or *there's a hair hanging from your beard.* Anticipations such as *I got a paper on my test* for *I got an A on my paper* or *how good is that for?* for *how long is that good for?* seem to begin as transpositions. However, when the speaker reaches the point where the second word is being produced, s/he inserts an associate of what was originally the second element, rather than inserting the original first element. Perseverations, on the other hand, are more likely to involve exact repetitions as in *the bed was lying on the bed* for *the bed was lying on the book* or *raccoons sometimes eat raccoons* for (raccoons sometimes eat frogs).

Morpheme loss occurs most often when a closed-class item does not reach selection threshold by the time its open-class item is read. Examples of morpheme loss with the missing items enclosed in parentheses include: *I just wanted to (ask) that, the points distribute the (electricity) out, you don't have to worry (about) that, see what (the) child does, one strategy for do(ing) everything,* and *he relax(es) when you go away.* Children also leave out items. However, it is difficult in child data to distinguish loss from nonacquisition.

5. MONITORING

So far, we have described how the lexical and syntax components work. Now we turn to questions of learning and development. Specifically, how are these syntactic and lexical rules acquired? A crucial claim in the dialectic model is that learning proceeds on the basis of identification of some error, i.e., some mismatch between the child's system and new data s/he is processing. Monitoring looks for two things: completeness and accuracy.

5.1 Completeness Monitoring

When people are talking, they can check to see if what they have said fails to include a part of what they wanted to say. When we detect such omissions, we may retrace or restart our utterances. However, if we have not yet acquired the needed item, we must simply confirm our desire to learn it. When people are listening, they can check to see if there is material in the verbal message that is unfamiliar. In either case, the language user is able to detect the existence of new and unfamiliar lexical items. By accepting partial regularities (MacWhinney, 1983; Menn and MacWhinney, in press), speakers indicate that they do, in fact, check to see if what they are going to say includes all of what they intended to say.

5.2 *Accuracy Monitoring*

Even when monitoring detects no mismatch between the verbal message and the situation, it may be able to detect formal inadequacies in the verbal message. This can occur in either production or comprehension. In production, the generation of a combinatorial or analogic form can facilitate retrieval of a weak rote item. Children can then check to see if there is a discrepancy between the weak rote receptive form and the combinatorial expressive forms. This mode of monitoring turns out to be quite effective for morphophonological acquisition (MacWhinney, 1978). However, applying accuracy monitoring above the level of the word requires that there be long rote units. In comprehension, these length limitations may be relaxed. While listening to incoming sentences, the language learner uses his system to generate his own versions of the target sentences. If these match the actual input, no error is present. If they do not match, and if the child places trust in the input, s/he must then pass the mismatch on to acquisition. This mode of monitoring is extremely powerful, since it provides acquisition with both new formal structures and interpretations of those structures. When accuracy monitoring works in comprehension, it can allow the child to outgrow even persistent, self-taught errors. Monitoring during comprehension is the main mode of monitoring in the ACT* stimulation of language acquisition.

6. *ACQUISITION*

In acquiring language, the child's task is to formulate a set of rules that can produce sentences appropriate to the speech community. Some of these rules are lexical rules and some are syntactic rules. Some are highly general and some are quite specific. In this section, we will examine a set of nine acquisitional strategies which, when taken together, can allow the language learner to acquire the lexical and syntactic rules of his language. These strategies are linked together in terms of the overall dialectic.

6.1 *Lexical Rules: Amalgam Acquisition*

When monitoring for completeness, the child may note a spatiotemporal contiguity between a phonological cluster produced by another speaker and some meaning cluster. When this occurs, the child can associate the phonological cluster to the meaning cluster as a new lexical item. What is important here are the principles that govern clustering or segmentation on the phonological and the semantic levels. On the phonological side, the claims are (a) that clustering is determined by intensity, pitch, and juncture; (b) that recent segments and stressed segments are stored most clearly; and (c) that presentation of a single intonational group in isolation enhances acquisition by precluding any need for segmentation. The idea of early words as phonological clusters is supported by a variety of acquisitional phenomena discussed in MacWhinney (1978):

1. When morphemes appear in several allomorphic shapes, the child tends to take the citation form as basic. This suggests that children are picking up words from utterances where the word is being produced by itself.
2. Affixes are acquired quite early, earlier than adpositions, but their first uses indicate that they function as integral parts of the stems with which they were learned. (See the discussion of rote forms in section 3.1.)
3. The importance of phonological packaging is reflected in the fact that children tend to preserve stressed syllables and final syllables in newly learned words.

On the semantic side, the assumption is that children are attempting to acquire words for meanings that they want to express and for which they think there ought to be a word. Clark (1982) calls this the principle of "conventionality" and holds that the child realizes that "for certain meanings, there is a conventional word or word-formation device that should be used in the language community."

6.2 *Inflectional Rules: Component Analysis*

When monitoring for completeness, the child may note that a word contains noncomprehended segments. If situational clues are present, the child can link this noncomprehended section to the semantic clue. This analysis of components out of amalgams makes the default assumption that words are compositions of continuous pieces. A variety of reports indicate that, in fact, reanalysing his own data from Mayan, as well as Brown's (1973) data on English, Pye (1979) has shown that the order of acquisition of grammatical morphemes in both English and Mayan is better predicted by ease of segmentability than by either semantic complexity or frequency.

6.3 *Syntactic Rules*

When monitoring for completeness, the child may understand, say, two words, but not have a rule to govern their syntactic relation. When this occurs, the child forms a new rule on both the free and bound levels. Rules on the free level must be formulated in terms of already available features and units. Rules on the bound level are formulated in terms of lexical items. Finally, in ACT*, rules may be formulated in terms of formal syntactic classes. For a complete discussion of these three levels of syntactic rules, details on the structure of each, and the evidence supporting the importance of each type, please consult MacWhinney (1982).

6.4 *Strengthening*

Strengthening serves to identify the correct rules and increase their probability of application. Every time a rule or item is used during either expression or reception and no error results, it gains in strength. Whenever a rule or item applies unsuccessfully, it loses strength. Frequency of correct application is an important factor in accounting for the development of both items and rules. In regard to lexical items, MacWhinney (1978) has shown that frequent forms tend to resist morphophonological overregularizations. Thus, in both children and adults, errors like *goed* are relatively less frequent than errors like *felled.* In languages that have extensive allomorphy, it is generally true that the allomorph that is overgeneralized is the one which is most frequent and, hence, strongest. There are now a total of 14 examples from different languages supporting this observation. In regard to rules, MacWhinney (1978) demonstrated that the order of acquisition of 15 rules in Hungarian morphophonology was closely correlated with their relative order of frequency of correct application. In other languages, detailed analyses of this type have not yet been conducted, but it has been reported that rules affecting affixes are generally acquired before rules affecting stems, apparently because of the fact that individual affixes are much more frequent that individual stems. In the area of semantics, similar effects have been reported. For example, the most frequently overextended polyseme of the Hungarian denominative verbalizer *-ol* is the agentive polyseme, which is also the most frequent in the language. In syntax, the complement structure for common verbs like *tell* is overgeneralized to replace that of less frequent verbs like *promise* (Chomsky, 1969).

6.5 *Generalization*

Generalization collapses many specific rules into a single general rule. For example, the child may have the adjective "good" encoded in two forms, one for the singular as in "good girl" and one for the plural as in "good girls". When the child realizes that these two forms are equivalent, s/he achieves a generalization. If this is done generally across all adjectives, many forms will be merged into a single rule. To take another example, in Hungarian the rule for final-a-lengthening may initially be stated to apply only when the suffix is the plural /-Vk/. When the child realizes that the rule applies with all suffixes that begin with vowels or deletable vowels, s/he achieves a significant generalization.

6.6 *Discrimination*

Discrimination adds extra features to overly general rules. For instance, if there is a rule that activates the same verb form in present or past, two different versions of it might be produced, one with a test for present tense and the other with a test for past tense. Whereas in generalization the focus is on the detection of extraneous conditions in rules, in discrimination the focus is on missing conditions in rules.

6.7 *Proceduralization*

Anderson, Greeno, Kline, and Neves (1981) underscore the importance of (pre)compilation of highly specific rules in achieving accuracy and automaticity. One compilation process is called proceduralization. It takes a general rule and makes it specific to a particular circumstance of application. So, for instance, one can imagine the following lexical rule:

P29: IF the goal is to communicate a feature set and a sound-structure has been used to communicate that feature set
THEN set as subgoals to communicate the components of that sound-structure.

Thus, if the speaker recalls hearing /d-a-d/ to communicate {[+parent] [+male]} this would lead to the subgoals of generating /d/, /a/, and /d/. However, through practice proceduralization will form a version of the rule specific to this lexical item:

THEN set as subgoals to:
1. activate /d/ in onset position
2. activate /a/ in nucleus position
3. activate /d/ in coda position

Because all of the subgoals here involve lexical activation, proceduralization can make P30 fully parallel.

6.8 *Composition*

The other compilation process is composition. It combines the effect of a number of rules into a single rule. Again, it occurs with practice. Thus, P23 and P26 given earlier might be composed into the following rule:

P23: IF the goal is to describe a proposition involving a relation between an agent and an object and the relation describes an ongoing action and the action is currently happening
THEN set as subgoals to:
1. lexicalize the agent,
2. activate "is"
3. lexicalize the action
4. activate "ing"
5. lexicalize the object

The effect of both proceduralization and composition is to make rapid, special-purpose rules. They serve to make the process of language generation more and more automatic. They also help the system in recovering from overgeneralization. Butler and MacWhinney (in press) have noted that composition may lead the child into self-taught errors. For example, composing attempts to add the regular past suffix to irregular verbs will lead the child to learning forms like **bringed* and **catched* by rote.

6.9 Inference

Bates and MacWhinney (1982) stressed the importance of functional characterizations of syntactic classes. There is evidence that children not only are able to infer the class of a word from cooccurrence data, but even can override semantics in placing items into classes. For example, Katz, Baker, and Macnamara (1974) found that, beginning around 17 months, girls who were given a proper name for a doll learned this name better than girls who were given a common noun. In the proper noun frame, girls were told that the doll was called "Zav"; in the common noun frame they were told that the doll was "a zav." Thus, even at this early age, children seem to realize that names with articles are common nouns and names without articles are proper nouns. This ability to infer the semantics of words on the basis of cooccurrence continues to develop. By age 8, Werner and Kaplan (1950) were able to show in their classic "corplum" experiment that children could acquire many aspects of the semantics of abstract nouns from highly abstract sentence contexts.

The degree to which conjugation, declension, part-of-speech, and grammatical role should be understood as formal rather than functional categories continues to be a topic of much investigation (Bates & MacWhinney, 1982). Most parties (e.g., Maratsos, 1982; Pinker, 1982) agree that categories are defined initially in functional terms. Even highly arbitrary systems such as German gender have been shown to have a partially functional basis (Kopcke & Zubin, in press). The ACT* model in Anderson (1983) describes a generalization scheme for forming such categories that can use both semantic and formal features.

7. CONCLUSION

The current model incorporates a number of important advances over our earlier independent efforts. Most improved is the theory of lexical activation, which now provides a unified account of the interaction of rote, analogy, combination, and selection while also dealing with the various types of speech errors. We next hope to focus our attention on a theoretical unification of the nine acquisitional strategies that we have just outlined. We believe that a similar type of theoretical unification can be achieved here too.

In this paper, our focus has been on the construction of an account of language development that is maximally grounded in the theories of cognitive psychology and linguistics. By emphasizing the connections between language structures, language processing, general cognitive processing, and general learning mechanisms, we believe that it is possible to construct a coherent account of the great mass of data that has been collected in the last 20 years of research in child language acquisition. We believe that unitized approaches of this sort avoid the "cognitive ugliness" of which Roger Brown has warned us. We also believe that the unified approach we have sketched out can also form an important part of the general theories of both psychology and linguistics.

REFERENCES

Anderson, J. R. (1976). *Language, memory, and thought.* Hillsdale, NJ: Erlbaum.

Anderson, J. (1977). Induction of augmented transition networks. *Cognitive Science, 1,* 125–157.

Anderson, J. (1978). Arguments concerning representations for mental imagery. *Psychological Review, 85,* 249–277.

Anderson, J. (Ed.). (1981). *Cognitive skills and their acquisition.* Hillsdale, NJ: Erlbaum.

Anderson, J. (1983). *The architecture of cognition.* Cambridge, MA: Harvard University Press.

Anderson, J., Greeno, J., Kline, P., & Neves, O. (1981). Acquisition of problem-solving skill. In J. Anderson (Ed.), *Cognitive skills and their acquisition.* Hillsdale, NJ: Erlbaum.

Baker, C. (1977). Comments on the paper by Culicover and Wexler. In P. Culicover, T. Wasow, & A. Akmajian (Eds.), *Formal syntax.* New York: Academic Press.

Bates, E., & MacWhinney, B. (1982). Functionalist approaches to grammar. In E. Wanner & L. Gleitman (Eds.), *Language acquisition: The state of the art.* New York: Cambridge University Press.

Bierman, A. W., & Feldman, J. A. (1972). A survey of results in grammatical inference. In S. Watanabe (Ed.), *Frontiers of pattern recognition.* New York: Academic Press.

Block, H., Moulton, J., & Robinson, G. (1975). Natural language acquisition by a robot. *International Journal of Man-Machine Studies, 7,* 571–608.

Blum, L., & Blum, M. (1975). Toward a mathematical theory of inductive inference. *Information and Control, 28,* 128–155.

Braine, M. D. S. (1971). The acquisition of language in infant and child. In C. Reed (Ed.), *The learning of language.* New York: Appleton-Century-Crofts.

Bresnan, J. (Ed.). (1982). *The mental representation of grammatical relations.* Cambridge, MA: MIT Press.

Brown, R. (1973). *A first language: The early stages.* Cambridge, MA: Harvard University Press.

Brown, R. (1977). *Word from the language acquisition front.* Invited address at the Eastern Psychological Association, Boston.

Butler Platt, C., & MacWhinney, B. (1983). Error assimilation as a mechanism in language learning. *Journal of Child Language, 10,* 401–414.

Chandrasekaran, B., & Reeker, L. H. (1974). Artificial intelligence—a case for agnosticism. *IEEE Transactions on Systems, Man and Cybernetics, 4,* 8–94.

Chomsky, C. (1969). *The acquisition of syntax in children from 5 to 10.* Cambridge, MA: M. I. T. Press.

Chomsky, N. (1980). On binding. *Linguistic Inquiry, 11,* 1–46.

Clark, E. (1982). Language change during language acquisition. In M. Lamb & A. Brown (Eds.), *Advances in Developmental Psychology* (Vol. 2). Hillsdale, NJ: Erlbaum.

Culicover, P., & Wexler, K. (1977). Some syntactic implications of a theory of language learnability. In P. Culicover, T. Wascow, & A. Akmajian (Eds.), *Formal syntax.* New York: Academic Press.

Dresher, B. E., & Hornstein, N. (1976). On some supposed contributions of artificial intelligence to the scientific study of language. *Cognition, 4,* 321–398.

Feldman, J. (1972). Some decidability results on grammatical inference and complexity. *Information and Control, 3,* 244–262.

Garrett, M. (1980). Levels of processing in sentence production. In B. Butterworth (Ed.), *Language production: Vol. 1. Speech and talk.* London: Academic Press.

Gold, E. (1967). Language identification in the limit. *Information and Control, 10,* 447–474.

Hamburger, H., & Wexler, K. N. (1973). Identifiability of a class of transformational grammars. In K. J. J. Hintikka, J. Moravcsik, and P. Suppes (Eds.), *Approaches to natural language.* Dordrecht-Holland: D. Reidel.

Hamburger, H., & Wexler, K. (1975). A mathematical theory of learning transformational grammar. *Journal of Mathematical Psychology, 12,* 137–177.

Harris, L. (1977). A system for primitive natural language acquisition. *International Journal of Man-Machine Studies, 9,* 153–206.

Hinton, G., & Anderson, J. (1981). *Parallel models of associative memory.* Hillsdale, NJ: Erlbaum.

Hooper, J. (1976). *An introduction to natural generative phonology.* New York: Academic Press.

Horning, J. J. (1969). *A study of grammatical inference* (Tech. Rep. No. CS 139). Palo Alto, CA: Stanford University, Computer Science Department.

Hudson, G. (1980). Automatic alternations in non-transformational phonology. *Language, 56,* 94–125.

Katz, N., Baker, E., & MacNamara, J. (1974). What's in a name? A study of how children learn common and proper names. *Child Development, 45,* 469–473.

Kelley, K. L. (1967). *Early syntactic acquisition.* (Tech. Rep. No. P-3719). Santa Monica, CA: Rand Corporation.

Kiss, G. (1973). Grammatical word classes: A learning process and its simulation. In G. Bower (Ed.), *The psychology of learning and motivation.* New York: Academic Press.

Klein, S., & Kuppin, M. (1970). An interactive heuristic program for learning transformational grammars. *Computer Studies in the Humanities and Verbal Behavior, 3,* 144–162.

Kopcke, K. & Zubin, D. (in press). Zur Frage der psychologischen Realitat von Genuszuweisenden Regeln zu den einsilbigen Nomen der deutschen Gegenwartssprache. *Linguistische Berichte.*

Langley, P. (1982). Language acquisition through error recovery. *Cognition and Brain Theory, 5,* 211–155.

Leopold, W. F. (1937–1949). *Speech development of a bilingual child: A linguist's record* (Vols. 1–4). Evanston, IL: Northwestern University Press.

Levelt, W. (1975). *Formal grammars in linguistics and psycholinguistics.* The Hague: Mouton.

MacWhinney, B. (1974). *How Hungarian children learn to speak.* Unpublished doctoral dissertation, University of California, Berkeley.

MacWhinney, B. (1975). Pragmatic patterns in child syntax. *Stanford Papers And Reports on Child Language Development, 10,* 153–165.

MacWhinney, B. (1978). The acquisition of morphophonology. *Monographs of the Society for Research in Child Development, 43,* Whole No. 1.

MacWhinney, B. (1982). Basic syntactic processes. In S. Kuczaj (Ed.), *Language acquisition: Vol. 1. Syntax and semantics.* Hillsdale, NJ: Erlbaum.

MacWhinney, B. (1983). Miniature linguistic systems as tests of universal operating principles. *Journal of Psycholinguistic Research, 12,* 467–478.

Maratsos, M. (1982). The child's construction of grammatical categories. In E. Wanner & L. Gleitman (Eds.), *Language acquisition: The state of the art.* New York: Cambridge University Press.

McClelland, J., & Rumelhart, D. (1981). An interactive activation model of context effects in letter perception: Part 1. An account of the basic findings. *Psychological Review, 88,* 375–402.

McMaster, I., Sampson, J., & King, J. (1976). Computer acquisition of natural language: A review and prospectus. *International Journal of Man-Machine Studies, 8,* 367–396.

Menn, L., & MacWhinney, B. (1984). The repeated morph constraint: Topward an explanation. *Language, 60,* 519–581.

Miller, G. (1967). *The psychology of communication.* New York: Basic Books.

Newell, A., & Simon, H. (1972). *Human problem solving.* Englewood Cliffs, NJ: Prentice-Hall.

Pao, T. W. L. (1969). *A solution of the syntactical induction-inference problem for a non-trivial subset of context-free languages* (Tech. Rep. No. 70-19). University of Pennsylvania: The Moore School of Electrical Engineering.

Pinker, S. (1979). Formal models of language learning. *Cognition, 7,* 217–283.

Pinker, S. (1982). A theory of the acquisition of lexical-interpretive grammars. In J. Bresnan (Ed.), *The mental representation of grammatical relations.* Cambridge, MA: MIT Press.

Pye, C. L. (1979). *The acquisition of grammatical morphemes in Quiche Mayan.* Unpublished doctoral dissertation, University of Pittsburgh.

Reeker, L. (1976). The computational study of language acquisition. In M. Yovits & M. Rubinoff (Eds.), *Advances in computers.* New York: Academic Press.

Siklossy, L. (1972). Natural language learning by computer. In H. A. Simon & L. Siklossy (Eds.), *Representation and meaning: Experiments with information processing systems.* Englewood Cliffs, NJ: Prentice-Hall, Inc.

Stemberger, J. (1982). *The lexicon in a model of language production.* Unpublished doctoral dissertation, University of California, San Diego.

Werner, H., & Kaplan, E. (1950). Development of word meaning through verbal context: An experimental study. *Journal of Psychology, 29,* 251–257.

Wexler, K. & Culicover, P. (1980). *Formal principles of language acquisition.* Cambridge, MA: MIT Press.

Wexler, K., Culicover, P., & Hamburger, H. (1975). Learning-theoretic foundations of linguistic universals. *Theoretical Linguistics, 2,* 215–253.

Wexler, K. N., & Hamburger, H. (1973). On the insufficiency of surface data for the learning of transformational languages. In K. J. J. Hintikka, J. Moravesik, and P. Suppes (Eds.), *Approaches to natural language.* Dordrecht-Holland: D. Reidel.

Wittgenstein, L. (1953). *Philosophical investigations.* Oxford: Blackwell.

Woods, W. (1970). Transition network grammars for natural language analysis. *Communications of the ACM, 13,* 591–606.

Chapter 2

Theoretical Issues in the Investigation of Words of Internal Report*

William S. Hall
University of Maryland

William E. Nagy
University of Illinois

I. INTRODUCTION

In this paper, we discuss in detail some of the theoretical issues related to the investigation of words of internal report (or, as we shall henceforth refer to them, *internal state words*). The categories presented are also intended to provide a basis for the quantitative analysis of internal state word usage in naturalistic data.[1]

* The research on which this paper is based was supported by a grant from the Carnegie Corporation of New York. The preparation of this manuscript was supported by the National Institute of Education under Contract No. US-NIE-C-400-76-0116, and The Department of Psychology, The University of Maryland, College Park.

The listing of authors for this paper is alphabetical. The preparation of this paper was a joint enterprise.

[1] These procedures are an outgrowth of the work reported in Gearhart and Hall (1979, 1983); the suggestions for investigating internal state words made there have been refined in substantial ways by applying them to large amounts of natural conversation from the corpus of data described in Hall (1978). Among the refinements are the following: Criteria for membership in the category "internal state words" have been sharpened, and a major new subclass ("Intentions and Desires", covering words such as *want, desire, decide, intend,* and *choose*) has been included. The resulting list of internal state words cannot of course be considered exhaustive, but, being based in part on a vocabulary list drawn from almost 300 hours of recorded conversation, it covers the overwhelming majority of internal state words occurring in the normal conversation of persons from diverse social and ethnic backgrounds. We have also included idioms and other multiple-word lexical units relating to internal states present in the data.

The motivation for investigating words of internal state has been discussed in some detail in Gearhart and Hall (1979; 1982) and elsewhere (cf. Wellman & Johnson, 1979). To recap briefly, it is based on the following hypotheses: (a) that the vocabulary in the internal state domain determines to a large extent the repertory of concepts in this area; (b) that certain types of internal state word usage will correlate with skill in metacognitive processes; (c) that therefore frequency of certain types of internal state word usage, and perhaps size of internal state word vocabulary, will correlate with greater readiness for, and success in, school; and (d) that situational variation exists in the function and use of words of internal state (cf. Hall, Nagy, & Nottenburg, 1981) (Tech. Report 212).

An increasing number of articles give evidence for the importance of metacognition (Palincsar & Brown, 1984 (Tech. Report 269); Kendall & Mason, 1982 (Tech. Report 263); Flavell, 1978; 1979). Metacognition refers to knowledge or cognition which has cognition as its object. We would argue that the broader construct of knowledge or cognition which has any internal state as its object is of even greater educational relevance. For example, successful reading requires not only an ability to monitor one's own comprehension, but also the ability to make judgements and inferences about the emotions and intentions of the characters of the story (Gearhart & Hall, 1979; 1983; Jose & Brewer, 1983 (Tech. Report 291); Brewer & Lichtenstein, 1982 (Tech. Report 265)). While cognition about cognition may form an important subclass of the more general construct, it seems clear that awareness of and knowledge about all types of internal states is important.

Metacognition, whether in the broader or narrower sense, clearly cannot be equated with the use of internal state words. However, it is true that every meaningful use of an internal state word does indicate an act of metacognition on the part of the speaker.

These hypotheses give a two-fold motivation for the study of internal state word usage: First, to test them in some empirical way, it is necessary to have accurate and insightful methods of designating internal state word usage. Second, to the extent that they are true, the study of internal state word usage will be of great significance to psychology, as well as several applied disciplines.

In the first section of the paper, we deal with the basic categories of words involved, discussing and illustrating theoretical (and practical) problems in defining critical components and boundaries; first, the class of internal state words as a whole, and then the four basic subclasses: (a) Cognitive,

---

The categories for investigating subclasses and differences in usage of internal state words have also been expanded and refined, and will be presented here in detail, illustrated with examples taken from natural conversation.

(b) Perceptual, (c) Affective, and (d) Intentions and Desires. In the second section, we deal with categories of usage.

IDENTIFYING INTERNAL STATE WORDS: DEFINING THE CATEGORY AS A WHOLE

The Overall Class: Prototypical Members

One purpose of this paper is to provide a detailed and explicit basis for procedures for investigating words of internal state that can be applied to naturalistic data. To this end, we must start by giving some criteria for determining what counts as an instance of an internal state word.

The nature and extent of the class we are considering is to a large degree intuitively obvious. The class of internal state words includes words about *cognition* (e.g., think, know, believe, remember, figure out), about *emotions* (e.g., fear, angry, sad, happy), about *perceptions*—both the five senses (e.g., see, hear, etc.) and more "internal" senses (e.g., dizzy, thirsty, ache) about *desires* (e.g., want, desire), and about intentions, choices, and decisions.

The overwhelming majority of instances of internal state words in everyday language use will be clear-cut cases of such words. For example, in a rough count based on two dinners of a professional class family (1353 turns of conversation), slightly over 70% of the 400 internal state word tokens recorded were instances of eight common internal state words: *know, remember, think, want, see, look, hear,* and *like* (and inflectional variations such as *knew, saw, thinks,* etc.). If five more common words are included (*guess, mean, watch, feel,* and *love*) 80% of the internal state word tokens are accounted for (cf. Hall, Nagy, & Nottenburg, 1981 (Tech. Report 212).

Problems in Classification

But even though such prototypical internal state words form the bulk of the internal state content of everyday conversation, there is need for more precise criteria. No matter how clear the prototypical members of a category may be, there will inevitably be borderline cases for which it will be difficult to decide whether or not they actually belong to the group in question. Especially if one is interested in measuring the size of internal state vocabulary used by an individual or group, it is important to have consistent and non-arbitrary criteria for defining the boundaries of this class. We will return shortly to a detailed discussion of some of the problems and issues that arise in trying to define the limits of the set of internal state words.

Another problem has to do with the imprecision of the word "word." The lexical units of a language (which is what we are really interested in) can be different from "words" in two ways: First, the same "word" can represent different lexical units, that is, it can occur with several distinct and unrelated meanings. Second, a lexical unit may consist of more than one word, as in the case of idioms.

For an example of the first case, consider the word *see.* It normally has a meaning that could be glossed "to perceive visually," which belongs in the Perceptual subcategory of internal state words. However, in a sentence like "He went to see his grandmother," the meaning of *see* is most likely (depending on the context) a different one, which might be glossed "visit," and is not an internal state meaning at all.

In talking about internal state words, we also include multiple-word units, for example idioms, as well as single words. The following list illustrates the kinds of idioms of internal state one may find in everyday language:

(1) *List of Idioms*
pay attention to
big on (=like)
keen on (=like)
figure out
have (half) a mind to
change one's mind
make a mental note of
be dying to
be first in (someone's) heart

While such idioms and phrases are relatively infrequent among internal state words, it is still important to recognize them as a potentially important part of the lexical resources of the language; indeed, one might underestimate the vocabulary of an individual or group by not taking them into account.

Fuzziness of Boundaries

We have already informally given some content to the notion "internal state" by listing some prototypical members of the basic subclasses. At this point we want to discuss some general problems in defining and limiting the class of internal state words as a whole.

The first problem has to do with the boundaries of the notion 'internal state'; that is, the problem of determining what can be considered a 'mental process or state.' In the case of the category Perceptual, words like *see* and *hear* are clearly focused on sensory experiences. This also goes for certain "internal senses" like *ache* or *hurt,* as in "my stomach hurts." Not all that far removed from these are words whose meanings seem more physical," like *relaxed, full* (having eaten enough), *sore,* etc. These seem to relate more directly to the state of the person's body than to the experience of internal states, although both are included in the meanings. In between are a number of words such as *tired, nauseous, hungry, thirsty, hot, cold, sleepy, comfortable,* and so on, which seem to straddle the border.

A similar group of words involve states with psychological effects or implications, but which don't seem to be "internal states" in the sense of the more prototypical members: *drunk, loaded, stoned,* etc.

Although the borderline cases here are not clearly categorizable, they illustrate one of the defining properties of internal states, namely, that they are psychological rather than physical. If we consider the nature of the boundary between 'psychological' and 'physical' phenomena, it is hardly surprising that some words will be difficult to assign clearly to one category or the other.

In the case of Affective words, it is not clear where the exact boundary is between temporary emotional states (happy, angry, sad) and relatively long-term personality characteristics (patient, optimistic, irritable, "chicken"). Many words can apparently be used in either area: for example, *nervous,* as in "he's a nervous person" vs. "I feel nervous right now." Some of the following words seem to be especially questionable as to whether they can be thought of as referring to temporary emotional states: *paranoid, confident, cross, grumpy, unselfconscious.*

Again, although the boundary may remain unclear, as well as the exact status of words like *nervous,* the problem serves to clarify another of the defining criteria of internal states: Internal states are things that people *experience,* rather than what they are, in the long-term sense of the word. They are generally *temporary* states or experiences.

Along similar lines, it has to be pointed out that "internal states" include processes and (relatively short-term) states, but not capacities and abilities. For example, *intelligence* would not be considered an internal state word, although it is definitely 'cognitive' in some sense of the word. Similarly, *smart, stupid, blind, deaf, perceptive,* and *sensitive* refer to capacities, abilities, or lack of them, rather than to internal states as such.

This leads to the perhaps surprising conclusion that the noun *memory* (as in "I have a good memory") is not an internal state word, since it refers primarily to the capacity. In the same way, we would probably want to exclude words like *reason* and *motivation,* although the exact dividing line between internal states and non-internal-states becomes unclear. In a sentence like "That must have been his reason for doing it," one is not talking about specific internal states, but rather analyzing connections. (On the other hand, in the case of the superficially similar sentence "His intention was to keep his parents from worrying," one might paraphrase 'his intention' with 'what he intended,' which seems to concern internal states more directly. The boundary here is obviously not very clear.

The Focus of Word Meanings. Another cause of "fuzzy boundaries" has to do with the complexity of word meanings. Even if we are able to determine precisely for a given semantic feature whether or not it belonged to the category "internal state," this would not make the categorization of word meanings trivial.

Take for example the word *lie:* to say that someone is lying says something both about their beliefs (they don't believe what they are saying) and their intentions (they intend to deceive the addressee). This deliberate deception involves the internal states of the addressee as well: the liar intends for the addressee to believe both the content of the lie, and that the liar believes what he/she is saying. Notice how complex the internal state component of the meaning of *lie* is: the person lying has intentions about the beliefs of the addressee, including the addressee's beliefs about the intentions and beliefs of the person lying.

Yet despite all this, we do not feel that *lie* should be considered an internal state word. If one were to take as a definition for "internal state word" something like "any word which has as some part of its meaning an 'internal state' component," this will necessitate expanding the class of internal state words to include not only *lie,* but a host of other words such as *propaganda, testimony, promise,* etc., which at least intuitively do not belong in the class of internal state words. Thus, it seems desirable to limit the category of internal state words to those words for which the internal state component of the meaning is the primary or focal component.[2]

---

[2] Such a restriction, although unavoidable, has the drawback of introducing a new dimension of 'fuzziness' to the category of internal state words. Not only is it sometimes hard to determine whether a particular component belongs to the internal state category; now there is the additional question, which will come up frequently, of which component in a word-meaning is the center or focus of that meaning.

Even a clearly defined criterion for determining what component constituted the focus of a word meaning would leave us with some borderline cases and arbitrary decisions. As it is, the situation seems to be a little worse: it may not be possible even in principle to determine which component of a word-meaning is central or focal in some absolute sense, because which component is central may depend on context. One example of such a case is the word *hope.*

The word *hope* is normally defined in terms of two components, "expectation" and "desire." (It so happens that both of these components fall into the category of internal state, so that no matter which one is focal, *hope* will be an internal state word, although its classification into the subclasses is still problematic. One can easily imagine, however, that there are analogous cases in which one of the two components involved was not in the category internal state.) In a sentence such as:

(a) John hopes Sue will come to the party, but I don't.

the component focused on in the first half, and negated in the second is "desire." But in a sentence like:

(b) We really can't hope for much progress in the next few weeks.

the focused component, which is also negated, is "expectation."

Thus, we have a case where it is not possible to determine, apart from context, which component of meaning in a given word is focal. This is problematic insofar as we would like to develop a system of categorizing word-meanings, and this process is made much simpler by the assumption that word-meanings are, at least in their essential structure, definable apart from any particular context.

In practice, it is possible to get around the sort of problem posed by the word *hope* by modifying our restriction about focal components slightly: Internal state words will include those words for which the internal state component *can be* the focal component of the meaning in some natural context.

One class of words which contain internal state meanings as a component of their overall meaning are what might be called "causatives" of internal state, such as the following:

(2)	persuade	=	cause to believe
	convince	=	cause to believe
	distract	=	cause to cease (momentarily) to pay attention
	teach	=	cause to learn
	show	=	cause to see
	fool mislead deceive	=	cause to believe (something not true)

A similar relationship seems to hold between certain transitive verbs and the corresponding adjective or past participle:

(3)	anger	=	cause to be angry
	upset	=	cause to be upset
	sadden	=	cause to be sad
	cheer	=	cause to be cheerful
	discourage	=	cause to be discouraged
	frighten	=	cause to be frightened/be afraid/fear

Two questions that might be asked are, (a) does a given meaning focus on the internal state produced, or on the activity which produces (or may produce) the associated internal state, and (b) can we answer this question for all the 'causative' verbs as a group, or is it necessary to examine each case individually?

As to the second question, we do not feel that one can treat all the examples just given as a group. On the one hand, the word *teach* seems to focus on the activity of the person teaching as much as or more than on the learning that is produced. It could be that there is even some degree of lexical ambiguity here, with *teach* meaning "to be engaged in teaching as a profession" or "to (habitually) perform the duties associated with teaching," and *teach* meaning "to cause (someone) to learn (something)" or "to help or facilitate the processes of learning." The difference between these two meanings is illustrated in the following two sentences:

(4a) He teaches sixth grade.
(4b) He tried to teach them macrame.

The difference between the two senses is also illustrated by the oddness of the following two sentences:

(5a) He tries to teach sixth grade.
(5b) He taught them macrame, but none of them learned how to do it.

The first (professional) meaning of *teach* is clearly not an internal state meaning, and even the second seems to focus on the activity than on the internal state, although this is not absolutely clear.

Perhaps the real problem with *teach* is that the embedded meaning *learn* is itself of questionable status with respect to membership in the group of internal state words. *Learn* seems, at least in some contexts, to focus on the activity that results in the acquisition of certain knowledge of skill itself. Thus, there is a difference in meaning between the sentences:

(6a) I spent the week learning to swim.
(6b) I spent the week coming to know how to swim.

In any case, both *learn* and *teach* seem to be less than full-fledged internal state words, apparently because there is a focus on the activities involved in the change of internal state as well as on the internal states themselves.

On the other hand, words like *sadden, discourage,* and *anger* all do seem to focus on the internal state produced, and thus qualify as bona fide internal state words.

It might be argued that there is a difference between true causatives such as *anger* (= cause to be angry) or *sadden* (= cause to be sad) and meanings such as *teach, show,* and perhaps also *deceive,* which imply or include in their meaning the causation of a change in internal state, but which cannot be analyzed simply as the addition of a simple abstract predicate CAUSE to some internal state meaning.

This leaves us with a decision about words like *persuade, convince, distract, fool, mislead,* and *deceive.*

First of all, we can note that the *convinced* of "I'm convinced that he's right" is an internal state meaning. However, it is not clear that this *convinced* is simply the past participle of the transitive verb *convince;* the sentence just cited as an example is not the result of the application of the passive transformation.

Secondly, true passives form contexts where the focus is more likely to be on the internal state than the activity that produced it, as in:

(7) I was distracted for a moment, and when I looked back at...

Even in this context, it isn't clear which of these words, if any, should be considered internal state words. For example:

(8) He was persuaded to join the club.
I was misled by the data.
Many were deceived by the politician's rhetoric.
They were fooled into thinking that the work on the project had been stopped.

In these cases, it is at least possible that the focus is still on the activity producing the internal state rather than on the change in internal state itself.

The example "they were fooled into thinking that work on the project had stopped" is especially helpful, for the following reason: If *fool* simply meant "to cause to believe" (something false), then "fool into thinking" would be as redundant as "to kill someone to death" or "to frighten someone into being afraid." The existence of phrases like "fool someone into thinking something" suggests that the internal state component is not the focus of the meaning of the word *fool.* Such phrases cannot be taken as absolute proof, since redundancy of various sorts is found in language at all levels, but it certainly constitutes significant evidence.

Our suggestion at this point is that the transitive verbs *convince, persuade, fool, trick, deceive,* and *mislead* be excluded from the class of internal state words, on the grounds that they focus on activity that result in an internal state, rather than focusing on the internal state itself. A more explicit justification for this decision would require more explicit criteria and tests for determining what the 'central component' of a word meaning is than we are able to propose right now.

There are words besides the "causatives" just discussed that are candidates for internal state words, since the internal state component of the meaning seems to be central to the word-meaning as a whole. Some of them are:

(9) favorite = the one I like best
remind = perceive as similar (or cause to remember)

The question remains, to what extent does the word-meaning as a whole focus on an internal state? In the case of the above examples, the internal state meaning does seem central.

Object of Perception vs. Act of Perception. The Perceptual subcategory of internal state words gives us another interesting problem in defining the limits of this category, a problem similar to the one of determining the focus of word-meanings. This one involves distinguishing between word-meanings relating to the 'act of perception' or 'experience of perception' on the one hand, and the 'content of perception' or 'object of perception' on the other.

To start with a clear-cut case, the word *red* is clearly a perceptual word, in some sense, and relates to internal states in some significant way; and yet it would seem inappropriate to label it as an internal state word. The word *see,* on the other hand, is about the process or experience of perception, clearly an internal state word. Between these two relatively clear-cut cases lie some more problematic cases, such as the following:

(10) That kind of cheese is usually pretty *smelly.*
That perfume *smells* good.
That music *sounds* discordant.
The pillow *felt* nice and soft.

The room *looked* clean.
Vitamic C *tastes* bitter.

On the one hand, such sentences can be used as reports of perceptual experiences. On the other hand, this is not sufficient grounds for saying that they contain internal state words: A sentence like "This room is a nice shade of beige" can be used to convey a perceptual experience, but this does not mean that *beige* is an internal state word. One can consider the sentences "This room is a nice shade of beige" and "Vitamin C tastes bitter" to be parallel in that both can be used as reports of sensory experiences, but both focus on the properties of the objects perceived rather than on the experience or process of perception. The word *tastes* in the latter sentence can be thought of as specifying the sensory channel, but still focusing on the object of content of the perception.

In the Cognitive subclass of internal state words, *interesting* and *fascinating* seem to be parallel cases. While they relate to internal states, they are more directly about qualities of some object.

A related problem concerns the use of *taste, smell,* and *feel* in sentences such as the following:

(11) Tom tasted the batter.
I bent over to smell the flower.
He felt the edge of the knife to see if it was sharp.

At first glance, these might be thought to be parallel in meaning to words of 'directed attention' in other sensory modalities, as in:

(12) I looked at the picture for a few minutes.
He stopped to listen to the band.

But the sentences with *taste, smell,* and *feel* are actually different, in that they seem to include significant content beyond the internal state component. The meanings of these particular usages might be paraphrased as follows:

(13) taste_i = to put something in one's mouth, to see how it tastes.
smell_i = to hold near one's nose while inhaling to see how it smells.
feel_i = to touch to see how it feels.

These paraphrases are not intended as serious semantic analyses, but they do ilustrate that there is content to the meanings of *taste, smell,* and *feel* (in the contexts cited) which goes beyond the internal state component. As to whether the internal state component is central—that is, whether these should be considered true internal state words—it is difficult to make a clear case in either direction.

One might ask at this point if there aren't any usages of *taste, feel,* and *smell* which are clearly internal state words. There are, in fact, in sentences such as the following:

(14) I can taste chlorine in the water.
I felt the wind blowing against my face.
If you smell smoke, say something.

The Role of Syntax in Defining the Category Internal States

Syntactic Categories. There are some syntactic categories that will be 'typical' of internal state words, but there are no syntactic criteria that will determine whether or not a word belongs in this class.

The majority of internal state words will be verbs with the experiencer (normally human) as the subject:

(15) I think that you should invite her.
John knows the answer.
He saw someone go into the building.
Did you hear something?
They felt sad.
I like chocolate.
I want to leave.
We decided to stay.

A large number—especially in the Affective category—are adjectives, again with the human experiencer as the subject of the sentence:

(16) He was angry
sad
astonished
delighted
aware of the problem

There are also a fair number of internal state words for which the human experiencer shows up as the object of the sentence:

(17) It bothered me.
It annoys me.
They surprised me.
It angers me just to think about it.
The whole thing upset me.

The frequency of the more common patterns—especially the ones where the human experiencer is the subject of the sentence—means that one has to be all the more careful not to miss internal state words that have different syntactic characteristics, and might therefore be easily overlooked. In addition to the case where the experiencer appears as the object (as in the above examples), there are also examples where the experiencer shows up as the object of a preposition:

(18) It finally dawned on me that...
It occurred to me that...

and sometimes cases where it doesn't show up overtly at all:

(19) It didn't click at first.
(=I didn't understand immediately)

Abstract Nouns. Some genuine internal state words are abstract nouns, which can occur in sentences not referring to a (specific) person's internal state at all. For example:

(20) It might be a good *idea*.
It's the *thought* that counts.
That would be a hard *choice* to make.
The *decision* will be left up to the appropriate committee.

Note that abstract nouns like this can also occur in phrases that amount to complex verbs of internal state:

(21) I *came to a decision* about it.
I *have an idea* about how to do it.
The *thought occurred* to me that we should act soon.
I've *made the choice* to stay here.

Note that *choice* can also mean alternative, which is not an internal state word, as in sentences such as:

(22) Here are the choices we have.

SUBCLASSES OF INTERNAL STATE WORDS

The Four Basic Categories

Having discussed the general extent of the class of internal state words, and some of the problems associated with drawing precise boundaries for this class, we move on to the definition of the four basic subclasses of internal state words—Cognitive, Affective, Perceptual, and Intentions and Desires.

To begin, we give some prototypical members of these classes, to give an approximate idea of their scope and content:[3]

---

[3] The types of problems that make it difficult to decide whether or not a given instance of a word is an internal state word also make it difficult at times to decide which subclass a given word belongs to.

For example, several words are ambiguous, having meanings in different subcategories of internal state words; however, which meaning is intended by the speaker is generally clear from the context:

Footnote 3 continued...

(23) Cognitive: know, remember, think, aware
Affective: like, love, hope, hate, afraid
Perceptual: see, hear, look, watch, feel
Intentions and Desires: want, decide, intend, choose

Theoretical Problems in Classification

A problem in categorizing internal state words that comes up fairly frequently in everyday language has to do with the use of utterances involving conversational implicature (cf. Grice, 1975, 1978; Gordon & Lakoff, 1971; Sadock, 1974). More specifically, assertions and questions about emotions, especially likes and dislikes, are used to imply questions and assertions about wants. For example:

(24)		
	I would love to go swimming.	(=I want to...)
	Would you like some tea?	(=do you want...)
	I would enjoy going swimming.	(=I want to...)
	I don't feel like going.	(=I don't want to...)
	Would you care for some more?	(=Do you want...)

The words under consideration here—*love, like, enjoy, feel,* and *care for*—are clearly in the Affective category as far as their meanings are concerned. But the implications of the sentences definitely involve desire as well, although the paraphrase with *want* do not all seem to be equally appropriate. The question therefore arises: should these be coded as belonging to the class Affective, according to the literal meanings of the words, or the class Intentions and Desires, according to the implied meaning?

One principle to take into account in trying to answer this question is that a sentence may have a number of implications, but this does not in itself mean that the literal meaning of the sentence was not also intended by the speaker. For example, at one point in our data, the father in a family fails to understand what the child has said, and asks the mother, "Did you understand him?" The mother says "Yes" and, without a pause, repeats what the child has said. This is of course in response to the father's implied request 'If you understand what he said, tell me what it is.' The mother both

---

(a)	I don't see anyone coming.	(Perceptual)
(b)	I don't see how they do it.	(Cognitive)
(c)	I don't feel cold at all.	(Perceptual)
(d)	How would you feel if they said that to you?	(Affective)
(e)	I don't feel he can handle the job.	(Cognitive)

Some words seem to hold 'double membership.' As was discussed above, *hope* has in its meaning both components of expectation (Cognitive) and desire (Intentions and Desires); in some contexts the expectation component seems focal, and in other contexts, the desire.

Words like *crave, yearn,* and *long for* seem to have components of meaning in both the Affective and Intentions and Desires categories.

answers the literal question and the implied request, showing that both levels of meaning are functioning. In such a case, the internal state word should be coded for the meaning it contributes to the literal meaning of the sentence.

This is pretty clearly the right way to treat a sentence like:

(25) I would enjoy going swimming.

The implication—'I want to go swimming'—is very clear, but the literal meaning is in no way ruled out.

On the other hand, one could argue that the phrase "would you like" is simply a polite idiom for "do you want," and that this is the one and only meaning of the phrase. There are two classes of data that can be taken as evidence that "would like" is actually an idiom meaning roughly 'want,' and belongs in the category Intentions and Desires, whereas the other examples listed above are bona fide members of the category Affective, whose conversational implications do not change their lexical meaning:

One kind of evidence has to do with the appropriateness of *please* (cf. Gordon & Lakoff, 1971, pp. 73–74; note that these examples do not follow all the generalizations suggested there). Since statements of want or desire can conventionally be used as requests, *please* can be appropriately added to a statement of the speaker's desires to emphasize its function as a request:

(26) I want another cup of coffee, please.

Would like functions just like want in this respect:

(27) I'd like another cup of coffee, please.

But the other Affective internal state words that imply wants and desires do not sound as natural with *please:*

(28) I'd love another cup of coffee, please.
I'd enjoy another cup of coffee, please.
I feel like another cup of coffee, please.

Another type of evidence is based on the difference between idioms and conversational implicatures (cf. Sadock, 1972). An idiom has two distinct senses, the literal sense and the idiomatic sense; these are independent of each other, since the idiom with its idiomatic meaning is a separate lexical item. Therefore, one can construct contexts where the idiomatic reading is sensible, and the literal meaning contradictory, or vice versa. In the case of a conversational implicature, however, since both meanings are functional in the interpretation of the sentence (that is, both the literal and implied meaning), you cannot contradict the literal meaning without making the whole sentence contradictory, since the implied meaning is conveyed only *via* the literal meaning.

The following sentences can be understood in a perfectly noncontradictory way, especially if one imagines a context in which the 'request' meaning is appropriate:

(29a) I'd like another cup of coffee, please—I don't actually like coffee, but I have to drive all night tonight.

(29b) I'd like to get a tetanus shot—I don't really like getting shots, but I understand it would be risky for me not to get one.

Parallel sentences with *would love* or *would enjoy* sound odd because the literal meanings of *love* and *enjoy* still contribute to the interpretation of the sentence:

(30a) I'd enjoy another cup of coffee—I don't actually enjoy coffee, but I have to drive all night tonight.

(30b) I'd love to get a tetanus shot—I don't really like getting shots, but I understand it would be risky for me not to get one.

Therefore, it seems appropriate to treat *would like* as an idiom belonging to the category Intentions and Desires—that is, when it occurs with the meaning *want.* There are of course contexts which allow only the literal meaning of *would like,* which would then be considered *Affective:*

(31) I would like owning a big car, but I don't want to buy one.

The other phrases mentioned—*would enjoy, would love to, don't* or *would care for,* and *feel like*—should be classed as Affective, even though they can be used to conversationally imply desire.

Another type of implication that blurs the distinction between categories is that between perception and knowledge.

Awareness and knowledge—part of the Cognitive domain—are often the result of perception. In more than one language the word for *know* is derived from the past tense of the word for *see.* The same connection is seen synchronically in English in the cognitive meanings of *see,* such as in sentences like:

(32) I want to see if I can add these up in my head.
I don't see how they can do it.

In some cases it really seems difficult to know which class *see* belongs in. In a sentence such as:

(33) I see that we may run into trouble.

One might judge *see* to be perceptual if the sentence was uttered by a mountain climber looking over the path ahead, and cognitive if uttered, for example, by a government arbitrator commenting on a new turn in some negotiations. *Foresee* seems more clearly cognitive.

In the other direction, it could conceivably be argued that *notice* (which we have classed as Cognitive) should be considered Perceptual.

Lists of Words Belonging to Each Subclass

List of "Cognitive" Words. This list contains the cognitive words that have been found to occur in our corpus (Hall, Nagy, & Linn, 1984). The subgroupings given are primarily to make the content and the boundaries of the category Cognitive more explicit.

(34a) *Consciousness/Knowledge/Understanding*

aware	head (can't get it out of my head)
conscious	mind (crossed my mind, come to mind)
notice	pick up (=learn)
know	find (out)
knowledge	dawn (on someone)
recognize	slip (one's mind)
experience (v)	track (keep track of, lose track of)
realize	blank (draw a blank)
recall	get (=understand)
remember	see (=understand, find out)
forgot	catch (=understand, perceive)
misunderstand	follow (I don't follow you=don't understand)
understand	
click	

(34b) *Directed Attention*

notice	(pay)attention
ignore	concentration
engrossed	concentrate
distracting	

(34c) *Thinking (as an activity)*

think	consideration
thought	pondering
concepts	concentrate
idea	figure (out)
conceivable	reason (verb)
consider	

(34d) *Mental states relative to a proposition: belief, certainty, etc.*

belief	curious	Figure, (I felt that would happen)
believe	convinced	impression (get the i., under the i.)
agree	sure	view (I view it as) seem (it seems to me=
accept	positive	I think) feel (I f. it would be best=think)
expect	satisfied	hope

anticipate	confidence
anticipation	certain
doubt	dream
bet	imagine
guess	imaginary
suppose	imagination
suspect	buy (I can't b. that)
suspicion	swallow (I can't s. that)

(34e) *Mental Acts relative to a proposition*

assume	make-believe
wonder	make up
conclusion	invent
pretend	

Wonder seems to be a complex meaning, but more appropriately classed as Cognitive than anything else.

The word see has one if not more cognitive meanings, as in:

(35) I want to see if I can add these up in my head.
I don't see how they can do it.

The following words are of questionable status, but might belong to the Cognitive category:

(36) careful
get used to
learn
teach
appear (it appears to me...)
seem (it seems to me...)
fool
deceive
confuse
confusion

"Perceptual" Words. The following list contains the words in the corpus that fall into the category Perceptual. This category breaks down into two basic subcategories, the 'five senses,' and the more 'internal senses.' As has been discussed above, the exact boundaries of the latter class are unclear.

(37a) *Perceptual words involving the "five senses"*

appear	see
feel	sight
hear	smell
hearing	taste

look
observe
peek
peep
view
watch

(37b) *Possible/questionable members of this group:*
notice
observation
seem
tart
touch
ear
sound

(37c) *"General body perceptions"*
beat (=tired)
hungry
hurt
sore
uncomfortable
warm
ache
appetite
cold
comfy
comfortable
dizzy
exhausted
nauseous
ravenous
sleepy
starved
thirsty
tired
zonked
comfort

(37d) *Possible/questionable members of this group:*
awake
relax
relaxed
stuffed
restless
satisfied

"Affective" Words. The next list contains words that belong (or seem to belong) to the Affective category, that is, words which relate to feelings and emotions.

(38) aback (taken a.)
afraid
afraid
agitate
alarm
alarmed
amazed
amusing
anger
anticipation
angry
annoy
annoyed
anxious
appalled
appreciate
approve
attitude
ashamed
astonished
bear (can't b.)
blue
blues
bother
bothersome
bored
bug
bummer
burns (b. me up)
care
cheer
cheerful
concern
concerned
cross
dazed
dejected
delight
delighted

depressed
depressing
desperate
desperately
desperation
displease
disappoint
disgust
disgusting
disillusioning
dismal
disturb
disturbing
delirious
down
encourage
encouragement
embarrass
enjoy
enjoyment
enthused
enthusiasm
envy
exasperated
exasperating
excited
exciting
favorite
fit (throw a f.)
flip (=like)
flip (out)
floor (it. fl.d him)
freaking (?)
frustrating
fuss
fear
fond
fright
frighten
frightened
fumes
furious
feel
glad
grief
hilarious
hurt
happy
hate
hateful
hysterical
heart (set one's h.on)
hope
infuriating
intimidated
interest
interested
interesting
irritated
jealous
joy
kicks
like
lonesome
love
look forward to
mad
maddening
miserable
miss
mixed up
mood
moody
nuisance
nervous
pity
possessed
proud
passion
peed (off)
piss(ed) (off)
please
pleasure
prefer
preferences
raging
raving
reacting
reactions
rejoice
reluctantly
regret
resent
resolve
resolution
serious
seriously
soul
spirit
stand (can't s.)
sympathy
sympathetic
sad
sadness
scare
scared
scary
scaredy (cat?)
shame
shock
shocked
shook
sick (of s.t.)
sickening
sorrows
sorry
stun
suffer
surprise
surprised
surprising
satisfied
tantrum
tempted
threaten
threatening
trust
tense
terror

thankful	uptight	respect
thrilled	yellow	worry
unhappy	zonked	worried
upset		

Some of the problems in defining the boundaries of this group have already been mentioned in the previous section.

Many words seem to have some 'affective' component, but have been categorized elsewhere, for example:

(39) curious
hope
doubt
certain
sure
convinced

All these have been included in the category Cognitive.

Some possible members of the Affective category, not listed in the main list, are:

(40) get used to
accustomed
acclimated
adjust

"Intentions and Desires." The members of this category are listed in several semantically defined subgroups, first to make the scope and content of this category more explicit, and second to make it easier to see how this category might be reanalysed. One might proffer, for example, that desires be classified in the Affective category, and intentions in the Cognitive category, rather than grouping them into one class. We concede that the suggestion is plausible, but feel that it would erase important basic distinctions in how these words of internal report were actually used.

(41a) *Wants and desires*

desires	tempted
want	heart (have one's heart set on)
wish	
would like	

(41b) *Intention, plan, purpose*

aim (to)	purpose
intend	plan
have (half) a mind to	mean

(41c) *Determination*

resolve
resolution
deliberately
determined

(41d) *Decisions and choices*

decide
choose
make up one's mind
pick
change one's mind

(41e) *Willingness*

willing
willingly
volunteer

The word *mean* is the most potentially problematic member of the group, since it has several meanings which, on the one hand, seem to be related, but on the other hand do not all belong in the category of internal state words.

Mean definitely belongs in the class Intentions and Desires when it can be validly paraphrased by *intend,* in sentences such as:

(42) Did you really mean to do that?

A little less clear is the case where *mean* can be paraphrased by *intend to say* or *attempt to convey,* as in:

(43) What I meant was that I wouldn't be able to come on time tomorrow night.
I mean that the people who are responsible should pay for it.

Although it isn't clear, it seems that the focus here is on the communication more than the intention; at best this is a borderline case of an internal state word.

There are of course several meanings of *mean* that are not internal state words at all; for example:

(44) Oh, you mean the one on the left.
What does that word mean?

INVESTIGATING THE USE OF INTERNAL STATE WORDS

Introduction to Investigation for Use: Motivation

In addition to identifying all occurrences of internal state words, we must specify in some way how they are used. Any internal state can be experienced without being verbalized, and any internal state word can be uttered in a meaningful sentence independent of anyone in the speech situation experiencing that internal state.

Therefore, in approaching the question of how the use of internal state words relates to internal states themselves, we must focus on the question: How are internal state words used to *communicate about* internal states?

Focusing on this more specific question—what is the relationship between use of internal state words and communication about internal states—one must still ask what sort of discrepancy there might be between the two. After all, one can talk indefinitely about a person without using that person's name, and not every utterance of the word *frank* necessarily refers to your friend Frank whom you sometimes talk about.

Thus, we can conceive of two types of discrepancy between use of internal state words and communication about internal states: (a) People can communicate about internal states without using internal state words, and (b) People can use internal state words without communicating about internal states.

It is of course possible to talk about internal states without using internal state words. There are syntactic devices such as 'dative of experiencer' as in "To me, he's too conservative" or "It looks beige to me" which convey the notion of internal state. It is also clearly possible to convey emotions and other internal states by other means, for example facial expressions, metaphors, and gestures.

Another way that people can talk about internal states and processes without using internal state words is exemplified by sentences such as the following:

(45) This problem is turning out to be really hard for me to work on.

The reasonable reference, that the problem here is an intellectual one, enables one to determine that the generic term *work on* (not an internal state word in itself) may refer to cognitive activity, hence internal states.

Thus, the use of internal state words to communicate about internal states is only a subset of the total communication about internal states that occur. Nevertheless, it must constitute a large and significant subset; it seems reasonable to assume that, to the degree that internal states and processes are actually the topic of the communication, internal state words are likely to be used.

This brings us to the question, to what extent and in what ways can people use internal state words without communicating about internal states.

Phrased in this negative way, the question focuses on the discrepancy between use of internal state words and communication about internal states. This discrepancy is captured by what we label the "semantic–pragmatic" distinction. From this perspective, an instance of an internal state word is considered 'semantic' if it is used to refer to—and hence to communicate about—an internal state; it is coded 'pragmatic' if its function in the sentence is something other than to communicate about internal states.

THE SEMANTIC/PRAGMATIC DISTINCTION

General Discussion: The Basis and Motivation of the Distinction

The question underlying the semantic/pragmatic distinction is: When are people using internal state words to communicate about internal states, and when are they using them for something else?

The first step in answering this question is to define more clearly and operationally what we mean by 'using an internal state word to communicate about an internal state.' We will approach this in terms of the role the literal internal state meaning of an internal state word plays in the intended meaning of the utterance which contains the word. (cf. Dixon, 1971). This will become clearer from an example where the distinction is clear-cut.

Assuming a normal context, when someone utters a sentence like "Jack knows the answer," the intended meaning of the utterance has something to do with Jack, knowledge, and the answer to some question; that is, the literal meaning of these words play a straightforward and obvious role in determining the meaning of the utterance. On the other hand, a sentence such as "You know, George could play shortstop" is normally not used to convey anything about knowledge as such. The literal meaning of the word *know* does not contribute to the propositional or logical content of the sentence.

To take another kind of example, consider a sentence such as "Do you want to take out the garbage, please?" when uttered with the intention of conveying a meaning that might be paraphrased "Please take out the garbage." While the literal meaning of the word *want* may be said to contribute to the intended meaning of the utterance, the contribution is indirect, and the intended meaning actually has little or nothing to do with the wants or wishes of the addressee. We will use the label 'semantic' for cases where the literal internal state meaning of a word contributes directly to the intended meaning of the utterance which contains it. 'Pragmatic' describes those cases where the literal internal state meaning of a word contributes indirectly if at all to the intended meaning of the utterance.

At this point, we will briefly mention some of the reasons why a token of an internal state word might be considered 'pragmatic'—that is, in what sorts of cases the internal state meaning of the word does not contribute directly to the intended meaning of the utterance:

One general class of such pragmatic usages might be labelled 'indirect speech acts.' This class might be characterized as utterances whose intended meaning can be inferred from the literal meaning by principles of conversation, or "conversational postulates" as they have been called (cf. Gordon & Lakoff, 1971). The indirect speech acts that are of interest to us are those whose literal meaning contains an internal state meaning which is not directly part of the implied or intended meaning. The example cited above, "Do you want to take out the garbage, please?" belongs in this class. Rhetorical questions ("You know what I'll do? I'll talk to the teacher about it") belong in the same class.

Another class of pragmatic usages can be labelled 'conversational devices and mannerisms.' These consist of highly stereotyped phrases containing (or consisting of) internal state words which have completely or almost completely, lost their literal content, as in the following examples:

(46) You know, I should do something about that leak.
Look, I don't want any trouble around here.

These two categories (indirect speech acts and conversational devices and mannerisms) form two fairly cohesive and clear-cut categories of pragmatic usages. There are some other categories of pragmatic usages, especially Attentional Devices and Hedges, that are somewhat more problematic. We will discuss these in the next section, where specific types of pragmatic usages are described and illustrated in detail.[4]

Criteria for Identifying Pragmatic Usages

Conversational Devices. Having discussed the general nature of the semantic/pragmatic distinction, we now want to examine in detail the kinds

---

[4] There are other vantage points from which one can look at the semantic/pragmatic distinction. One is in terms of the role that a word plays in the hearer's interpretation of an utterance. From this point of view, pragmatic instances of internal state words are less crucial to the interpretion of the utterance; one can so to speak ignore conversational devices and mannerisms like 'ya know' and still have an accurate understanding of the propositional content of the sentence.

Another related perspective is the degree to which a given instance of an internal state word might be helpful to a child in acquiring the corresponding internal state concept. A sentence such as "I don't remember where I left my keys," uttered in the right context, might provide information that would help a child acquiring the corresponding internal state concept. A sentence such as "I don't remember where I left my keys," uttered in the right context, might provide information that would help a child learn what the word 'remember' means. On the other hand, the *know* in 'ya know' does little if anything that would help a child develop his/her concept of knowledge.

These two perspectives illustrate the educational and pysychological significance of the categories 'semantic' and 'pragmatic.' But they also highlight the fact that the semantic/pragmatic distinction, although it may have to be treated as a dichotomy for coding purposes, is also in some respects a continuum. In indirect speech acts, for example, although the internal state word does not contribute directly to the meaning of the utterance, it does contribute, to the extent that the hearer knows the rules of conversational inference. The lexical meaning of the internal state word definitely plays more of a role in the indirect speech act than in the conversational device or mannerism. The same seems to be true in the case of concept acquisition; since children begin to use indirect speech acts at a fairly early age (cf. Ervin-Tripp, 1977), it is quite possible that the occurrences of internal state words in indirect speech acts could be of some use to the child in forming internal state concepts (or developing familiarity with them). On the other hand, conversational devices and mannerisms seem to be 'pragmatic' in an absolute sense; the internal state meaning would seem to have no part in their use or interpretation, and be of no value in the acquisition of the associated concepts.

of pragmatic usages of internal state words that occur in naturalistic data. We will start with the most clear-cut cases of pragmatic usage, namely, conversational devices.

Conversational devices are pragmatic usages of internal state words which (a) tend to be highly conventionalized; (b) contribute minimally to, and are not tightly integrated into, the propositional content of the context; and (c) function mainly in terms of the process of conversation rather than its content, that is, filling pauses, getting or maintaining the addressee's attention, or to indicate to the other person that one is in fact aware of what is being said.[5]

Pragmatic functions can be performed by non-internal-state words as well, for example, *hey, say,* and *well* in sentences such as:

(47a) Hey—let's go to the movies.
(47b) Say, do you want to see what's on TV?
(47c) Well, let's wait at least five more minutes.

or *mhm* or some other minimal token of affirmation a speaker often expects from the addressee as a sign that the addressee is in fact alive, awake, and aware (at least to some extent) of what the speaker is saying.

Perhaps the most prototypical case of a conversational device is the mannerism *you know* used as in the following examples:

(48a) You're not serving the children, you know.
(48b) You know, I think something should be done about it.

To say that these usages are 'pragmatic' is not to say that *know* is meaningless in this sentence, or does not contribute to the understanding of the utterance. If it were meaningless, there would be no difference between:

(49a) You know, I think something should be done about it.
(49b) You see, I think something should be done about it.
(49c) I mean, I think something should be done about it.

But on the other hand, it is clearly not tightly integrated into the propositional content of the rest of the sentence. That is, the two following sentences are not at all synonymous:

(50a) You know, I think something should be done about it.
(50b) You know that I think something should be done about it.

---

[5] One must note that not all conventionalized usages of internal state words are necessarily pragmatic. For example, in a sentence like:

(60) You're not supposed to eat like that, *and you know it.*

The phrase *and you know it* seems highly stereotyped, and yet also seems to have its full literal meaning.

This use of *know* is highly conventionalized. One proof of this is that it does not allow modification; that is, sentence (51) can be interpreted as parallel to (50b) but not (50a):

(51) You surely know I think something should be done about it.

Exactly what the mannerism *you know* does contribute is hard to determine out of context. It may serve as a way for "getting a word in edgewise," that is, claiming a turn in the conversation; it may be an unconscious attempt to maintain the addressee's attention, or serve simply as a pause-filler.

(52) You don't need a bow, remember, just a...

(53a) It's well you see it's a very sweet little thing.
(53b) See, her mike and my mike are independent.

Some Perceptual internal state words also have similar functions:

(54) Look, I don't want to waste any time.
(55) Listen, if a word of this ever gets out....

The *mean* in *I mean* is similar as well:

(56a) That's right, I mean, just be....
(56b) I mean, the topics they talk about aren't even the same as truck drivers around here.

Another type of conversational device, acknowledgements and back-channel responses, function as *mhm* does when it is used by the addressee to give the speaker permission to continue speaking, or reassure that speaker that the addressee is following what the speaker is saying. Some examples of this are:

(57a) I know.
(57b) I see.

This category might also be considered to include the following:

(58a) Let's hope so.
(58b) Well, I hope so.
(58c) I feel that way too.
(58d) My sentiments exactly.

On the other hand, these might be taken to be semantic usages of the internal state words; that is, that the lexical meanings of the words contribute directly to the interpretation of the utterance. It must be remembered that an internal state word can contribute to some definable conversational function without losing its contribution to the propositional content of the sentence; therefore, the fact that a sentence such as "let's hope so" serves a particular conversational function is not sufficient evidence in itself to demonstrate that the word *hope* in that sentence must be pragmatic rather than semantic.

Another conversational device that seems to function mostly as a pause-filler is *let's see* (or *let me see*). The *see* in this case seems to be Cognitive rather than Perceptual.

The related phrase *Let me think,* on the other hand, seems to retain its literal meaning. It is also not as conventionalized, allowing modification, as in *Let me think for a minute.*

It should be noted at this point that there are several usages of *see* that are cognitive but are not conversational devices. For example:

(59a) Let's see if you can play the piano blindfolded.
(59b) Let me see if I can do it.

Sometimes it isn't clear whether *see* is cognitive or perceptual; although it seems to be cognitive in (59), the parallel sentence (60)seems more Perceptual:

(60) Let's see if the picture looks better on the other wall.

The context here may be deceptive, though, and *see* may still have an essentially cognitive meaning something like "find out."

Two further uses of internal state words have become so conventionalized that it isn't clear whether to treat them as pragmatic usages of internal state words, or idioms which are based on internal state words, but which have their own new lexical meanings. The first is the use of *see* in expressions *like see you later* or *see you in a little while.* The second is the use of *sorry* in apologies. *Sorry* does often occur with a genuine semantic internal state word meaning, in sentences like:

(61a) I'm sorry I ever decided to go to college.
(61b) I'm sorry now that I didn't take care of it sooner.

But although apologies may indicate genuine regret on the speaker's part, "I'm sorry" is sometimes equivalent only to "I apologize," which is not in itself an internal state meaning. Thus, a sentence such as the following would be best considered pragmatic:

(62a) Sorry about that.
(62b) I'm sorry, Melissa, there is nothing sour or bitter about these greens.

There are additional pragmatic usages of internal state words that seem to be conversational devices, although they don't fall into the groups discussed above. One is *believe me* (and the alternative *believe you me*) when used as a marker of emphasis, rather than as an exhortation for the addressee to believe something, as in:

(63) They'll bump into it, believe me.

Indirect Requests and Suggestions. Conversational Devices are the 'most pragmatic' of the pragmatic usages of internal state words; that is, they constitute the cases in which the lexical meaning of the internal state word contributes the least to the meaning of the utterance in which it occurs. In addition, they are also characterized by the fact that they are minimally integrated into the propositional content of the context. Indirect Requests and Suggestions constitute a different type of pragmatic usage, where the internal state word is closely connected with the literal meaning of the sentence in which it occurs, but the sentence is used to convey not this literal meaning, but rather a meaning which is implied by the literal meaning of the sentence. A typical example of this would be a sentence such as the following:

(64) Do you want to take out the garbage, please?

On the one hand, *want* is an integral part of the literal meaning of this sentence, both syntactically and semantically. On the other hand, by a conversational implicature that has become conventionalized in English, this sentence is normally used to convey, not a question about the addressee's desires, but a request, which could be paraphrased:

(65) Please take out the garbage.

(The fact that *please* can be used in (64) shows that this implication has become conventionalized.) Thus it can be said that *want* does contribute to the meaning of (64), but only indirectly.

In our data, there are several instances of *want* being used in ways that should probably be classed as Indirect Requests and Suggestions. For example:

(66a) Now that you have nine blocks, wanna make them in a straight line?
(66b) When you find out her brain pattern, you want to tell us where the brain is actually located?

In both cases, it seems that the intended meaning is a request; that is, that these could be validly paraphrased as:

(66a′) Now you have nine blocks—why don't you put them in a straight line?
(66b′) When you find out her brain pattern, tell us where the brain is actually located.

In other cases, it may not always be clear whether the speaker is making a request or suggestion, or actually asking about the desires of the addressee. Trying to paraphrase with an explicit request (as we have just done) is probably the best test to determine the intended meaning. However, since it is possible for a speaker to intend to convey both the literal meaning of a sentence *and* its implications, it would seem best to consider pragmatic only those usages where the literal meaning of *want* seems clearly not to be intended.

Another use of *want* that may belong to the category Indirect Requests and Suggestions is exemplified by the following sentence:

(67) I want to know why there's—how come there's six people up on the loft.

The literal meaning of the sentence is a statement about the speaker's desire to know something; but in this case the words *I want to know* are used to convey a request. Thus, (67) can be validly paraphrased by (67 ′):

(67 ′) Why are there six people up on the loft?

Another type of sentence that seems to belong to the category of Indirect Requests and Suggestions involves the use of *think:*

(68a) Don't you think we should decide what we're going to do tomorrow?
(68b) Do you think you could take out the garbage?
(68c) Think we should start moving the furniture?

Such sentences are used to make suggestions and requests, and thus might be treated as belonging to the same category as the sentences with *want* discussed above. On the other hand, second-person questions with *think* of which the above examples are only a subset, seem to form a unified although problematic category which will be discussed in more detail below.

Rhetorical Questions. When conversational implicatures become conventionalized, a sentence whose literal meaning conversationally implies some other meaning can come to be used to convey that other meaning directly.

Rhetorical questions are an instance of this same phenomenon. A sentence such as "Do you want to know what happened next" can be meant perfectly literally, but an almost unavoidable implication is that the speaker wants to tell the addressee what happened next, and is requesting some indication of interest on his/her part. If the question is taken literally, the exchange might look like this:

(69a) Do you want to hear what happened next?
(69b) Yes, I'd like to. What happened next?
(69c) John went up to Frank and said. . . .

In everyday language use, however, such an explicit answer to the literal question would be rare. More frequently, the addressee responds directly to the implication (that the speaker wants permission from the addressee to continue, or some sign of the addressee's interest) and ignores the literal question, as in the following exchange:

(70a) Do you want to hear what happened next?
(70b) What?

(70c) John went up to Frank and said. . . .

We will also count as rhetorical questions, cases where the conversational process is abbreviated still more, in that the speaker doesn't give the addressee time to respond at all:

(71) Do you want to hear what happened next? John went up to Frank and said. . . .

In this case, the question apparently functions (or is intended) to heighten the addressee's interest or attention.

These two functions might for some purposes be best treated as separate phenomena, but we will use the term Rhetorical Questions for both.

In determining whether a question is rhetorical or not, in terms of the functions just specified, the most straightforward criterion is to look at what follows immediately. Thus, for example, the very same question will be considered literal in (69) and rhetorical in (70) and (71). It seems then that we could define rhetorical questions as questions which are not answered according to their literal meaning, but which count as an attempt by the speaker to elicit from the addressee either renewed attention, or permission to continue speaking.[6]

Finally, it must be noted that the category "Rhetorical Questions" is not necessarily limited to syntactic questions. Why this is so follows from the nature of questions: Questions are requests for information, and thus can be validly paraphrased by imperatives. Compare (72a) and (72b):

(72a) How old are you?
(72b) Tell me how old you are.

---

[6] This definition is however much more restricted than the normal usage of the term rhetorical question. Normally, the term includes questions such as the following, which are rhetorical in that the answer is obvious, so that the question is not intended as a question in the strict sense of the word:

(a1) Who could have imagined that this is what would happen?
(a2) Would anyone dare to doubt that what he says is true?
(a3) Who is more aware than I of the great danger involved?

There is an important difference, however, between the questions listed in (a) and those in (b).

(b1) Do you know what I did? I put it on the table.
(b2) Did you ever hear about the animal that was in my bed? Well. . . .
(b3) Would you like to hear what it was? It was a. . . .

The difference is the following: Although there are internal state words in the sentences of (a), the rhetorical nature of the question does not change or reduce in any way the contribution of the internal state word to the meaning of the sentence as a whole. On the other hand, the questions in (b) are, if taken literally, questions about the knowledge, beliefs, and desires of the addressee; but in their function as rhetorical questions they do not actually constitute either questions or assertions about the internal states of the addressee.

It should be clear why only this latter type of rhetorical question is of interest to us: only in this type does the rhetoricalness of the question contribute to the pragmaticity of the internal state word.

Since questions can be rhetorical, it is also possible for requests which are syntactically imperatives to be rhetorical as well. The following examples from our data illustrate what might be called 'rhetorical requests':

(73a) Guess what. We have no milk.
(73b) And guess what—the woman had a cat...

Exam Questions. Closely related to Rhetorical Questions are what we will call Exam Questions. They are another case where the desired response to a question is not the answer to the literal question itself, but a response to what the question implies. A typical exam question might look like:

(74) Johnny, do you know who discovered America?

A literal answer "Yes" would be considered uncooperative in most contexts. The implication (in the contexts where (74) would function as an exam question) is that the speaker wants to determine the extent of the addressee's knowledge by hearing the answer to the implied Wh-question "Who discovered America?"

Thus, exam questions can be defined in terms of two criteria: (a) as to their surface form, they are yes–no questions about the addressee's knowledge; (b) they count as (that is, are answered as) Wh-questions.

As with Rhetorical Questions, Exam Questions can be identified as such by looking at answers to them. If someone answers (74) with "Yes" or "No," it was understood as a literal question, not an exam question. If the answer is "Columbus" or some other name, the question was understood as an exam question. Note that the exact same question, could count as a literal, exam, or rhetorical question, depending on the answer, as in (75), (76), and (77), respectively:

(75a) Do you know how much money Harry won?
(75b) No I don't.

(76a) Do you know how much money Harry won?
(76b) $30.

(77a) Do you know how much money Harry won?
(77b) How much?

Normally, exam questions use the word *know,* but *remember* and other Cognitive words are also possible:

(78a) Do you remember how they used to start it when they didn't have matches?
(78b) Rub sticks.

Typically, exam questions have a third property, namely, that the speaker already knows the answer to the question. This is true of the typical classroom use of the exam question. However, there are cases such as the following where the first speaker probably does not know the answer to the question:

(79a) Do you know what time it is?
(79b) Three o'clock.

In this case, the first two criteria for exam questions are met. While this type of question does differ in terms of the knowledge of the speaker, there is justification for grouping it in the same class with other exam questions; namely, that the role of the lexical meaning of *know* is the same in both cases.

Normally exam questions are in the second person:

(80) Do you know who discovered America?

It is also possible to question the addressee's knowledge without using the second person, as in:[7]

(81) Does anybody know who discovered America?

Hedges. The next kind of pragmatic usage we will discuss is 'Hedges,' the use of cognitive internal statc words to convey uncertainty. Like some of the other pragmatic usages we have discussed, Hedges involve conversational implicatures. We will start by illustrating the kind of implicature involved in a non-internal-state context.

---

[7] There is a very similar implicational jump in third questions. For example:

(a) Did Glen know what day Mary was going to be here?
(b) Tomorrow, I think.

It isn't as clear, though, that this occurrence of *know* should be considered pragmatic; it might be argued that the meaning of *know* contributes substantially to the overall utterance meaning. Consider the following questions, all of which might appropriately be answered with "Tomorrow, I think":

(c) Did Glen *say* what day Mary was going to be here?
(d) Did Glen *decide* what day Mary was supposed to be here?
(e) Did Glen *specify* what day Mary was going to be here?
(f) Did Glen *write* what day Mary was going to be here?

It seems safe to say that all of the italicized words contribute their full literal meaning to the sentence, and that the fact that the question might not be answered literally does not change this fact. Therefore, it would seem best to consider *know* in a parallel sentence to be semantic rather than pragmatic.

This of course raises the question of whether the *know* in second-person exam questions shouldn't also be considered semantic rather than pragmatic, since failure to literally answer a question about knowledge does not necessarily imply that the word *know* did not contribute to the meaning of the question.

The word *adequate* is listed in Webster's New World Dictionary of the American Language (College Edition) as having two meanings:

1. Equal to a requirement or occasion; sufficient; suitable
2. Barely satisfactory; acceptable but not remarkable

The second meaning is clearly derivable from the first by some very general rules of conversational implication, which probably fall under the Quantity maxim of the Cooperative Principle (Grice, 1975; 1978). The principle is a little difficult to state explicitly, but it is transparent enough; if you say, for instance, that the service at a restaurant was "adequate," by saying this, you imply that it is only, or just barely, adequate.

This principle has implications for the use of words like *believe, think, bet, feel, guess, suppose,* and *opinion* in everyday conversation. In some contexts, *believe, think,* and words of similar meaning have what one could call a 'neutral' meaning, that might be paraphrased as "to consider to be true" or "to hold the opinion," as in:

(82) Some astronomers believe that the universe will continue to expand indefinitely.

However, because of the principle that the speaker should use 'stronger' words like *know* or *certain* if they in fact fit the situation, the use of *believe* or *think* often emphasizes the uncertainty or lack of verifiability that differentiate *believe* and *know*. One context in which this is the case is when contrastive stress is on the word *believe* or *think:*

(83) John *thinks* he's going to be invited to the party.

The words think and believe do not necessarily mean that the propositional content of their complements is doubtful, but in (83) the implicit contrast with *know* does convey this.

Another context in which this is the case is in first person assertions about beliefs, as in:

(84) I think it's going to rain.

The basic reason for this is as follows: The word *think* in such a sentence is largely redundant. If you say "It's going to rain," it is clear (assuming normal contexts and use of language) that you believe it is going to rain; there is no need to assert that you believe what you assert. Therefore, to use the word *think* in such a sentence is to implicitly emphasize it. The effect is more or less the same as in the contrastive stress example mentioned above (83)—what is conveyed is not the fact that you have an opinion, but rather the fact that what you are asserting is dubious or uncertain because it is based only on belief, and not knowledge.

This is a matter of degree; the following sentences seem to exhibit increasing uncertainty:

(85a) It's going to rain.
(85b) I think it's going to rain.
(85c) I *think* it's going to rain.

The next question is whether the use of *think* in any of the following sentence types should be considered pragmatic:

(86a) I think it's going to rain.
(86b) I *think* it's going to rain.
(86c) *I* think it's going to rain.
(86d) It's going to rain, I think.

The distinction between semantic and pragmatic here relates to the function of the two aspects of meaning we have been discussing: first, the 'literal' meaning, concerning someone's opinion, or what one considers true, and second, the implication of doubt or uncertainty. To say that a usage of *think* is semantic is to say that the first or 'literal' meaning was intended by the speaker. (This does not exclude the second being implied as well, of course.) A usage would be labeled pragmatic if the second meaning, the implied doubt or uncertainty, were intended by the speaker, with the literal meaning either not intended at all, or only marginally involved in what the speaker was trying to communicate.

Using this as a guideline, we would categorize the examples in (86) as follows:

First (86d), "it's going to rain, I think." This can fairly safely be classed as pragmatic. The "I think" in this sentence does not specify that the prediction about rain is the speaker's opinion or belief; rather, it expresses chiefly some doubt or uncertainty on the speaker's part.

The same can be said of other tags, such as *I bet, I guess, I suppose.*

Second, (86c) "*I* think it's going to rain" can without question be classified as semantic. It is about the speaker's opinion, and does not convey uncertainty at all.

A little more problematic is the case of (86b), "I *think* it's going to rain." On the one hand, the implied meaning of doubt or uncertainty is obviously the main thing conveyed by such a sentence. On the other hand, in almost all other pragmatic usages we have examined up to now, the internal state word has been peripheral to the intended meaning of the utterance, and could be deleted without loss of essential content.

One possible direction for a criterion for classifying such a sentence would be a paraphrase test of the following sort: If a sentence such as "I think we have everything," *taken in context,* can be validly paraphrased by a genuinely pragmatic hedge, "We have everything, I think," then it can be classed as a Pragmatic usage.[8]

Finally, related to the hedges we have already discussed in function, although not in form, is the use of phrases like "I don't know" to convey uncertainty rather than literal lack of knowledge, as in:

(87) Well I don't know, they come from a bakery....

Somewhat similar to this are usages such as:

(88) I don't know about you, but I'm going to....

There are also uses of *know* that are perhaps difficult to classify:

(89) One never knows.
I don't know about that.
I don't know if they would....

It seems clear that the use of *know* in (87) is pragmatic, but the rest of these cases seem questionable, and probably better classified as semantic.

Opinion Questions. We have noted that first-person assertions with words like *think* (e.g., I think it's going to rain) are problematic: On the one hand, the word *think* is somewhat redundant in such a sentence, and doesn't contribute much other than to express some doubt or uncertainty on the part of the speaker. On the other hand, it is not absolutely clear that the literal meaning of *think* contributes so little to the sentence that it should be considered a pragmatic usage.

Second person questions with *think* seem similar in some respects; the *think* in sentences such as the following seems a little redundant, for example:

---

[8] It must be noted that the problem of classifying sentences such as (I think we have everything) applies specifically to first-person assertions. In the third person, for example, it is clear that it is the opinion or belief of the individual that is being talked about:

She probably thought you didn't like it.
Julia thinks that peas are from corn on the cob.

(Second-person questions constitute a special case which will be discussed below.)

First person assertions in the past tense generally convey information about the speaker's former beliefs and opinions, and thus are semantic, as in the case of the following:

I thought the place was flooded.

However, if there is some implicit or explicit disagreement, the speaker can distance him/herself from an opinion by putting it in the past tense:

(a) I thought he wanted you to leave it on.
(b) I thought grandma grew it in her back yard.
(c) Four, I thought you said.

Such usages seem more like hedges, and therefore are presumably pragmatic.

(90a) Why do you think the fire went out?
(90b) What do you think he wants?

In some cases, where this category overlaps with Indirect Requests and Suggestions, *think* seems so redundant that it can be left out without affecting the sense very much. Thus, compare the sentences of (91) with their paraphrases without *think* in (92):

(91a) Don't you think we should decide what we're going to do?
(91b) Do you think you could take out the garbage?
(91c) Think we should start moving the furniture?

(92a) Shouldn't we decide what we're going to do?
(92b) Could you take out the garbage?
(92c) Should we start moving the furniture?

However, in the case of the sentences in (90), it isn't clear that the word *think* is quite that redundant. The question is, basically, are the sentences in (93) more like those in (94) or (95), in terms of what the speaker is trying to convey?

(93a) Why do you think the fire went out?
(93b) What do you think he wants?

(94a) In your opinion, why did the fire go out?
(94b) In your opinion, what does he want?

(95a) Why did the fire go out?
(95b) What does he want?

Again, we have a problematic case, since the answer is not absolutely clear. With some intonation patterns, of course, it is easier to make the decision. For example, (96) is clearly closer in meaning to (94a) than to (95a):

(96) Why do *you* think the fire went out?

One way to make a decision is to ask what *think* contributes to the sentences in (93); that is, what is the difference between "What happened?" and "What do you think happened?"? The difference seems to be that, in the latter, the speaker explicitly recognizes that the addressee doesn't (or may not) have sure knowledge of the answer, so that the speaker is asking for a belief or opinion rather than a statement of knowledge. But this is exactly what the literal content of *think* contributes to the sentence, so it seems wrong to call the usage of *think* in (93) pragmatic.

The Indirect Requests and Suggestions in (91), however, do seem to be instances of pragmatic usage. There are also cases of second-person questions with *think* that are Rhetorical Questions, which are therefore also to be coded as pragmatic:

(97a) What do you think happened next?

(97b) What?

(98) And do you think he came to visit me? Of course not.

Attentional Devices. Attentional Devices are uses of Perceptual words which function primarily to get the addressee's attention. They can be divided into two basic categories:

(A) Imperatives of verbs like *look, listen,* and *watch:*

(99) Look what I did!
But then look what happened, see!
Look. Hey Julia, look. Julia, look what I did with yours.
Look at that!
Look it! This guy only got no arms and only one leg.
Watch out!
Look at Matilda!

(B) Questions and reduced questions with *see:*

(100) You see that? Put your finger on this?
The small circles go in the curved section. See?
Oh! See that? A spark.
See, they're showing you all kinds of fires.
See, look at the needles jump.

On the one hand, it seems clear that such usages are not as pragmatic as most of the pragmatic usages we have already discussed. While the major purpose of saying "Look!" may be to get the addressee's attention, it is probably also the case that, in this case, visual attention (rather than listening) is being requested; thus, the literal meaning of the internal state word is playing an important role in the intended meaning of the utterance.

On the other hand, there is a real difference between, for example, a music teacher saying "Listen!" in a loud voice to the class to get their attention, and the same teacher saying "Listen carefully to this next part where the trumpets come in." It can be argued that the lexical meaning of *listen* plays a more substantial role in the second case than in the first. The second is also much more likely to cause the addressee to reflect on the process of listening.

We can intuitively characterize Attentional Devices as uses of perceptual internal state words where the function of getting the addressee's attention is more important than the specific lexical meaning of the word; but it is difficult to give any precise criteria for how to identify such instances in texts.

It is possible (and important) to distinguish between Attentional Devices and several other superficially similar pragmatic usages. For example, consider the following pairs of sentences, where the (a) version illustrates an Attentional Device, and the (b) version a Conversational Device:

(101a) Look! I can do a cartwheel!
(101b) Look, I paid a lot of money for this car and I expect. . . .

(102a) Listen! I have something important to tell you.
(102b) Listen, if you think you can get away with. . . .

(103a) See? Her mike and my mike are independent.
(103b) See, her mike and my mike are independent.

There is also a superficial similiarity between some Attentional Devices and Rhetorical Questions. Compare the following two examples, where the former is an attentional device, and the latter a rhetorical question:

(104a) See that? A spark!
(104b) Did you see that show? It was fantastic.

Actually, it is hard to come up with a good rhetorical question with *see* that would be confused with an Attentional Device. But the difference can be stated fairly clearly: A rhetorical question draws the addressee's attentional device, especially one with *see,* draws the addressee's attention to some object or event in the speech situation.

Miscellaneous. Finally, we just want to mention as an apparent example of a pragmatic usage that doesn't fit into any of the preceding categories the use of *know* in a sentence like:

(105) You know how sick people act.

Another type of pragmatic usage that doesn't fit into the major categories of pragmatic usages well is the use of *afraid* in a sentence such as:

(106) I'm afraid I didn't think of it.

This usage seems to be pragmatic in that there is no real fear expressed by the speaker. This probably falls into the same category as the use of *sorry* in apologies and similar uses where real sorrow or regret is not necessarily part of the meaning:

(107) I'm sorry, Melissa, there is nothing sour or bitter about these greens.

Perhaps we could establish a class of "conventionalized used of Affective words," for which other members are likely to be found.

SUMMARY

This chapter has outlined an approach to the study of internal state words. First, we have explored some of the theoretical problems and issues associated with defining this class, determining its boundaries, and breaking it down into the four major subclasses: Cognitive, Perceptual, Affective, and

Intentions and Desires. We have found the primary problems in this area to be: (a) lexical ambiguity and (b) determining whether an internal state component in a complex word meaning is the central component of that meaning.

Secondly, we have outlined two basic categories of usage. The Semantic/Pragmatic distinction relates to whether the lexical meaning of an internal state word contributes directly, indirectly, or not at all, to the intended meaning of the utterance in which it occurs. At one extreme, there are perfectly literal usages, e.g., "John knows the answer." At the other extreme are almost meaningless conversational devices and mannerisms, such as the phrase 'ya know.' In between, there are a variety of types of usage in which the contribution of the internal state word to the meaning of the utterance is diminished or made indirect by various conversational implicatures and conventions. Among these are Indirect Requests and Suggestions, such as "Do you want take out the garbage, please," and Hedges, such as "He's in his office, I think."

REFERENCES

Brewer, W. F., & Lichtenstein, E. L. (1982). *Stories are to entertain: A structural -affect theory of stories* (Tech. Report No. 265). Urbana: University of Illinois, Urbana-Champaign.

Dixon, R. M. W. (1971). A method of semantic description. In D. Steinberg & L. Jakobovits (Eds.), *Semantics: An interdisciplinary reader in philosophy, linguistics, and psychology* (pp. 436–471). Cambridge, England: Cambridge University Press.

Ervin-Tripp, S. (1977). "Wait For Me, Roller Skate!" In S. Ervin-Tripp & C. Mithcell-Kernan (Eds.), *Child discourse* (pp. 165–188). New York: Academic Press.

Flavell, J. (1978). *Cognitive monitoring.* Paper Presented at the Conference on Children's Oral Communication Skills, University of Wisconsin.

Flavell, J. (1979). *Metacognition and cognitive monitoring.* Unpublished paper.

Gearhart, M., & Hall, W. S. (1979). *Internal state words: Cultural and situational variation in vocabulary usage* (Tech. Report No. 115). Urbana: University of Illinois, Center for the Study of Reading.

Gearhart, M., & Hall, W. S. (1983). Cultural and situational variation in vocabulary usage. In L. Waterhouse (Ed.), *Individual variation in language acquisition* (pp. 89–136). Hiroshima, Japan: Bunka Hyoron.

Gordon, D., & Lakoff, G. (1971). Conversational postulates. In *Papers from the Seventh Regional Meeting of the Chicago Linguistic Society* (pp. 63–84). Chicago, Chicago Linguistic Society.

Grice, H. P. (1975). Logic and conversation. In P. Cole & J. Morgan (Eds.), *Syntax and semantics: Speech acts* (Vol. 3). New York: Academic Press.

Grice, H. P. (1978). Further notes on logic and conversation. In P. Cole (Ed.), *Syntax and semantics: Pragmatics* (Vol. 9). New York: Academic Press.

Hall, W. S. (1978). *Cultural and situational variation in language function and use: A program of research* (Working Paper No. 15). New York: Rockefeller University, Laboratory of Comparative Human Cognition and Institute for Comparative Human Development.

Hall, W. S., Nagy, W. E., & Linn, R. (1984). *Spoken words.* Hillsdale, NJ: Erlbaum.

Hall, W. S., Nagy, W.E., & Nottenburg, G. (1981). *Situational variation in the use of internal state words* (Tech. Report No. 212). Urbana: University of Illinois, Center for the Study of Reading.

Jose, P. E., & Brewer, W. F. (1983). *The development of story liking: Character identification, suspense, and outcome resolution* (Tech. Report No. 291). Urbana: University of Illinois, Center for the Study of Reading.

Kendall, J. R., & Mason, J. M. (1982). Metacognition from the historical context of teaching reading (Tech. Report No. 263). Urbana: University of Illinois, Center for the Study of Reading.

Palinscar, A. S., & Brown, A. L. (1984). Reciprocal teaching of comprehension fostering and comprehension monitoring activities. *Cognition and Instruction, 1,* 117–175.

Sadock, J. (1972). Speech act idioms. In P. Peranteau, J. Levi, & G. Pharess (Eds.), *Papers from the Eighth Regional Meeting of the Chicago Linguistic Society.* Chicago: Chicago Linguistic Society.

Sadock, J. (1974). *Toward a linguistic theory of speech acts.* New York: Academic Press.

Wellman, H., & Johnson, C. (1979). Understanding of mental processes: A developmental study of "remember" and "forget." *Child Development, 50,* 79–88.

Wellman, H., & Johnson, C. (1979). Understanding of mental processes: A Developmental Study of "Remember" and "Forget." In *Child Development* (Vol. 50). Chicago: University of Chicago Press.

Chapter 3

Some Relations Between Children's Knowledge of Metalinguistic and Metacognitive Verbs and Their Linguistic Competencies*

David R. Olson
Nancy G. Torrance
Ontario Institute for Studies in Education

There is some evidence that children's knowledge of one part of the metalanguage, that part used for referring to the structure of language per se, is important to learning to read. As Reid (1966), Downing and Leong (1982), Wells (1985), and others have shown, children's knowledge of such concepts as word, letter, sentence, and sound is highly correlated with their progress in learning to read. Another way to say this is that children's knowledge of the metalinguistic nouns *sentence, word, letter,* and *sound* is important to learning to read and write an alphabetic, word-based script.

But only a small part of the metalanguage is represented in these structural nouns. Also important is the more general set of metalinguistic verbs implicated in the theories of language developed by such philosophers as Austin (1962), Grice (1957), Vendler (1970) and Searle (1979). A central point of these theories is that there is a rather direct relation between the structures of thought and the structures of talk. That link is specified in the theory of speech acts. For each distinctive type of speech act, such as asserting, requesting, and promising, there is a distinctive type of mental state. Their relations are made explicit in the set of speech act verbs and mental state verbs, what we may call metalinguistic verbs and metacognitive verbs. Specifically, in order to sincerely *assert* x, one must *believe* x; in order to

* This research was funded jointly by the Spencer Foundation, the Social Sciences and Humanities Research Council of Canada, and the Ontario Ministry of Education under its Block Transfer Grant to OISE.

sincerely *request* y, one must *want* or *desire* y; in order to sincerely *promise* z, one must *intend* z.

A child may carry out these speech acts and entertain the corresponding mental states without knowing the metalinguistic verbs *say, ask, promise,* or the metacognitive verbs *believe, desire,* or *intend.* Yet, just as the speech acts are tied to mental states, so knowledge of speech act verbs may be tied to knowledge of mental state verbs. Simply, the verbs *say* and *think* may be related.

But the relations between the speech acts and mental states, on one hand, and the verbs representing those speech acts and mental states, on the other, are not at all clear. As we mentioned above, surely it is possible to believe something without knowing the verb *believe* (or *think*). But is it possible to promise something without knowing the meaning of the verb *promise?* These issues are pursued more fully in Olson and Astington (in press).

Certainly, it is difficult to test for children's knowledge of beliefs and intentions without using the corresponding verbs. There is no way to ask about the meaning of words without using the terms *meaning* and *word,* as for example, "What does the word *x* mean?" To ask "what is an x?" is to ask about the object, not about the word denoting that object (Watson & Olson, in press).

Further, it may be the case that what is referred to as metacognitive knowledge (Flavell, 1981), as indicated in children's difficulty in recognizing failures to understand (Markman, 1979) reflects the fact that young children do not know what *understand* or *comprehend* mean, and they consequently do not know what the experimenter is referring to. Thus, Markman gave first and third grade children the task of advising someone on writing instructions for a magic trick. Although the instructions contained glaring omissions, young children claimed to understand them. Evidence of failure of understanding was taken to be the child's claim that he or she did not understand or "get it," or requested further information. What should be noted is that children could only indicate a failure to understand if they knew first what understanding required and secondly, what the term *understand* means.

For less complex metalinguistic and metacognitive verbs such as *say* and *think,* it would seem to be unnecessary to learn to use these verbs in order to carry out either the acts of saying things or thinking things. That is, there would seem to be no necessity in knowing the verb in order to carry out the action or to entertain the mental state. Surely children can carry out the speech act of requesting before they learn the metalinguistic verb *ask* or *request.* And surely they can carry out the speech act of asserting before they learn the metalinguistic verb *say.* Yet studies of early child language by Limber (1973) and Bloom, Lahey, Hood, Lifter, and Fiess (1980) have shown that the metalinguistic verbs *ask, say,* and *tell* and metacognitive verbs *want, think,* and *know* appear extremely early, somewhere around the middle of the third year. But not until about 5 years of age can children successfully differentiate metacognitive verbs such as *know* and *think* (Johnson & Maratsos, 1977), *know* and *guess* (Miscione, Marvin, O'Brien, and Greenberg, 1978) and *remember* and *forget* (Johnson, 1981). Again, it is not clear that concepts of speech acts and mental states are acquired before the corresponding metalinguistic and metacognitive verbs; there is no evidence on this point.

There is another reason for thinking that the metalinguistic and metacognitive verbs may be closely tied to the use of particular speech acts and the entertaining of particular mental states. Some theorists (Ross, 1970) have argued that there is an implicit speech act verb in every speech act. The assertion "It's noon" has in its deep structure the full embedding construction, "I assert that it's noon." It is not clear that a similar argument could be made for the metacognitive verb as in "I believe (think) that it's raining", although theories of propositional attitudes (Dennett, 1978; Fodor, 1978) do argue that all mental representations consist of propositions marked by some propositional attitude which indicates how that proposition is to be taken.

Our suggestion is that metalinguistic verbs and metacognitive verbs, the verbs of saying and the verbs of thinking/meaning are at the heart of the problem of language and thought. Like Vendler, we would argue that the thoughts a child or adult can think are closely related to the utterances the child or adult can generate and/or comprehend. And one important means of examining children's thought and language is via their knowledge of the corresponding verbs of saying and meaning.

These verbs are interesting for the reason suggested at the outset, namely, that competence with the metalanguage can reasonably be related to literacy. The preservation of text in written form preserves what was said, the linguistic form, but not the intended meaning which must then be reconstrued on the basis of the linguistic form. Writing, we may say, solves the "memory problem" but it creates a "meaning problem". We have argued (Olson, 1977; Olson & Torrance, 1983) that, for this reason, literacy is an important factor in coming to differentiate what was said from what was meant.

Our concern in this paper is with children's acquisition of a small set of metalinguistic and metacognitive verbs, the relations between acquisition of the metalinguistic verb and its corresponding metacognitive verb—*say* with *think, ask* with *want, deny* with *doubt, promise* with *intend,* and with the relations between competence with such verbs and the child's literacy skills. We have not yet examined these verbs in a way that permits a direct answer to our questions, but results of some early studies suggest that there is a relation between the verbs of thinking and saying, and of these in turn with literacy.

In one of our early studies (Robinson, Goelman, & Olson, 1983), we pursued Robinson's finding that preschool and first grade children in a referential communication task tend to blame the listener in cases of communication failure, while second graders begin to correctly blame the speaker and his ambiguous message. We examined the possibility that "listener blamers" failed to blame the message because they did not clearly differentiate what was *said* from what was *meant*. Results indicated that children who distinguish what is said from what is meant are the very ones who can differentiate an informationally adequate message from an inadequate one. Furthermore, the ability to distinguish what was actually said from what the speaker had meant to say is directly associated with their management of the contrast between the metalinguistic verb *say* and the metacognitive verb *mean*. Linguistic awareness of what was said may be nothing other than competence with the corresponding metalinguistic and metacognitive terms. Interestingly, in an examination of the transcriptions of some of these children's speech collected in the home, Robinson found that the children who were more sophisticated in this task, the "speaker blamers," tended to have mothers who had, in fact, used some of these metalinguistic and metacognitive verbs in their conversations with children, saying, for example, "What do you mean?" or "I don't understand."

As mentioned, the other reason for examining children's mastery of these metalinguistic and metacognitive verbs has to do with our interest in literacy. In our longitudinal study of oral language competence and its relation to the acquisition of literacy skills (Torrance & Olson, 1985), we found that one of the best predictors of early reading was children's use of such metacognitive verbs as *think, know, decide,* and *remember* in their conversational interactions with peers. Hall and Nagy (1979) too, in a very thorough analysis of terms for describing internal states, found large social group differences in children's use of these verbs. They have not yet looked to see if their use was related to children's progress in school.

We have also designed a series of experimental tasks to allow us to explore children's competence with a range of metalinguistic and metacognitive verbs and the relation between that competence and their progress in learning to read. Again, the findings of our longitudinal study indicate that, by Grade 1, good and poor readers differ in their use of this set of verbs in their oral conversations. The tasks presented here are intended to permit us to make a more thorough assessment of children's comprehension of these verbs. Long range plans include both a fuller analysis of these verbs in the transcripts that were made for the longitudinal study, and further experimental studies of children's competence with these verbs.

METHOD

Subjects

Tasks were administered to the 34 children who are subjects in the longitudinal study. The children are native English speakers drawn from two Toronto schools, one in a predominantly working class neighbourhood and the other in a predominantly middle class neighbourhood. The children were approximately 5½ years old when the study began, and were approximately 7½ years old when the current tasks were administered. Reading and vocabulary test scores were collected a year earlier, when the children were 6½ years old.

Procedure

Each of the four tasks was administered individually in the same session, lasting approximately 25-30 minutes. Each child was given the tasks in the same fixed order—Say and Mean, and Think, Know and Pretend, Forced Choice, and Mean-Intend.

The Say and Mean Task. The children were told that they would be read some very short stories and then asked some questions about the story. The task consisted of 3- or 4-line stories—all of which involved the same set of characters. The stories ended with a direct quotation, two of them with: "That was a clever thing to do," and two concluded with: "There's a car." The content of two of the stories was such that the final direct quotation could be interpreted literally in one case, while, in the other, it would be interpreted indirectly, that is as sarcasm or as an indirect request. To illustrate, the two contexts that accompanied the utterance, "That was a clever thing to do, Jonathan," either led to the interpretation that Jonathan had indeed performed a clever action (the direct meaning) or that he had done something stupid (the indirect, sarcastic meaning). In the "There's a car" stories, that ending was a simple assertion in one context, while in the other it indirectly expressed a warning.

After each paragraph, the children were asked (a) What did ——— say? (b) What did ——— mean? (c) Why did s/he say that?

The Think, Know, Pretend Task. The second task contrasted the verbs "think," "know," and "pretend." These verbs were used to construct complex sentences consisting of an embedding construction with one of the metacognitive verbs—John thinks, John knows, John pretends—and an embedded sentence complement. Six different complements were used with each verb: two were factual complements (the ball is round; the house has a roof); two were false or counter-factual (ice cream tastes bad; snow is warm); and two were neutral (the book is lost; the bicycle is under a tree).

Each of these complex sentences was followed by a question of the form: "If John thinks (knows, pretends) it, is (the complement) true?" These 18 statements were read to the children in random order. Each child was asked to respond yes, no, or maybe to the question following each statement, and then was asked to justify his/her response.

The Pretend/Imagine, Doubt/Deny, Realize/Remember, Decide/Wonder Forced Choice Task. Four pairs of verbs were examined by presenting short 3 or 4 line stories which concluded with two endings, one involving each member of the pair of verbs, only one of which correctly completed the story. Each verb of the pair appeared once appropriately and once inappropriately.

After hearing each story, the subject was asked to choose the best ending and to tell why they thought it best.

The Mean/Intend to Task. This task, based on Astington's (1980) study of complex expressions of intention, consisted of 6 complex statements in which the metacognitive predicates "intends to," "intended to," and "didn't intend to," as well as "means to," "meant to," and "didn't mean to," made up the embedding clause, and various simple statements served as the embedded complements. Corresponding to each of these 6 complex statements were a series of cartoon-like drawings. For each statement, there were three picture choices: one picture corresponded to the intention expressed by the verb, one picture served as a distractor item by showing either a completed action or an action done on purpose, and the third picture was a neutral item. The subjects were asked to choose the picture that *best* corresponded to the presented sentence.

RESULTS

We shall first present the results on each of these tasks separately, and subsequently examine the relation between these tasks and our other measures, primarily reading, oral competence, and intelligence test scores.

Say and Mean

Responses to the questions "What did x say?" and "What did x mean?" were asked after each story presented in this task. Responses were categorized as follows:

Verbatim:	Subjects repeat the final sentence of the story.
Intention:	Subjects attempt to retrieve an intention which lies behind the words used in the final sentence.
Contextual:	Subjects paraphrase the sentence in providing an explanation.
Inappropriate:	Subjects fabricate a response or fail to respond.

Children's responses were scored as correct as follows: For stories which concluded with either the indirect statement or the direct statement, the correct answer to the "Say" question was the verbatim answer. For the story concluding with an indirect statement, the correct answer to the "Mean" question was the Intention response; for that ending with a direct statement, the correct response was the Verbatim response or the Contextual response or an appropriate Intentional response. The number of children responding correctly to one or both of each type of item is presented in Table 1. Clearly, the majority of these second graders differentiate say/mean questions, and they have little difficulty arriving at the meanings of sentences used indirectly whether they occur as sarcasm or as indirect requests. However, they have more difficulty saying that literal sentences mean exactly what they say; they tend not to simply repeat the final sentence verbatim, but rather to attempt to construct some meaning which differs somewhat from the meaning of the verbatim sentence.

Again, by and large, these children have little difficulty with these verbs, but the little variability that does occur correlates, as we shall see, with children's performance on the vocabulary test and on the reading test.

Think, Know, and Pretend

Correct response to the *know* questions was "Yes," to the *pretend* questions was "No," and to the *think* questions was "Maybe." Further, the responses were classifed in terms of the embedded complements which can be described as factual, neutral, or counterfactual. The number of correct responses per cell is shown in Table 2. There were two significant effects, one for the verb ($F = 13.17$, $df = 2{,}64$ $p < .01$) and one for the interaction between

Table 1. Number of Children Responding Correctly to the Say/Mean Question ($N = 34$)

	Question	
Story	**Say**	**Mean**
Direct	31	21
Indirect	30	29

Table 2. Number of Correct Responses to *Think, Know, Pretend* Questions with Factual, Neutral, or Counterfactual Complements ($N = 34$)

	Verb			
Complement	**Think**	**Know**	**Pretend**	**Mean**
Factual	.88*	1.91	.97	1.25
Neutral	1.00	1.68	1.44	1.37
Counterfactual	.85	1.12	1.65	1.20
Mean	.91	1.57	1.35	

* Maximum score per cell is 2.00

the verb and the form of the complement ($F = 18.77$, $df = 4{,}128$ $p < .001$). The verb *know* was easier than the verb *pretend,* which, in turn, was easier than the verb *think*. These differences, however, have to be qualified by the fact that our children appear to be reluctant to say "maybe" to the *think* questions; our young Ss appear to prefer either "yes" or "no" responses which they then justify by some fabrication.

Consider, however, the interaction between the complement types, factual, neutral, and counterfactual, and the verb involved. An examination of Table 2 shows that it is easy to say "yes" to the verb *know* when it takes a factual or neutral complement clause, but difficult when it takes a counterfactual clause—for "John knows the ice cream tastes bad. If John knows it, does the ice cream taste bad?", children tended to say "no" and thus get this counterfactual item incorrect.

For *pretend,* just the opposite pattern holds. It is easy to say "no" to a *pretend* sentence when the complement is a counterfactual, and difficult to say "no" when the complement is factual. "John pretends the ball is round. If John pretends it, is the ball round?" The correct answer is "no," but children were as likely to say "yes" as "no." Preliminary evidence suggests that some adults do much the same thing, while others respond solely on the basis of the verb, regardless of the truth of the complement.

Our young subjects were not, however, ignoring the verb altogether. If they simply said "yes" to all sentences containing factual complements and "no" to those containing counterfactual complements, while ignoring the embedding verb, the number of "yes" and "no" responses would be consistent across verbs and different for the three conditions. The relevant data are shown in Table 3a and 3b. Indeed, "yes" responses are much more com-

Table 3a. Number of "Yes" Responses

	Think	Know	Pretend	% of Yes Resp.
Factual	37	96	26	47
Neutral	16	84	10	33
Counterfactual	7	56	6	20
% of Yes Responses	18%	70%	12%	338

Table 3b. Number of "No" Responses

	Think	Know	Pretend	% of No Resp.
Factual	20	1	50	19
Neutral	36	11	73	33
Counterfactual	51	40	83	48
% of No Responses	29%	14%	56%	365

mon for the factual items (47%) and "no" for the counterfactuals (48%). Nevertheless, the verb *know* gets by far the largest number of "yes" responses (70%), while the verb *pretend* gets the majority of the "no" responses (56%). Thus, the child's response is influenced both by the verb and by the plausibility of the complement clause.

Just how subjects are treating these verbs is more clearly indicated in the justifications they offered for their choice of responses. Justifications were coded in terms of whether subjects appealed to the verb, to their general knowledge of the world, or to some "on the spot" fabrication. If they appealed to the verb in explaining their choice, it was further noted if the appeal was an adequate justification or simply an appeal. These categories are listed in full in Table 4.

As the various appeals to wording, that is to the verb *think, know,* or *pretend,* all gave much the same result, we will report only that for adequate appeals to the verb. The mean number of correct appeals to the verb in the three conditions is shown in Table 5. Justifications tend to mirror the results for correct responses in that there are significant verb differences ($F=4.99$, $df=2,64$, $p<.01$), *know* being appealed to more often in justifying a response than either *think* or *pretend,* and *think* more often than *pretend.* Secondly, there is a significant condition effect ($F=8.40$, $df=2,64$, $p<.01$), the neutral complement leading children to appeal to the verb more often than the factual or counterfactual complements.

One incidental finding illustrates the importance of the truth of the complement in determining children's judgments. The two counter-factual complements occurring with the verb *know* differed in that one was a general

Table 4. Coding Scheme for Think/Know/Pretend/Justify

(1) Correct appeal to wording (implicit and explicit). "If he knows it, it's true."
(2) Correct appeal to definition. "Because *know* means it's gotta be true."
(3) Incorrect appeal to definition. "You *pretend* something, then it's true."
(4) Appeal to general knowledge. "All balls are round."
(5) General knowledge and appeal to wording. "Balls are round and besides he knows it."
(6) Fabrication.
(7) Fabrication and appeal to wording.
(8) Irrelevant. "I don't know" or no response.

Table 5. Mean Number of Correct Appeals to the Verb

	Think	Know	Pretend	Mean/Condition
Factual	1.15*	1.18	.82	1.04
Neutral	1.32	1.44	1.26	1.34
Counterfactual	1.03	1.18	.73	.98
Mean/Verb	1.16	1.27	.94	

* Out of 2 responses per child

statement: "that snow is warm," while the other was a specific one: "that *the* ice cream tastes bad," the latter marked by the presence of the definite article. While the general statement could not be false, the specific one could. That is, the definite statement is more plausible than the general one. Although this factor was not counterbalanced, it appears that children did indeed note the difference, rejecting the general statement some 71% of the time and the specific one only 40% of the time.

These results can be summarized briefly. First, judgments are made by reference to the truth of the complement clause. Factual and counterfactual complements tend to elicit "yes" and "no" responses respectively; hence, justification for these choices tends to be based more on general knowledge and less on the verb in question. In the neutral complement condition, there is no reasonable general knowledge base to appeal to, so Ss tend to appeal to the verb in justifying their answers. Some children are more likely to do this than others, as we shall see in the correlational analysis.

Imagine/Pretend, Realize/Remember, Doubt/Deny, Wonder/Decide

In this task, children had to choose the verb which best completed the final sentence of a brief story. Responses were scored both for their correctness for each verb and for the justifications children offered—again primarily for an appeal to the verb in which the child defined or attempted to define the correctly chosen verb.

Children tended to correctly select some verbs more often than others. These means are shown in Table 6. Again, differences in the number of children correctly selecting a particular verb are difficult to interpret, in that each verb falls in a different story context and is drawn from a different pair of alternatives. Hence, the justification of choices in terms of provision of a correct definition may be a better indication of children's knowledge of these verbs. The number of correct appeals to definitions for each verb is shown in the bottom row of Table 7. These verbs differ significantly from each other ($F=2.62$, $df=7{,}224$ $p<.05$), with *wonder, remember,* and *doubt* being among the easiest to define, and *imagine, decide, pretend,* and *deny* the most difficult.

Table 6. Number of Children Choosing and Justifying the Correct Verb in Forced-Choice Task ($N=34$)

	Remember	Decide	Imagine	Wonder	Doubt	Realize	Pretend	Deny
Correct verb choice	31	30	29	26	23	22	22	21
Correct appeal to definition	9	3	4	13	8	6	5	5

It may be more appropriate to take these verbs as pairs rather than singly, since subjects had to choose between the members of a pair in each case and these verbs were chosen to be contrastive. Hence, a subject who failed to discriminate the verbs but simply chose the same one every time would tend to get one verb right and the other wrong. If we take performance on the pair as an indication of competence in differentiating the two verbs, we find that some of the verb pairs are, in fact, somewhat easier than others: *Doubt/Deny* was the most difficult, with 14 subjects getting both correct; followed by *Imagine/Pretend,* with 17 correct; *Realize/Remember,* with 20 correct; and *Wonder/Decide,* the easiest, with 22 children getting both correct.

As we shall see, competence with this task correlates with our measure of vocabulary. Indeed, there is a significant difference between children who score above the median on the Vocabulary test and those who score below, for the number of adequate definitions given on this verb choice task ($F = 5.36$, $df = 1,32$ $p < .05$). We shall return to a consideration of this relationship as well as the relationship between performance on this task and reading level.

Means To and Intends To

This task is taken from Astington's picture choice task (Astington, 1981). In the present tense, these verbs (e.g., intends to) express prior intention as opposed to the completed action. In the past tense (e.g., intended to), they express the difference between intentional and accidental actions. Astington found that, prior to age 8, children ignored these verbs of intention, selecting pictures of the completed action rather than the preparation for the action in the first case, and failing to discriminate intentional from accidental in the second. By age 8, they got most of these items correct. In the present study, the percentage of children choosing the correct picture for each of these verbs is presented in Table 7. Although there is some variability on this task, by and large our second grade children performed well above chance on all of the items. The differences between the verbs is slight. The verb *means to* used in the present, as in "John means to take a bath," strikes even adults as somewhat odd, and that presumably accounts for the somewhat poorer performance on that verb. Nor is there any indication that the

Table 7. Percentage of Children Choosing the Correct Picture in Response to Sentences Employing Verbs of Intention

intends to	86%
means to	57%
didn't mean to	80%
meant to	89%
intended to	74%
didn't intend to	83%

expressions of prior intention "intends to" are any different than the expressions of deliberate action "intended to."

Again, the individual differences appear to be more important than the verb differences in that, as we shall see in more detail presently, children's performance on this task also correlates with their vocabulary and reading test scores.

Metalinguistic Verbs, Metacognitive Verbs, and Other Aspects of Oral and Literate Competence

When we consider these verbs not in terms of their structure but rather in terms of the differences between children in their competence with them, we find that performance on these tasks is quite strongly related to other aspects of oral and literate competence. The matrix of intercorrelations is shown in Table 8. Measures of oral and literate competence include vocabulary score, conversational rating (the mean score of two independent raters judging conversational skill from videotapes of children in cooperative play settings—see Torrance and Olson, 1985, for further detail), and reading score on the Durrell Analysis of Reading Difficulty. The scores from the four metalinguistic and metacognitive verb tasks described above that were included in this analysis were the number of correct items on the say/mean task (maximum = 4), the number of pairs correctly differentiated on the forced-choice task (max. = 4), the number of correct items on the *means to/ intends to* task (max. = 8), the number of correct items on the *think, know, pretend* task for the neutral complement condition only (max. = 6), and the number of justifications that appealed to a definition of the verb (correct or attempted) in the forced-choice task (max. = 8).

From Table 8, it may be noted first that the measures on the metalinguistic and metacognitive verbs are all reasonably intercorrelated, these correlations ranging up to .48. Generally, children who are good at one task will be good at the remaining tasks in the set.

Next, consider the relationship between performance on these tasks and the measures of oral and literate competence that we included in the analysis. Children's performance on the verb tasks correlate positively with each of the independent measures of language competence, these correlations ranging from .14 to .47. These correlations indicate that performance on these tasks is strongly related to aspects of both oral and literate competence. In particular, differentiating the verbatim from intended meaning (say/ mean task), choosing the correct verb to complete a short story (forced-choice task), correctly choosing a picture which illustrates an intention (means to/intends to task), and appealing to a definition of the verb in justifying the correct verb choice in the forced-choice task, all correlate significantly with ability to define words in the WISC Vocabulary subtest. Taking the verb into account in the neutral complement condition of the *think,*

Table 8. Correlations among Performance on Metalinguistic and Metacognitive Verbal Tasks and Oral and Literate Competence

	Vocabulary	Conversation	Reading	Say/Mean	Forced-Choice	Mean/Intend	TKP-Neutral	Appeal to Def'n.—Forced-Choice
Conversation	.35*							
Reading	.29	.01						
Say/Mean	.47**	.25	.17*					
Forced-Choice	.47**	.21	.26	.26				
Mean/Intend	.36*	.14	.19	.25	.48**			
TKP-Neutral	.20	30*	.14	.27	−.02	.22		
Appeal to Def'n.—forced-choice	.36*	43**	.36*	.03	.29	.18	.30*	
Total Score —combined	.61**	43**	.38*	.50**	.77**	.65**	.47**	.62**

* $p < .05$, ** $p < .01$

know, pretend task, and appealing to a definition of the verb in justifying correct verb choices in the forced-choice task, correlates significantly with a subjective measure of conversational competence, namely ability to successfully launch and maintain topics in a conversation. Finally, appealing to a definition of the verb in the forced-choice task correlates significantly with reading score on the Durrell. Thus, we find that performance on these verb tasks tends to correlate most strongly with the vocabulary test results, and to a lesser degree with conversational competence. Also, performance on the forced-choice task, particularly appealing to a verbal definition, correlates with reading. We see such an appeal to definition as equivalent to an appeal to "text," or sentence meaning as opposed to speaker's meaning (Olson, 1977). In other words, the better readers are able to restrict the justification for their responses to the very wording or "text" of the item. We have discussed elsewhere this relationship between the ability to treat language as having a meaning in its own right, the sentence meaning and literacy (Olson & Torrance, 1983). We shall return to this point in our conclusion.

Finally, as Table 8 shows, a total score on the four verb tasks was obtained for each child and entered into the analysis. This total score consisted of the sum of the five measures entered individually in the analysis and listed in Table 8. As can be seen at the bottom of Table 8, this total score correlates with the measures of oral and literate competence better than any of the individual scores on these tasks. As could be expected, given the individual results, the correlation is strongest with vocabulary, is weaker with conversational competence, and is weakest with reading performance. However, all three correlations are significant at the .05 level.

CONCLUSION

We remarked at the outset that one of the reasons for measuring children's competence with metalinguistic and metacognitive verbs in the early school years was the correlation we obtained between reading ability in Grade 1 children and the variety of metalinguistic and metacognitive verbs they used in their conversational speech. Indeed, lexical range on these verbs was the best predictor of reading success of the dozen or so measures of lexical, structural, and conversational aspects of children's speech. Further, it was from the set of the verbs occurring in these transcripts that verbs were chosen for the tasks described here, which were presented 1 year later. While performance on one of these tasks, the forced-choice task, did correlate with reading ability, the obtained correlation was less than that obtained the previous year with lexical range of these verbs in spontaneous speech (.36 as opposed to .59). This suggests that, while competence with these verbs accounts for part of the variance in our young subjects' reading ability, a more important factor is simply their use of such verbs in a conversational setting. Most of our young subjects had sufficient mastery of the terms involved to be able to correctly solve the problems presented to them in these four tasks. But not all of these children make use of these particular verbal expressions in their everyday interactions with peers. And those who do so tend to be our better readers.

This suggests an interesting hypothesis with regard to the relation between these metacognitive and metalinguistic verbs and the acquisition of literacy skills. It may be that these verbs, many of which have been available in the child's vocabulary since the age of 3 (Limber, 1973), are part of a system of concepts for decontextualizing language and thought, for making language and thought subjects in their own right. Basic to this system are the verbs which mark an understanding of the relation between speaker's meaning and sentence meaning, as well as verbs which mark the psychological commitment of the speaker to what is said, verbs such as *know, think, guess, believe, doubt,* and so on. It may be that, in learning to cope with a literate environment, the child comes to master and use concepts that permit him or her to deal with both language and thought in a new way, so that language and thought can be differentiated and decontextualized. Language no longer merely expresses the intention of the reader or writer, but comes to have a meaning in its own right, what we have called the sentence meaning. Similarly, the attitudes to propositions come free from the propositions they mark and can, therefore, be interrogated and discussed in their own right. It may be this altered stance to language and thought that we are witnessing in the conversations of our young readers. To be sure, mastery of the concepts is important and continues to be the subject of much of our research with schoolchildren, but the endpoint of this mastery may mark the beginning of a new development, one that may be critical for the child who is learning to live in the world of autonomous, decontextualized texts.

REFERENCES

Astington, J. (1981). *Children's understanding of verbal expressions of intention.* Unpublished Master's thesis, University of Toronto.

Austin, J. L. (1962). *How to do things with words.* Edited by J. O Urmson. New York: Oxford University Press, 1962.

Bloom, L., Lahey, N., Hood, L., Lifter, K. & Fiess, K. (1980). Complex sentences: Acquisition of syntactic connectives and the semantic relations they encode. *Journal of Child Language, 7,* 235–261.

Dennett, D. C. (1978). *Brainstorms.* Montgomery, VT: Bradford.

Downing, J. & Leong, C. K. (1982). *Psychology of reading.* Toronto: Macmillan.

Flavell, J. H. (1981). Cognitive monitoring. In W. P. Dixon (Ed.), *Children's oral communication skills.* New York: Academic Press.

Fodor, J. A., (1978) Propositional attitudes. *Monist, 61,* 501–523.

Grice, H. P. (1957). Meaning. *Philosophical Review, 3,* 377–388.

Hall, W. S., & Nagy, W. E. (1979). *Theoretical issues in the investigation of words of internal report.* Technical report, Center for the Study of Reading, University of Illinois.

Johnson, C. N. (1981). Acquisition of mental verbs and the concept of mind. In S. Kuczaj (Ed.), *Language development: Syntax and semantics* (Vol. 1). Hillsdale, NJ: Erlbaum.

Johnson, C. N., & Maratsos, M. P. (1977). Early comprehension of mental verbs: Think and know. *Child Development, 48,* 1743–1747.

Limber, J. (1973). The genesis of complex sentences. In T. E. Moore (Ed.), *Cognitive development and the acquisition of language.* New York: Academic Press, 1973.

Markman, E. M. (1979). Realizing that you don't understand: Elementary school children's awareness of inconsistencies. *Child Development, 50,* 643–655.

Miscione, J. L., Marvin, R. S., O'Brien, R. G., & Greenberg, M. T. (1978). A developmental study of preschool children's understanding of the words know and guess. *Child Development, 49,* 1107–1113.

Olson, D. R. (1977). From utterance to text: The bias of language in speech and writing. *Harvard Educational Review, 47,* 257–281.

Olson, D. R., & Astington, J. W. (1986). Children's acquisition of metalinguistic and metacognitive verbs. In W. Demopoulos & A. Marras (Ed.), *Language learning and concept acquisition: Foundational issues.* Norwood, NJ: Ablex.

Olson, D. R., & Torrance, N. G. (1983). Literacy and cognitive development: A conceptual transformation in the early school years. In S. Meadows (Ed.), *Issues in childhood cognitive development.* London: Methuen.

Reid, J. F. (1966). Learning to think about reading. *Educational Research, 9,* 56–62.

Robinson, E., Goelman, H., & Olson, D. R. (1983). Children's understanding of the relation between expressions (what was said) and intentions (what was meant). *British Journal of Developmental Psychology, 1,* 75–86.

Ross, J. R. (1970). On declarative sentences. In R. A. Jacobs & P. S. Rosenbaum (Eds.), *Readings in transformational grammar.* Boston: Ginn-Blaisdell.

Searle, J. R. (1979). Intentionality and the use of language. In A. Margalit (Ed.), *Meaning and use.* London: Reidel.

Torrance, N. G., & Olson, D. R. (1985). Oral and literate competencies in the early school years. In D. R. Olson, N. G. Torrance, & A. Hildyard (Eds.), *Literacy, language and learning: The nature and consequences of reading and writing.* New York: Cambridge University Press.

Vendler, Z. (1970). Say what you think. In J. L. Cowan (Ed.), *Studies in thought and language.* Tucson, AZ: University of Arizona Press.

Watson, R., & Olson, D. R. (in press). From meaning to definition: A literate bias in the structure of meaning. In R. Horowitz & J. Samuels (Eds.), *Comprehending oral and written language.* New York: Academic Press.

Wells, G. (1985). Preschool literacy-related activities and success in school. In D. Olson, N. Torrance, & A. Hildyard (Eds.), *Literacy, language and learning: The nature and consequences of reading and writing.* New York: Cambridge University Press.

PART II

TEXT AND TEXT PROCESSING

Chapter 4

An Interaction Between Morphology and Discourse

Joseph E. Grimes

Cornell University and Summer Institute of Linguistics

Whether our position on universal grammar begins with the supposition that a number of innate, genetically conditioned attributes of humankind interact to make language be what it is, as Noam Chomsky wants to assume (1980), or whether we simply recognize that, for one reason or another, there are some things without which a human language cannot really be a human language, there is an implication that any phenomenon we find in our field studies, however unfamiliar it may seem to us, may point to something very deep-seated about language. Chomsky, for example, identifies the difference between proximate and obviative in Hopi as "one of the devices provided by universal grammar" which also "figures in English and presumably in all languages" (1980, p. 169).

While neither he nor anyone else would claim to be able to describe the components of universal grammar that account for this device, or even to distinguish them clearly from others, the notion that we humans are put together in such a way that we can respond consistently in terms of that kind of difference is not one to be taken lightly. The further notion that every human being has the capability of responding in a similar way to the rest, given similar activation, is not far off from the other.

Perhaps by historical accident, the discussion of such universal properties of language has concentrated on phonology and sentence grammar. These are the areas where modern linguistics developed most rapidly; linguists for many decades were not very good at thinking about discourse or meaning, but they are good at sounds and sentences. But when we open up the broader question Chomsky raises—the question about what there is in human nature that renders us capable of language—in the light of recent work in discourse and semantics, the complexity goes up.

Though I have no background myself to discuss the biological side of the question, on the linguistic side of it I have come to see from my field experience that, for nearly any feature of discourse, no matter how bizarre it may appear or how delicately it may be hidden in the sentences that manifest it, that feature is almost certain to be laid out in some other languages in a way that is more accessible than hidden.

It is something like the well-known phenomenon that afflicts second language learners: the minute you learn a new word or a new form of expression, everyone around you seems to start using it right away, as if they had conspired to keep quiet until the moment you tumbled to it. They didn't, of course; you merely were not ready to notice it when they used it. In the same way, discourse features we are only beginning to become aware of turn out to be manifested in many ways once we start to observe them in different languages.

To put it another way, some languages seem to conceal part of the way they do things so successfully that only a sophisticated grammarian will even notice that anything is going on, whereas other languages put the same things right up front. For example, Russian has ways of communicating definiteness—the means by which the speaker tells his hearer that he believes the hearer can identify what he is referring to without further talk. But definiteness in Russian is something even a Russian has difficulty explaining, because it is wrapped up in subtleties of word order and other things grammarians tend to shy away from. On the other hand, one can hardly get through one's first lesson on English without coming face to face with definiteness, because it is forced into attention by the choice of articles that confronts the speaker in nearly every sentence: I count twelve places in this sentence up to the beginning of this clause, for example, where one has to decide whether what he is saying involves it. So if one wants to understand definiteness, an ideal language to work it out in is English, and an ideal language to refine one's understanding of it is Russian, but not the other way around.

When we look at what needs to be subsumed under universal grammar in this light, Chomsky's statement about Hopi as evidence for a universal trait of human speech seems less odd. What is present though barely noticeable in English is spread all across Hopi; our task is to account for it in both.

One such phenomenon that has held my attention recently is the way we shape our utterances so as to give our hearer the maximum chance of following what we are saying. We do not simply enunciate propositions; we express them in such a way as to guide the hearer through them.

I use the term *topic* to refer to this phenomenon. This is not the only use of 'topic' in linguistics, and there are other terms like 'theme' and 'focus' that are also used for it; but in this discourse I restrict myself to this one use.

Jeanette Gundel (1974) laid out several properties of this feature of language: in the referential field that consists of all the things a speaker could refer to at any point in the discourse, he gives special expression to a subset of the field which shares two properties. First, any referents that are treated in this special way have to be things that it is reasonable for the speaker to refer to as presumably existing as entities that the hearer can identify. Second, of the possible referents that fill the first requirement, one or more are made active at each point in the discourse as the link in understanding between the speaker and the hearer; the hooks from which the speaker hangs his comments, so to speak. The idea of topic is not restricted to singular referents, of course; nor is it restricted to objects or even objectified things, but may include entire situations.

In English, the topic may be hard to identify because it is so closely bound up with the notion of subject. The referent treated as topic is often the subject of the sentence; even when it is not, it commonly comes at the beginning of a sentence, and it may be set off by intonation or even by special wording such as *now concerning. . . .* In addition, English provides for a hierarchy of topics: in order for me to tell you about this, you must first let me talk about that, and later we will get back to the first thing (Grimes, 1981).

The signals by which topics are established, carried along, shifted, pushed down, and popped back up in English are to say the least subtle. Chafe has pointed out at least five factors that cluster together with the topic in English (1976), yet none of them is expressed distinctively enough to enable it to be segregated out totally from among the others.

There are languages, however, that simplify matters for us. If we can identify what is going on in languages such as these, where parts of the topic-related complex are made explicit, that knowledge will help us understand what is happening in other languages that are not so favored, keeping within the assumption that both kinds of languages manifest something deeply grounded in the human language faculty.

Bacairi of Brazil was the first language to come to my attention that made topic explicit. There James Wheatley observed (1973) that there seems to be an overabundance of pronouns for the third person, even allowing for a pervasive distinction between animate and inanimate. The pronouns all have a demonstrative use; but in text there are four pronoun sets that are not distinguished in any of the usual ways—by deictic category, case, or gender.

It became clear to Wheatley what all those pronouns are there for once he began to plot the way they are used in texts. Working from a transcript, one can almost visualize through these pronouns a set of stage directions for presenting the situations given in the texts. For example, one of the third person singular pronouns, *maca,* is like an instruction to turn the spotlight on one of the referents so that everything else is seen in relation to that referent as long as the pronouns do not change. All the other referents get other pronouns, which I would now think of as nontopic pronouns, in the same texts.

```
DEICTIC USE

                        DEFINITE        INDEFINITE

NONLOCAL                 inara            mangue (animate)
  verbal                   ila              manrin (inanimate)

HERE                     mira
  by speaker               xira

                    +------------+--------------+--------------+
                    |            |              |              |
THERE               |  auaca     |   uanca      |   NONTOPIC   |
  nearby            |    auara   |     uanran   |              |
                    |            |              |              |
                    +------------+--------------+--------------+
                    |            |              |              |
OVER THERE          |  maca      |   mauanca    |   TOPIC      |
  farther           |    mara    |     mauanran |              |
                    |            |              |              |
                    +------------+--------------+--------------+
                    |            |              |
                    |  TOPIC     |   NONTOPIC   |
                    |            |              |
                    +------------+--------------+
                          SUBSIDIARY                MAIN

                                                    TOPICAL USE-
```

Figure 1. Deixis, two levels of topic, and animateness in Bacairi third person pronouns. After Wheatley (1973).

In more complex texts in Bacairi, there is a topic embedding carried by the other pronouns. The main topic pronoun in those texts refers to what might be called the principal topic referent of that part of the text, at the highest level or in a global sense, but the nontopic referents require additional differentiation. It comes about in a two-by-two scheme given by the boxes in Figure 1. One pronominal distinction is between topic and nontopic on a high level of the text—Wheatley uses the terms 'thematic' and 'athematic'—and the other is between topic and nontopic on a subsidiary level, which Wheatley calls 'focal' and 'nonfocal.' Thus, when the main topic referent is also being treated as the topic of a subsidiary part of the text, the pronoun *maca* is used for an animate referent; when the main topic referent is mentioned in a subsidiary part while something else is the topic of that part, *mauanca* is used; a subsidiary topic that is not the main topic receives *auaca;* and anything that is not topic at either level is referred to by *uanca*. It was here that I began to see how some languages clarify mechanisms that in other languages are hard to even notice because they are communicated so subtly.

More recently, in early 1982, I had opportunity to observe Mapudungun, the language of the Mapuche of south central Chile, through the cooperation of the Summer Institute of Linguistics, particularly Robert Croese and

Timothy Sandwig and their wives, the Universidad de la Frontera, the Pontífica Universidad Católica, Sede Temuco, and Adalberto Salas of the Universidad de Concepción. Mapudungun brings topics to our attention by building the topic–nontopic distinction into its verb morphology. There it has to be dealt with every time a finite verb is uttered.

The first attempts at explaining Mapudungun verbs were made during the colonial period. In the early part of this century, Fray Félix de Augusta (1903), followed by P. Ernest Wilhelm de Moesbach (1962) and Rodolfo Lenz (1944), analyzed the referential system in terms of what they called 'transitions' or subject-object pairs. Since many languages make cross reference to both subject and object, this seemed plausible, except that the things called subject were not always subject and the things called object were not always object.

María Beatriz Fontanella de Weinberg in 1967 gave a componential analysis of the system that went in the right direction. Her features were 'speaker,' 'addressee,' 'focal,' 'plural,' 'transitive,' and 'reflexive.' These interact at three levels: 'distant' involving third person, 'middle' involving you-to-me interaction, and 'immediate' me-to-you. Neutralizations at each level effectively loosen up the connection between the two grammatical subsystems and subject and object.

There are indeed two portions of the suffix string of Mapudungun that refer in pronoun-like fashion. They may, however, be equated sometimes with subject, sometimes with indirect object, sometimes with direct object, applicative (benefactive or malefactive), or even with a remote referent connected indirectly through the applicative. The suffixes that come around the end of the verb, the final slots that are usually equated with the subject, cover first, second, and third person reference, but they may stand in any of the relations just named rather than necessarily being the subject. The suffixes that come in the nonfinal slots and are traditionally equated with the object though they may be in other roles, however, are restricted to second and third person, never first.

The most telling insight into the system has been provided by Adalberto Salas (1970a, b, 1971a, b, 1974, 1978a, b, 1981) through a series of articles that show conclusively that subject and object are not what the system is about. The final referential elements in the word point to what he calls the *axis* of *satellite* reference. Putting this into the context of much current discussion in linguistics, it is possible to simply identify the final obligatory elements as referring to the *topic* and the others as referring to some *nontopic*.

Which of the elements is translated as subject and which as object depends on the way they are set up. Very often, as the older analyses stated, the final topic element is the subject and the nonfinal nontopic referential element is the object, as in

(1) mïtrïm-FI-i-M-I[1]
(call-HIM-indicative-YOU-SINGULAR)
'you called him'

The order of subject and object may, however, be the opposite, with the object as the topic and the subject as the nontopic referent, as in

(2) mïtrïm-a-E-N
(call-future-YOU-INDICATIVE + ME)
'you will call me'

Given the restriction that first person occurs only in the final topic position, such a reversal is only to be expected. What is important is the rationale behind it.

Figure 2 shows most of the systematic choices that enter into the referential system of Mapudungun verb suffixes.[2] They are presented using the conventions for Halliday's systemic grammar that were proposed by Hudson (1976). Feature labels stand for the semantic choices. They take on positive or negative values, shown on Figure 2 by Y or 'yes' for positive and N or 'no' for negative, depending on what the speaker intends to say. Vertical lines that end in Y and N join such alternatives.

The choice of a value for one feature can be an entry condition into the choice of a value for another feature. Linked brackets indicate restriction of choice. Braces, on the other hand, join choices all of which must be made simultaneously. The next section goes through the system of choices.

The two features by which entry is made into the whole subsystem of reference are labeled *finite* and *bivalent*. Nominalizations are [– finite], ordinary verbs [+ finite]. [+ bivalent] verbs have a [– topic] referent, whether [+ finite] or not; monovalent verbs have a [+ topic] referent if [+ finite] or a nominalizer if [– finite] that I think also fits in with topic reference, but may involve levels of topical embedding. Verbs may be lexically bivalent, or else the valency of a monovalent verb may be increased by adding an applicative or associative suffix. On the other hand, in redundant discourse positions, lexically bivalent verbs may be treated as morphologically monovalent.

[1] The examples are normalized morphophonemically so as to show the internal makeup of the word more clearly. Adjacent vowels that are identical in this normalization collapse under certain circumstances. High vowels at the end of words, or surrounded by vowels, or between a vowel and a consonant that is not word final, become semivowels as explained in Grimes (1985). The sounds are transcribed phonemically: stops p, t̪ (dental), t, k, affricates tr (retroflex), ch (alveopalatal), r (retroflex fricative or approximant), nasals m, n̪ (dental), n, ñ, ng (velar), laterals l̪ (dental), l, ll (alveopalatal), semivowels, y, w, γ (back unrounded), and vowels a, e, i, o, u, and ï (unrounded from high close to open and from central to back).

[2] The details of the system are laid out in the articles by Salas. I have gone over them in a more compact way in Grimes (1985). The examples I give here are taken either from cited articles or from the text collected by Croese that is given in Loos and Croese's report.

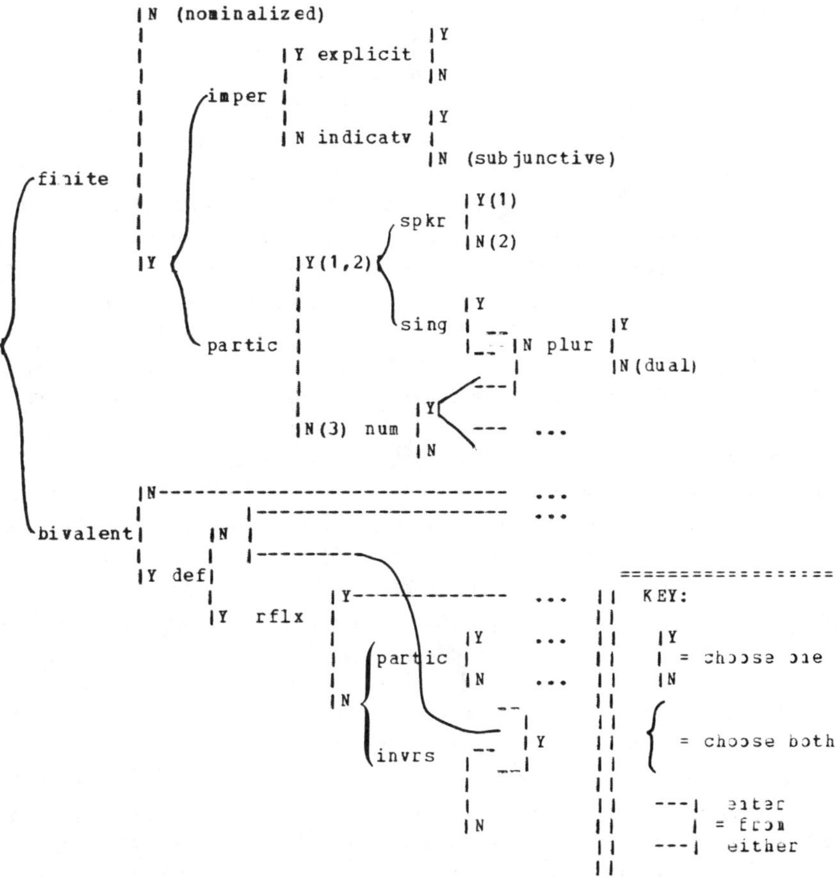

Figure 2. Systems of choice in Mapudungu verbs.

For any finite verb, two more choices have to be made: *imperative* or not, and *participant* or not.

Imperatives can be *explicit* or implicit, forms that need not concern us now. Nonimperatives are *indicative* or [– indicative], that is, subjunctive as in 'if' clauses. This set of choices defines the mode system.

A [+ participant] topic refers to one of the participants in the speech situation; that is, either to the speaker (first person) or to the hearer (second person), as distinguished further by the feature *speaker*. Any topic participant must also be specified as *singular* or not, and if not, whether it is *plural* or not, in which case [– plural] denotes dual number.

A topic that does not refer to a participant in the speech situation corresponds to our usual notion of third person. Here a choice of singular or plural is not obligatory, but if the speaker does decide to highlight a non-singular through choice of the *number* feature, then he tags it as dual or plural. This choice and some others also have consequences that are not of interest here, as is indicated by the ellipsis marks in Figure 2.

If there is a nontopic referent (that is, if the verb is treated as [+bivalent]), it may be *definite* or not. The indefinite nontopic *-nge* 'somebody' or 'something' is always translatable as an indefinite subject, as is indicated by its affinity with the feature [+inverse] that is described later. The indefinite nontopic is often spoken of in the literature as if it were a passive, which it is not, because it does not change transitivity or any of the mappings between the semantic actants of the verb and their grammatical manifestation.

The [+definite] nontopic may be *reflexive* or not. It is the [−reflexive] nontopics that make the referential system rich, because they may be *inverse* on a scale of relative activity regarding the situation described in the verb. Roughly speaking, [+inverse] nontopics are usually translated into English as subjects, while [−inverse] nontopics are translated as indirect or direct objects or referents that are involved in an action in a subsidiary way. Noninverse (or "direct") nontopics are lower on a scale of semantic role ranking than the topic referent (Grimes, 1975, p. 265).

The term "inverse" comes from comparing two scales. The primary scale is that of topical ranking, in which first person always outranks second, and second always outranks a [+definite] third person, which in turn always outranks [+definite, −topic] and [−definite] third person. The final referential element can never be outranked by the nonfinal one, which explains why nontopic referents are never first person.

The secondary scale is that of semantic role (Chomsky's thematic or theta-role). On this scale the final topic element outranks the nontopic one if the directionality is not inverted, but the nonfinal one outranks the topic if it is. This interplay between topic ranking, called "obviation," and semantic role ranking is well known from the Algonquian languages (Hockett, 1966) and has been found in other parts of the world as well.

In addition, nontopic referents must be calibrated as *participant* or not, just as topic referents are, when they denote a participant in the speech situation who is interacting with a [+participant] topic. Since nontopics can be first person only when they are [+reflexive] because of the topic ranking principle, by process of elimination all [−reflexive] participants must be second person. [−participant] nontopics are then third person. Two other features, *minimal* and *separable,* are part of the referential system but are not needed to elaborate the point of this paper.

Back to the topic referent: it enters into a greater number of relationships within the sentence than the nontopic referent can. Either one can be subject or object or indirect object or goal or source or possibly range (in the semantic role terminology I develop in Grimes, 1975). But in addition the topic can be benefactive or even malefactive when inflected additionally with *-lel* 'benefactive' or *-ñma* 'applicative' respectively. These make it refer to a person who is secondarily affected by an action in the sense that something is brought to him or taken from him.

The topic can also be cast as remotely affected by the use either of *-ma* after *-lel* or of a second *-ñma* after the first one. The sense is then that of a vague connection such as is suggested by the possessive with the person that is secondarily affected, who is not himself referred to explicitly in the verb; Salas gives numerous examples in his articles.

The loose tie between topic or nontopic reference and grammatical relation becomes especially apparent when both topic and nontopic are third person. Third person ([– participant]) topic reference combines with third person ([– participant]) nontopic reference in two different ways:

(3) pe-FI-i
(see-nonparticipant + noninverse-indicative)
'he saw him'

(4) pe-E-i-EU
(see-nonparticipant + inverse-indicative-nonparticipant + inverse)
'he saw him'

In (3) the nontopic suffix *-fi* 'nonparticipant, noninverse; him' is taken as object together with the bare indicative, which is implicitly third person topic. The noninverse topic is subject because its thematic role in the clause outranks that of the nontopic at the same time as its topic status outranks that of the nontopic. In (4), on the other hand, the nontopic suffix *-e. . . -eu* 'nonparticipant, inverse; he,' which has two discontinuous parts, is taken as subject in relation to the bare indicative, which is still implicitly third person topic; but the inverse relation says that the thematic role of the nontopic outranks that of the topic.

If topic simply meant subject and nontopic meant object, there would be no need for two sets of terms and there would be no problem. But the inversion principle is needed to account for the fact that the two structural positions or slots do not line up consistently with grammatical or even semantic categories; instead, the relative rank of the role of the nontopic implies what is often thought of as the grammatical category. In this light, it is possible to ask whether grammatical relation terms are needed at all for Mapudungun; but I am not prepared to pursue that question yet.

The true function of topic and nontopic is better explained in discourse terms by considering the referent here called "topic" to always refer to a central referent, whatever its grammatical relation may be to the other referents, and assigning the nonfinal element to one of the nontopic referents. The further specification of [± inverse] narrows down the possible range of grammatical function.

This is my current hypothesis about the topical structure of Mapudungun texts. It is undoubtedly not rich enough to cover all topic phenomena, but it seems to hold as far as it goes.

For example, in a description of traditional house building collected by Croese (Loos & Croese, 1979), there are three groups of referents: a family group that owns a house being built, a man and woman they select to organize the house raising, and some people who do the work on the house for the family of owners under the direction of the pair chosen as leaders. After the house is put up, there is a feast, and after the feast

(5a) Fey entu-i ñi ngïlam ti pu ngenke ruka
(then express-indicative 3 + possessive counsel definite plural owner house)
'Then the owners of the house expressed their views.'

(5b) ruka-ya-lu mañum-i,
(house-formative-participle appreciate-indicative)
'That they (the owners) appreciated the housebuilding'

(5c) mañum-fi-i-ng-ïn tal ti kïlla wentru ka ti kïlla domo.
(appreciate-nonparticipant + noninverse-indicative-number-plural ? definite foreman man and definite foreman woman)
'and that they (the owners) appreciated the man and woman who headed it up.'

(5d) Fewla fey kontentu-reke mïle-lu yeng-ïn feyta,
(now then happy-as be-participle number-plural then)
'So as they (the owners) were feeling happy,'

(5e) pïru-ñma-fi-i-ng-ïn ti ruka.
(dance-applicative-nonparticipant + noninverse-indicative-number-plural definite house)
'they danced around them (the owners) on account of the house.'

Clauses (5a) to (5c) tell what the owners of the house did. The reference to them is explicit because the topic uses the optional plural number sequence *-ng-ïn,* which cannot refer to the man and woman in charge of the work because then it would have to be the dual *-ng-u.* The nontopic *-fi* in (5c), which is not tagged for number, is what refers to the two leaders; it casts them as noninverse of lower thematic rank than the topic, which in this case is equivalent to indirect object.

In (5d) and (5e), it would be tempting to guess that the topic reference, and therefore the topic, shifts to the people working or to the whole crowd. The double introducer *fewla fey* 'now then' in (5d) is compatible with topic shift, but the *ñma* 'applicative' in (5e) has the sense 'dance around [the topic].' Furthermore, the topic is explicitly plural even though the situation involves only one house, and so only the owners of the house remain as possible candidates for the topic reference. The nontopic *-fi* 'nonparticipant, noninverse' therefore represents some other referent that cannot be as high on the scale of involvement as the topic is. But since the topic is nothing but a spatial reference point for the dancing, I hesitatingly suggest that *-fi* refers not to the dancers, who are more highly involved and therefore would have to be [+inverse] if they were referred to, but to the house *ti raka* 'on account of the house.'

The text goes on with the topic continuing to refer to the family that owns the house. The dancers are now referred to only with the indefinite *-nge* 'somebody,' which can usually be translated as an English agentless passive even though it is not a passive in Mapudungun grammar

(6a) Wïne ngilla-tu-ñma-nge-i, kime fele-al,
(first ask-do-applicative-indefinite-indicative, good be-thus-nominal)
'First there was a supplication ceremony made for them, for them to be well,'

(6b) depues upan i-i-ng-ïn
(after after eat-indicative-number-plural)
'and later they ate'

(6c) fey pïru-ñma-nge-i.
(then dance-applicative-indefinite-indicative)
'then [people] danced around them.'

At this point there is an explanatory aside, a parenthetical that probably casts *ti ruka* 'the house' as a temporary embedded topic:

(7) Epu puerta niye-i ti ruka.
(two door have-indicative definite house)
'[You need to understand that] the house has two doors.'

After this interruption of the topic sequence, the topic shifts to the people who are dancing; they are the ones referred to from then on by the topic slot:

(8a) Kon-pu-i kiñe puerta-mu
(enter-there-indicative one door-at)
'They went in one door'

(8b) ka puerta-mu tripa-i-ng-ïn.
(and door-at exit-indicative-number-plural)
'and came out at the other.'

Other texts show the same pattern with the topic referent. They also show the alternation of grammatical roles between the topic and the nontopic by means of the alternation of [+inverse] and [−inverse] nontopic forms that was illustrated in (3) and (4). This helps corroborate the central idea of this paper: Features of text organization that appear to be present in all languages, but are not too evident in some, nevertheless can come to the fore in certain languages. Their prominence in those languages may, however, bring with it the consequence that some of the categories Western linguists feel comfortable with may be less easily perceived.

REFERENCES

Augusta, Fray Félix José de. (1903). *Gramática araucana.* Valdivia, Chile: Imprenta Central J. Lampert.

Chafe, Wallace. (1976). Givenness, contrastiveness, definiteness, subjects, topics, and point of view. In Charles N. Li (Ed.), *Subject and topic.* New York: Academic.

Chomsky, Noam. (1980). *Rules and representations.* New York: Columbia University Press.

Fontanella [de Weinberg], María Beatriz. (1967). Componential analysis of personal affixes in Araucanian. *International Journal of American Linguistics, 33,* 305–308.

Grimes, Joseph E. (1975). *The thread of discourse.* The Hague: Mouton.

Grimes, Joseph E. (1981). Topics within topics. In Deborah Tannen (Ed.), *Georgetown University Round Table on Linguistics and Language Teaching for 1981.* Washington, DC: Georgetown University Press.

Grimes, Joseph E. (1985). Topic inflection in Mapadungun verbs. *International Journal of American Linguistics, 51,* 141–163.

Gundel, Jeannette K. (1974). The role of topic and comment in linguistic theory. Unpublished doctoral dissertation, University of Texas. (Reprinted by the Indiana University Linguistics Club, 1977).

Hockett, Charles F. (1966). What Algonquian is really like. *International Journal of American Linguistics, 32* (1), 59–73.

Hudson, Richard A. (1976). *Arguments for a non-transformational grammar.* Chicago: University of Chicago Press.

Lenz, Rodolfo. (1944). *La oración y sus partes: Estudios de gramática general y castellana* (4th ed.) Santiago de Chile: Nascimento. (Original work published 1922).

Loos, Eugenio, & Croese, Robert A. (1979). *Segundo informe semestral a la Universidad Austral de Chile.* Unpublished manuscript.

Moesbach, P. Ernesto Wilhelm de. (1962). *Idioma Mapuche.* Padre Las Casas, Chile: Imprenta San Francisco.

Salas, Adalberto. (1970a). Notas sobre el verbo en el mapuche de Chile (I). *Segunda Semana Indigenista,* pp. 59–95. Temuco, Chile: Ediciones Universitarias de la Frontera.

Salas, Adalberto. (1970b). Notas sobre el verbo en el mapuche de Chile (II). *Stylo, 10,* 119–134.

Salas, Adalberto. (1971a). Notas sobre el verbo en el mapuche de Chile (III). *Boletín de Filología de la Universidad de Chile, 22,* 99–116.

Salas, Adalberto. (1971b). Notas sobre el verbo en el mapuche de Chile (IV). *RLA, Revista de Lingüística Teórica y Aplicada, 9,* 75–101.

Salas, Adalberto. (1974). Notas sobre el verbo en el mapuche de Chile (V). *RLA, Revista de Lingüística Teórica y Aplicada, 12,* 49–88.

Salas, Adalberto. (1978a). *Semantic ramifications of the category of person in the Mapuche verb.* Unpublished doctoral dissertation, State University of New York at Buffalo.

Salas, Adalberto. (1978b). Terminaciones y transiciones en el verbo mapuche: Crítica y bases para una nueva interpretación. *RLA, Revista de Lingüística Teórica y Aplicada, 16,* 168–179.

Salas, Adalberto. (1981). La expresión de la circunstancia de compañía en mapuche. *Revista Latinoamericana de Estudios Etnolingüísticos, 1,* 101–134.

Wheatley, James. (1973). Pronouns and nominal elements in Bacairi discourse. *Linguistics, 104,* 105–115.

Chapter 5

Robot Plans and Human Plans: Implications for Models of Communication*

Bertram Bruce

Bolt Beranek and Newman Inc.

The Peanuts comic strip has a character named Lucy who is always trying to take advantage of one named Charlie Brown. Because Charlie is very trusting, her tricks often succeed. One of her favorite tricks occurs in the fall, when football season is getting underway: Lucy holds a football and says, "Come on, Charlie Brown! I'll hold the football for you. You come and kick it". Charlie runs as fast as he can, swings his leg back and tries to kick the ball. At the last second, Lucy yanks the ball away, Charlie's feet fly up in the air, and he lands on his back. His pride is wounded as well as his bottom.

One year, Charlie started thinking,

> "She says she's going to hold the ball so I can run up and kick it, but I know she's going to pull it away. She always pulls it away. She thinks that I don't know what she's planning to do, but, in fact, I do. I also know that she thinks that I don't know. I'm going to trick her. Instead of running up and kicking the ball I'll just run up and stop. Then she can't pull the ball away and make me fall on my back."

But then he goes further,

> "She can figure out that I know what her plan is. She's probably not going to yank the ball away after all. I'll run up, stop, and be embarrassed, this time because there'll be no trick."

---

* I would like to thank Andee Rubin, Behrooz Tavakoli, and Harry Blanchard for comments on this paper, Kathleen Starr for her artwork and Cheryl Przekwas for preparing the manuscript. The research was supported by the National Institute of Education under Contract No. NIE-400-81-0030.

Following this line of reasoning, he finally concludes that the best strategy is just to run as hard as he can and kick the ball. He runs right up and swings his leg back. As he does so, Lucy jerks the ball away and Charlie lands flat on his back, in the process setting himself up for next year's football season.

We live in a world of intentionality, a world in which we assign meaning to objects, relations, and events. One of the primary kinds of meaning that we assign is planful behavior. That is, we look at what people do and say, "What are their goals? What are the actions that they are going to carry out to achieve those goals? What are their plans?" We seek interpretations of actions in terms of plans, even in cases where behavior may not be all that planful. Referring to an action as aimless only highlights the fact that it is very unusual for people to act without some goal in mind.

This chapter discusses the role of plans in understanding discourse. It looks briefly at an example of what might be called a "robot model", or perhaps the "standard AI model" for plans, a model used widely not only in Artificial Intelligence, but in a wide variety of other disciplines as well. It then presents some problems that arise when this standard model is used to account for general human action. A contrasting model, the "mutual-belief model," is then presented by means of an example from the Hall corpus (Hall, Nagy, & Linn, 1984) of children's conversations. In a simple episode, we see something of the richness of human planfulness. Finally, some open questions are presented.

THE STANDARD AI MODEL FOR PLANNING

Plans have been used in a wide variety of ways in the study of discourse: to look at interactions of characters in stories (Bruce & Newman, 1978; Wilensky, 1981), to look at the interactions of the plans and purposes of an author with the plans and purposes of a reader (Brewer & Lichtenstein, 1982; Bruce, 1981), to look at the various plans of participants in conversation. Most of these analyses have relied on some form of information processing model that provides an explicit representation of actions, states of the world, goals, and the process of planning. There is a long tradition to this work, going back to Miller, Galanter, and Pribram (1960). The example to follow is a bit of a caricature of this view of planning and problem solving, but it suggests how people have been using terms like "operators" and "states" and the kinds of problems that can be solved.

Robot Worlds

First of all, one needs to have some way to represent a state of the world. Typically, what's done is to define a world state by a list of propositions. Figure 1 shows a simple world in which there are five points, or places where something can be; there are boxes A, B, and C; and there is a robot, who

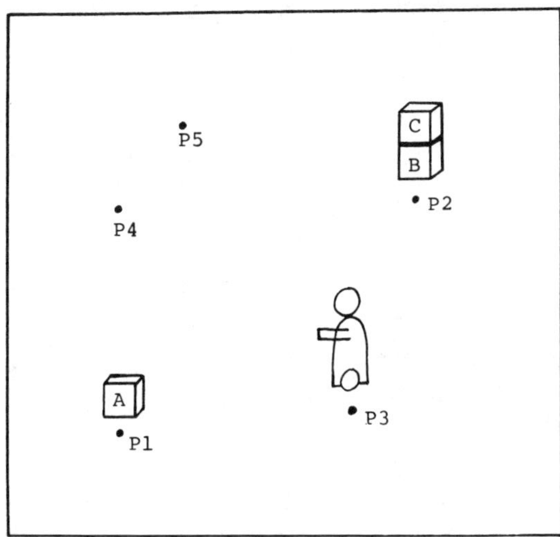

Figure 1. Initial state in the robot world.

can move the boxes around. To represent a state of this world we might use a set of propositions like the following:

Initial State

[On (Box-A, Floor)]
[On (Box-B, Floor)]
[On (Box-C, Box-B)]
[At (Box-A, P1)]
[At (Box-B, P2)]
[At (Robot, P3)]

This says that Box-A is on the Floor at point P1, the Robot is at point P3, and so on.

Planning becomes relevant when we have operators which can change states of the world. An example of an operation in the micro-world might be for the robot to pick up a box. Operators are typically defined in terms of enabling conditions, and outcomes, or effects:

Operator:	pick-up (X)
Enabling conditions:	$(\exists P)$ [At (Robot, P) & At (X, P)]
	$\sim (\exists Z)$ Hold (Z)
	$\sim (\exists Z)$ On (Z, X)
Effects:	Hold (X)

The pick-up operator can be used only in certain states: for example, the robot and the thing to be picked up have to be in the same location. Also,

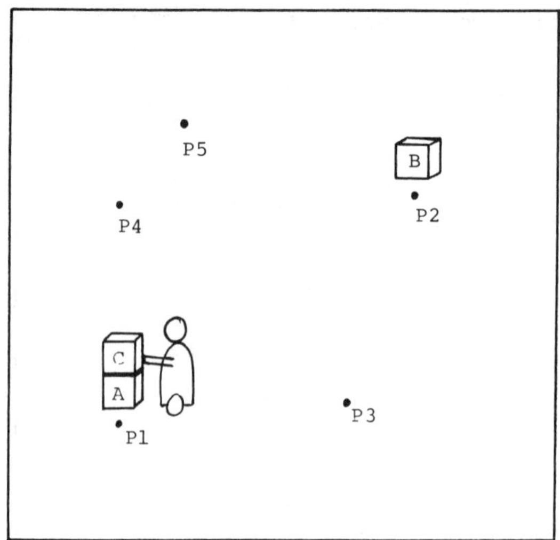

Figure 2. Goal state in the robot world.

the robot cannot be holding anything and there can be nothing on the thing to be picked up. If the pick-up operator is applied, the effect is that a proposition is added to our description of the world: The robot now holds the box.

Now, let's set up another state—a goal state (see Figure 2). Let's say you wanted Box C on Box A and the robot at P1. This looks like the initial state with the exception of a couple of propositions:

Goal State

[On (Box-A, Floor)]
[On (Box-B, Floor)]
[On (Box-C, Box-A)]
[At (Box-A, P1)]
[At (Box-B, P2)]
[At (Robot, P1)]

A planner can now operate to generate a sequence of operators, such as: "the Robot moves to P2, picks up Box-C, moves to P1, puts down Box-C." We call this sequence of operators a "plan."

The Plan

Move (P2)
Pick-up (Box-C)
Move (P1)
Put-down (Box-C)

More elaborate examples than this can easily be constructed, such as planning programs to write computer software or to solve complex assembly tasks. In various fields, people have used similar models to examine problem solving, composition, the reader interaction with characters in stories, conversations, and so on. It's fair to say that most planning research has relied on models of this general form.

Limitations of the Standard AI Model

Unfortunately, there are limitations to the standard AI model that appear when we try to account for human planning behavior (Most of these are acknowledged by those who have used such a model in their research.)

The first problem is that robot planning is basically planning for an individual. There is one robot moving around in its little micro-world. In contrast, human plans are essentially social, that is, people operate in a social environment in which they compete or cooperate with others. Even if there is another robot in the robot's world, the plan constructed is an individual plan; the other robot is an aspect of a passive environment. In human plan cases, even some things that are apparently individual, say, a teacher preparing a lesson for the next day, working at home, is still inherently social in that the teacher must imagine social contexts for his/her actions.

Secondly, the robot operates in a world of facts. There's a set of propositions that are simply true or false. There may be some uncertainty about them, and they may change, but they're essentially treated as solid facts. In contrast, in human planning situations virtually everything has a belief status. People act on the basis of what they believe to be true, and what they believe about other's beliefs. In conversations, for example, the operators are defined in terms of changes to other's beliefs or questions about what they believe. Moreover, these beliefs are recursive: It's not just your beliefs, and your beliefs about someone else's beliefs, but your beliefs about what they believe about you. For example, Charlie Brown is trying to figure out his beliefs about Lucy's beliefs about his beliefs.

Third, the standard AI model presupposes a fixed set of operators, state variables, and goals. Neither the operators nor the state variables change in the process of planning. There is no way to add new locations or new boxes. Also, the goal is fixed. The robot works to achieve the goal and either succeeds or fails. In the human planning situation, there is an ongoing, and even a retrospective, establishment of meaning.

For example, Gearhart and Newman (1980) report nursery school interactions in which a teacher talks to kids in the nursery school about the pictures they have drawn. She says, "Here, let me see your picture." Until that moment, the child might have been drawing with the crayon on the paper, on the desk, or on the wall. By her statement, the teacher seeks to establish that the object in question is a picture and that the activity that the child was doing was drawing a picture. When she points to an orange glob on the paper and says "Oh, that must be the sun," that orange circle suddenly takes on a new status. This establishment of meaning through interaction is a typical feature of human interactions; we define the rules of the game as we go along.

Fourth, the standard AI model tends to focus on the design and execution of plans. That is, given an initial state, a goal state, and operators, the task is to construct the most efficient plan to get from the initial state to the goal state, or, given a plan, to execute it. In contrast, in human planning situations, explicit planning is unusual, and there are few times when one just carries out a plan. More often, people talk about plans, they communicate plans to one another, and they use plans to achieve other goals. Plans become part of what one communicates: A plan is announced because of the effect that information is likely to have on someone else. These ways of dealing with plans require more sophisticated representations than those provided by the standard models.

Fifth, the standard AI model tends to separate the generation process from the recognition process. Producing a plan is one problem: How can we take an initial state and a sequence of operators and get to a goal state? Recognizing a plan is a separate problem: How can we infer a plan from a sequence of actions? For human plan models, these processes need to be considered together. Generating a plan is done while recognizing what plans others are carrying out. One's own path may have to change in light of the recognition of what others are planning. Similarly, if others recognize your plan in a certain way, their plans may alter while you are in the process of recognizing them. Recognition may depend upon simulating the generation of a plan, understanding why somebody might have produced the kind of plan they did.

Finally, in the standard AI model, plans are generally reversible. Certainly in the box example, we can switch the goal state and initial state and make the same point. Exceptions occur only when the domain introduces a directionality, say, in breaking an egg. In contrast, human plans are basically historical. Actions are nonreversible, because they interact with and are even defined in terms of a complex history of previous actions.

MUTUAL BELIEF MODEL

Several researchers have been trying to find ways to represent intentions and beliefs in order to model social plans as well as individual plans. Some of this work has been done with computer modelling (Cohen, 1981; Perrault & Allen, 1980; Sidner & Israel, 1981); some through analysis of conversations, stories, and skits. This section presents one such attempt based on the centrality of mutual belief (cf. Clark & Marshall, 1981; Cohen & Perrault,

1979; Schiffer, 1972). We mention here the major elements of a notation system that is being used in these analyses. For further details, see Bruce (1980) or Bruce and Newman (1978).

The notation system assumes an underlying facility for representation of actions and states. Every proposition is represented as embedded within a belief. A set of beliefs is indicated by a *belief space.* Figure 3 shows essentially equivalent representations, to say that a proposition is within the beliefs of some character or participant. We also need to represent intentions of at least two kinds. One is the intention to achieve something, to bring about a new state of affairs (Figure 4). The second is the intention to maintain some state (Figure 5).

An important concept built out of individual beliefs is that of *mutual belief.* Mutual belief means not only that one person believes something that the other person believes, but also that each believes that the other person believes it and that the other believes that the first believes it, and so on indefinitely (Schiffer, 1972). Using the notation presented thus far, we can

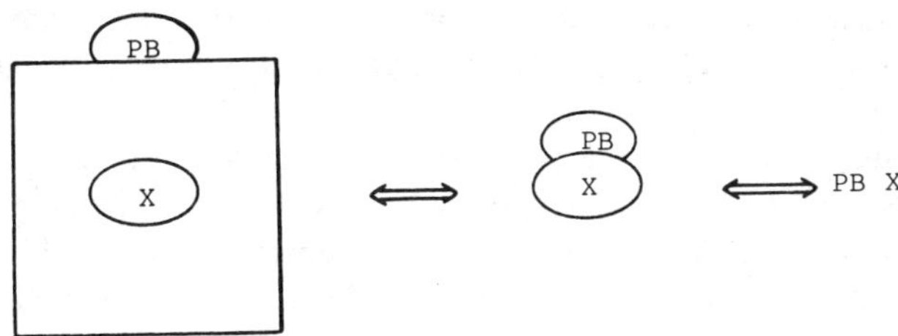

Figure 3. Representation of beliefs: Person P believes proposition X.

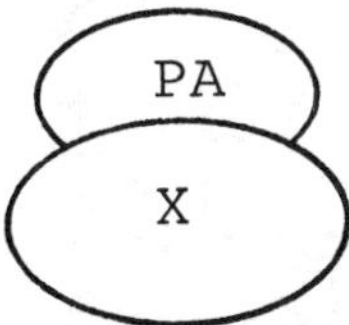

Figure 4. Representation of intentions: P intends to achieve X.

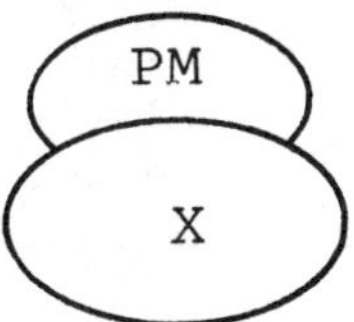

Figure 5. Representation of intentions: P intends to maintain X.

give two define mutual belief (MB) of a proposition, X, between two actors, F and R, as follows:

MB (F, R, X) < = = > FB X
RB X
FB RB X
RB FB X
FB RB FB X
RB FB RB X
.
.
.

Closely related to the mutual belief concept is that of the *social episode* (Figure 6). People can create a frame for their interactions within which they establish social facts to be true for the duration of that episode. Within the episode, participants have well defined roles. There are many conventional social episodes: For example, in a supermarket, there is the checkout person and the customer, with corresponding expectations about what each should do and know.

The more interesting case is when people create new social episodes. There is then a set of initiating actions to establish the episode and a set of actions to close it. A social episode is represented as a mutual belief state, with the participants' role specified. Each side holds one participant's beliefs, intentions, and actions. The entire episode resides within the larger belief space of one of the participants.

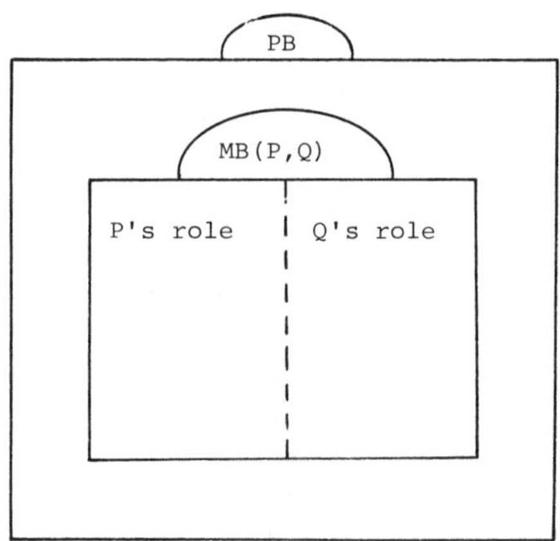

Figure 6. A social episode.

There are also rules for operating on these representations. For example, we have found it useful to allow the representation of a belief about one's own belief. But in general we collapse this representation by invoking a rule of the form:

SB SB X ===> SB X

Figure 7 shows how, using this rule and the definition of mutual belief, one can derive various equivalences within the notation system, e.g., that although "P believes it is mutually believed that X" *is not* equivalent to "Q believes it is mutually believed that X," the conjunction of these two *is*

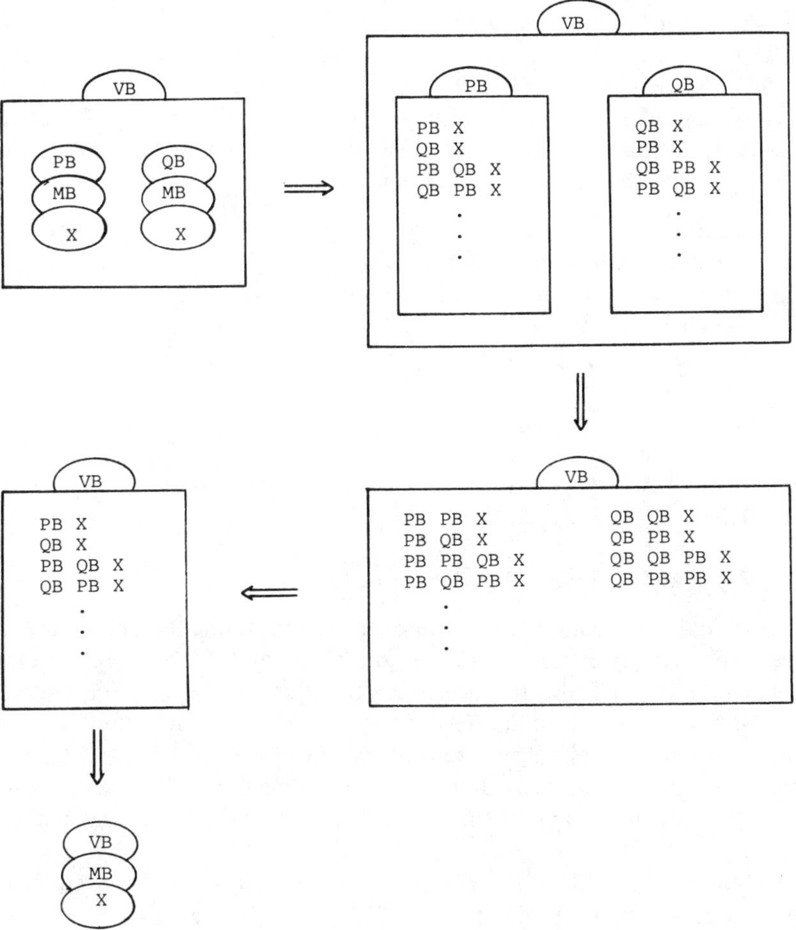

Figure 7. Equivalences among belief representations.

equivalent to mutual belief. Such manipulations are useful, since one of the most interesting things that has emerged in the examples that we have looked at is a shifting in and out of mutual belief—successive establishments of mutual belief, breakdowns, and then re-establishments.

TODD AND THE TOYS

In this section, we look at a formal representation of a dialogue to see how mutual belief is established and manipulated in order to achieve personal goals. This analysis is not some magical device to see into the participants' heads, but rather a way to represent one observer's interpretation (mine) which might be compared then to someone's else's. Thus, the analysis is necessarily limited to a point of view.

The example is taken from a corpus of natural conversations collected by W. Hall (see Hall et al., 1984). The particular excerpt is from a conversation between a mother and her 4½-year-old son. Let's call the boy "Todd" and the mother "Susan." Todd is in the living-room playing with his father's tools and his mother is in an adjoining room:

1. Susan: Go into your room and play, Todd, and...
2. [She comes into the room,
3. and helps Todd put his father's tools away.
4. Todd holds a tool.]
5. S: What have you got now?
6. That's not a toy!
7. Todd: We're putting them back.
8. S: You're putting it back? Very...
9. T: Can I have these batteries?
10. S: No,
11. yeah, the batteries....
12. and how many times did Daddy say not to go in his kit?

Our analysis will allow us to address certain puzzling features of the dialogue. For example, notice that, in lines 5, 6, and 8, Susan refers in the singular, whereas Todd, in line 7, uses the plural to refer to the same object(s). Note also that, in line 7, Todd says that the two of them ("we") are putting away the objects, whereas Susan, in line 8, says that it is Todd's ("you") action which is in question. Are these examples of miscommunication? Do they just represent "noise" that one should expect in normal conversation? Do Todd and Susan see the object(s) in question as respectively singular and plural? Do they have different views about who is carrying out the actions in question?

The analysis to follow will make the case that, far from being noise, such apparent mismatches are crucial to understanding what the dialogue is all about. In particular, the difference arises because of simultaneous, but conflicting attempts to manipulate mutual belief.

ESTABLISHING MUTUAL BELIEF

Let's start with the dialogue at the point at which Susan says, "Go into your room and play, Todd." The essential thing Susan believes at this point is that they are entering into a social episode, working together for a common goal, which involves on Todd's part, getting the tools in the box. Figure 8 shows her belief that Todd wants to achieve the state, "tools in box." Meanwhile, Todd believes that Susan believes that it's a mutual belief that that's exactly what they are doing. But he is still playing with the tools. He also realizes that there is a conflict (represented by the dotted arrow) between his intention to play and the intention she wishes him to have—to get the tools into the box (Figure 9).

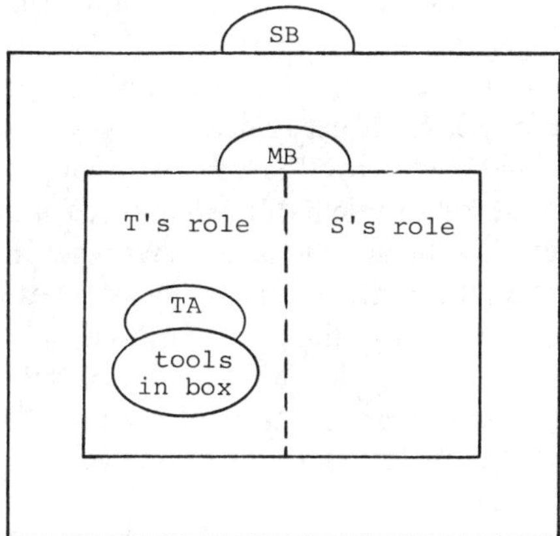

Figure 8. Susan's initial model: Cooperative action.

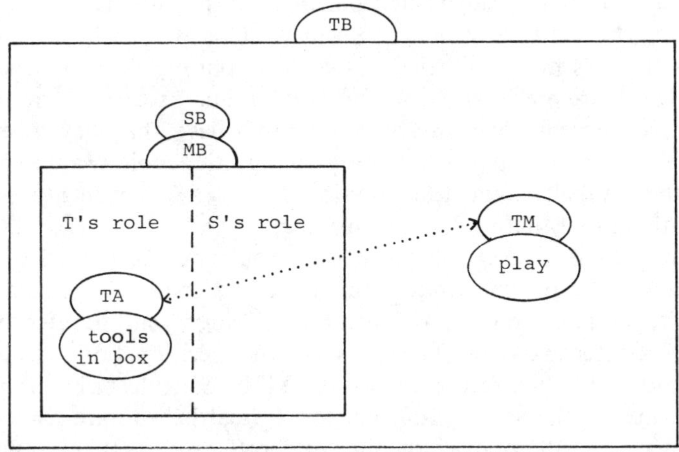

Figure 9. Todd's initial model: Goal conflict.

Now let's consider Susan's view of the world in more detail. She believes Todd has the intention to play in his room, which means he must go in the room and play with his toys there. But she also wants him to get the tools in the box. Achieving that intention will take away the toys Todd is playing with, which, Susan understands, would be a conflict for Todd if he were, in fact, intending to play. But that conflict would be resolved by the fact that, once he gets into his room, there will be other toys to play with.

Todd is holding a tool in a manner that suggests play. He's clearly not putting it away. When Susan realizes that Todd doesn't have the intention of putting away the tools her belief about their mutual belief changes. The social episode starts to dissolve, and she must re-establish it as a social fact. Figure 10 says that Susan want to re-achieve the mutual belief space that corresponds to this social episode. Within that intention is re-establishing Todd's intention to get the tools in the box.

Recognizing the conflict between the intention she wants him to have and the one she believes he has leads her to act. She says (lines 5 and 6), "What have you got now? That's not a toy!" This is an attempt to change his intention by a retrospective establishment of meaning—defining what counts as a toy. She's also redefining the action, saying that what they are doing is not just putting tools away, it is putting nontoys away. These assertions directly address Todd's plan to play with the tools. Susan is saying, "If you look at what you are trying to do, you'll see that it's contradictory to the actual state of affairs." Note that Susan is acting on the basis of her interpretation of Todd's goals, forming hypotheses in the same way that we, as observers, are doing.

Todd (line 7) replies, "We're putting them back." He affirms that he wants to get the tools into the box; but to achieve that state he has to have the tools in his hand. Having a tool in his hand is a necessary subgoal to achieve the goal that Susan wanted all along. He may still have the intention of playing, but he clearly wants to achieve the state in which his mother believes that it's mutually believed that he is putting the tools away (See Figure 11). More precisely, his use of "we" in line 7 suggests that he either believes, or, more likely, wants his mother to believe, that they are engaged in a true social action in which they are *both* putting tools away. Regardless of whether he really wants to be putting them away, he wants to make his mother think that that's what's happening.

Susan continues (line 8) with a skeptical, "You're putting it back? Very. . . ." She wants to keep things moving along so she confirms his reassurance despite her doubts about his true intentions. Using "you" to refer to Todd, and "it" to refer to the tool, she focuses on the specific act of putting a dangerous tool away. In effect, she asserts that if his statement and his physical actions support the assumption that the mutual belief state has been re-established, she will not question him further. She asserts that it is mutually

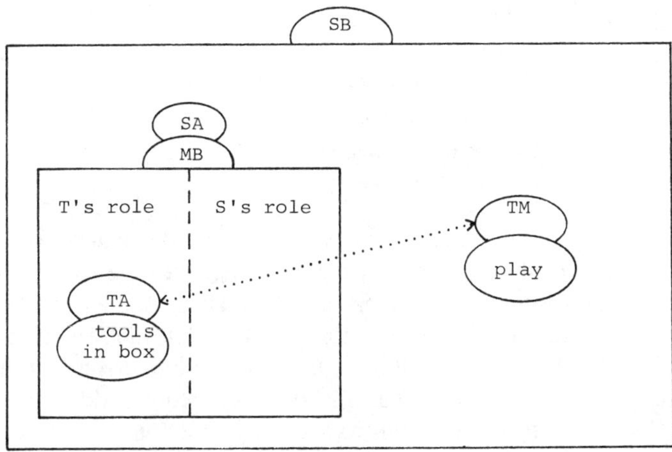

Figure 10. Susan's recognition of the goal conflict.

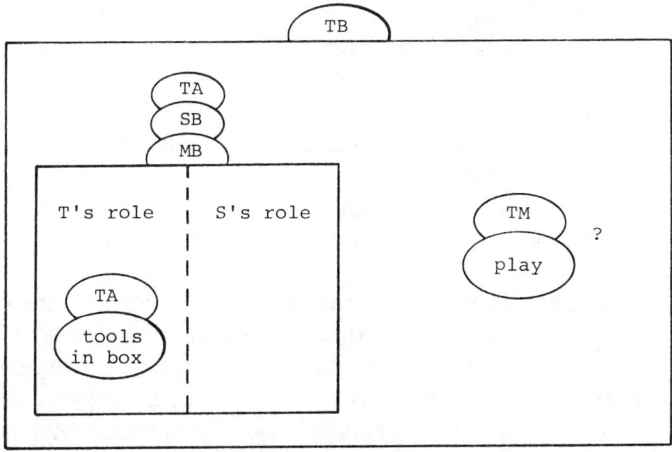

Figure 11. Todd's goal of conflict resolution.

agreed they are putting the tools away (as in Figure 8), even though she may believe at some level that Todd still has the beliefs shown in Figure 11. Later (line 12) she reinforces this settlement and turns it into a teaching activity regarding what things count as toys.

Apparent Miscommunication

With the foregoing analysis in mind we can return now to consider the "them" versus "it" problem mentioned above. It may help in doing this to consider two hypothetical dialogues:

(A) Susan: Let's put *these tools* away.
Todd: OK. Where should we put *them?*
Susan: Put *the big ones* on the table and *the little ones* in the box.

(B) Todd: Let's play with *the hammer.*
Susan: OK. What should I do with *it?*
Todd: Use *it* to pound the table.

Dialogue (A) manifests the Put-Away view of the world. Note that, under this view, all the references are plural, i.e., they are to "tools" as a collection of undifferentiated objects, all of which are to be put away. Dialogue (B) manifests the Play view. In contrast to (A), the references in (B) are to a singular object ("the hammer"). Playing implies assigning singular, significant status to the objects used in the play. How Todd thinks of the tool may be more important than its nominal function, in fact, its usual function is only one idea for how it might be used in play.

Our analysis of the real dialogue suggests that it is Todd who has the Play view and Susan who wants to Put-Away. But notice how each refers to the tool(s). It is Todd who says, "We're putting *them* back," Susan who says, "*That's* not a toy," and "You're putting *it* back?" Thus, they seem to switch roles.

There are two levels of reference to consider here. First, whether the, let's say, hammer, is one of many tools or a singular, interesting toy is a matter of individual beliefs and intentions. Thus, reference to it/them is conditioned by what participants believe. In the social world, we must hypothesize about a person's beliefs even to infer what objects are physically available for reference.

Second, Susan and Todd are in a true dialogue in which they are attempting to understand and alter each other's beliefs and intentions. What appears as a talking past each other in fact is a reflection of their coinciding attempts to take account of the other's beliefs. Thus, Susan, who wants the two to be in a Put-Away social episode, uses the singular reference, not because she sees the hammer as a plaything, but because she sees that Todd does, and wishes by her focus on it in his terms to more effectively alter his intentions. Similarly, Todd, who is undoubtedly in Play mode, probably has specific plans for the hammer as a singular, significant object. Nevertheless, he refers to it as part of a "them" because he sees that Susan is viewing it that way, and, moreover, he sees that she intends for him to view it likewise. Independent of his decision whether to go along with her desires, he decides it is useful strategically to appear to cooperate with her intention about what he should intend. His action appears in his form of reference.

The strategic use of reference to the "tools"—Susan's saying "it" because she believes Todd is thinking "they" when she wishes him to think otherwise (vice versa, in Todd's case)—is paralleled in the reference to the actor(s) involved. Thus, Todd says "we" because he believes Susan believes he is not engaged in the desired plan (i.e., that she believes that he doesn't intend to put away the tools), and he wants to have her change this belief about his intentions. Susan says "you" for converse reasons.

From this we see a resolution of the questions presented previously. Effective communication is not a function of exact reference, even if such a thing were possible. Instead, apparent misreference may actually reflect a high degree of coordination and understanding between participants who are operating in a dynamic social setting in which references are actions to communicate about and change one another's beliefs, intentions, and plans.

OPEN QUESTIONS

The approach presented here has been applied in studies of natural conversations, stories, and Sesame Street skits. These studies raise a number of important questions about the role of the author (in the case of presented social interactions), the effects of modality, discourse conventions, representation of process, the size of planning units, complexity, and background knowledge. One interesting phenomenon that emerges in the studies done thus far concerns the role of the author (or lack thereof). We saw this in our analysis of "Hansel and Gretel" (Bruce & Newman, 1978): Hansel goes along a path dropping pebbles. But he stops each time he drops one, so that his mother and father become suspicious and say, "What are you stopping for now?" Hansel replies, "Oh, I'm looking at the cat that's on the roof." They say, "That's not a cat, that's just the sunlight reflecting on the roof."

This interaction is unnecessary from the point of view of just marking a trail. One of the reasons it happens is that the authors are trying to highlight the importance of Hansel's actions for the reader, and also to indicate who believes what. They're showing (a) that Hansel is deliberately dropping pebbles, (b) that he knows what's going on, and (c) that his parents don't. When we're analyzing "Hansel and Gretel," we might temporarily ignore the author and just look at Hansel and Gretel in their interactions with their parents. But such an analysis is necessarily tentative. In general, one must integrate the character level analysis with analysis of the interaction of plans and beliefs between the author and the reader.

We need to investigate the extent to which models of planning can be used in rhetorical theory (see Brewer & Lichtenstein, 1982), in particular, the relationship between author and reader in terms of author's goals and reader's goals, author's beliefs about reader's beliefs, reader's beliefs about what the author believes about the reader, and so on. When there are stories within stories each of the levels adds two more participants, each of whom has beliefs about each other, and also about characters in their stories (Bruce, 1981).

Closely related to questions about author/reader relationship are questions about discourse structure and convention. How much does the carrying out of a plan by a character constrain the discourse structure that can be produced? How do we separate the conventional aspects of a story (e.g., setting, character stereotypes, and so on) from the underlying plans?

There have been some efforts at computer simulation of social planning (Cohen & Perrault, 1979; Perrault & Allen, 1980). This work is beginning to address the limitations of the robot work model mentioned above (see Sidner, Bates, Bobrow, Goodman, Haas, Ingria, Israel, McAllester, Moser, Schmolze, & Vilain, 1983). Designing systems that can cope with belief-based models is a formidable task.

Another question concerns the size of planning units: To what level should we break down actions? For example, should the action of putting away tools be taken as a unit? It is a subpart of the action of going into the bedroom to play and has subparts such as picking up tools and putting them in a box. The appropriate level of representation appears to be a consequence of the interaction itself. This raises all sorts of questions about the formal representation of plans.

Another interesting question regards complexity: Producing plans and recognizing plans are both complex tasks, but what is the main contributor to complexity? Newman (1981) has analyzed several Sesame Street skits (starring Bert and Ernie) showing various degrees of complexity in the skits themselves and in viewers' interpretations. For example, one skit has six distinct interpretations. From this work, it appears that the degree of embedding of intentions and beliefs is not the primary source of complexity differences. What appears more salient is the complexity of beliefs that need to be maintained outside of the mutual belief space.

A final question is how background knowlege comes into play. In the Sesame Street skits, it helps to know that Ernie typically tricks Bert, despite Bert's greater knowledge about some domains. Similarly, in "Hansel and Gretel," beliefs about cutting wood, building fires, and so on, are crucial both for characters in the story and the reader.

SUMMARY

This chapter has examined the role of plan recognition and plan generation in communication. One idea that emerges from this examination is that people in interaction with others appear to organize their perceptions of a social situation in terms of plans. They do this even when the others' plans are poorly formulated. They use their models of others' plans in formulating their own plans. Much of what occurs in discourse centers on a continual communication about and reformulation of one's own plans and one's models of other's plans.

A second idea that emerges is that formal methods for describing and analyzing plans are now available. Such methods allow us to be more explicit in our hypotheses about social interaction. Unfortunately, the classical formalisms for planning are derived from a robot world model that fails to generalize sufficiently to account for typical human planning situations.

By pushing the classical model, we come to the third main idea of this chapter, namely, that a model of planning with concepts such as mutual belief at its core may take us further in our studies of discourse and other forms of social interaction.

In particular, such a model addresses a number of characteristics central to human planning: Plans are essentially social, involving cooperation and/or conflict between individuals. They operate in a space of social facts, not just physical states. As such, they are built upon participants' beliefs and their beliefs about each other's beliefs. The classical model's state variables, operators, and goals are then beliefs of participants that evolve throughout the interaction. This is one reason why the human planning world emphasizes talk about plans, not just design and execution of them. Moreover, generation and recognition of plans become necessarily intermingled, since each individual's plan is only part of a larger social plan. Finally, the human plan has a historical character to it. Each action produces irreversible changes in others' beliefs, including, of course, the belief that the given action was carried out.

Using a mutual belief model that attempts to take account of these characteristics of human plans we looked at a simple dialogue. It is clear from the analysis that elements of the model, e.g., mutual belief, social episode, goal conflict, and so on, are necessary for modeling such dialogues, but not sufficient. More complex dialogues and texts will undoubtedly require further elaboration of the model.

REFERENCES

Brewer, W. F., & Lichtenstein, E. H. (1982). Stories are to entertain: A structural-effect theory of stories. *Journal of Pragmatics, 6,* 473–486.

Bruce, B. C. (1980). Analysis of interacting plans as a guide to the understanding of story structure. *Poetics, 9,* 295–311.

Bruce, B. C. (1981). A social interaction model of reading. *Discourse Processes, 4,* 273–311.

Bruce, B. C., & Newman, D. (1978). Interacting plans. *Cognitive Science, 2,* 195–233.

Clark, H. H., & Marshall, C. R. (1981). Definite reference and mutual knowledge. In A. K. Joshi, I. Sag, & B. Webber (Eds.), *Elements of discourse understanding.* Cambridge, England: Cambridge University Press.

Cohen, P. R. (1981, August). The need for identification as a planned action. *Proceedings of the International Joint Conference on Artificial Intelligence, Vancouver, B.C.*.

Cohen, P. R., & Perrault, C. R. (1979). Elements of a plan-based theory of speech acts. *Cognitive Science, 3,* 177–212.

Gearhart, M., & Newman, D. (1980). Learning to draw a picture: The social context of an individual activity. *Discourse Processes, 3,* 169–184.

Hall, W. S., Nagy, W., & Linn, R. (1984). *Spoken words: Effects of situation and social group on oral word usage and frequency.* Hillsdale, NJ: Erlbaum.

Miller, G. A., Galanter, E., & Pribram, K. H. (1980). *Plans and the structure of behavior.* New York: Holt.

Newman, D. (1981). *Children's understanding of strategic interaction.* Unpublished doctoral dissertation, City University of New York.

Perrault, C. R., & Allen, J. F. (1980). A plan-based analysis of indirect speech acts. *American Journal of Computational Linguistics, 6,* 167–182.

Schiffer, S. R. (1972). *Meaning.* London: Oxford University Press.

Sidner, C. L., & Israel, D. J. (1981, August). Recognizing intended meaning and speaker's plans. *Proceedings of the International Joint Conference on Artificial Intelligence, Vancouver, B.C.*.

Sidner, C., Bates, M., Bobrow, R., Goodman, B., Haas, A., Ingria, R., Israel, D., McAllester, D., Moser, M., Schmolze, J., & Villain, M. (1983). *Research in knowledge representation for natural language understanding.* Cambridge, MA: Bolt Beranek and Newman.

Wilensky, R. (1981). Meta-planning. Representing and using knowledge about planning in problem solving and natural language understanding. *Cognitive Science, 5,* 197–234.

PART III

GRAMMARS, PARSERS, AND LANGUAGE COMPREHENSION

Chapter 6

The Mapping Between Grammar and Processor*

Lyn Frazier

University of Massachusetts, Amherst

The relation between a theory of language competence and a theory of language performance is of central interest to linguists and psycholinguists for several obvious reasons. If it should turn out that there is a single function which, when applied to any grammatical rule, translates the rule into a psychological operation in the theory of performance, then knowledge of the psychological role of any one grammatical rule would automatically place tight constraints on performance theory by constraining the nature of the translation function. On the other hand, if different grammatical rules may serve distinct roles in performance theory, then a wide variety of translation functions may be needed to specify the performance interpretation of grammatical rules. In principle, there might be a different translation function for each rule of the grammar. It seems more likely, however, that a single translation function will operate on all of the rules within a single component of the grammar, thereby establishing modules in a performance theory that correspond to the modules of the competence theory. If this modular view should turn out to be correct, then an understanding of the translation function for each grammatical module might help us to construct psycholinguistic theories. Ultimately it might also help elucidate the nature of grammars by helping to explain the reasons for the particular vocabulary, operations, domains and substantive constraints characteristic of particular grammatical subsystems.

---

* This work was supported by NIMH Research Grant MH35347 to C. Clifton and L. Frazier, and NSF Research Grant 17600 to K. Rayner and L. Frazier. I am grateful to Charles Clifton for very helpful comments on an earlier draft of this paper.

In this paper, we will examine a variety of studies published in the psycholinguistic literature, emphasizing their implication for the relation between linguistic competence and performance. We will then explore some interesting implications of this relation for the theory of language acquisition.

I. COMPETENCE HYPOTHESES

Specific hypotheses about the relation between language competence and language performance have been offered under a variety of different guises. Under one guise, the competence-performance distinction amounts simply to a general statement of the problem involved in studying human cognition or knowledge processing systems. An insightful description of the structure of the knowledge being processed is probably essential to the task, since this structure is likely to both constrain and be constrained by the structure of the processing system, at least in empirical domains where biological organisms are the object of inquiry. At this level, drawing a distinction between language competence and performance amounts only to separating out different aspects of the larger problem of developing a theory of the representation and processing of linguistic knowledge. (See Pylyshyn, 1972, 1973, for discussion.)

A particular hypothesis about the relation between competence and performance may also be adopted as a research strategy, guiding the development of competence theories and performance theories alike. (See, for example, Bresnan, 1978, 1982). In this case, the research strategy is typically characterized by the attempt to juggle the theories of competence and performance to permit a maximally direct or transparent mapping between the two.

Given a particular theory of competence, a specific hypothesis about the relation between that theory and the best (most explanatory) theory of human language performance may also be offered as an empirical claim. It is this latter (empirical) class of hypotheses that we will be concerned with in this paper. In particular, the attempt will be to assess the validity of the following hypotheses:

A. All and only the rules of the grammar describe the operations that can be performed on linguistic representations during the comprehension of sentences.
B. Each of the theoretical constructs in the grammar plays a role in the best psychological theory of the acquisition, production or comprehension of language.

I will argue that Hypothesis A is too restrictive and that Hypothesis B needs to be strengthened along the lines suggested by the above discussion of the modular view of the translation function between the grammar and the theory of performance.

2. *SYNTACTIC EVIDENCE*

In the early 1960s psychologists by and large ignored the role of phrase structure rules in their theorizing about sentence processing. Instead, they focused on the role of transformational rules, hypothesizing that each transformational rule of the grammar corresponded to a psychological operation performed during sentence processing. The initial success and subsequent failure of this approach is now well-known (cf. Fodor, Bever, & Garrett, 1974).

More recent psycholinguistic investigations provide relatively direct evidence for the use of phrase structure rules in the online processing of sentences. Much of this evidence derives from studies used to motivate, test, and provide an explanation for the Minimal Attachment strategy. This parsing strategy specifies that perceivers incorporate each word of an input lexical string into a constituent structure representation of the sentence, using the fewest syntactic nodes consistent with the well-formedness constraints of the language.

Frazier (1979) originally used a variety of experimental findings drawn from the psycholinguistic literature, and intuitions about the preferred interpretation of sentences, to motivate this strategy. She then tested the generality of the strategy using a grammaticality judgment experiment, by showing that, in a wide variety of constructions, sentences consistent with the phrase structure analysis selected by the strategy (e.g., (1a)) take less time to process than corresponding sentences where the chosen syntactic analysis turns out to be incorrect (e.g., (1b)).

(1a) Sally was relieved when she found out *the answer to the physics problem.*
(1b) Sally found out *the answer to the physics problem* was in the book.

In (1a), the temporarily ambiguous phrase *the answer to the physics problem* may be incorporated into the constituent structure representation of preceding items by minimally attaching it to the VP node dominating the preceding verb; in (1a), this will turn out to be correct, but in (1b), an additional (S) node will have to be postulated when subsequent items are processed. Some of the structures in which the predictions of Minimal Attachment have been experimentally tested are represented schematically in (2), where the circled nodes in the right-hand column indicate potentially unnecessary nodes which, according to Minimal Attachment, will not be postulated unless or until the processor receives evidence demanding their postulation.

(2a) Direct object vs. sentential complement of a verb.

Minimal Attachment *Nonminimal Attachment*

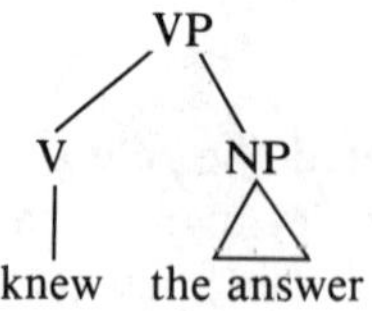

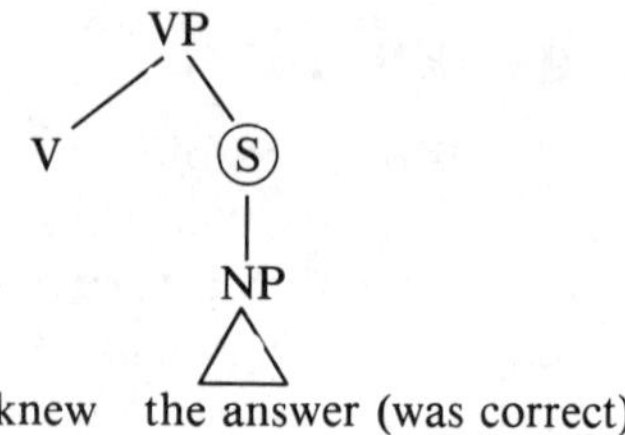

(2b) NP vs. S conjunction

Minimal Attachment *Nonminimal Attachment*

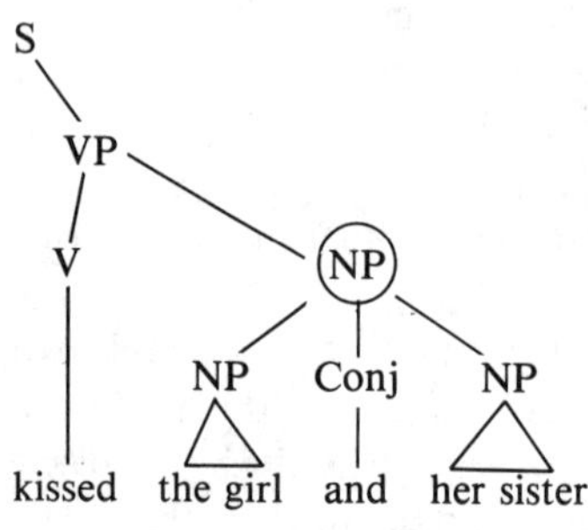

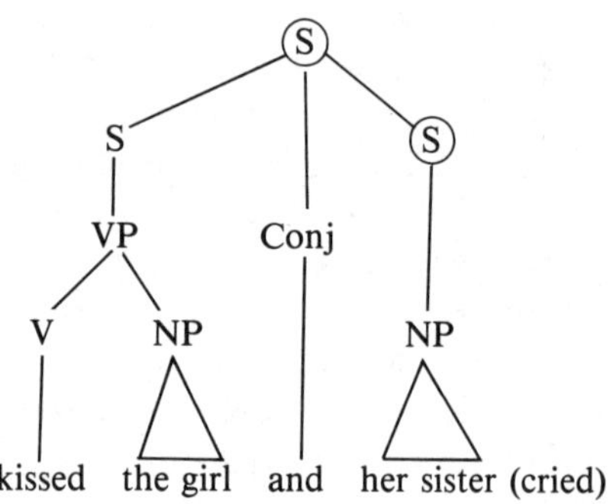

(2c) NP vs. S complement of a preposition or adverb.

Minimal Attachment *Nonminimal Attachment*

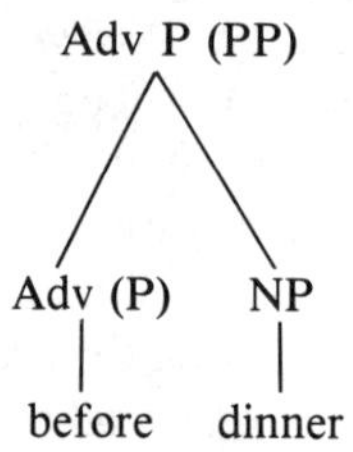

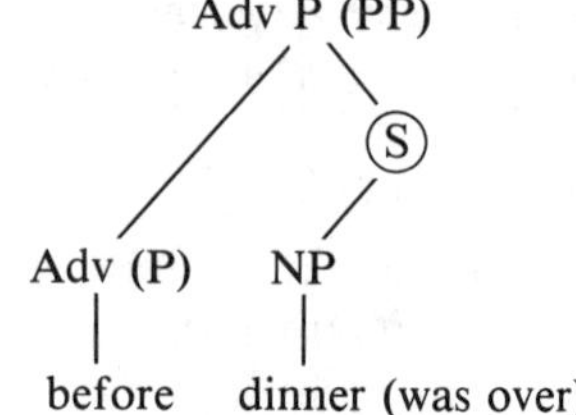

(2d) Main clause vs. reduced relative in double object construction

Minimal Attachment

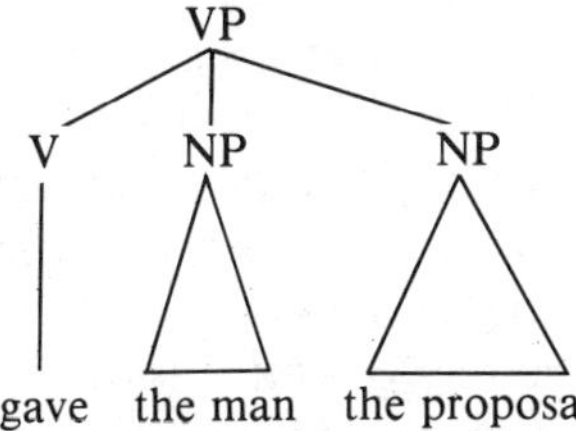

Nonminimal Attachment

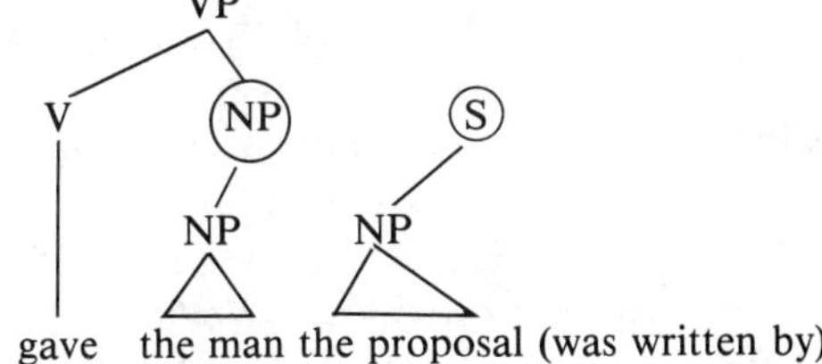

(2e) Main clause vs. reduced relative in subject position

Minimal Attachment

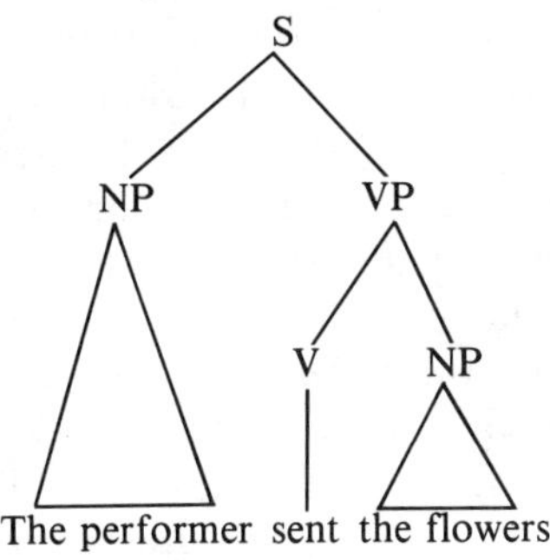

Nonminimal Attachment

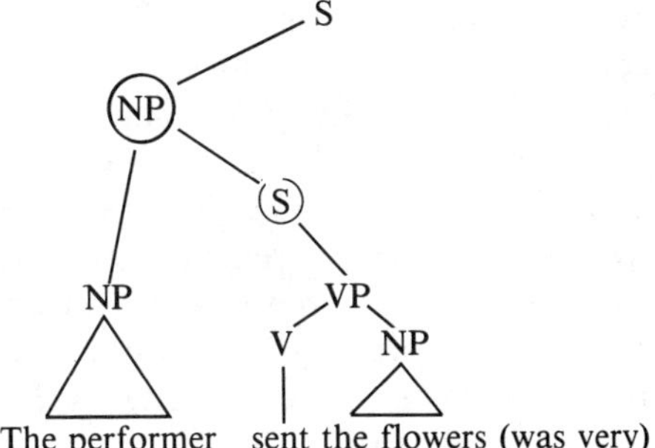

(2f) PP in VP vs. in NP

Minimal Attachment

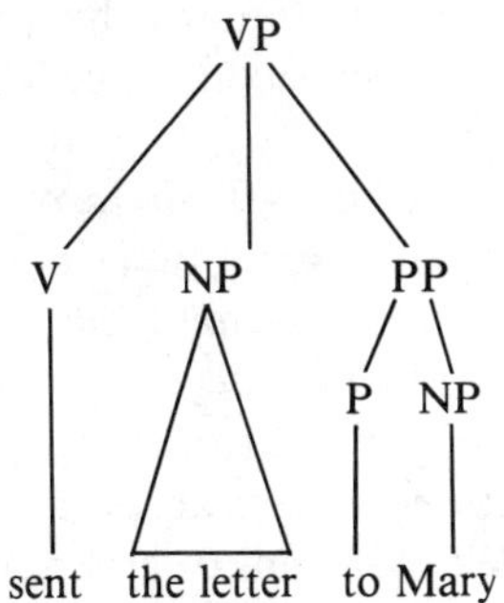

Nonminimal Attachment

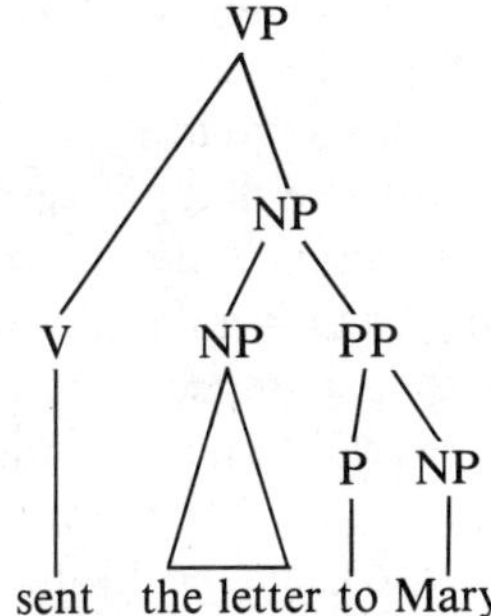

The predictions of Minimal Attachment in the structures in (2a), (2e), and (2f) have also been tested by recording eye movements as subjects read sentences (cf. Frazier & Rayner, 1982; Rayner, Carlson, & Frazier, 1983). The results of these studies have provided striking confirmation of the predictions of Minimal Attachment, showing for example that the average duration of fixations is significantly longer on the very first fixation on the disambiguating region of nonminimal attachment sentences. In short, the predictions of the Minimal Attachment strategy have now been confirmed in a large range of structures, using several experimental techniques.

These results provide clear evidence that perceivers use the information contained in phrase structure rules to construct a constituent structure representation of a sentence as the words of the sentence are encountered. However, these results by themselves do not suffice to show that this phrase structure information is represented in the form of traditional phrase structure rules (i.e., context free rewriting rules). But there is good reason to suppose that this is the case, i.e., that phrase structure information is mentally represented by a series of statements, each containing information only about the possible daughter nodes permitted by some mother node. Frazier and Fodor (1978) argue that the reason why different perceivers adopt the Minimal Attachment strategy is because it is the first analysis of the lexical string available to the sentence processor. On the assumption that it takes more time to access more phrase structure rules, the Minimal Attachment analysis of a sentence will simply be available before any nonminimal analysis of the string, since the latter will require the accessing of additional phrase structure rules. Hence, an explanation of the Minimal Attachment strategy requires the assumption that phrase structure rules are accessed during the processing of sentences. (Note that it will not suffice to say that it simply takes more time to postulate more nodes. Garden-path effects noted in nonminimal attachment structures are not observed in sentences containing information in left-context, which unambiguously requires the same number and type of nodes to be postulated as eventually becomes necessary in a garden-path sentence.)

Further evidence that phrase structure rules are used directly in the online processing of sentences derives from a study by Clifton, Frazier, and Connine (1984). Using an ungrammaticality detection task, they show that facilitation effects due to a sentence form matching the preferred subcategorization of its verb are overlaid on a general bias for transitive sentence forms. This set of effects can be explained on the assumption that perceivers access a general verb phrase rule (specifying all of the possible expansions of an English verb phrase) and use it to predict the occurrence of a following noun phrase. This predicted noun phrase node is then deleted, entered into the developing constituent structure representation of the sentence, or taken to be a noun phrase gap, depending on the preferred (most frequent) subcategorization frame of the verb. If this interpretation of the findings is correct (see Clifton et al. for discussion), it too provides striking evidence for the online use of phrase structure rules in sentence processing, since it shows that phrase structure rules are accessed, and influence the processing of the sentence, even when more specific lexical information in principle would have sufficed to determine the analysis of the lexical string.

In short, considerable psychological evidence shows that phrase structure information is used during the online analysis of sentences and, further, that phrase structure information is mentally represented in the format current theories of competence would lead us to expect, i.e., as a series of rules or definitions each of which specifies the number, order, and syntactic type of all possible daughters of a phrase.

Recently, Stowell (1981) has argued that all of the properties of the phrase structure rules of a language may be explained by appeal to independently motivated grammatical constraints. This observation is extremely important and very likely to enter into an account of how children manage to acquire the phrase structure rules of their language. However, the evidence discussed here suggests that it would be a mistake to assume that having an explanation for the properties of some set of grammatical rules automatically permits us to dispense with those rules in the theory of grammar.

We turn now to the processing of filler-gap dependencies (i.e., dependencies between a phonetically null position in the phrase marker and the phrase which controls the interpretation of this position). Investigations in the ATN framework (cf. Wanner & Maratsos, 1978), as well as investigation of the grammatical constraints on possible filler-gap dependencies (Fodor, 1978) and intuitions concerning the possible meanings of (Swedish) sentences with multiple filler-gap dependencies (cf. Engdahl, 1983) suggest that perceivers rely on the heuristic of assigning the most recent potential filler to the first gap encountered. (If phrases encountered more recently are more readily available in memory, this strategy, like Minimal Attachment, may simply be an automatic consequence of the processor adopting the first syntactic analysis available.) In many sentences (e.g., (3a) and (4a)), a recent filler decision will turn out to satisfy the grammatical constraints of the language; however, in others (e.g., (3b) and (4b)), it will not and the decision will have to be revised.

(3a) This is *the girl* (who) *the teacher* wanted _____ to talk to _____ at the meeting.

(3b) This is *the girl* (who) *the teacher* wanted _____ to talk at the meeting.

(4a) This is *the girl* (who) *the teacher* started _____ to talk to _____ at the meeting.

(4b) This is *the girl* (who) *the teacher* forced _____ to talk at the meeting.

In a comprehension experiment, Frazier, Clifton, and Randall (1983) show that reading times are longer for the (b) versions of the above sentence pairs, where assignment of the most recent filler to the first gap turns out to be incorrect. Frazier et al. propose that the processor initially assigns filler-gap dependencies using the Most Recent Filler strategy, and only later checks the grammatical constraints on permissible filler-gap assignments. If this interpretation of the data is correct, then we have a clear counterexample to the more restrictive competence hypothesis which claims that all and *only* the rules of the grammar describe the operations that can be performed on linguistic representations during the comprehension of sentences. The recent filler strategy clearly does not correspond to a grammatical rule; indeed, in sentences like (4b) it leads to an ungrammatical filler-gap assignment (though see Crain and Fodor (forthcoming), where it is suggested that the recent filler strategy only operates in cases of ambiguity).

3. MORPHOLOGICAL EVIDENCE

Most psychological investigations of word recognition have focused on the recognition of monomorphemic words. But there are some interesting exceptions that can be culled from the literature. It is well known that, in a lexical decision experiment (where subjects are asked to judge whether a letter string corresponds to a word of their language), repetition of a word during the course of the experiment speeds up decision times for the second occurrence of the word. Stanners, Neiser, Hernon, and Hall (1979) exploited this whole word repetition effect to explore the processing of the regular and irregular inflected forms of a word. They found that prior occurrence of a regularly inflected form of a verb (e.g., BURNING, BURNS, or BURNED) facilitates later recognition of the stem (BURN) in just the same manner as prior occurrence of the stem itself. This is precisely what we would expect to find if the inflected form of words were recognized and produced by rule, rather than being stored as fully specified lexical entries. Irregular inflected forms (e.g., HUNG) also facilitated later recognition of the stem (HANG), but not to the same degree as prior presentation of the stem itself. Hence, the facilitation effect observed for regularly inflected forms can not be attributed simply to the fact that inflected forms are mentally represented in the same lexical entry as their stem, or to the existence of a close semantic relation between an inflected word and its stem. (Also see Murrel and Morton (1974) for a demonstration showing that these effects cannot be attributed simply to the visual similarity of items.) Further evidence for the hypothesis that the regularly inflected forms of words are computed by rule, and not prestored in the lexicon, derives from speech errors, such as producing **goed* for *went.*[1]

[1] Taft (1979) presents evidence which, taken by itself, might appear to provide a counterexample to the generalization that regular inflectional rules correspond to psychological computations performed by perceivers. He showed that the frequency of occurrence of a particular inflected form of a verb, as well as the frequency of occurrence of the uninflected word, influenced recognition times. Given the evidence discussed in the text, the most plausible interpretation of these data is that computations that are performed more often take less time to perform.

Bradley (1979) used the lexical decision task to examine the recognition of words derived from neutral derivational affixes, such as *-ness, -ment,* and *-er,* and words derived from non-neutral derivational affixes, such as *-ion* and *ity*. (Though the distinction between neutral and nonneutral derivational affixes is cast in somewhat different terms in different grammatical theories, any theory must capture the fact that nonneutral affixes may not occur 'outside' neutral affixes, that only the nonneutral affixes may alter the phonological composition of the items they attach to, etc.) Bradley very cleverly exploited the fact that the frequency of occurrence of a word is known to influence the recognition time of a word. Essentially what she did was to ask whether it was the frequency of occurrence of the derived form of a word or the frequency of its base that would predict the recognition time of the derived form. Thus she compared recognition times for pairs of words that were matched only in the frequency of their base (e.g., *heavy* occurs as often as *happy,* but *heaviness* does not occur as often as *happiness*) with pairs of derived words that were themselves matched in frequency, though the frequency of the base words differed (e.g., *briskness* occurs as often as *sharpness,* though *brisk* does not occur as frequently as *sharp*). In the case of each neutral derivational affix tested, she found that it was the frequency of the base word that predicted recognition times, suggesting that words derived from neutral derivational affixes are stored together with their base forms. By contrast, in the case of words derived from nonneutral derivational affixes, it was the frequency of the derived word that predicted recognition times, suggesting that these words have lexical entries distinct from the entry of their base and are not recognized by reference to their base words.

Using the whole word repetition effect described earlier, Stanners et al. also examined the recognition of words derived from rules of nonneutral derivational affixes. They show that prior presentation of a word derived from a nonneutral derivational affix (e.g., SELECTIVE) did facilitate recognition of the base (SELECT), though not as much as did the prior presentation of the base itself. Further, there was no difference between derived words in which the affix altered the phonological composition of the base (e.g., DESCRIPTIVE) and those where the affix did not (e.g., SELECTIVE). This suggests that it is the particular rule or affix involved, and not some particular application of the rule, which determines the psychological role that the rule will play.

Taken together, the results of these experiments show that rules of nonneutral derivation establish a relation between distinct lexical entries. Bradley's results argue that words derived from these affixes cannot be stored together with their base, but Stanner's results show that there is some relation between the lexical entry of the base and the lexical entry of the derived form. By contrast, neutral derivational rules apparently determine which morphologically related items are stored together in a single lexical entry. Inflectional rules apparently play an even more active role; speech error data, as well as whole word repetition effects in recognition, suggest that these rules correspond directly to psychological computations performed in the recognition and production of words.

4. THE CONSISTENT REALIZATION HYPOTHESIS

Recall the restrictive competence hypothesis discussed above. It specified that all and only the rules of the grammar describe the operations performed on linguistic representations during the comprehension of sentences. We have now seen examples of both logically possible types of counter-example to this claim. In the case of long distance dependencies, it appears that an operation (assignment of the most recent filler to the first gap detected) is performed on linguistic representations, even though that operation does not correspond to any grammatical rule. On the other hand, nonneutral derivational rules seem to capture a psychologically real generalization in that they establish relations between distinct lexical entries, though they do not correspond to operations performed on linguistic representations during the comprehension of sentences. Thus, as an empirical claim, the restrictive competence hypothesis (A) seems to be false.

The alternative competence hypothesis (B) considered above merely claimed that each of the theoretical constructs of the grammar plays some role in the best psychological theory of acquisition, production, or comprehension. But the evidence examined here suggests that a stronger hypothesis is warranted by the data, namely, that rules of the same formal type receive the same interpretation in a theory of language comprehension. Generalized slightly to extend it to other performance systems, this hypothesis may be stated as the Consistent Realization Hypothesis formulated in (5).

(5) Consistent Realization Hypothesis:
Any two rules of the same formal type will receive a consistent interpretation in any given performance system (production, comprehension, acquisition)

Let us briefly review the evidence that supports this hypothesis. In the case of phrase-structure rules (of the traditional variety, i.e., without slashed nodes), we have seen evidence that the rules are used online during the immediate processing of the lexical string. By contrast, the (limited) evidence currently available suggests that grammatical constraints on legitimate filler-gap dependency assignments do not guide the immediate processing of the lexical string. That these two types of grammatical well-formedness conditions should play different roles in the processing of sentences comes as no surprise, given the division of grammatical theory into distinct components. Even in theories such as Generalized Phrase Structure Grammar (cf. Gazdar, 1981) which attempt to provide a uniform grammatical characterization of all syntactic well-formedness constraints, there remains a distinction between the basic phrase structure rules of the language and the derived rules, which capture long distance filler-gap dependencies. (It should be noted, however, that the attempt to collapse basic and derived phrase structure rules using parenthesis notation seems to be desirable if these rules are to be used in parsing sentences, but it would seem to neutralize the formal distinction between rule types.)

The evidence concerning inflectional rules showed that all of the (regular) inflections tested (the PRESENT, PAST, and PROGRESSIVE morphemes) behaved in the same manner and defined actual computations performed on linguistic representations. Similarly, all of the neutral derivational affixes tested (*-ment, -ness,* and *-er*) behaved in a like manner, defining the contents of a single lexical entry. The evidence concerning nonneutral affixes suggested that all affixes of this type merely establish a relation between distinct lexical entries. Further, in the case of the nonneutral derivational affix *-ive,* it made no difference whether or not it altered the phonological makeup of a particular derived form; instead, it seems to be the formal status of the affix itself (whether it attaches to stems or words, cf. Selkirk, 1982) which determines the role it plays in a psychological theory of language performance.

It might easily have turned out that some rules of neutral derivation would behave like rules of nonneutral derivation, or that the interpretation of different inflectional rules in a theory of performance would depend on their phonological consequences, their frequency of occurrence, or the like. Of course, it is possible that further testing of morphological rules will turn up some exceptions to the above generalizations. Nevertheless, it is really quite striking that all rules tested of a given formal type showed evidence of playing the same role in a psychological theory of the representation and processing of words.

The evidence discussed here not only provides interesting and rather surprising support for the Consistent Realization Hypothesis, but it cries out for explanation. Why should each type of rule assume the particular performance role that it does? Why should two rules of the same type play the same performance role, apparently without regard for the frequency or phonological consequences of individual rules or rule applications? And why should the same performance interpretation of a rule be observed across different perceivers of the language?

Certainly the most obvious explanation of these facts would claim that the acquisition process is governed by the Consistent Realization Hypothesis. The uniform performance interpretation of morphological rules and rule types in the adult comprehension system is then explained quite simply. Each rule type can serve the particular performance function noted above but none of the rule types discussed could systematically assume a more 'active' function. Regular inflectional rules may correspond to psychological operations performed on linguistic representations because the output of such rules is totally predictable and thus the derived forms need not be stored. The output of some neutral derivational rules must be stored because they are associated with idiosyncratic or unpredictable meanings (compare the meaning of *attachment* and *merriment,* for example). Thus, as a class, neutral derivational rules could not assume the fully active role of regular inflectional rules. There are a variety of reasons why forms derived from nonneutral derivational rules could not systematically assume a more active role in performance by determining what derived forms are stored in the lexical entry of their base. Perhaps the most compelling reason is that nonneutral affixes may alter the phonological composition of the initial syllable of the base (e.g., compare *nation* and *national*), and, thus, storing a word derived from a nonneutral affix in the lexical entry of its base would in such cases prevent the derived form from being accessed on the basis of its initial segments. (See Marslen-Wilson and Tyler (1980), where it is argued that the initial segments of a word are used to determine the set of candidate lexical representations against which a perceptual input is matched.) We have just seen that the Consistent Realization Hypothesis, together with the hypothesis that children use grammatical generalizations in the most active manner possible, explains the uniformity observed in the adult comprehension system. We turn now to the implications of these hypotheses for a theory of language acquisition.

5. THE LANGUAGE ACQUISITION SYSTEM

If there is any obvious fact about children acquiring their native language, it is that children are phenomenally good at extracting regularities from the data they are exposed to. However, to account for the fact that all children do acquire their language in a fixed amount of time, it must be assumed that children are predisposed to notice certain regularities (the grammatically viable ones) and not others. These considerations alone strongly suggest that the child is innately equipped with the universally available vocabulary each grammatical component or subsystem has at its disposal for stating grammatical well-formedness conditions.

Given the hypothesis that, in performance, children exploit grammatically viable generalizations in the most active manner possible (up to the limits imposed by the Consistent Realization Hypothesis and the need to store idiosyncratic information and to recognize words efficiently), it must be assumed that the child formulates cautious generalizations. Children clearly do not treat each datum as being isolated and providing information only about itself; rather, they form generalizations. But to prevent totally unconstrained overgeneralizations, the child must hypothesize rules that apply to the smallest natural class consistent with both the data in hand and the vocabulary available for stating grammatical rules.

This immediately raises the issue of how the child determines the appropriate vocabulary for stating some generalization. In some cases, this will not be problematic. The vocabulary available to the child for couching grammatical generalizations may itself dictate that a generalization may be stated only in some particular subsystem of the grammar, e.g. phonological generalizations simply could not be represented in the vocabulary available in the phrase structure component of the grammar or long-distance syntactic relations in the vocabulary of lexical rules. In other cases, the appropriate vocabulary for stating a generalization may be indeterminate, due to an overlap in the vocabulary available to various grammatical subsystems. The need to formulate cautious generalizations entails that, in cases where the vocabulary appropriate for stating some generalization is shared by several subsystems, the generalization must initially be couched in terms of the subsystem with the richest vocabulary, i.e., the one capable of drawing the most distinctions. If it is assumed that lexical rules may make reference to syntactic categories, thematic restrictions, and predicate-argument structures, then the vocabulary of lexical rules is clearly richer than that available to syntactic rules. And if "structure preserving" syntactic dependencies are viewed as dependencies between phrases in argument positions, then the subsystem available for stating the well-formedness conditions pertaining to these dependencies may presumably refer to syntactic category and thematic relations but not predicate-argument structure. The vocabulary available for stating long-distance syntactic dependencies appears to be even more restrictive, since it is generally assumed that these dependencies may not be restricted by either thematic relations or predicate-argument structure. Hence, if possible, the child must initially couch generalizations about relations between syntactic phrases in terms of the vocabulary of lexical rules, generalizing the rule to the smallest natural class consistent with the data encountered and the vocabulary of lexical rules. (Of course, any of several types of evidence may force the child to later reformulate a generalization in terms of the vocabulary of a different grammatical subsystem, including evidence about the domain needed to state the generalization, evidence about the general constraints a rule is subject to, or evidence about the interaction of a hypothesized rule with other rules of the grammar.)

The hypothesis that children form cautious generalizations (limited to the smallest natural class provided by the grammatical subsystem with the richest appropriate vocabulary) is supported by various experimental studies of language acquisition, not just by the absence of rampant and unconstrained overgeneralizations. For example, recent empirical studies show that children acquire verbal passives class by class, passives with action predicates before passives with nonaction predicates (cf. Maratsos, 1978; also Jill deVilliers, personal communication). Roeper, Lapointe, Bing, and Tavakolian (1981) also imply that rules are initially cast as lexical rules if they can be, and their experimental studies show that passives form part of a "hypothesis chain" involving rules that are clearly lexical. Thus there is evidence from passives that rules are initially formulated as lexical rules if possible, and that they are initially restricted to the smallest natural class possible, i.e., in the case of passive, to dyadic predicates taking an agent and theme argument. It has been proposed here that the need for children to form cautious generalizations explains why this is the case.

Let us pause briefly to review the structure of the above arguments. To account for the surprising regularities in the adult comprehension system, it was hypothesized that language acquisition is governed by the Consistent Realization Hypothesis and by the strategy of using grammatically viable generalizations in the most active manner possible in language performance. These hypotheses in turn required us to assume that children form cautious generalizations, since otherwise the child could formulate grammatical hypotheses using the most impoverished vocabulary available, leading to over-generalizations from which the child could not retreat without the aid of considerable negative evidence. (Note that the same problem would not arise if the child used grammatical viable generalizations in the least active manner possible, i.e., as a redundancy rule.)

Instead of overgeneralizations due to the child formulating a rule to apply to an overly general class of items, the present hypotheses predict the existence of a class of overgeneralizations due to overly active deployment of rules in the language performance system. According to the above hypotheses, we would expect the child to initially use any grammatical generalization as a processing operation to produce and analyze novel forms. Thus we would expect a child to produce a form like **sadment* until the child received evidence that rules of neutral derivation cannot play such an active role (e.g., evidence that forms derived from neutral derivational rules need to be stored). However, as soon as the child receives evidence that rules of neutral derivation must play a less active role in the developing language performance system, this overgeneralization, together with all other overgeneralizations due to rules of neutral derivation, should disappear as a class, due to the Consistent Realization Hypotheses (though, of course, only once the child has his generalizations couched in the correct grammatical subsystem). In short, the Consistent Realization Hypothesis offers an explanation for how entire classes of overgeneralizations may disappear without the need for negative evidence and on the basis of very limited evidence.[2]

[2] The examples I am aware of where an overgeneralized form coexists for a period of time with a correct form all involve cases governed by the Elsewhere Condition (cf. Kiparsky, 1982). See, for example, the discussion of ongoing competition between the correct and over-regulated form of the past tense of irregular verbs in Slobin (1978). By contrast, evidence consistent with the claim that an entire class of overgeneralizations may disappear together once the child has established a particular grammatical generalization appears, for example, in the work of Randall (1982). She argues that subcategorization frames incorrectly inherited by deverbal derived forms disappear for entire classes of items once the child discovers particular grammatical differences between a derived form and its verbal stem.

The Consistent Realization Hypothesis also helps to account for the robustness of language acquisition. The hypothesis entails that information about the status or performance interpretation of any randomly selected rule of a given formal type should suffice to determine the status of all formally indistinguishable rules; it should not matter at all which particular rule provides the child with a crucial bit of evidence. Thus the Consistent Realization Hypothesis helps explain why language acquisition is insensitive to the particular nature and order of the input data.

The question now arises of why the child would be cautious about the statement of generalizations extracted from the data, but then (in apparent contrast) be aggressive about using those generalizations in the most active manner possible. This apparent tension cannot be resolved simply by appeal to the expressive needs of children to convey a wide range of messages. Overgeneralizations in rule-formation as well as in rule use may under certain circumstances increase the range of messages the child may attempt to convey.[3] Further, active use of overly general grammatical hypotheses, as well as of cautious grammatical hypotheses, would permit the child to aggressively test hypotheses, creating opportunities for the child to receive evidence about the correctness of the hypothesis (perhaps in the form of indirect negative evidence due to an adult's failure to understand an utterance or prompting the adult to supply useful positive evidence). Indeed, it might seem that the strategy of formulating cautious generalizations is completely misdirected, because it will not lead to maximally disconfirmable hypotheses (cf. Williams, 1981), since a broader generalization would be more readily disconfirmed than one which applies to a smaller natural class of items.

Though maximally general hypotheses may be more readily disconfirmed, disconfirmation of the hypotheses is not likely to be very informative about the nature of the correct hypothesis. Like overt corrections that a child might receive, evidence disconfirming an overly general rule is likely to be uninterpretable, since it would be unclear what property of an error due to a maximally general rule was responsible for the error signal the child receives (e.g., a correction, failure to communicate, or the occurrence of positive disconfirmatory evidence). For example, consider a circumstance where the child has received evidence that /p/, /t/, and /d/ undergo some phonological process when they occur in a particular environment. If the child postu-

[3] Aronoff's (1976) "Blocking Convention" which specifies that derived forms are blocked if they correspond to underived forms already present in a language might be taken as evidence that the expressive needs of the child to create a pressure for overgeneralizations, since an overgeneralization will not be needed to express some concept if the child already has available to him some form for expressing that particular concept. The fact that "Blocking" is merely a tendency in the case of forms produced by rules of derivational affixation, and not an absolute constraint on rule application, suggests that the Blocking Convention does indeed require some performance explanation and should not be subsumed under a formal condition such as the Elsewhere Condition.

lated a phonological rule that applied to all consonants occuring in that environment, positive evidence that some consonant should be excluded from the rule would be easy to obtain, but it would provide little information about what feature of that consonant was responsible for its exclusion from the rule. By contrast, if the child postulates a rule that applied only to the smallest natural class which includes /p,t,d/, any disconfirmatory evidence he receives will be more informative. Of course, in either case, the child would eventually be able to learn the correct rule on the basis of positive evidence alone, in this example, but simultaneous overgeneralization of other phonological rules, together with uninformative error signals, would be expected to complicate the acquisition system enormously, given the possible interactions of several incorrect hypotheses. By contrast, active use of cautious generalizations permits the child to actively try to disconfirm generalization that are sufficiently limited for the disconfirmation to be informative with respect to the appropriate domain of application of the rule. This suggests that the child's formation of cautious grammatical generalizations and aggressive use of those generalizations in performance are simply two specific consequences of one general acquisition principle of maximal informativeness. Active use of hypothesized rules permits quick disconfirmation of hypothesized rules, cautious hypotheses permit disconfirmations to be informative, permitting the child to incrementally test his hypotheses, natural class by natural class.

The hypothesis that language acquisition is guided by the Consistent Realization Hypothesis has offered an explanation for certain regularities in the adult comprehension system. It also predicts that children can retreat from large classes of overgeneralizations on the basis of very limited data. It further helps to account for the insensitivity of language acquisition to the specific nature and order of input data. In addition, it places a strong and interesting constraint on the mapping between the grammar and the processor which is supported by a fairly wide range of empirical evidence about the relation between the grammar and the adult language comprehension system.

6. CONCLUSIONS

The purpose of this paper has been to assess the validity of several empirical claims about the relation between the grammar and the human language performance system. A variety of different types of evidence show that there is a principled correspondence between the two, module by module. Formal grammatical distinctions that characterize subsystems of grammatical rules influence and constrain the mapping between grammatical rules and the language performance system.

REFERENCES

Aronoff, M. (1976). *Word formation in generative grammar.* Cambridge, MA: MIT Press.

Bradley, D. (1978). Lexical representation of derivational relations. In M. Aronoff & M. L. Kean (Eds.), *Juncture.* Cambridge, MA: MIT Press.

Bresnan, J. (1978). A realistic transformational grammar. In M. Halle, J. Bresnan, & G. A. Miller, (Eds.), *Linguistic theory and psychological reality.* Cambridge, MA: MIT Press.

Bresnan, J. (1982). *The mental representation of grammatical relations.* Cambridge, MA: MIT Press.

Clifton, C., Frazier, L., & Connine, C. (1984). Lexical and syntactic expectations in sentence comprehension. *Journal of Verbal Learning and Verbal Behavior, 23.*

Crain, S., & Fodor, J. D. (forthcoming). How can grammars help parsers? In D. Dowty, L. Karttunen, & A. Zwicky (Eds.), *Syntactic theory and how people parse sentences.*

Engdahl, E. (forthcoming). Interpreting questions. In D. Dowty, L. Karttunen, and A. Zwicky (Eds.), *Natural language parsing.* Cambridge: Cambridge University Press.

Fodor, J. A., Bever, T. G., & Garrett, M. F. (1974). *The psychology of language.* New York: McGraw Hill.

Fodor, J. D. (1978). Parsing strategies and constraints on transformations, *Linguistic Inquiry,* 9, 427–473.

Frazier, L. (1979). *On comprehending sentences: Syntactic parsing strategies.* Unpublished doctoral dissertation, University of Connecticut.

Frazier, L., Clifton, C., & Randall, J. (1983). Filling gaps: decision principles and structure in sentence comprehension. *Cognition,* 13, 187–222.

Frazier, L., & Fodor, J. D. (1978). The sausage machine: a new two-stage model of sentence parsing. *Cognition,* 6, 291–325.

Frazier, L., & Rayner, K. (1982). Making and correcting errors during sentence comprehension: eye movements in the analysis of structurally ambiguous sentences. *Cognitive Psychology,* 14, 178–210.

Gazdar, G. (1981). Unbounded dependencies and coordinate structure. *Linguistic Inquiry,* 12, 155–184.

Kiparsky, P. (1982). *Lexical morphology and phonology.* Unpublished manuscript.

Maratsos, M. (1978). New models in linguistics and language acquisition. In M. Halle, J. Bresnan, & G. A. Miller (Eds.), *Linguistic theory and psychological reality.* Cambridge, MA: MIT Press.

Marslen-Wilson, W., & Tyler, L. (1980). The temporal structure of spoken language comprehension. *Cognition.* 8, 1–71.

Murrell, G. A. & Morton, J. (1974). Word recognition and morphemic structure. *Journal of Experimental Psychology,* 102, 963–968.

Pylyshyn, Z. (1972). Competence and psychological reality. *American Psychologist,* 27, 546–552.

Pylyshyn, Z. (1973). The role of competence theories in cognitive psychology. *Journal of Psycholinguistics Research,* 2, 21–50.

Randall, J. (1982). *Morphological structure and language acquisition.* Unpublished doctoral dissertation.

Rayner, K., Carlson, M., & Frazier, L. (1983). The interaction of syntax and semantics during sentence processing: eye movements in the analysis of semantically biased sentences. *Journal of Verbal Learning and Verbal Behavior, 22,* 358–374.

Roeper, T., Lapointe, S., Bing, J., & Tavakolian, S. (1981). A lexical approach to language acquisition. In S. Tavakolian (Eds.), *Language acquisition and linguistic theory.* Cambridge, MA: MIT Press.

Selkirk, E. (1982). *English word structure.* Cambridge, MA: MIT Press.

Slobin, D. (1978). A case study of early language awareness. In A. Sinclair, R. J. Jarvella, & W. J. M. Levelt (Eds.), *The child's conception of language.* Berlin: Springer-Verlag.

Stanners, R. F., Neiser, J. J., Hernon, W. P., & Hall, R. (1979). Memory representation for morphologically-related words. *Journal of Verbal Learning and Verbal Behavior,* 18, 399–412.

Stowell, T. (1981). *Origins of phrase structure.* Unpublished doctoral dissertation.

Taft, M. (1979). Recognition of affixed words and the word frequency effect. *Memory & Cognition,* 7, 263–272.

Wanner, E., & Maratsos, M. (1978). An ATN approach to comprehension, In M. Halle, J. Bresnan, & G. A. Miller (Eds.), *Linguistic theory and psychological reality.* Cambridge, MA: MIT Press.

Williams, E. (1981). Markedness and phrase structure. In S. L. Tavakolian (Eds.), *Language acquisition and linguistic theory.* Cambridge, MA: MIT Press.

Chapter 7
Modularity and Lexical Access*

Mark S. Seidenberg
McGill University
Michael K. Tanenhaus
University of Rochester

I. INTRODUCTION

Although recognizing the words in a text or utterance is an important part of language comprehension, the complexity of the recognition process is sometimes overlooked because of the skill and rapidity with which it is accomplished. Psycholinguistic research on lexical processing has been concerned with a number of issues, including: (a) how information is represented in the mental lexicon; (b) which types of lexical information are accessed in comprehension; and (c) the extent to which lexical processing is contingent upon the linguistic or extra-linguistic context in which a word occurs.

This research is important to an understanding of natural language processing for several reasons. First, the rapidity of the comprehension process suggests that a great deal of information becomes available as individual words are heard or read, and that this information is almost immediately integrated with the perceiver's developing representation of the message (Marslen-Wilson, 1975). The basic facts about the time course of the comprehension process emphasize the importance of lexical processing.

In addition, the processing of individual words—identifying them, determining their meanings and grammatical functions—influences subsequent processing events. A simple example is provided by (1) and (2),

(1) John put the ball away.

(2) John threw the ball away.

* This work was supported in part by grants from the Natural Science and Engineering Research Council of Canada (A7924), the Quebec Ministry of Education (EQ-2074), the National Science Foundation (IST 80-12439), and the National Institute of Child Health and Development (HD 16019-01).

where information associated with the verbs *put* and *throw* affects processing later in the sentence. *Put* is subcategorized for an obligatory location; for *threw,* the location is optional. Having processed *put,* the reader or listener can anticipate the occurrence of the obligatory element, knowing that the sentence is not complete following *the ball. Throw* functions quite differently, as it is unclear whether (2) is complete following the definite noun-phrase or not. Recent evidence suggests that readers access information concerning the subcategorization of verbs, and that it influences the processing of subsequent noun-phrases (Clifton, Frazier, & Connine, 1984). Thus processing that occurs later in a sentence is conditioned by the results of prior lexical processing, the use of subcategorization information providing only one example of this phenomenon.

The comprehension of individual lexical items also directs the access of information that is relevant to understanding a passage, but not explicitly stated. Recent theories of language comprehension emphasize that the reader or listener must "go beyond the information given" in order to construct a representation of what is meant. This elaborative process draws upon information stored in memory, and individual lexical items may influence the access of contextually appropriate information. In a sequence such as (3),

(3) John was killed yesterday. The murderer was one of John's friends.

the definite noun-phrase "the murderer" serves to trigger the inference that John was murdered, which links the two sentences. Such linking inferences are generated immediately following the triggering lexical item (Tanenhaus & Seidenberg, 1981). A comprehensive theory of lexical processing, then, would explain not only the processing of individual words, but also the events that follow from such processes.

Understanding the representation of lexical information in memory, and the access of such information in natural language processing, is also important given recent developments in linguistic theory. Lexical-functional grammar (Kaplan & Bresnan, 1982), government-binding theory (Chomsky, 1981), and generalized phrase structure grammar (Gazdar, 1982) all involve conceptions of the lexicon far richer than in previous theories (e.g., Chomsky, 1965). The fact that all of these theories are being construed as the basis of computational theories of language processing (see Berwick & Weinberg, 1983, and the papers in Dowty, Karttunen, & Zwicky, 1985) makes it important to understand the "psychological reality" of lexical structures and processes.

A fourth reason for investigating lexical processing is its role in certain acquired and developmental language disorders. Most children exhibiting specific reading disability ("dyslexia") have severe problems in decoding words, even though they possess adequate grammatical and world knowledge (as indicated by their ability to produce and understand spoken language). Similarly, many language disorders consequent upon stroke or other brain injury are manifested as various dysfunctions in lexical processing (Coltheart, Patterson, & Marshall, 1980). Thus, theories of lexical representation and access may be important in understanding both language disorders and the representation of language in the brain.

Most important perhaps is the fact that recent research on lexical processing provides the clearest evidence to date concerning the so-called modularity of cognitive structures and processes (Marr, 1982; Fodor, 1983). Marr's principle of modular design is "the idea that a large computation can be split up and implemented as a collection of parts that are as nearly independent of one another as the overall task allows" (1982, p. 102). As applied to language comprehension, the principle suggests that different types of linguistic knowledge and the processes by which this knowledge is utilized in comprehension may be conceptualized as relatively separate sub-systems. This general idea has appeared repeatedly in slightly different guises. In linguistics, it underlies Chomsky's conception of the components of the grammar (Chomsky, 1965, 1980). In computer science, it appears in the concept of structured or modular programming. In psychology, it is represented by Posner's (1981) notion of "isolable sub-systems," and by Pylyshyn's (1981) notion of "cognitively impenetrable processes." It is also related to the notion of automatic processes proposed by Posner and Snyder (1975), Shiffrin and Schneider (1977), and Hasher and Zacks (1980). Fodor (1983) elaborates the idea.

While these proposals differ in detail, they all suggest that components of complex processes such as language comprehension may be construed as relatively independent modules. The suggestion from recent research on lexical processing is that it represents just such a module (Forster, 1979). If this is true, it represents an important confirmation of the utility of the modular approach. In the following sections, we consider the claim more closely.

1.1 Autonomous Lexical Processes

In an important paper, Forster (1979) outlined the idea that lexical processing functions as an independent sub-system in language comprehension. He suggested that a primary characteristic of lexical processing is its autonomy. It is clear that, in skilled language use, word recognition processes are automatic, in the sense that they occur rapidly, without conscious effort, and without utilizing limited capacity processing resources (Posner & Snyder, 1975). The idea that lexical processing is automatic provides a basis for hypothesizing that it is also autonomous, that is, that it occurs independently of other aspects of the comprehension process (Seidenberg, Tanenhaus,

Leiman, & Bienkowski, 1982). To the extent that lexical processes are automated, they may become isolated from other such processes, occurring in the same manner regardless of the nature of a particular context or comprehension task.

Two important predictions stem from the claim that lexical processing occurs within an autonomous module. First, the information made available as a consequence of lexical processing should be invariant across contexts. Second, the speed with which that information is made available should be unaffected by the processing context. These predictions can be contrasted with those made by "interactive" models of lexical processing (e.g., Rumelhart, 1977; Marslen-Wilson & Welsh, 1978; Marslen-Wilson & Tyler, 1980). In these models, contextual information is combined with sensory information during lexical processing. In one class of interactive models, exemplified by the cohort model developed by Marlsen-Wilson and colleagues, contextual information combines with sensory information to select from among a candidate set of words which have been activated by sensory input. This model predicts that the speed with which a word can be recognized depends on the information made available by the context in which the word is presented. Words in rich contexts are processed more rapidly than words in impoverished or misleading contexts. Under a stronger version of this model, context can influence which candidates are initially activated by priming words that are congruent with the processing context. In these models, different information may become available in different contexts.

In the remainder of this chapter, we will survey recent research from several domains concerning the question of contextual influences on word recognition. Before doing so, it is necessary to explicate what is at stake. The autonomy claim is not that word processing is unrelated to other comprehension processes. A basic part of comprehension is determining how each word relates to previously given information. This much is obvious. However, the idea that lexical information must be integrated with prior context is quite different from the idea that the access of lexical information differs depending on the content and availability of contextual information. It is the latter claim that the autonomy hypothesis denies in its strongest form. In evaluating this claim, it is also necessary to consider which aspects of the comprehension process could be influenced by context. Word recognition is itself a complex process occurring over time; contextual information could influence some aspects of lexical processing but not others. We will distinguish three temporally distinct aspects of word recognition, each of which must be evaluated with regard to putative contextual effects. *Prelexical processes* involve the decoding of a written or spoken word, that is, the analysis of the sensory stimulus. *Lexical access* involves the retrieval from memory of information associated with particular lexical items, including the semantic, phonological, and orthographic codes, and other information as well (e.g., syntactic). *Post-lexical processes* involve the selection, elaboration, and integration of lexical information for the purpose of comprehending a text or utterance. Defined in this way, it is clear that post-lexical processes are influenced both by information provided by the context and by other knowledge of the perceiver. As such, they are not autonomous. Indeed, numerous studies have demonstrated how the reader or listener's representation of the meaning of a sentence varies depending upon the availability of other information (Bransford & Franks, 1971; Bransford & Johnson, 1972; Merrill, Sperber, & McCauley, 1981). We shall consider in detail, however, the extent to which empirical evidence supports the idea that both pre-lexical and lexical processes are autonomous, focussing on four claims.

First, research on the activation of lexical codes provides strong direct support for the idea that lexical processes are autonomous. Second, the only robust "pre-lexical" contextual effects are due to lexical priming, which is itself a consequence of the organization of lexical information in memory, and thus internal to it. These intra-lexical effects (Forster, 1979) do not violate the autonomy notion. Third, some pre-lexical contextual effects only occur under conditions of degraded stimulus presentation or extreme predictability which have little relevance to skilled reading or spoken language comprehension. Finally, many apparent cases of contextual effects on word recognition reported in the literature are in fact post-lexical, preserving the idea that pre-lexical and lexical processing are autonomous.

2. *AUTONOMOUS ACCESS OF LEXICAL CODES*

On the view of word recognition sketched above, an intermediate stage of lexical access can be distinguished from pre-lexical decoding and post-lexical integration with context. There is strong evidence for the autonomy of lexical access. Much of it derives from research on a particular aspect of word recognition, the resolution of lexical ambiguity. Homonymous words (such as *tire* or *watch*) have multiple meanings, only one of which is appropriate to a particular context (ignoring degenerate cases such as puns, double entendres, and the like). Determining how the appropriate meaning is selected is an important problem for theories of language comprehension, and for computer programs that process natural language. In lexical access, the meanings of words are retrieved from semantic memory. If this process were influenced by the information provided by the linguistic context, it might be expected that a reader or listener could use this information to restrict access to the contextually appropriate reading and no other. If lexical access is autonomous, however, access of meaning should not vary as a function of the demands of particular contexts. This implies that more than the single contextually appropriate reading of an ambiguous word may be accessed in a given context.

A good deal of research now suggests that access of the meanings of ambiguous words is essentially autonomous. In this research (Onifer & Swinney, 1981; Seidenberg et al., 1982; Simpson, 1981; Swinney, 1979; Tanenhaus, Leiman, & Seidenberg, 1979), a chronometric priming methodology was used which provided evidence concerning the availability of word-meanings over time. It shows quite clearly that, across a variety of contexts containing different types of information, meaning access is not determined by context. When ambiguous words have two or more common readings, there is transitory activation of more than a single meaning, followed by selection of the contextually appropriate reading. Both the initial access of meaning and the selection process are rapid and unconscious. The processing of ambiguous words seems to depend upon their structure—that is, the number and relative frequencies of alternative meanings—rather than the nature of the information provided by a particular context. For example, in hearing a sentence such as (4), listeners initially access both of the common readings of *tire,* and

(4) John began to tire.

rapidly (within about 200 msec) select the one reading appropriate to the context, suppressing the alternative (Tanenhaus et al., 1979; Seidenberg et al., 1982). It is quite easy to imagine a model in which access of the meanings of an ambiguous word such as *tire* were contingent upon the context. Listeners might use the context to selectively access the contextually appropriate meaning of an ambiguous word. However, this outcome is not observed. Rather, subjects initially access multiple meanings in a non-contingent manner, and use contextual information to subsequently select the correct reading. This research provides a clear illustration of the distinction between lexical and post-lexical processes. The *access* of meaning, a lexical process, is autonomous. The *selection* of a particular meaning, a post-lexical process, is determined by the demands of a particular context.

A further illustration is provided by recent studies by Lucas (1983) and by Hudson and Tanenhaus (in preparation) that examined the time course of ambiguity resolution. In the Lucas study the prior context strongly biased one reading of an ambiguous word, while in the Hudson and Tanenhaus study the prior context was neutral in that it was consistent with both primary readings. Multiple readings of the ambiguous word were initially accessed in both studies. However, one reading—the contextually appropriate one—was selected within 200 msec when the contexts contained biasing information, while both readings remained available for 350 msec when the contexts were neutral between the two readings. Thus, the operation of the lexical module is not modified by other modules, but they do operate upon its *output*.

2.1 Other Implications

The ambiguity research suggests that at least one important aspect of word recognition, the access of meaning, is autonomous. Before considering other evidence, and some possible counter-evidence, for autonomy, we briefly consider two other implications of the ambiguity research. First, there is a methodological point. The ambiguity research suggests that it may be possible to obtain behavioral evidence concerning very rapid, unconscious processes in language comprehension. Listeners are not aware of entertaining alternate senses of an ambiguous word, and they complete the assignment of meaning extremely rapidly. Nonetheless it was possible to observe this process using a relatively simple methodology, whose important features are (a) that it reflects language comprehension processes as they occur (i.e., it is an "on-line" method), and (b) that it can be used to examine the operation of such processes over time (i.e., the method is chronometric), and (c) it is sensitive to mental representation.

Second, the ambiguity research demonstrates that there are times in the comprehension process when information becomes available that ultimately is not incorporated into the interpretation of an utterance. In the case of meaning access, the processing system makes available the common meanings of a word, those most likely to be relevant to any context. Some of this information (e.g., a contextually inappropriate reading) is superfluous from the point of view of the final representation assigned to the utterance. However, the access of such extraneous material is probably a necessary consequence of autonomous processing. If autonomous linguistic modules only communicate at output, access of extraneous information is likely. In fact, access of more information than is ultimately required by a particular context (e.g., multiple meanings, structural assignments, parses, etc.) may be *diagnostic* of autonomous processes. It may be that the comprehension system is constructed so as to facilitate the access of information likely to be relevant to any context, rather than the specific information relevant to a particular context. It follows, of course, that access of this information must not come at great cost to the processor (e.g., in terms of memory or processing load), and that the system must have the capacity to rapidly determine which information is to be retained.

2.2 Access of Other Lexical Codes

The notion that an autonomous process may make available more information than is required for the completion of a particular task is illustrated by research on the access of the other codes of a word. Words are represented in terms of various codes, including orthographic, phonological, and semantic. The ambiguity research suggests that access of the semantic code is essentially autonomous; does the same hold for access of the other codes?

Words are recognized through an analysis of either their orthographic code (in reading) or the phonological code (in listening). Recent research suggests that recognition makes available both sensory codes, regardless of input modality. Classic studies suggest that reading a letter or word results in the access of information concerning its sound or pronunciation (for review, see McCusker, Hillinger, & Bias, 1981). It is not a logical or functional requirement of the reading task that this information become available, and congenitally deaf, non-speaking persons can in fact learn to read. Nonetheless, phonological information is accessed across a wide variety of conditions.

More striking, perhaps, is the fact that the converse also holds, namely auditory word recognition results in the access of information related to spelling. Consider the following experiment (Seidenberg & Tanenhaus, 1979). A subject is presented with a cue word followed by a list of semantically unrelated target words. The task is to indicate which word in the target list rhymes with the cue. All stimuli are presented auditorally. In this rhyme monitoring task, similarly spelled rhymes (e.g., *pie–tie*) are detected more rapidly than dissimilarly spelled rhymes (e.g., *pie–rye*), even though subjects see no stimuli. The results suggest that subjects accessed the orthographic code for the stimulus words, even though the task did not require it. Again there is access of information that is extraneous from the point of view of the immediate task. This orthographic interference effect has been replicated several times, in experiments which control for subjects' response biases in performing the rhyming task (Donnenwerth-Nolan, Tanenhaus, & Seidenberg, 1981), in experiments with young readers (Waters, Tanenhaus, Seidenberg, & Hudson, in preparation), and, importantly, in experiments using a non-rhyming task (Stroop), in which access of orthographic information as a negative effect on performance of the primary task (Tanenhaus, Flanigan, & Seidenberg, 1980). Taken in conjunction with the ambiguity studies and those of phonological coding, these results suggest that the output of the word recognition process is access of multiple codes for words, regardless of input modality or task. The conclusion seems to be that, acting as an autonomous module, lexical processing makes available several types of information, not all of which will be necessary for completion of a particular task.

3. *APPARENT VIOLATIONS OF AUTONOMY*

We have seen that the autonomy hypothesis is nicely supported by the results of ambiguity studies and the studies of lexical code activation. However, research in several different areas seems to require that the hypothesis be abandoned. Common to these studies is the idea that prior context, in the form of a word or a phrase, can facilitate or interfere with the recognition of a subsequent word. In the following sections we survey those contextual effects which appear most damaging to the autonomy hypothesis: lexical priming; transitional probability (expectancy); pragmatic and syntactic context; and "backwards" priming. We will argue that the only genuine contextual effects on word recognition result from lexical priming, which is due to semantic or associative relations between words; this process does not violate autonomy because it is wholly internal to the lexicon. The remaining effects are post-lexical, reflecting decisions made after a word has been recognized; thus they do not violate autonomy either.

3.1 *Contextual Effects Due to Lexical Priming*

A well-known class of contextual effects on word recognition result from a process termed lexical priming (sometimes termed "associative" or "semantic" priming); these are consistent with Forster's proposal and are discussed extensively in his 1979 paper. Individuals form associations among words, for example, *doctor–nurse, bread–butter,* etc. Recognition of one of the words in an associated pair may facilitate recognition of the other member if it is subsequently encountered. Such effects are typically attributed to a spreading-activation process (Collins & Loftus, 1975). The entries in the mental lexicon are conceptualized as represented in a network structure; entries that are associated are "closer" (in terms of number of intervening nodes, or a distance metric) than unrelated words. Recognition of an input results in "activation" of its node in memory; activation spreads through the network to the nodes for related words. The recognition latency for a word is a function of its activation level; thus, as a consequence of spreading activation, an associated word will have a higher activation level than an unassociated word. Hence, reading *doctor* will increase the activation level of a word such as *nurse,* but not *computer;* thus, only *nurse* is facilitated. This is a case in which the context (a priming word) facilitates the recognition of a subsequent word (the target). Fischler and Bloom (1977) have also shown that facilitation results when stimuli are semantically related but unassociated (e.g., *bread–cake*).

Two facts should be noted about this process. First, it is entirely a consequence of the relations that hold among lexical items, the manner in which they are represented in memory, and the spreading activation process. As such, the phenomenon occurs entirely within the lexicon, and does not involve other sources of knowledge, such as episodic memory or knowledge of the grammar. Forster terms the process "intra-lexical," and notes that it is accommodated by his proposal. Second, priming has its effect by increasing the activation level of a lexical entry *before* it is encountered. It appears that the decoding of the input word proceeds exactly as in the unprimed case; the only difference is that the target word passes recognition threshold more rapidly because it has been primed.

Lexical priming is a theoretically important phenomenon, because contextual effects that result from this process do not violate the autonomy hypothesis. Recent research suggests, however, that the scope of this phenomenon is rather limited. Although activation spreads to the nodes for high associates of the input, and to the nodes for highly semantically related, but unassociated, words, it does not spread a step further to the associates of the primed associates (deGroot, 1983). Thus the pool of primed items is probably very small. The related words also must be closely contiguous in time for facilitation to occur (Blank & Foss, 1978). These facts limit the importance of this process in natural language processing.

3.2 *Perception of Degraded Stimuli*

Potentially more damaging to the autonomy hypothesis are demonstrations that contextual information can facilitate the identification of degraded stimuli. A number of well-known studies have demonstrated this fact (e.g., Becker & Killion, 1977; Meyer, Schvaneveldt, & Ruddy, 1975). For example, Tulving, Mandler, and Baumal (1964) had subjects read context words that were followed by a tachistoscopically presented target word. Recognition thresholds were lower when targets were preceded by semantically related words. Such results could be interpreted as evidence that higher-order contextual information and bottom-up stimulus information combine interactively during lexical processing to facilitate recognition. However, the relevance of these results to normal listening or reading is unclear. Degraded stimuli may induce subjects to use a guessing strategy that is neither required nor efficient under normal conditions. Subjects might generate a prediction based on the context and then determine whether it is consistent with the gross characteristics of the stimulus. Some models of the reading process (e.g., Goodman, 1970; Hochberg & Brooks, 1970) suggest that this process is characteristic of normal reading. However, Stanovich (1980) has argued that this mode of processing is only characteristic of *poor* readers. On his view, the bottom-up analysis of the input signal permits a good reader to identify a word with little contextual assistance. Poor readers' abilities to perform this analysis are limited, forcing them to rely upon supplemental contextual information. Thus, studies involving degraded stimuli force good readers to use the processing strategy used by poor readers under normal conditions. Below we consider independent evidence that an expectation-based reading strategy would be counterproductive in normal skilled reading (and listening) because the transitional probabilities of words in context are usually low, and the costs associated with wrong predictions are very high.

3.3 *Transitional Probabilities*

A well-known study that appeared to suggest that prediction may be more generally useful was reported by Morton and Long (1976). Using a phoneme-monitoring task, they showed that the transitional probability of a word in context influenced recognition latency. For example, in the context "At the sink, Mary washed a . . ." the word *plate* has a higher probability of occurrence than the word *pan* (as indicated by sentence-completion norms). Subjects were faster to detect the target phoneme *p* in *plate* compared to *pan*. This appeared to indicate that context facilitated the decoding of the expected word, a clear violation of autonomy under conditions where the stimuli were not degraded. In a recent study, however, Foss and Gernsbacher (1983) demonstrated that the effect was due to a subtle artifact in Morton and Long's materials. Phoneme-monitoring latencies are influenced by the length of the vowel in a monosyllabic word carrying the phoneme (among other factors; Mehler, Segui, & Carey, 1978; Newman & Dell, 1978). Morton and Long's high transition probability stimuli tended to have longer vowels than the low transition probability stimuli (as in the above example). With vowel length equated across conditions, Foss and Gernsbacher found no effect of transition probability.

The most detailed investigation of the effects or predictability on visual word recognition was conducted by Fischler and Bloom (1979). In this study, subjects read a context phrase and then made a lexical decision to a target word which either formed a sensible or anomalous sentence. Target words forming sensible completions varied in terms of their predictability, given the context. Examples of predictable, unpredictable, and anomalous sentences are given in (5), (6), and (7).

(5) John brushed his teeth.

(6) John brushed his car.

(7) John brushed his truth.

Facilitation (faster decision latencies compared to neutral controls) obtained only when the target was extremely predictable (90% or greater as measured by a Cloze procedure). While it is doubtless the case that the predictability of words in text varies greatly as a function of such factors as type of word and text, words in actual contexts are almost never predictable enough for context to be useful, if 90% is used as a benchmark. For example, Gough, Alford, and Holley-Wilcox (1981) looked at subjects' abilities to guess the words in various types of texts. Correct guesses ranged from 20 to 39%, which is in agreement with Aborn, Rubenstein, and Sterling's (1959) estimate of 25% for sentence-final words. The only exception was a subject who was asked to guess the words in the first paragraph of a textbook he had written; about 75% of his guesses were correct.

It appears that words in natural language contexts rarely approach the 90% predictability that Fischler and Bloom found to be necessary for context to be beneficial. On this basis alone, it seems unlikely that the processing system would have evolved so as to rely upon transitional probability.

Moreover, the costs associated with generating incorrect predictions based on context will usually outweigh the benefits obtained from correct predictions. Neely (1977) demonstrated that generating expectancies is a controlled process (in the sense of Posner & Snyder, 1975), and that it is accompanied by substantial inhibition when a prediction is incorrect. The low probability that predictions will be correct, taken with the high costs associated with disconfirmed predictions, suggests that a highly top-down, expectation-driven processing system would be inefficient.

3.4 *Does Context Inhibit Inappropriate Alternatives?*

One aspect of Fischler and Bloom's results is potentially damaging to the autonomy hypothesis. They found substantial inhibition (longer decision latencies) to words that were anomalous given their contexts. Rather than directly facilitating the identification of a particular target word, context could be used to inhibit irrelevant words. A possible mechanism for such inhibition is provided by the cohort model proposed by Marlsen-Wilson and Welsh (1978). In the cohort model, bottom-up information provided by an analysis of the input signal activates a candidate set, or cohort, of lexical representations. Candidates are evaluated against the demands of contextual information; if a candidate is inconsistent with context, it is eliminated from consideration. This process continues until the target is the only remaining item in the cohort. In this way, contextual information could facilitate recognition by inhibiting incongruent candidates.

Contextual inhibition of this sort would clearly violate the autonomy assumption. However, recent work by Stanovich and West (1979, 1983; West & Stanovich, 1982) suggests that contextual inhibition of this sort is not the mechanism responsible for the inhibition obtained by Fischler and Bloom (1977). In many of their studies (e.g., Stanovich & West, 1979), subjects read a context and then read aloud a target word which was either congruous or incongruous in the context. When the target word followed immediately after the context, congruous targets were named faster than targets presented in neutral contexts. In contrast to Fischler and Bloom's results, no inhibitory effects obtained for incongruous targets. When several hundred milliseconds intervened between context and target, incongruous targets were inhibited. Stanovich and West interpret their results within the Posner and Snyder (1975) dual-process model of attention. The absence of early inhibition suggests that the facilitation for congruous targets is automatic; West and Stanovich (1982) later argued that it was due to associative priming, since their congruous contexts included words that are associatively or semantically related to the target word. The inhibition at longer target delays was attributed to subjects having had time to generate conscious expectancies.

These results are consistent with the autonomy hypothesis; however, they differ from the results of Fischler and Bloom who obtained facilitation for predictable targets, and inhibition of incongruent targets, immediately following their contexts. West and Stanovich (1982) have provided an explanation of these differing results which, if correct, further strengthens the autonomy claim. Their explanation has to do with the nature of the lexical decision task, which is often taken to provide a relatively direct, uncontaminated measure of lexical processing. It is generally assumed that subjects make lexical decisions by waiting until a lexical entry has been identified and then making the "word" response. Subjects set a deadline for making a response; if no entry is identified by the deadline, the subject responds "nonword." This model of lexical decision, labelled a "direct knowledge" account by Tanenhaus, Carlson, and Seidenberg (1985), while simple, is implausible for several reasons. First, on this account, it must be assumed not only that lexical access makes lexical information available, but also that it makes available to consciousness the fact that a lexical entry has been accessed. Given that much of the language comprehension system operates without awareness and that the lexical processor was not structured so as to facilitate lexical decisions, it is unclear how this additional awareness comes about. There is an important difference between accessing lexical information and the metalinguistic awareness that this has occurred.

More important, perhaps, is that the direct knowledge model cannot accommodate a number of important facts about performance of the lexical decision task. It does not explain why lexical decisions are usually slower than other lexical tasks such as pronunciation and rhyme and category decision tasks (Forster & Chambers, 1973; Frederiksen & Kroll, 1976). Lexical decisions are influenced by subject strategies, a fact that is hard to explain given the widespread and, to our thinking, reasonable assumption that lexical access is an automatic process. For example, the type of nonword distractor has a large effect on the speed with which lexical decisions are made, and the magnitude and types of priming effects obtained (Shulman, Hornak, & Sanders, 1978). Lexical decisions are also influenced by a number of other variables which are arguably non-lexical, such as the ease with which a context can be imagined for a word (Schwanenflugel & Shoben, 1982). All of these facts suggest that making a lexical decision involves more than simply accessing an entry in memory.

An alternative to a direct knowledge account takes seriously the idea that lexical decision involves a conscious decision. According to the view developed by Forster (1979) and West and Stanovich (1982), lexical decisions are made by a central processor which has access to the outputs of different components of the language comprehension system, including the lexical processor. Information made available as a consequence of lexical access will contribute most to the lexical decision. However, other information which may bear on whether or not the target is a word may also be taken into account. One likely factor is whether or not the target makes sense in the context. In the typical lexical decision experiment, the subject must discriminate between words and nonwords that are very similar in orthographic and phonological structure. The slowness of this decision (compared, for example, to simply naming a word aloud) suggests that this discrimination is fairly difficult. When the target is presented in context, however, the central processor has another source of information to use in discriminating the word and nonword, namely whether or not the target makes sense in the context. The subject could reliably identify nonwords in this manner: they never make sense in context. The only problematic case, of course, is one in which the target is a word but fails to make sense—the incongruous targets, which yield inhibition.

Why would the central processor responsible for the lexical decision take into account contextual congruity when this information necessarily must become available *after* lexical access? Given that lexical processing makes available sufficient information for the lexical decision to be made, why do any contextual effects result? The likely answer is that higher-order contextual information usually becomes accessible to consciousness more rapidly than does lower-order lexical information (Forster, 1979). This information produces Stroop-like interference with lexical processing. In the Stroop task, subjects must identify the color that a word is printed in, but cannot ignore the meaning of the word itself, even when it has a negative effect on performance. In the lexical decision task, subjects must make a word–nonword decision, but cannot ignore contextual congruency, producing inhibition for anomalous targets. If the decision stage takes into account contextual congruity, as well as the results of lexical processing, decisions to incongruous words should be slow and subjects should make many errors. This is exactly the pattern obtained by Fischler and Bloom.

The claim, then, is that the inhibitory effects obtained by Fischler and Bloom are not due to context inhibiting all inappropriate words through an automatic mechanism. Rather, contextual incongruity influences a post-lexical decision stage that is specific to the lexical decision task. On this view, contextual information influences lexical *decisions,* but not lexical *access.* Note that this process will not be involved in naming, which does not involve a word–nonword discrimination. And, in fact, the inhibition to anomalous targets observed with lexical decision does not obtain with naming (West & Stanovich, 1982).

4. *TASK DIFFERENCES DIFFERENTIATE PRE- AND POST-LEXICAL CONTEXTUAL EFFECTS*

The view of the lexical decision task we are promoting suggests that it is properly interpreted as a signal detection task in which the subject must discriminate between words (signals) and nonwords (noise) which can vary along a number of dimensions, including orthographic structure, phonological structure, meaningfulness, and whether or not they make sense in a given context. Subjects adopt different decision criteria based on the dimension(s) along which the two types of stimuli can best be discriminated. This account is clearly consistent with the range of strategic effects reported in lexical decision studies. It also accounts for why there are no inhibitory effects of incongruous contexts when the naming task is used. Unlike lexical decisions, naming does not require an explicit word–nonword decision. Rather, it relies upon knowledge of how to pronounce a word which is either stored procedurally or can be rapidly computed (Seidenberg, Waters, Barnes, & Tanenhaus, 1984a). Thus, naming should be less sensitive to post-lexical variables than is lexical decision.

If this view is correct, there should be systematic differences between lexical decision and naming with only the former task being sensitive to post-lexical processes. Note that both tasks should be influenced by associative priming, the intra-lexical process. The evidence for the latter hypothesis is clear (e.g., see Seidenberg, Waters, Sanders, & Langer, 1984b); we turn now to evidence that several types of contextual effects obtain with lexical decision but not naming.

4.1 *Syntactic Context Effects*

Two recent studies have been interpreted as providing evidence that syntactic context can influence lexical access. In one study, lexical decisions to nouns in Serbo-Croatian were faster when preceded by an appropriate preposition (Lukatela, Kostic, Feldman, & Turvey, 1983). In the other study, lexical decisions were faster when prime-target pairs formed a grammatical constituent (e.g., *the–laugh*) than when they did not (*it–laugh;* Goodman, McClelland, & Gibbs, 1981). These results have been interpreted as evidence that spreading activation can occur between words that form a constituent. A spreading activation account seems implausible, however, as activation would have to spread to all words of a particular syntactic class (e.g., verbs). An alternative explanation assumes that the locus of facilitation due to syntactic appropriateness is the subject's post-lexical judgment that the sequence is grammatical. This yields the clear prediction that syntactic facilitation should only occur with the lexical decision task, not naming; this has been confirmed (Seidenberg et al., 1984b).

4.2 *"Backwards Priming"*

A curious contextual effect interpreted as being due to automatic spreading activation but probably due to post-lexical processes is the "backwards priming" effect obtained by Koriat (1981). In this experiment, lexical decisions to targets were facilitated when a preceding primer word was an associate of the target, but the target was *not* an associate of the prime. For example, *apple* is a high associate of *fruit,* but *fruit* is not a high associate of *apple.* Lexical decisions to targets were facilitated both when the sequence was *fruit–apple,* the normal associative priming effect, and when the pair was *apple–fruit,* a "backwards" effect. Koriat argued that the backwards effect was due to spreading activation, while the forwards effect was due to subject expectations.

This interpretation accommodates the data but is far from satisfying. First, it represents a radical reinterpretation of forwards effects that had received a clear interpretation under the Collins and Loftus (1975) model of spreading activation. Second, it does not provide a plausible basis for backwards spreading activation in the absence of forwards spread. There are two alternative interpretations, however, that place the locus of the backwards priming effect after the target has been recognized. One is that it is simply due to subjects' post-lexical recognition of prime-target relatedness. The stimuli are processed independently, but following access subjects notice that they are related in a backwards direction. Having noticed the unusual, backwards association between a prime and target, subjects may become very sensitive to this characteristic. Indeed, it is difficult to ignore. A second possibility is that the backwards effect is simply due to contextual incongruity, as in the Fischler and Bloom experiment. The prime creates a context in which the subject expects a forward associate as target; this expectation is disconfirmed in the case of backwards associates. A similar mechanism was proposed by Schwanenflugel and Shoben (1982) to account for their effects of context imaginability. Evidence that "backwards priming" is post-lexical is provided by Seidenberg et al. (1984b), who obtained the effect with lexical decision (replicating Koriat), but not with naming. The effect also fails to obtain with the Stroop task (Warren, 1972).

4.3 Proportionality Effects

Finally, Tweedy, Lapinski, and Schvaneveldt (1977) found that the size of the associative priming effect depended on the proportion of related stimuli. This result seems to present a problem for a simple spreading activation model, in which lexical priming is thought to be an unconscious, reflexive consequence of the manner in which entries are organized in memory. As we have seen, lexical priming of this sort is the only type of contextual effect which is compatible with the autonomy assumption. Again, however, Tweedy et al. (1977) used the lexical decision task as a response measure. Seidenberg et al. (1984b) examined this effect using both lexical decision and naming tasks. The results for lexical decision replicated Tweedy et al., showing a larger priming effect with a greater proportion of related items. However, with the naming task, the size of the priming effect did not increase with proportion. Furthermore, the priming effects in lexical decision were larger than in pronunciation. The interpretation of these results is that associative or very close semantic relations produce facilitation through an automatic spreading activation process; these effects appear in both tasks. In the lexical decision task, there is an additional post-lexical component due to subject expectations concerning the relatedness of the stimuli. This produces both the proportionality effect, and the larger amount of priming with this task.

In sum, a wide range of contextual effects which at first appear to present difficulties both for the autonomy hypothesis and for a simple spreading activation model of lexical priming apparently are due to post-recognition processing. Although these types of contextual effects superficially resemble lexical priming, in that a prime word or context influences responses to a target, they result from processes that occur after lexical access for the target has been completed.

5. *SUMMARY*

The autonomy hypothesis fares well when considered with respect to the available evidence. Although the literature appears at first glance to abound with studies that are inconsistent with Forster's proposal, it is clear that most of the observed contextual effects either obtain under conditions of stimulus degradation or excessive predictability, or reflect post-lexical processes. It appears that autonomous lexical processing is characteristic of skilled language processing under normal reading or listening conditions. Heavy reliance upon context to facilitate initial decoding appears to be the exceptional strategy, used when bottom-up decoding processes fail, either because the requisite level of decoding skill has not been achieved (as with poor readers), or because the stimulus conditions do not permit normal processing.

Before accepting the autonomy hypothesis prematurely, several cautions should be considered. First, most of the studies consistent with this view have been concerned with the processing of common, monosyllabic words. The recognition of short, morphologically simple, high-frequency words may be quite different from the recognition of longer, morphologically complex, low-frequency words. The acoustic forms of the latter words will be more extended in time, possibly allowing more time for the utilization of contextual information. Similarly, these words may require multiple fixations in reading (Rayner & McConkie, 1977), again allowing for contextual intervention. This issue can only be resolved through further research. The principal questions concern the timing of the utilization of contextual information relative to the bottom-up extraction of information from the signal, and the relative costs and benefits of an interactive recognition process compared to a strictly bottom-up process.

Second, there may be important differences in the extent of contextual effects as a function of modality, with greater effects in speech than in reading. The modalities clearly differ in important respects. In speech, the signal necessarily is distributed over time, even for monosyllabic words. Although not all of the stimulus information is available simultaneously in reading words that require multiple fixations, it is clear that reading offers more potential for parallel processing of different parts of the stimulus. It may be for this reason that the studies seeming to demonstrate the clearest contextual effects on word recognition involve the processing of multisyllabic spoken words (Marslen-Wilson & Welsh, 1978; Marslen-Wilson & Tyler, 1980; Tyler & Wessels, in press). Although some of these effects may be due to degraded stimulus presentation, they could reflect genuine modality differences.

Finally, there are important unresolved questions concerning the conditions that comprehending natural text or discourse present. It is clear, for example, that lexical priming influences word recognition, and that predictable contexts function differently than other contexts. So little is known about the ecology of texts and discourse that it is difficult to know how greatly these processes contribute to comprehension outside the laboratory. It is important not only to demonstrate that contextual information facilitates word recognition under some conditions (e.g., stimulus degradation), but to consider whether such conditions hold in more natural reading or listening tasks. Gough et al.'s (1981) study of textual predictability is a step in the appropriate direction, and much more research of this kind is in order.

Similar considerations hold for speech. For example, Marslen-Wilson and Tyler's (1980) cohort model of auditory word recognition suggests that contextual information facilitates the discrimination of an auditory input from a cohort of phonetically similar alternatives. It may be possible to demonstrate the operation of such a process, just as it was possible to demonstrate that highly predictable words are read more quickly than unpredictable words. Marslen-Wilson and Tyler's model provides an elegant mechanism by which context could facilitate recognition. However, the importance of this mechanism to the recognition process depends on facts about the relative discriminability of words that are unknown. Consider a hypothetical language in which no two words begin with the same phoneme. Presumably the bottom-up analysis of the signal would provide sufficient information for rapid recognition, obviating reliance upon contextual support entirely. More realistically, the question for a language such as English is, how discriminable are spoken words from each other, given the facts about the distribution of acoustic-phonetic forms in the lexicon, the timing of speech events, and the existence of phenomena such as co-articulation? In other words, given the facts about English, how well can an autonomous lexical processor do? This requires a characterization of the distribution and discriminability of acoustic-phonetic forms English, something which does not at present exist, and would be difficult to obtain.

6. *AUTONOMOUS VS. INTERACTIVE: A FALSE DICHOTOMY?*

Most studies of contextual effects on word recognition, such as the ones reviewed above, have been concerned with determining the extent to which the *literal* context in which a word appears influences recognition. As indicated above, this influence appears to be limited because of the facility of lexical decoding processes. Recently, however, several models have appeared which suggest that the information relevant to word recognition is provided not by the literal context, but by the perceiver's knowledge of relations that hold among lexical items. This knowledge represents the *virtual* context of occurrence. It may be that earlier research on word recognition overestimated the importance of the literal context relative to the virtual context.

Consider, for example, McClelland and Rumelhart's (1981) interactive model of word recognition. The model was developed in order to accommodate word superiority effects (i.e., the fact that a letter is easier to identify in an orthographically legal nonword than in isolation, and in a word than in a nonword), but it represents a general theory of the word recognition process. In this model, as in several other recent models (e.g., Paap, Newsome, McDonald, & Schvaneveldt, 1982; Marslen-Wilson & Tyler, 1980), word recognition is seen as requiring the perceiver to discriminate a word from a cohort of alternatives. As featural and letter information are decoded over time, various candidates are partially activated, with recognition occurring when all but one of the alternatives are eliminated. The difficulty of identifying a word, then, depends on the relations that hold among the input and similarly spelled or pronounced words. Note that only the actual stimulus input is present; the virtual context is provided by the perceiver's knowledge of the lexicon. Thus it is in the head, rather than in the literal context. These models are "interactive," but the locus of the interactions is not between the information provided by the literal context and knowledge of the lexicon, but rather between different types of lexical information stored in memory that are activated by the input.

These models provide additional mechanisms by which the literal context could be used to facilitate the identification of the signal. As we have argued, there is little evidence that these mechanisms are actually used. The reason is clear. Powerful interactive recognition processes internal to the lexical module yield rapid and effortless recognition. The important question, then, is not whether word recognition is interactive or autonomous, but rather, whether interactive processes can be construed as occurring within autonomously functioning modules. We have suggested that a broad range of evidence supports this view of lexical processing, providing at least prima facie support for the modular approach.

REFERENCES

Aborn, M., Rubenstein, H., & Sterling, T. D. (1959). Sources of contextual constraint upon words in sentences. *Journal of Experimental Psychology, 57,* 171–180.

Becker, C. A., & Killion, T. H. (1977). Interaction of visual and cognitive effects in visual word recognition. *Journal of Experimental Psychology: Human Perception and Performance, 5,* 252–259.

Berwick, R. C., & Weinberg, A. S. (1983). The role of grammars in models of language use. *Cognition, 13,* 1–62.

Blank, M. A., & Foss, D. J. (1978). Semantic facilitation and lexical access during sentence processing. *Memory and Cognition, 6,* 644–652.

Bransford, J. D., & Franks, J. J. (1971). The abstraction of linguistic ideas. *Cognitive Psychology, 2,* 331–350.

Bransford, J. D., & Johnson, M. K. (1972). Contextual prerequisites for understanding: Some investigations of comprehension and recall. *Journal of Verbal Learning and Verbal Behavior, 11,* 717–726.

Chomsky, N. (1965). *Aspects of the theory of syntax.* Cambridge, MA: MIT Press.

Chomsky, N. (1980). *Rules and representations.* New York: Columbia University Press.

Chomsky, N. (1981). *Lectures on government and binding.* Dordrecht: Foris.

Clifton, C., Frazier, L., & Connine, C. (1984). Lexical expectations in sentence comprehension. *Journal of Verbal Learning and Verbal Behavior, 23,* 696–708.

Collins, A. M., & Loftus, E. F. (1975). A spreading-activation theory of semantic processing. *Psychological Review, 82,* 407–428.

Coltheart, M., Patterson, K., & Marshall, J. (1980). *Deep dyslexia.* London: Routledge & Kegal Paul.

de Groot, A. M. B. (1983). The range of automatic spreading activation in word priming. *Journal of Verbal Learning and Verbal Behavior, 22,* 417–436.

Donnenwerth-Nolan, S., Tanenhaus, M., & Seidenberg, M. (1981). Multiple code activation in word recognition: Evidence from rhyme monitoring. *Journal of Experimental Psychology: Human Learning and Memory, 7,* 170–180.

Dowty, D. R., Karttunen, L., & Zwicky, A. M. (Eds.) (1985). *Natural language parsing: Psychological, computational, and theoretical perspectives.* Cambridge, England: Cambridge University Press.

Fischler, I., & Bloom, P. (1977). Semantic facilitation without association in a lexical decision task. *Memory and Cognition, 5,* 335–339.

Fischler, I., & Bloom, P. (1979). Automatic and attentional processes in the effects of sentence contexts on word recognition. *Journal of Verbal Learning and Verbal Behavior, 18,* 1–20.

Fodor, J. A. (1983). *Modularity of mind.* Cambridge, MA: Bradford Books-MIT Press.

Forster, K. I. (1979). Levels of processing and the structure of the language processor. In W. E. Cooper & E. C. T. Walker (Eds.), *Sentence processing: Psycholinguistic studies presented to Merrill Garrett.* Cambridge, MA: MIT Press.

Forster, K. I., & Chambers, S. (1973). Lexical access and naming time. *Journal of Verbal Learning and Verbal Behavior, 12,* 627–635.

Foss, D. J., & Gernsbacher, M. (1983) Cracking the dual code: Toward a unitary model of phoneme identification. *Journal of Verbal Learning and Verbal Behavior, 22,* 609–632.

Frederiksen, J., & Kroll, J. F. (1976). Spelling and sound: Approaches to the internal lexicon. *Journal of Experimental Psychology: Human Perception and Performance, 2,* 361–379.

Gazdar, G. (1982). Phrase structure grammar. In P. Jacobson & G. Pullum (Eds.), *The nature of syntactic representation.* Dordrecht: Reidel.

Goodman, K. S. (1970). Reading: A psycholinguistic guessing game. In H. Singer & R. B. Ruddell (Eds.), *Theoretical models and processes of reading.* Newark, DE: International Reading Association.

Goodman, G. O., McClelland, J. L., & Gibbs, R. W., Jr. (1981). The role of syntactic context in word recognition. *Memory and Cognition, 9,* 580–586.

Gough, P., Alford, J. A., & Holley-Wilcox, P. (1981). Words and context. In O. J. L. Tzeng & H. Singer (Eds.), *Perception of print.* Hillsdale, NJ: Erlbaum.

Hasher, L., & Zacks, R. T. (1980). Automatic and effortful processes in memory. *Journal of Experimental Psychology: General, 108,* 356–388.

Hochberg, J., & Brooks, W. (1970). Reading as intentional behavior. In H. Singer & R. Ruddell (Eds.), *Theoretical models and processes of reading.* Newark, DE: International Reading Association.

Hudson, S., & Tanenhaus, M. K. (in preparation). *Lexical ambiguity resolution in biasing and neutral contexts.*

Kaplan, R., & Bresnan, J. (1982). Lexical-functional grammar: A formal system for grammatical representation. In J. Bresnan (Ed.), *The mental representation of grammatical relations.* Cambridge, MA: MIT Press.

Koriat, A. (1981). Semantic facilitation in lexical decisions as a function of prime-target association. *Memory and Cognition, 9,* 587–598.

Lucas, M. (1983). Lexical access during comprehension: frequency and context effects. In *Proceedings of the Fifth Annual Meeting of the Cognitive Science Society.* University of Rochester.

Lukatela, G. Kostic, A., Feldman, L. B., & Turvey, M. (1983). Grammatical priming of inflected nouns. *Memory and Cognition, 11,* 59–63.

Marr, D. (1982). *Vision.* San Francisco: Freeman.

Marslen-Wilson, W. D. (1975). The limited compatibility of linguistic and perceptual explanations. In R. Grossman, J. San, & T. Vance (Eds.), *Papers on the parasession on functionalism.* Chicago: Chicago Linguistic Society.

Marslen-Wilson, W. D., & Tyler, L. K. (1980). The temporal structure of spoken language comprehension. *Cognition, 8,* 1–71.

Marslen-Wilson, W. D., & Welsh, A. (1978). Processing interactions and lexical access during word recognition in continuous speech. *Cognitive Psychology, 10,* 29–63.

McClelland, J. L., & Rumelhart, D. E. (1981). An interactive activation model of context effects in letter perception: Part 1. An account of basic findings. *Psychological Review, 88,* 375–407.

McCusker, L. X., Hillinger, M. L., & Bias, R. G. (1981). Phonological recoding and reading. *Psychological Bulletin, 89,* 375–407.

Mehler, J., Segui, J., & Carey, P. (1978). Tails of words: Monitoring ambiguity. *Journal of Verbal Learning and Verbal Behavior, 17,* 29–35.

Merrill, E., Sperber, R. D., & McCauley, C. (1981). Differences in semantic coding as a function of reading comprehension skill. *Memory and Cognition, 9,* 618–624.

Meyer, D. M., Schvaneveldt, R. W., & Ruddy, M. G. (1975). Loci of contextual effects on visual word recognition. In P. M. A. Rabbitt & S. Dornic (Eds.), *Attention and Performance V.* New York: Academic Press.

Morton, J., & Long, J. (1976). Effect of word transitional probability on phoneme identification. *Journal of Verbal Learning and Verbal Behavior, 15,* 43–52.

Neely, J. H. (1977). Semantic priming and retrieval from lexical memory: Roles of inhibitionless spreading activation and limited-capacity attention. *Journal of Experimental Psychology: General, 106,* 226–254.

Newman, J. E., & Dell, G. S. (1978). The phonological nature of phoneme monitoring: A critique of some ambiguity studies. *Journal of Verbal Learning and Verbal Behavior, 6,* 364–371.

Onifer, W., & Swinney, D. A. (1981). Accessing lexical ambiguities during sentence comprehension: Effects of frequency of meaning and contextual bias. *Memory and Cognition, 9,* 225–236.

Paap, K. R., Newsome, S. L., McDonald, J. E., & Schvaneveldt, R. W. (1982). An activation-verification model for letter and word recognition: The word-superiority effect. *Psychological Review, 89,* 573–594.

Posner, M. I. (1981). *Chronometric explorations of mind.* Hillsdale, NJ: Erlbaum.

Posner, M. I., & Snyder, C. R. (1975). Attention and cognitive control. In R. L. Solso (Ed.), *Information processing and cognition: The Loyola Symposium.* Hillsdale, NJ: Erlbaum.

Pylyshyn, Z. (1981). The imagery debate: Analogue media versus tacit knowledge. *Psychological Review, 88,* 16–45.

Rayner, K., & McConkie, G. W. (1977). Perceptual processes in reading: The perceptual spans. In A. S. Reber & D. L. Scarborough (Eds.), *Toward a psychology of reading: The proceedings of the CUNY conferences.* Hillsdale, NJ: Erlbaum.

Rumelhart, D. E. (1977). Toward an interactive model of reading. In S. Dornic (Ed.), *Attention and Performance VI.* Hillsdale, NJ: Erlbaum.

Schwanenflugel, P. J., & Shoben, E. (1982). Differential context effects in the comprehension of abstract and concrete verbal materials. *Journal of Experimental Psychology: Learning, Memory, and Cognition, 9,* 82–102.

Seidenberg, M. S., & Tanenhaus, M. K. (1979). Orthographic effects on rhyme monitoring. *Journal of Experimental Psychology: Human Learning and Memory 5,* 546–554.

Seidenberg, M. S., Tanenhaus, M. K., Leiman, J. L., & Bienkowski, M. (1982). Automatic access of the meanings of ambiguous words in context: Some limitations of knowledge-based processing. *Cognitive Psychology, 14,* 489–537.

Seidenberg, M. S., Waters, G. S., Barnes, M. A., & Tanenhaus, M. K. (1984a). When does irregular spelling or pronunciation influence word recognition? *Journal of Verbal Learning and Verbal Behavior, 23,* 383–404.

Seidenberg, M. S., Waters, G. S., Sanders, M., & Langer, P. (1984b). Pre- and post-lexical loci of contextual effects on word recognition. *Memory and Cognition, 12,* 315–328.

Shiffrin, R. M., & Schneider, W. (1977). Controlled and automatic human information processing II. Perceptual learning, automatic attending and a general theory. *Psychological Review, 84,* 127–190.

Shulman, H., Hornak, R., & Sanders, E. (1978). The effects of graphemic, phonemic, and semantic relationships on access to lexical structures. *Memory and Cognition, 6,* 115–123.

Simpson, G. B. (1981). Meaning, dominance and semantic context in the processing of lexical ambiguity. *Journal of Verbal Learning and Verbal Behavior, 20,* 120–136.

Stanovich, K. E. (1980). Toward an interactive-compensatory model of individual differences in the development of reading fluency. *Reading Research Quarterly, 16,* 32–71.

Stanovich, K. E., & West, R. F. (1979). Mechanisms of sentence context effects in reading: Automatic activation and conscious attention. *Memory and Cognition, 7,* 77–85.

Stanovich, K., & West, R. F. (1983). On priming by a sentence context. *Journal of Experimental Psychology: General, 112,* 1–36.

Swinney, D. A. (1979). Lexical access during sentence comprehension: (Re)consideration of context effects. *Journal of Verbal Learning and Verbal Behavior, 18,* 645–660.

Tanenhaus, M. K., & Seidenberg, M. S. (1981). Discourse context and sentence perception. *Discourse Processes, 4,* 197–220.

Tanenhaus, M. K., Carlson, G. N., & Seidenberg, M. S. (1985). Do listeners compute linguistic representations? In D. Dowty, L. Kartunnen, & A. Zwicky (Eds.), *Natural language parsing: Psycholinguistic, theoretical and computational perspectives.* Cambridge, England: Cambridge University Press.

Tanenhaus, M. K., Flanigan, H., & Seidenberg, M. S. (1980). Orthographic and phonological code activation in auditory and visual word recognition. *Memory and Cognition, 8,* 513–520.

Tanenhaus, M. K., Leiman, J. L., & Seidenberg, M. S. (1979). Evidence for multiple stages in the processing of ambiguous words in syntactic contexts. *Journal of Verbal and Learning and Verbal Behavior, 18,* 427–441.

Tulving, E., Mandler, G., & Baumal, R. (1964). Interaction of two sources of information in tachistoscopic word recognition. *Canadian Journal of Psychology, 18,* 62–71.

Tweedy, J. R., Lapinski, R. H., & Schvaneveldt, R. W. (1977). Semantic-context effects on word recognition: Influence of varying the proportion of items presented in an appropriate context. *Memory and Cognition, 5,* 84–89.

Tyler, L. K., & Wessels, J. (in press). Quantifying contextual contributions to word recognition processes. *Perception and Psychophysics.*

Warren, R. E. (1972). Stimulus encoding and memory. *Journal of Experimental Psychology, 94,* 90–100.

Waters, G. S., Tanenhaus, M. K., Seidenberg, M. S., & Hudson, S. (in preparation). *Development of lexical code integration in children.*

West, R. F., & Stanovich, K. E. (1982). Source of inhibition in experiments on the effect of sentence context on word recognition. *Journal of Experimental Psychology: Learning, Memory, and Cognition, 8,* 385–399.

PART IV

SCIENTIFIC REASONING AND PROBLEM SOLVING

Chapter 8

The Organization of Medical Disorders in the Memories of Medical Students and General Practitioners*

Georges Bordage

Université Laval, Québec

Investigators of the reasoning process in general (for example, De Groot, 1965) and of medical reasoning in particular (for example, Barrows, Feightner, Neufeld, & Norman, 1978; Elstein, Shulman, & Sprafka, 1978) have reached common conclusions about the critical role of memory in problem solving. Thus, Elstein, Shulman, and Sprafka (1978) conclude: "the differences between experts and weaker problem solvers are more to be found in the repertory of their experiences, organized in long-term memory, than in differences in the planning and problem solving heuristics employed" (p. 276). Barrows and Tamblyn (1980) also note that "generations of students in conventional curricula have expressed the desire to repeat basic science courses when they enter their clinical years, testimony to their frustration over their inability to recall subject-based information from earlier years" (p. 12). Hence, How is medical knowledge organized in the memories of medical students and physicians? and Are different structures related to different learning outcomes or clinical performances?

Because of theoretical and methodological shortcomings, there are still no decisive answers to these significant questions. However, most investigators in the field agree on the importance of categorization as a basis for the

---

* Based on a paper presented at the 1982 Annual Meeting of the American Educational Research Association, New York, N.Y., March 23, 1982 as well as on a paper by G. Bordage and R. Zacks published in *Medical Education,* 1984, *18,* 406–416. By permission of the publishers.

understanding of memory organization. Most often, categories of objects or events are viewed as rule-defined entities derived from a criterion and expressed within definite boundaries inside which all instances sharing the criterial feature(s) have a full and equal degree of memberships. While this traditional deterministic view is most common, recent investigations have shown that the internal structure of categories in a person's memory may be of a different nature. Rosch and coworkers in particular have shown for color and object categories that they are represented in memory in terms of "prototypes," the clearest cases or best examples of the category, surrounded by other instances of decreasing similarity to the prototypes and of decreasing degree of membership (1975, 1978; Rosch & Mervis, 1975).

PURPOSES

The purpose of the present study is twofold: (a) to determine whether the concept of prototypes as developed by Rosch and coworkers is applicable to the mental categorization of medical disorders, and (b) to describe the influence of clinical experience on those memory structures. Four experiments were conducted with 100 pre-clinical medical students (n_s) and 77 experienced physicians (n_p).

SAMPLES

The two samples represent contrasting levels of diagnostic skills. It is hypothesized that prototypes become more clearly defined as a result of experience and that the categories contain a richer, more closely woven network of information. It is also expected that the experts would have quicker access to the information in the categories than the novices.

The pre-clinical medical students, representing the novice diagnostician, had completed the basic science part of the curriculum, including study of the various system pathologies, and were just beginning their in-hospital training or clerkships. Because of limited resources, only one medical school population was sampled: the 152 third-year medical students at Laval University in Québec City. They were solicited by letter and participation was voluntary. Two thirds accepted to participate and were subsequently randomly assigned to the four experiments. Based on their respective GPA scores (a score believed to be correlated with the dependent variables in the study since both are measures of medical knowledge), the participants ($\bar{x}$ = 4.22, s = 0.38) did not vary significantly (α = .1; t (150) = 0.78, p = 0.22) from the nonparticipants ($\bar{x}$ = 4.27, s = 0.36). The average age of the Laval participant was 23.8 years (21–32). Two thirds were male and all were French speaking. Most were bilingual (all could read English and about half of the textbooks were in English. The courses were organized according to a traditional discipline-oriented curriculum. The students participated in the study some 2 to 3 months prior to their clerkships during their 3 months of introduction to clinical methods.

Because of the prevailing trend of many medical schools to emphasize family practice in their curriculum, the experienced physicians were limited to general practitioners who (a) do not have any specialty training, except possibly a certification from the College of Family Physicians; (b) have at least 1 year of active practice; and (c) have seen patients on a regular weekly basis. The physicians were selected either from the greater Québec City chapter of the Québec Fédération of General Practitioners for the first and third experiments, or from participants attending one of two continuing medical education conferences for the remaining two experiments. Four fifths (81%) of the physicians solicited agreed to participate. Participation was anonymous and voluntary. All of the participants (except one) graduated from one of the three French-speaking medical schools in the Province of Québec, and all practiced in predominantly French-speaking communities. They had practiced for an average of 8.5 years (2–28) and saw an average of 104 patients per week (15–200). Most worked in group practice (78%) in an urban setting (73%). Only 17% were certified family physicians.

EXPERIMENTS

The distinctiveness of categories can be achieved in two ways: by means of formal, necessary, and sufficient criteria for category membership; or by conceiving of each category in terms of its clear cases. The arguments in favor of the latter view come from the operational definition of two concepts—prototypes and family resemblance. The level of typicality of an item is derived from people's perception of how good an example various members are of a category (Rosch, 1973, 1978). The degree of agreement among the judgments is an indication of how applicable the concept is. Prototypes, like categories themselves, develop through the maximization of family resemblance: "members of a category come to be viewed as prototypical of the category as a whole in proportion to the extent to which they bear a family resemblance to (have attributes which overlap those of) other members of the category" (Rosch & Mervis, 1975, p. 575). Rosch and Mervis (1975) have shown, for categories of concrete nouns, that the more typical of a category a member is rated, the more attributes it has in common with other members of that category.

Four experiments, based on Rosch (1975) and her colleagues' research strategy, were designed and conducted to form a logical and converging sequence of evidence about the internal structure of 14 categories of medical disorders (see Table 1). These categories were chosen because, like in Rosch's initial experiments (1973, 1975), they represent broad and widely accepted category names. The eight organ-system categories were drawn from the classification of medical problems of the Royal College of General Practitioners and the remaining six names from standard medical references.

Experiment 1: Category Norms

The list of disorders contained in the categories was obtained seperately from the two samples by means of a production task ($n_s = 42$; $n_p = 21$). These lists provided the basis of the materials for the following three experiments on internal structure.

Experiment 2: Typicality Ratings

Using a 7-point scale, the subjects were asked to rate the degree of examplariness of 8 disorders taken from each of the categories ($n_s = 13$; $n_p = 19$).

Experiment 3: Family Resemblance

The lists of attributes (symptoms, signs, pathophysiological characteristics) for six of the disorders rated for typicality were obtained by means of a production task ($n_s = 31$; $n_p = 12$). Two hypotheses were tested about these attributes: (a) that each disorder in a category has at least one, if not several, attributes in common with one or more other disorders in the category (the family resemblance view), but none, or few, of the features are common to all disorders (the criterial view); and (b) that the disorders with the highest typicality ratings in a category are those with the greatest number of attributes in common with the other disorders in the category.

Experiment 4: Response Time

To test the effect of typicality on the cognitive processing of the categories, response time to category membership statements of the type "Diabetes mellitus is a kind of endocrine disorder" was obtained for disorders with high typicality ratings (central members) as opposed to those with lower ratings (peripheral members) ($n_s = 14$; $n_p = 14$). The hypothesis was tested that the central members would be recalled faster than the peripheral ones.

All four experiments were conducted in French. If the internal structure of the categories in the long-term memories of the subjects was a prototypical one, then the results from all, if not most, experiments should point toward that conclusion.

RESULTS

There were three basic and converging findings from this series of experiments.

First, the striking structural feature of the categories resides in the presence of prototypical disorders as opposed to some common criterial attribute(s)—few attributes are listed which are common to all six disorders in a category. Only rarely is an attribute common to all, or even to the majority, of the disorders. The distribution in Figure 1 also illustrates that the number of attributes decreases as the number of disorders to which the attribute is applicable increases. Both the students and the physicians found the rating task meaningful and made reliable judgments about the degree of exemplariness of selected members from each category. The ratings in all 14 categories departed significantly from a chance distribution (Friedman tests: $p < .001$; see Table 1). Overall, the disorders with the highest typicality ratings are recalled earlier in the production task than the less typical ones; the median Spearman rank-order correlation coefficients between the ratings and the item output ranks are 0.83 and 0.85 for the students and the physicians respectively ($p < .025$).

To derive the measure of family resemblance, each attribute received a score ranging from 1 to 6, representing the number of disorders in a category that shared that attribute. The measure of degree of family resemblance for a given disorder is the sum of the weighted scores of each of the attributes

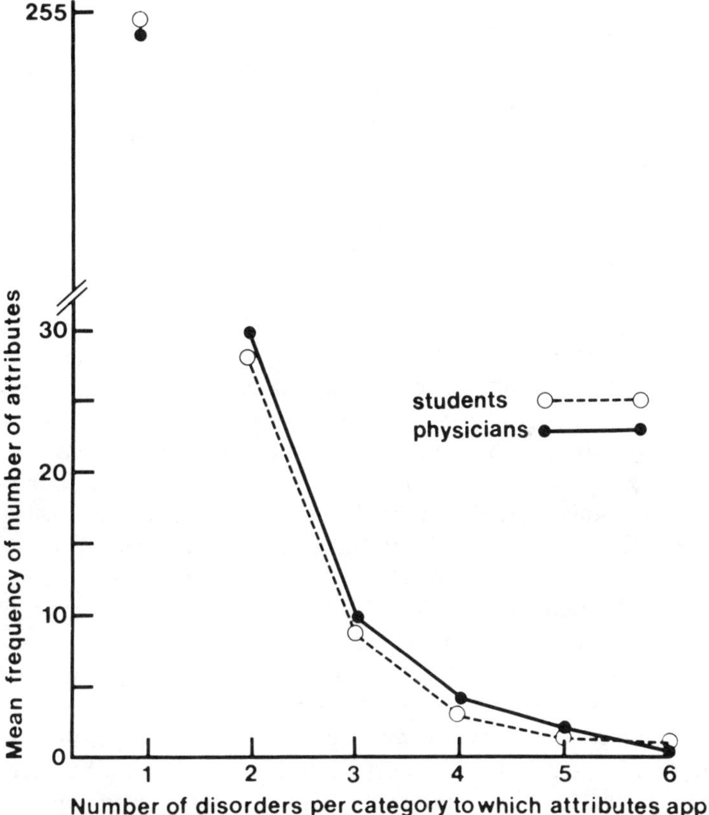

Figure 1. Frequency distribution for the mean number of attributes applied to each number of disorders per category.

Table 1. **Mean Typicality Ratings Obtained in Experiment 2**

	Students' Frequency Range from First Experiment					Physicians' Frequency Range from First Experiment				
	Top	**High**	**Mod.**	**Low**	**Out**	**Top**	**High**	**Mod.**	**Low**	**Out**
Categories										
1. Respiratory	7.0	6.35	5.80	5.05	1.0	6.7	6.80	6.35	4.95	1.00
2. Cardiovascular	6.9	6.45	5.90	5.25	1.0	7.0	6.50	6.25	5.40	1.05
3. Genitourinary	6.3	6.80	5.85	4.80	1.0	6.5	6.30	6.15	5.75	1.00
4. Gastrointestinal	6.9	6.55	5.70	5.35	1.2	6.8	6.25	6.05	5.50	1.05
5. Endocrine	6.8	6.85	5.75	4.15	1.0	6.7	6.50	6.60	5.30	1.00
6. Musculoskeletal	6.8	6.30	6.05	5.15	1.0	6.0	6.55	5.15	5.80	1.20
7. Neurological	6.7	6.05	5.60	5.65	1.0	6.8	4.70	6.50	5.60	1.00
8. Hematological	6.5	6.85	6.20	3.15	1.0	7.0	6.75	6.20	3.90	1.20
9. Infections	6.7	6.70	5.50	4.50	1.2	6.4	6.30	5.85	6.50	1.40
10. Neoplasms	6.8	6.00	4.80	6.50	1.2	6.4	6.85	6.45	5.85	1.05
11. Inflammations	6.7	6.30	5.05	3.25	1.2	6.5	6.30	5.75	4.50	1.20
12. Dyspnea	6.8	5.30	5.75	4.65	1.2	7.0	5.55	5.50	4.25	1.00
13. Abdominal pain	7.0	6.35	3.75	4.10	1.0	6.9	6.60	5.55	4.90	1.30
14. Joint pain	6.8	6.20	4.65	4.30	1.0	6.6	6.45	6.05	4.20	1.05
Mean total:	6.76	6.36	5.45	4.70	1.07	6.66	6.31	6.03	5.17	1.11

that are listed for that item (attributes with scores of one or two were not included). Overall, the higher the typicality rating of an item, the higher its family resemblance score; the scores for each level of typicality are statistically different from one another (Friedman tests: $\chi_r^2 = 17.3$ and 21 for the students and physicians respectively, $p < 0.001$). In other words, the disorders with the highest typicality ratings in a category are also the ones with the greatest number of attributes in common with the other members (see Tables 2 and 3). The median Spearman rank-order correlation coefficients between the family resemblance scores and the ratings are 0.62 and 0.59 for the students and the physicians respectively. These correlations are not as high as those obtained by Rosch and Mervis (1975) for semantic categories of concrete objects: that is, 0.88 to 0.94. A possible explanation may be because they used 20 items per category to perform their experimentation as opposed to only six items here. The call for further experimentation is well founded since there is a definite positive trend between the two measures.

Second, typicality affects the cognitive processing of the categories. It took less time for the students and physicians to make judgments about the category membership of central disorders as opposed to peripheral ones ($F(1,24) = 5.07$, $p < .05$; see Table 4). There is no interaction between subject types (students and physicians) and disorder types (central and peripheral). Furthermore, while the judgments are virtually error-free for the central members, many more classification errors are made for the peripheral ones (some 17 to 20 times more; Mann-Whitney U-tests: $U=0$, $p<.05$; see Table 4).

Third, clinical experience affects the internal structure of the categories. Although there is a high degree of similarity in the individual disorders listed by the students and the physicians in the production task, the general practitioners had a richer and more tightly woven network of knowledge than the students. The physicians used a narrower range of points on the typicality rating scale (Wilcoxon matched-pairs signed-ranks tests formed by the 14 categories: $T=18$, $p<.05$) and responded faster to category membership statements than the students ($F(1,24)=9.24$, $p<.01$). Both of these results suggest that the associative strength between a disorder and its category label is stronger for the physicians than for the students. Also, the physicians have higher family resemblance scores, (Sign tests for the 84 pairs of scores: $Z=3.38$, $p<.001$), thus indicating that they have more explicit ties among the members of their categories than the students. Despite their

Table 2. Students' Family Resemblance Scores for the Two Items at Each Level of Typicality

Category	High Typicality Ratings		Moderate Typicality Ratings		Low Typicality Ratings	
1. Respiratory	48	54	33	30	40	27
2. Cardiovascular	30	24	14	18	17	13
3. Genitourinary	18	6	21	15	15	15
4. Gastrointestinal	51	50	38	60	42	30
5. Endocrine	23	8	13	16	16	10
6. Musculoskeletal	38	24	32	28	11	21
7. Neurological	28	36	31	22	22	22
8. Hematological	25	25	25	17	7	30
	(32.6)[a]	(28.4)	(25.9)	(25.8)	(21.3)	(21)
	(30.5)		(25.8)		(21.1)	
9. Infections	44	37	45	31	43	31
10. Neoplasms	38	45	40	34	31	23
11. Inflammations	19	13	22	19	6	3
	(33.7)	(31.7)	(35.7)	(28)	(26.7)	(19)
	(32.7)		(31.8)		(22.8)	
12. Dyspnea	20	33	30	27	10	15
13. Abdominal pain	31	31	24	18	13	21
14. Joint pain	35	52	32	45	44	37
	(28.7)	(38.7)	(28.7)	(30)	(22.3)	(24.3)
	(31.6)		(29.3)		(23.3)	
TOTAL	32	31.3	28.6	27.8	23.6	21.3
	(31.7)		(27.9)		(22)	

[a] Average scores in parentheses.

Table 3. Physicians' Family Resemblance Scores for the Two Items at Each Level of Typicality

Category	High Typicality Ratings		Moderate Typicality Ratings		Low Typicality Ratings	
1. Respiratory	58	55	40	50	51	33
2. Cardiovascular	36	33	30	17	30	12
3. Genitourinary	49	45	40	29	16	12
4. Gastrointestinal	57	46	53	36	57	21
5. Endocrine	19	9	16	7	13	6
6. Musculoskeletal	20	17	6	11	10	13
7. Neurological	17	45	20	39	30	30
8. Hematological	51	44	29	40	16	30
	(38.4)[a]	(36.8)	(29.3)	(28.6)	(27.9)	(19.6)
	(37.6)		(28.9)		(23.8)	
9. Infections	36	45	46	30	30	53
10. Neoplasms	35	52	44	50	44	31
11. Inflammations	14	21	14	17	13	14
	(28.3)	(39.3)	(34.7)	(32.3)	(29)	(32.7)
	(33.8)		(33.5)		(30.8)	
12. Dyspnea	40	26	32	33	36	24
13. Abdominal pain	54	50	27	36	55	12
14. Joint pain	86	60	51	64	58	30
	(60)	(45.3)	(36.7)	(44.3)	(49.7)	(22)
	(52.7)		(40.5)		(35.8)	
TOTAL	40.9	39.1	32	32.8	32.8	22.9
	(40)		(32.4)		(27.9)	

[a] Average scores in parentheses.

Table 4. Mean Response Times and Error Proportions for Central and Peripheral Sets, Experiment 4

	Response Times (in seconds)	Error Proportions: False for a True Item	Error Proportions: True for a False Item
STUDENTS			
Central ($n = 7$)	222.9 (25)[a]	0.016	0.000
Peripheral ($n = 7$)	338.6 (116.6)	0.269	0.006
PHYSICIANS			
Central ($n = 7$)	180.1 (55.7)	0.031	0.006
Peripheral ($n = 7$)	246.4 (88.2)	0.181	0.006

[a] Standard deviations in parentheses.

increased clinical experience, the general practitioners did not tend, in general, to list any more than the students did the names of disorders that are encountered most often in the family practice setting. While frequency may play a role in the formation of some prototypes (55%), others most likely arise from the overlapping structure of the attributes of the various members in a category, the family resemblance structure.

DISCUSSION AND CONCLUSION

Cantor, Smith, French, and Mezzich (1980), in a study of the categorization of nine psychiatric disorders, also found that the internal structure of the categories was better described by the "correlated features" of the prototype view than the "defining features" of the traditional deterministic view. They also studied psychiatric diagnosis as a "prototype-matching process" and found that the accuracy and confidence of diagnosis increases with typicality. In their analysis of the changes in the latest edition of the APA's diagnostic manual of mental disorders, they note that "Diagnostic criteria are now presented as prototypes—larger sets of correlated features rather than selected defining ones; guidelines for diagnosis also emphasize the potential heterogeneity of the symptoms of like-diagnosed patients.... From the perspective of the prototype view, these changes are important because they help to emphasize, rather than obscure, the probabilistic nature of diagnostic categorizations" (pp. 190, 192). And they add, "Diagnoses can be made on the basis of degree of fit between the patient's cluster of symptoms and the prototypes for various different categories" (p. 192).

These observations are also consistent with the differences found between experts and novices. For example, Larkin, McDermott, Simon, and Simon (1980) state that "although a sizable body of knowledge is prerequisite to expert skill, that knowledge must be indexed by large numbers of patterns that, on recognition, guide the expert in a fraction of a second to relevant parts of the knowledge store" (p. 1336). Medical textbooks and much classroom teaching abound in the presentation of detailed lists of disorders, features, and therapeutic actions to the students. More often, both fail to provide a categorization scheme that is best suited for their retrieval in a clinical problem-solving situation. The prototypes, with their overlaping attributes, their representativeness, may serve as an indexing scheme for the clinician's knowledge. Although both the medical students and the physicians in the present study exhibited a prototypical structure, the experienced practitioners had a richer and more readily accessible store of knowledge than the novices.

Given the results of the present study and those of Cantor and coworkers in psychiatry, there is a growing body of evidence to the effect that prototypes may be better suited to describe the internal structure of medical categories than the traditional deterministic view. Furthermore, the notion of prototypes offers a promising means by which the learning and diagnostic process of becoming and being an expert clinician can be analyzed, understood, and eventually improved.

REFERENCES

Barrows, H. S., Feightner, J. W., Neufeld, V. R., & Norman, G. R. (1978). *Analysis of the clinical methods of medical students and physicians.* McMaster University, Hamilton, Ontario.

Barrows, H. S., & Tamblyn, R. M. (1980). *Problem-based learning: An approach to medical education.* New York: Springer.

Cantor, N., Smith, E., French, R., & Mezzich, J. (1980). Psychiatric diagnosis as prototype categorization. *Journal of Abnormal Psychology, 89*(2), 181–193.

DeGroot, A. D. (1965). *Thought and choice in chess.* The Hague: Mouton.

Elstein, A. S., Shulman, L. S., & Sprafka, S. A. (1978). *Medical problem solving: An analysis of clinical reasoning.* Cambridge, MA: Harvard University Press.

Larkin, J., McDermott, J., Simon, D., & Simon, H. (1980). Expert and novice performance in solving physics problems. *Science, 208,* 1335–1342.

Rosch, E. (1973). On the internal structure of perceptual and semantic categories. In T. E. Moore (Ed.), *Cognitive development and the acquisition of language.* New York: Academic Press.

Rosch, E. (1975). Cognitive representations of semantic categories. *Journal of Experimental Psychology: General, 104,* 192–233.

Rosch, E. (1978). Principles of categorization. In E. Rosch & B. B. Lloyd (Eds.), *Cognition and categorization.* Potomac: Erlbaum.

Rosch, E., & Mervis, C. B. (1975). Family resemblances: studies in the internal structure of categories. *Cognitive Psychology, 7,* 573–605.

Chapter 9

Cognitive Factors in Programming: The Good, The Bad, and The Ugly*

Elliot Soloway
Yale University

Kate Ehrlich
Honeywell Information Systems

I. INTRODUCTION

When someone comes to learn a new subject, there are bound to be difficulties. One source of those difficulties is the mismatch between what the learner brings to the subject—his *naive* theory—and what is to be learned. Such mismatches have been documented in the fields of physics and mathematics (DiSessa, 1982; Gentner & Stevens, 1982). We of the Cognition and Programming Project at Yale have focused on the domain of programming. In what follows we will describe two types of mismatches in a computer programming context.[1]

- *The Ugly:* In the first type of situation, the difficulty caused by the mismatch seems to persist and give advanced programmers as well as novice programmers significant difficulty.
- *The Bad:* In the second type of situation, the difficulty caused by the mismatch seems to be only temporary.

---

* This work was sponsored by the National Science Foundation, under NSF Grant SED-81-12403, and NSF Grant IST-81-14840. Approved for public release; distribution unlimited. Reproduction in whole or part is permitted for any purpose of the United States Government.

A previous version of this paper, was delivered to the American Educational Research Association Meeting, 1982. We would particularly like to thank the members of the Cognition and Programming Project—Valerie Abbott, Paul Barth, Jeff Bonar, Lewis Johnson, Eric Rubin, and Beverly Woolf—for their valuable contributions to the research that we have reported in this paper.

[1] See Bonar and Soloway, 1983; Bonar and Soloway, 1982; Bonar, 1985 for additional examples of mismatches.

It can work the other way too: domain knowledge that is consistent with what the learner brings can facilitate the building of new knowledge.

- *The Good:* We will also present an instance where programming appears to tap into learners' procedural notions, and facilitates the transfer of those notions to another domain: algebra.

Interestingly, most of the *ugly* and *bad* mismatches that we will be describing can be remedied by a simple redesign of the programming language. That is, unlike physics, programming is a "design" discipline—programming languages are developed by people for people. Up until recently, however, programming languages were designed with the computer in mind, not with the programmer. While people are very adaptable, and, with sufficient practice, often capable of accommodating themselves to even the most baroque of constructs, there is no need to make programming unnecessarily difficult. By looking to the problems programmers have—and identifying their cognitive origins—we are in a position to help shape the development of programming.

2. THE UGLY: PASCAL'S WHILE LOOP

Our example of an *ugly* problem is drawn from our recent research on the **while** loop in Pascal (Soloway, Bonar, & Ehrlich, 1983). Wegner (1979) and Knuth (1974) have both pointed out that the **while** loop, as used in Pascal, requires an "awkward" coding strategy. As we will argue, the **while** loop is more than awkward, it is downright confusing.

Consider the problem in Figure 2-1. The stylistically correct solution to this problem in Pascal, also shown in Figure 2-1, uses a **while** loop (Wirth, 1974). The loop must *not* be executed if the test variable has the specified value, and this value could turn up on the first read; thus, a **read** outside the loop is necessary in order to start the loop off. Thus, the loop begins with summing the number that was read in on the previous iteration and finishes with reading in the next number; the ith input is processed, and then the next ith (i + 1) is fetched. If we step back from the code, we notice that the strategy which underlies this loop can be characterized as:

```
read first-value
while (test ith value)
    process ith value
    read next-ith value
```

We call this looping strategy the "process i/read next-i" strategy. The strategy can be described informally as, "do something to a number that you got the last time and then get the next number." In contrast, we believe that the preferred strategy is to, "get a number and then do something to it." We call this latter strategy, "read i/process i." In Figure 2-2 we show an exam-

Problem. Write a program which repeatedly reads in integers until it reads the integer 99999. After seeing 99999, it should print out the **correct** average. That is, it should not count the final 99999.

```
program Example(Input, Output);
    var Count, Sum, Number : integer
        Average : real
    begin
    Count : = 0;
    Sum : = 0;
    Read (Number);
    while Number < > 99999 do
          begin
          Sum : = Sum + Number;
          Count : = Count + 1;
          Read (Number)
          end;
    if Count > then
        Average : = Sum / Count
      else Average : = 99999;
    Writeln (Average)
    end.
```

Figure 2-1. A Sample Program: The Running Total Loop Plan

```
program Example2(Input, Output); ;
    var Count, Sum, Number : integer ;
        Average : REAL;
    begin
    Count : = 0;
    Sum : = 0;
    loop
        Read (Number);
        if Number = 99999 then leave;
        Sum : = Sum + Number;
        Count : = Count + 1
    again;
    if Count > 0 then
        Average : = Sum / Count
      else Average : = 99999;
    Writeln (Average)
    end.
```

Figure 2-2. Coding Read/Process with a loop. . .leave **Construct**

ple of a program which uses a read/process strategy to solve the problem given in Figure 2-1. The program uses a **loop. . .leave** construct, which is a variant of a construct that is used in the new programming language, ADA.[2]

In order to compare the performance of programmers using these two constructs, the **while** construct and the **loop-leave** construct, we conducted the following experiment. We asked three different groups of student programmers (novices, intermediates, and advanced) to write a program to solve the problem in Figure 2-1 in either standard Pascal or in modified-Pascal, a language that was the same as Pascal except for having the **loop. . . leave** construct as the only looping construct. Students using modified-Pascal were given a one-page description of the new construct, while students using standard Pascal were given a one-page description of the standard Pascal constructs. The subjects were all Pascal programmers with varying amounts of experience. In order to elicit students' preferred strategy for solving the problem, we asked all subjects to write a plan in English to solve the problem before we asked them to write a program to solve the problem.

We were interested in the following questions:

1. Do students prefer one strategy over another, in their plans and programs, and if so, which one?
2. Do students write correct programs more often when they use the construct that facilitates their natural strategy?
3. Does experience affect how people prefer to think about the problem?

We found that students overwhelmingly adopted a read/process strategy on their plans; 82% of the novices, 91% of the intermediates, and 67% of the advanced students used a read/process strategy on their plans, when we were able to discern any plan at all. These results show that read/process does appear to be the preferred strategy. It is also interesting to note that, among the advanced programmers, who had been programming for three semesters or more, there was a higher proportion of students who used a process/read strategy.

As predicted, we found a greater proportion of correctly written programs amongst the students who used modified-Pascal as compared with the students who used standard Pascal. The results are shown in Table 2-1. In many ways, these results are surprising. Given that students generally perform poorly on written tests (see next section) and that they had been using the Pascal constructs for at least a semester, we were quite amazed

---

[2] Note that the **while** construct facilitates a process/read strategy but it does not restrict people to using that strategy. One can add extra code to a **while** loop (e.g., an embedded boolean test) to realize a read/process strategy. Similarly, the **loop. . .leave** construct facilitates a read/process strategy but does not restrict people to just that strategy. For instance, the **loop. . .leave** construct could be used to simulate a **while** loop by simply putting the **if** test at the top of the loop. Thus students could use the **loop. . .leave** construct to code a process/read strategy if they so desired.

that students could learn a new construct from a one-page description in about 4–6 minutes, and then go on to use it correctly![3] We feel that these data provide support for the claim that people will find it easier to program when they can use a program language construct that facilitates their natural problem solving strategies.

The difficulty with the **while** loop is quite general and extends beyond simply reading an element. Consider the simple program depicted in Figure 2-3. There we see a **while** loop being used to search through an array. We

Table 2-1. Program Correctness With Respect to Language

	Correct[1]	Incorrect[1]	*N*	Significance[2]
NOVICES				
Modified Pascal	24% *(14)*	76% *(44)*	58	not significant
Standard Pascal	14% *(8)*	86% *(50)*	58	
INTERMEDIATES				
Modified Pascal	61% *(36)*	39% *(23)*	59	($\chi^2 = 7.08$)
Standard Pascal	36% *(19)*	64% *(34)*	53	$p = 0.01$
ADVANCED				
Modified Pascal	96% *(25)*	4% *(1)*	26	($\chi^2 = 6.58$)
Standard Pascal	69% *(18)*	31% *(8)*	26	$p < 0.02$

[1] The numbers in parenthesized italics represent actual numbers, not percentages.
[2] Chi-Square test was used in this comparison.

```
program Get/Process-Example(Input, Output);
    var sum, i : integer; a : Array[1..10] of integer;
begin
  (*                                                      *)
  (* there is code here that fills up the array with data values *)
  (*                                                      *)
  Sum := 0;
  i := 1;
  while a[i] <> -1 do
    begin
      sum := sum + a[i];
      i := i + 1
      end
  (*                                   *)
  (* there is code here to output the result *)
  (*                                   *)
end.
```

Figure 2-3. Generalizing a Get a Value/Process a Value

[3] Students were given as much time as they wanted to do this problem; typically they only used 10 to 15 minutes in total.

can view the incrementing of i as equivalent to reading the next element. In other words, we can generalize the underlying strategy from process i/read next-i to process i/get next-i. We are currently carrying out experiments to explore the performance of programmers on problems of this sort.

2.1 *Summary: The Ugly*

Even though programming can be facilitated by providing language constructs which match people's natural strategies, one might argue that in fact we need to break people of their bad habits and teach them new strategies. A case in point is our success with the **loop...leave** construct. A common argument in the structured programming paradigm is that jumping out of the middle of the loop is a poor programming practice (Wirth, 1974): one should enter a loop at the top, and leave either via the bottom or the top of the loop. Thus, on this view, by advocating a strategy that encourages programmers to write programs with an exit from a loop body, we are encouraging the development of bad habits. However, one look at the data shows that, in fact, the **while** loop is giving less-advanced programmers such difficulties that it could be said they are not learning *any* habits! Moreover, Sheppard, Curtis, Milliman, and Love (1979) recently showed that jumping out of the middle of a loop was not at all detrimental to programmers in comprehension and debugging tasks.

3. *THE BAD: SOME COMMON CONFUSIONS*

In this section we will describe two language constructs which, while not as glaring as the **while** construct, still seem to give novices difficulties.

3.1 *The "Demon" in the While Loop Test*

In the previous section we discussed a major difficulty with Pascal's **while** loop. In this section, we point up another, though less serious, confusion which students have with this looping construct. In particular, based on our examination of student programs, we felt that there was significant confusion surrounding the time at which the terminating test in the **while** loop gets evaluated: is it evaluated once, at the top of the loop, or is the test continually evaluated during the execution of the body of the loop? To examine this issue, we included the program below on a test to 31 novice programmers, and asked them to tell us how many '*' and how many '/' would be printed out by this program.

```
program Problem4(Input, Output);
    var Count : integer;
    begin
    Count := 0;
    while Count<7 do
```

```
        begin
        Writeln ('*');
        Count : = Count + 1;
        Writeln ('/')
        end
    end.
```

This program will print out 7 '*' and 7 '/'. However, if students felt that the terminating test was evaluated continually, then the loop should terminate before an '/' would be printed, and thus there would be one more '*' printed out as compared with the number of '/' printed out. Of the 31 students, 34% made just this mistake. Apparently, the test in the while loop is viewed as if it were a "demon," watching the statements in the loop body, and waiting for its condition to become true; once true, the loop is exited immediately. Given the ubiquity of the **while** construct in programs, and given the lateness in the course (the end of the semester), we felt that this was a surprisingly high error rate.

We feel that the basis for this confusion is grounded in the mismatch between the semantics of **while** in a programming language context, and the semantics—the meaning—of "while" in every day experience. In the latter case, "while" has a global sense: during the course of some event. In contrast, the programming language **while** requires a local, narrow interpretation: at a specific point in time. Again, we see a conflict between what the learner brings to programming and what the learner must acquire. Moreover, the language construct could be named something other than **while**—or, the test condition could be made to work like a demon!

3.2 Counter Variable vs. Running_Total Variable: Update Problems

We have observed that students often have difficulty in understanding the use of variables in programs (Ehrlich & Soloway, 1984). For instance, a variable that is used to accumulate a running total of numbers, a *Running_Total Variable,* will be written in a program in the following fashion: SUM : = Sum + New, where New is the variable representing the new number that is added into the total. Students often have some early difficulties in grasping the dynamic use of variables that allows the same variable (i.e., Sum) to appear on both sides of the "equation." There are other problems that variables pose for students. Consider the following problem (the same one as we gave in the previous section):

> Write a program which repeatedly reads in integers until it reads the integer 99999. After seeing 99999, it should print out the correct average. That is, it should not count the final 99999.

To solve this problem, the program needs to keep track of the running total, e.g., Sum : = Sum + New, and it needs to keep a count of the number of numbers read in, e.g., Count := Count + 1. Typically, instructional texts treat the update of the *Counter Variable* and the update of the *Running_Total Variable* as instances of the same basic construct, i.e., the assignment statement. If students treat the two types of variables as the same, we would expect to see no difference in performance; students should be as likely to handle correctly the *Counter Variable* update as the *Running_Total Variable* update. However, data we have collected from novice and intermediate level student programmers, suggest otherwise. The discussion here is based on a study with two groups of student programmers: a novice group of 31 students in an introductory Pascal programming course, and an intermediate group of 52 students in a second course in Pascal programming. The former group was tested at the end of the semester, while the latter group was tested in the 10th week of a 16-week semester.[4] We found that, in the problem just given, 100% of the novices wrote a correct *Counter Variable* update, while only 83% wrote a correct *Running_Total Variable* update. The difference in performance was significant ($\chi^2 = 4.38$, $p < 0.05$). In contrast, the intermediates performed essentially the same on both updates: 91% correct on the *Counter Variable* update versus 95% correct on the *Running_Total Variable* update.

Why should the *Running_Total Variable* update be "harder" than the *Counter Variable* update for the novices? After all, both require assignment statements of the same form. Below, we list three hypotheses which could account for this observation.

1. The activity of counting and the activity of accumulating a total are **different** activities. Whereas counting is naturally represented as a "successor function" (i.e., increase the previous number by 1), one does not traditionally add up a column of numbers using a running total algorithm. (With the increasing use of pocket calculators, this might change.) However, the standard assignment statement does not distinguish between these two cases, and in fact requires that both activities be encoded in the same way. Thus, the mismatch between one's standard algorithm and the programming language results in the *Running_Total Variable* update being harder to learn than the *Counter Variable* update.
2. Students might learn the notion of a counter as a special entity, i.e., they see the instructor and the textbook always using I := I + 1 whenever a counter is needed, and thus they memorize this pattern as an indivisible unit. In other words, they do not decompose I := I + 1 into a left hand variable which has its value changed by the right hand expression. By this hypothesis, students are not viewing I := I + 1 as an example

[4] A fuller discussion of the study can be found in Soloway, Ehrlich, Bonar, and Greenspan (1982).

of an assignment statement.[5] When faced with developing an assignment statement for the "running total function," students must really confront their understanding of the particular type of assignment statement needed in this context. The poorer performance in this situation reflects a misunderstanding of how the assignment statement works, and how to encode a running total with this type of statement.

3. The assignment statement in the *Running_Total Variable* update case requires a variable while the assignment statement in the *Counter Variable* update case requires only a constant; the difference in performance reflects the fact that variables are "harder" than constants for novices. While this hypothesis might seem like the obvious one, it unfortunately does not provide an adequate *explanation* for the data. Why should variables be harder than constants? At the syntactic level, writing down a symbol string does not seem all that much harder than writing down a number. At the semantic level, both are the same—the value of the name is used in the computation. One must go after deeper differences, differences which get at why and when variables are used as opposed to when constants are used. Hypotheses 1 and 2 above attempt to explain the performance difference by describing the circumstances under which each entity is most appropriate. This hypothesis, while appealing on the surface, lacks the explanatory power that we seek.

Another curious coding technique, which we observed in the same students' programs, provides additional supportive evidence that students did perceive the *Running_Total Variable* differently from the *Counter Variable*. The program in Figure 3-1 contains a *Running_Total Variable* update which is "fractured," i.e., split over two lines of code (Y: = X + Z, Z: = Y). While not incorrect, this technique is not good programming practice. It probably reflects a confusion of the equal sign in traditional algebra with the assignment operator in programming. If students perceived the *Counter Variable* update to be of the same sort as the *Running_Total Variable* update, then we would expect to see "fractured updates" used in both the *Counter Variable* update and the *Running_Total Variable* update. Fractured updates were observed in seven programs from the novice group. However, in all instances this occurred with respect to a *Running_Total Variable* update, not a *Counter Variable* update! While the numbers are small, and thus conclusions drawn from them must be treated with caution, these data nonetheless are consistent with our claim that students do perceive the two variables as being different.

---

[5] Performance data on Problem 3 suggest some intriguing corroborating evidence. More novices got the count action correct (e.g., I : = I + 1) than got the count initialization correct (e.g., I : = 1)! Maybe this was due to sloppiness. However, if I : = I + 1 is a unit unto itself, then possibly the students do not see the need to initialize the variable.

```
program Student21_Problem3(Input, Output);
    var C, X, Y, Z : integer ;
        begin
    C := 0;
    Z := 0;
    while X<99999 do
        begin
        Read (X);
        C := C+1;
        Y := X+Z;
        Z := Y
        end;
    A := Y div C;
    Writeln (A, ' Average')
    end.
```

The above student program contains a fractured *Running_Total* assignment statement in the body of the **while** loop.

Figure 3-1. A Fractured Running-Total Update

3.3 *Summary: The* Bad

In this section we have described two examples in which novice programmers had difficulty understanding programming concepts. Moreover, the root of the difficulty appears to be in the mismatch between how the student wanted to think about the concept, and how that concept was defined in the programming context. We rank these difficulties as only *bad,* since they do not seem to persist. In the case of the *Running_Total Variable* vs. *Counter Variable* difficulty, we have data that indicates that by the time students have reached the level of intermediate programmers they no longer have a problem with *Running_Total Variables.* While we do not have the same comparison between novice and intermediate programmers for the **while** demon problem, it is hard to imagine anyone progressing in programming without getting that confusion straightened out.

4. *THE GOOD: PROCEDURALITY*

In the preceding sections, we outlined some of the troublesome features of programming. In this section, we will review a set of experiments which indicate that programming can have a positive impact on problem-solving skills. Specifically, we will show that programming can tap into a student's existing procedural skills to facilitate the transfer of those skills to the domain of algebra word problems.

4.1 *Background: Interpretation of Algebra Experiments*

In a previous study, Clement,. Lockhead, and Monk (1981) uncovered several ostensibly simple algebra word problems which gave students great difficulty. In Table 4-1, we list two of these problems and typical performance results. Among college freshman engineering students, 37% missed the first problem, while 73% missed the second. In their experiments, Clement and his colleagues were able to eliminate algebraic manipulation and tricky wording as major sources for the errors.

The errors made on problems 1 and 2 were largely of one kind; most were *reversals:* 6S = P instead of S = 6P and 4C = 5S instead of 5C = 4S. In order to pursue the source of these errors, Clement et al. (1981) conducted audio and video-taped interviews with 20 students who were asked to think out loud as they solved these and other problems. On Problem 1 in Table 4-1, they were able to identify several strategies which led to the reversal error. In one strategy, the student simply assumes that the order or contiguity of key words in the English language problem statement map directly into the order of symbols appearing in the algebraic equation. Weaknesses in this type of *direct translation strategy* have previously been analyzed by (Paige & Simon, 1966). Clement and his colleagues also uncovered evidence of other incorrect strategies. Students seemed to be confused about what the variables represented. For instance, many students treated P and S, from Problem 1, as representing *a professor* rather than *the number of professors.* Students also seemed to treat the equal sign as expressing a comparison or association rather than equivalence. Both of these strategies represent a *descriptive* approach to algebraic equations.

Table 4-1. Examples of Algebra Word Problems

PROBLEM 1

Given the following statement:

"There are six times as many students as professors at this University."

Write an equation to represent the above statement. Use S for the number of students and P for the number of professors.

- Result: 63% correct
- Typical wrong answer: 6S = P

PROBLEM 2

Given the following statement:

"At Mindy's restaurant, for every four people who order cheesecake, there are five people who order strudel."

Write an equation to represent the above statement. Use C for the number of cheesecakes ordered and S for the number of strudels ordered.

- Result: 27% correct
- Typical wrong answer: 4C = 5S

The *direct translation strategy* and the *descriptive* approach contrasts with the correct equation S = 6P, which needs to be viewed as expressing an active operation being performed on one number (the number of professors) in order to obtain another number (the number of students). The correct equation, S = 6P, does not describe sizes of groups in a literal or direct manner. Rather, it describes an equivalence relation that would occur if one were to make the group of professors six times larger. The key to fully understanding the correct translation lies in viewing the number, 6, as an *operation* which transforms the *number* of professors into the *number* of students. In summary, these results suggest that many students fail to treat their equations as representing an active process for obtaining the value of one variable when supplied with the value of the other variable.

4.2 Computer Programs vs. Algebraic Equations: Experimental Results

On the basis of the foregoing analysis, we developed the following hypothesis: if students were placed in an environment which could induce them to take a more active, procedural view of equations, then the error rate on these problems should go down. One clear candidate for such an environment, as Papert (1971, 1980) has frequently pointed out, is that of computer programming. That is, a computer program is a definite prescription for action; it is a set of commands which produces some result.

Initial support for the beneficial effects of programming came from a study by Soloway, Lockhead, and Clement (1982), in which they found that students who were enrolled in courses on machine and assembly language programming wrote more correct equations when asked to write a computer program than when asked to write an equation. Half the class were given problem 1 in Table 4-2 and half the class were given problem 2. The difference in performance on the two problems was significant (Chi-squared test: $\chi^2 = 5.18$, $p < 0.05$).

In a subsequent study, Ehrlich, Soloway, and Abbott (1982), examined whether the improved performance was due to the wording of the instructions given in the two problems (Table 4-2); the instructions for writing an equation. In this study, we included a set of instructions for writing an equation that had the same wording as the instructions for writing a computer program. Examples of all three sets of instructions are shown in Table 4-3. We administered these three problems to students in an introductory programming course at the end of the semester. One-third of the class were given problem 1, 1/3 were given problem 2, and 1/3 were given problem 3. We also administered problems 1 and 3 to a group of students who had not taken any programming courses. The results of this study, which are shown in Table 4-4, indicate that the programmers could write more correct equations when either asked to write a computer program or when given the procedural instructions. However, the students with no programming experience were no more accurate when given the procedural instructions than when they were given the standard instructions. These results suggest that students can and do respond to the procedurality in instructions—but only if they have first been exposed to a domain such as programming in which procedurality is emphasized.

Table 4-2. Comparisons of Writing Programs and Writing Equations

PROBLEM 1: PROGRAM INSTRUCTIONS

Given the following statement:

At the last company cocktail party, for every 6 people who drank hard liquor, there were 11 people who drank beer.

Write a computer program in BASIC which will output the number of beer drinkers when supplied (via user input at the terminal) with the number of hard liquor drinkers. Use H for the number of people who drank hard liquor, and B for the number of people who drank beer.

Sample Size	% Correct	% Incorrect
52	69	31

PROBLEM 2: NEUTRAL INSTRUCTIONS

Given the following statement:

At the last company cocktail party, for every 6 people who drank hard liquor, there were 11 people who drank beer.

Write an equation which represents the above statement. Use H for the number of people who drank hard liquor, and B for the number of people who drank beer.

Sample Size	% Correct	% Incorrect
51	45	55

Table 4-3. Examples of Problem Instructions

Given the following statement:

"At Mindy's restaurant, for every four people who order cheesecake there are five people who order strudel."

PROBLEM 1: NEUTRAL INSTRUCTIONS

Write an equation to represent the above statement. Use C for the number of cheesecakes ordered and S for the number of strudels ordered.

PROBLEM 2: PROGRAM INSTRUCTIONS

Write a computer program which can be used to calculate the number of cheesecakes ordered when supplied with the number of strudels ordered. Use C for the number of cheesecakes ordered and S for the number of strudels ordered.

PROBLEM 3: PROCEDURAL INSTRUCTIONS

Write a mathematical function which can be used to calculate the number of cheesecakes ordered when supplied with the number of strudels ordered. Use C for the number of cheesecakes ordered and S for the number of strudels ordered.

Table 4-4. The Number of Subjects Responding Correctly and Incorrectly as a Function of Instructions and Subject Group

Programmers				Nonprogrammers		
	Procedural	Neutral	Program		Procedural	Neutral
Correct	41	27	41	Correct	36	33
Incorrect	27	38	20	Incorrect	26	33
Neutral vs. Program ($\chi^2 = 8.35$, $p < 0.01$)				Neutral vs. Procedural: N.S.		
Neutral vs. Procedural: ($\chi^2 = 4.68$, $p < 0.05$)						
Procedural vs. Program: N.S.						

4.3 *The Effect of Programming on Algebra Word Problems*

In order to examine the effect of programming more fully, Ehrlich, Soloway, and Abbott (1982) compared the performance of a group of students who had just completed an introductory programming course with a similar group of students who had no programming experience. The purpose of this study was to examine whether the students who had completed the programming course would perform better on the algebra word problems than the students who had never taken a programming course. Evidence of better performance by the programmers would indicate support for our claim that programming can encourage students to develop problem-solving skills which can transfer to other domains.

We administered a large diagnostic test to both groups of students. The problems in the test included a variety of algebra word problems of the kind we have been discussing so far, as well as other kinds of problems such as rate problems or problems involving percentages. All of the problems had the standard equation wording (i.e., neutral wording). Over the set of 12 algebra word problems, the programmers averaged 69% correct, whereas the nonprogrammers averaged only 54% correct. The difference between the groups was significent (*t* test: $t_{11} = 5.57$, $p < 0.0005$). We were also able to examine the data more closely to explore some of the reasons why programming helps performance on algebra word problems. In particular, two interesting observations emerged from the data.

The first observation was that the programmers seemed to have particular skill in coping with more complex problems. In the study there were four problems in which only one number, other than 1, has to be considered in forming the equation (see Problem 1 in Table 4-1). We label these problems as *Integral*. In addition, there were four matching problems in which two numbers have to be considered in forming the equation. (see Problem 2 in Table 4-1) We label these problems as *Non-Integral*. The Integral problems are generally easier to solve correctly than the Non-Integral ones, as evidenced by the data given in Table 4-1 in which there was a difference of 36 percentage points in accuracy between Problem 1 and Problem 2. The data from Ehrlich et al. (1982), shown in Table 4-5, indicated a similar difference

Table 4-5. Percent Correct for Integral and Non-Integral Versions of Equation Generation Problems

		Nonprogrammers ($N=26$)	Programmers ($N=31$)
Generate	Correct Answer	% Correct	% Correct
Non-Integral At Mindy's restaurant for every 4 people who ordered cheesecake, there were 5 people who ordered strudel.	4S = 5C	39%	67%
Integral At a Yankees game for every 3 hot dog sellers there is a Coke seller.	H = 3C	62.5%	68%

Task: Write an equation to represent the statement

between Integral and Non-Integral problems, but only for the nonprogrammers. The programmers found the Non-Integral problems just as easy as the Integral problems. (The interaction between problem complexity and subject group was significant at the .10 level, ANOVA: $F_{1, 55} = 2.85$, $p < 0.10$). Thus, the programmers seem to have found a method for coping with the added complexity of the Non-Integral problems. A method they may have used is the following. Programming teaches students the skill of breaking down a complex problem. By breaking the problem down the student is able to create sub-problems which are easier to solve than the complex whole. In fact, some students use this skill explicitly. For instance, we have seen students who solve the problems by writing their equations as a two step sequence of operations, e.g., $X = C/4$; $S = 5 * X$, instead of as a single equation, i.e., $S = 5/4 * C$.

The second observation we made was that programming gives students practice in writing equations. Moreover in a program, most equations are written in a form in which a single variable is isolated on one side of the equation; for instance, $C = 4/5 * S$. This form of equation may help to break the "set" of associating the number and nearest name on one side of the equation, as exemplified by the equation, $4C = 5S$. This latter equation represents an incorrect solution to Problem 2 in Table 4-1. In the study we gave students partial equations to complete to see whether the form of the equation could induce differences in performance. The set of problems we used and the results are shown in Table 4-6. An analysis of the data from these problems indicated that programmers only did better than nonprogrammers when the equation was presented in the form in which a single variable is isolated on one side of the equation (example A). In this example, the difference between the programmers and nonprogrammers was significant (Chi-squared test: $\chi^2 = 4.03$, $p < 0.05$). Since this is the form used

Table 4-6. Percent Correct Responses for the Equation Completion Problems

Complete the Equation	Equation Given	Correct Answer	Nonprogrammers ($N=26$) % Correct	Programmers ($N=31$) % Correct
A: Single Variable Form of Equation				
When the slot machine at Rosie's bar gives a jackpot, there are 6 nickels for every 5 quarters.	$N = \frac{?}{?} Q$	$N = \frac{6}{5} Q$	35%	61%
B: Ratio Form of Equation				
In Fairmont Hills there are 8 plumbers for every 3 electricians.	$\frac{?}{?} = \frac{P}{E}$	$\frac{8}{3} = \frac{P}{E}$	65%	77%
C: Multiple Form of Equation				
When Elizabeth Taylor goes to Tiffanys she buys 3 rubies for every 2 emeralds.	?R = ?E	2R = 3E	35%	48%

Task: Complete the given equation by replacing the question marks

to write equations for computer programs, we interpret this result as evidence that students who took a programming course learned to write correct equations in the form of a single variable and that they were able to transfer this skill from programming to the domain of algebra word problems.

4.4 *Summary: The Good*

What is it about programming that is responsible for the enhanced problem solving performance? In Soloway, Lockhead, and Clement (1982), we present a number of specific hypotheses about which factors in programming might be responsible for the improved performance. They all come down to one basic issue: the procedurality in programming (input, output, assignment, etc.) provides a model which can be integrated into people's underlying problem solving strategies to facilitate problem solving.

There are two specific implications of our work: for mathematics education and programming language design. With regards to the former, it seems clear to us that a redefinition of what counts as mathematics is in order. In particular, it would seem that the integration of what is now taught as mathematics and what is taught as programming has the potential of producing a synergistic effect on the mathematical literacy of our population. Given the growing incorporation of computers in primary and secondary schools this integration is happening defacto.

Second, our data support the claim that keeping procedurality in programming languages is important, at least for the novice and casual user. That is, the growing trend in programming languages is towards "non-procedural" languages, in which, for example, explicit looping is eliminated. One major motivation behind this trend is the desire to develop languages which are more tractable mathematically. The thought here is that expert programmers can better develop—and analyze—their programs in such a language. While it is not even clear that this type of language will help to alleviate the "software crisis," we think it will be disastrous when applied to novice programmers. If programming languages get to look more and more like algebra, one can bet that fewer and fewer people will master them. Before we lock just plain folk out of computers, as, for the most part, they have been from mathematics, more research is needed into "cognitively appropriate programming languages." We see the above work as a step in that direction.

5. CONCLUDING REMARKS

In this paper, we have focused on the mismatches and matches between what the learner brings to programming and what he is trying to learn. For the *ugly* and *bad* mismatches, we have argued that they can often be remedied by a redesign of the programming language. For the *good* match, we have argued that what counts as mathematics needs to be redefined to include programming notions—if we want people to learn that body of knowledge. Clearly, the work reported here is only a beginning. We need to develop a better understanding of programming—an understanding that goes beyond the syntax and semantics of programming language constructs now being taught—and we need to understand how people understand the notions involved in programming.

REFERENCES

Bonar, J. (1985). *The bugs and misconceptions of novice programmers.* Unpublished Ph.D. dissertation. University of Massachusetts, Amherst.

Bonar, J., & Soloway, E. (1982). *Uncovering principles of novice programming.* SIGPLAN-SIGACT Tenth Symposium on the Principles of Programming Languages, Austin, TX.

Bonar, J., & Soloway, E. (1983). *The Bridge Between Non-Programmer and Programmer.* Baltimore, MD: National Educational Computing Conference.

Clement, J., Lockhead, J., & Monk, G. (1981). Translation difficulties in learning mathematics, *American Mathematical Monthly, 88,* 26–40.

DiSessa, A. A. (1982). Unlearning Aristotelian physics: A study of knowledge-based learning. *Cognitive Science, 6,* 37–75.

Ehrlich, K., & Soloway, E. (1984). An empirical investigation of the tacit plan knowledge in programming. In J. Thomas & M. L. Schneider (Eds.), *Human Factors in Computer Systems.* Norwood, NJ: Ablex.

Ehrlich, K., Soloway, E., & Abbott, V. (1982). *Transfer effects from programming to algebra word problems: A preliminary study.* Technical Report No. 257, Computer Science, Yale University.

Gentner, D. & Stevens, A. (Eds.). (1982). *Mental Models.* Hillsdale, NJ: Erlbaum.

Knuth, D. (1974). Structured programming with GO TO statements. *ACM Computing Surveys, 6(4),* 261–301.

Paige, J., & Simon H. (1966). Cognitive Processes in solving algebra word problems. In B. Kleinmutz (Eds.), *Problem solving: Research, method and theory.* New York: John Wiley and Sons.

Papert, S. (1971). *Teaching Children to be Mathematicians Versus Teaching About Mathematics.* Technical Report No. 249, MIT AI Lab.

Papert, S. (1980). *Mindstorms, Children, Computers and Powerful Ideas.* New York: Basic Books.

Sheppard, S. B., Curtis, B., Milliman, P., & Love, T. (1979). Modern coding practices and programmer performance. *Computer, December,* 41–49.

Soloway, E., Bonar, J., & Ehrlich, K. (1983). Cognitive strategies and looping constructs: An empirical study. *Communications of the ACM, 26,* 853–861.

Soloway, E., Ehrlich, K., Bonar, J., & Greenspan, J. (1982). What do novices know about programming? In A. Badre & B. Shneiderman (Eds.), *Directions in Human-Computer Interactions.* Norwood, NJ: Ablex, Inc.

Soloway, E., Lockhead, J., & Clement, J. (1982). Does computer programming enhance problem solving ability? Some positive evidence on algebra word problems. In R. Seidel, R. Anderson, & B. Hunter (Eds.), *Computer Literacy.* New York: Academic Press.

Wegner, P. (1979). Programming language—concepts and research directions. In P. Wagner (Ed.), *Research Directions in Software Technology.* Cambridge, MA: MIT Press.

Wirth, N. (1974). On the composition of well-structured programs. *ACM Computing Surveys, 6(4),* 247–259.

PART V

LANGUAGE AND THE BRAIN

Chapter 10

The Optimal Level of Abstraction for Models of Cerebral Representation of Language Processes: The State of the Question

Michel Paradis
McGill University

According to Chomsky (1967), "A person who knows a language has represented in his brain some very abstract system of underlying structures, along with an abstract system of rules. . . . Possession of this grammar is a fact which psychology and neurophysiology must ultimately account for" (p. 81). "When a person has command of a language, some information is in some fashion represented in his nervous system" (p. 76).

The question the neurolinguist will then ask is, "What kind of information is represented? And how is it represented in the nervous system?"

Chomsky (1965) tells us on the one hand that competence is a basic component of a performance model, yet, on the other hand, performance is not the use (together with other factors) of a generative grammar as described by the linguist, although a generative grammar is a characterization of competence. That is to say, the generative grammar which describes competence is not a component a speaker-hearer uses to produce sentences.

Many linguists, psycholinguists, and neurolinguists complain that transformational grammar produces a theory of competence so highly abstract that it is difficult to determine how it might relate to psychological and neurological hypotheses. Whitaker (1970), among them, argued that, if the notion of functional equivalence is to have any meaning, some attempts must be made to find levels in the respective models which can be correlated.

Because "competence" is defined in such a way that it is of use only to linguistic theory and that it is virtually impossible to relate it to empirical psycholinguistic investigation, Whitaker (1970) abandoned investigation of competence as a theoretical construct for which empirical evidence might be found.

Bever (1970) even suggested that the relation between transformational grammar and language performance may not just be "abstract" but may be "nonexistent."

Whitaker (1971) argued that competence, to be a useful notion for the neurolinguist, must be a real property of the brain, and as such must be affected by brain damage.

It is not necessary that the linguist's theory of grammar "be consistent with the neurophysiologist's theories" as Katz (1964) demanded, but a neurolinguistic theory certainly must. A neurolinguistic model must be adequate from both linguistic and neurological ends.

It is indeed possible, as Hutchinson (1974) suggested, to study competence without doing neurophysiology. "It is possible to go for the logic of the machine even in ignorance of its physical constitution." That is precisely what theoretical linguists are doing.

But if we are to concern ourselves with neurolinguistics, then a theory of mind is not sufficient. The linguist may investigate the abstract conditions that neural structures must meet, but surely the neurolinguist, in addition, must study what these structures are. If we are to take the search for the physiological basis for language seriously, a number of current metaphors must be made explicit and more clearly defined.

What does it mean, for instance, to say that language functions are lateralized to one or the other hemisphere? What does it mean to say that a particular area of cortex "subserves" a certain language function? What does it mean to be "a neural substrate" for a particular cognitive function? How is linguistic information processing carried out by neural systems? How is language related to its neurophysiological representation?

This latter question is one manifestation of the mind-body problem, as Schnitzer (1978) pointed out. He then went on to ask the question "Is competence a neuropsychologically real component of a normal human mind-brain, or is it merely a fiction abstracted by the analyst from the variety of performances which human beings engage in?" (p. 343). If we are to answer Whitaker's (1974) title question "Is the grammar in the brain?" affirmatively, then competence must refer to the structure of the system in its potential to operate, and performance to the same system with the structure put into operation. Hence neurolinguistic competence, as Schnitzer sees it, is the language system in its static aspect; performance, the (same) language system in its dynamic aspect.

Schnitzer (1978) then went on to reason that, unlike transformational grammar in any of its variants, stratificational grammar is at least compatible with a neurophysiologically plausible model. It would be capable of relating mentalistic descriptions of linguistic phenomena to physical descriptions of neurophysiological phenomena.

Discussing Schnitzer's proposal to use stratificational grammar as an idealized metaphor for relating language and brain, Buckingham (1983) noted that the metaphor implies that the isomorphism relates stratificational networks with neurons in their static structure or with neurons actively firing electrical impulses, but that it cannot be related to networks of protein molecules or other biochemical processes in the nervous system. The metaphor of the impulse can only relate to nervous electrical activity—not to chemical processes, which may very well underlie much language behavior. Buckingham concluded that "the stratificational model offers *only one* type of isomorphism with the brain." (I would personally think that one is better than none.)

This brings us to the question under debate: what is the optimal level of abstraction for models of the representation of language in the brain?

The list of possible levels is indeed extensive. Psycholinguists have concerned themselves with the psychological reality of linguistic theoretical constructs. Their level of investigation is therefore the mind and behavior. The *neuro*linguist on the other hand must concern himself with *the brain.* He may first look at the gross anatomical level such as right vs. left hemisphere, and show that the left hemisphere is involved in language processing in a way that the right is not. This is in fact the level of language–brain correlation first attempted in the middle of the 19th century: Language was a function of the left hemisphere, soon to be localized in specific areas: first Broca's area, (i.e., F_3), and was later extended to include Wernicke's area, T_1 T_2, the angular gyrus, and the supramarginal gyrus.

We still rely on this notion of a hemisphere "subserving" language functions every time we give a Wada test to a patient or a dichotic listening test to a subject in an experimental setting.

More specific localizations have been made possible with electrical stimulation of the brain, and more recently, regional cerebral blood flow studies have allowed to differentiate between areas involved in listening to intelligible speech, speaking spontaneously, reading out loud, or reading silently.

Once we go beyond the representation of some language modality as a whole, we must speak in terms of the representation of grammar or of specific aspects of linguistic structure, at the phonological, morphological, syntactic, and narrowly linguistic semantic levels.

As early as 1931, Arnold Pick was interested in the microgenesis of a sentence, that is, the processes that lead to the production of a sentence from the conception of the message to its acoustic realization. This is surely a legitimate domain of inquiry for the neurolinguist.

One may then ask what is the optimal level of abstraction for models accounting for the microgenesis of a sentence. Is it the physical level of brain matter in terms of electrons? the biochemical level? the physiological level? the level of electrical impulses as picked up by EEG? the anatomical level? or are we to be content with a neurofunctional level?

If language is an emergent property of systems of neurons, as Bunge (1980) would propose, then it seems legitimate to study the physiological basis for language in terms of circuits of neurons if an acceptable isomorphism can be shown to exist between a particular description of competence and a neurophysiologically plausible model. One would be much better off than with a description of grammar so highly abstract that it cannot relate to *any* level of physiological and neurological hypotheses.

In the framework of Bunge's emergentist materialism, the microgenesis of a sentence is regarded as a special biological event. Speech is an external manifestation of specific neural processes. It is some subsystem of the CNS that controls verbal behavior and plans the sentence. The basic functional unit capable of being in a mental state is not a single neuron (let alone a molecule or a biochemical reaction), nor the brain as a whole, but specialized subsystems of the brain. Hence the optimal level for speaking of a microgenesis of a sentence seems to be the level of neural interconnections. Marshall (1982) reproached most models from the 19th century diagram makers to their modern descendents with postulating only two defined levels of representation—a psychological and an anatomical level. This two-level assumption naturally lends itself to accounts in which a one-to-one mapping is postulated between the levels, though on occasion one finds one-to-many or many-to-one mappings.

However, relevant generalizations simply seem to disappear when the mapping between psychology and anatomy is many-to-many. Modern physiology has learned much about the operations of the individual nerve cell, but disconcertingly little about the meaning of the circuits that they compose in the brain.

The first step towards remedying this state of affairs, according to Marshall, is to disavow explicitly a theoretical style in which there are only *two* defined levels of representation, and to insist upon four-level theories:

- At the lowest level, there is the basic component and circuit analysis: how do neurons or synapses work?
- The second level is the study of particular mechanisms: adders, multipliers and memories, these being assemblies made from basic components.
- The third level is that of the algorithm, the schema for a computation;
- and the top level contains the *theory* of the computation.

The contributors to this section each have something to say about each other's work, and have some proposals of their own.

Hopefully after this debate we will be closer to the beginning of an answer to the question: "What is the optimal level of abstraction for models of the representations of language in the brain?" or perhaps the question should be "Is there an optimal level?" Perhaps the answer should be "no." There should perhaps be different levels of abstraction for different purposes. It has been my experience that the question "what is the best way to..." always turned out to be a bad question because it presupposed that there was "the" best way, when in fact there is only "a" best way, given a number of conditions, and another "best way" given a different set of conditions. Let us hope the deliberations of this workshop will throw some light on the question, or at least on the way it should be formulated.

REFERENCES

Bever, T. G. (1970). The cognitive basis for linguistic structures. In J. R. Hayes (Ed.), *Cognition and the development of language.* New York: Wiley.

Buckingham, H. W., Jr. (1983). Biological perspectives on language: An argument for psychological parallelism. In S. K. Ghosh (Ed.), *Human language—Biological perspectives.* Ghent, Belgium: E. Story-Scientia.

Bunge, M. (1980). *The mind-body problem.* Oxford, England: Pergamon.

Chomsky, N. (1965). *Aspects of the theory of syntax.* Cambridge: MA: MIT Press.

Chomsky, N. (1967). The general properties of language. In C. H. Millikan & F. L. Darley (Eds.), *Brain mechanisms underlying speech and language* (73-88). New York: Grune & Stratton.

Hutchinson, L. G. (1974). Grammar as theory. In D. Cohen (Ed.), *Explaining linguistic phenomena.* Washington, DC: Hemisphere.

Katz, J. (1964). Mentalism in linguistics. *Language, 40,* 124–137.

Marshall, J. (1982). What is a symptom-complex? In N. A. Arbib, D. Caplan, & J. C. Marshall, (Eds.), *Neural models of language processes* (389–409). New York: Academic Press.

Pick, A. (1931). Aphasie. In A. Bethe et al. (Eds.), *Handbook der normalen und pathologischen Psychologie* (Vol. 15, pt 2, pp. 1416-1524). Berlin.

Whitaker, H. A. (1970). A model for neurolinguistics. *Occasional Papers, 10,* Language Center, University of Essex, Colchester.

Whitaker, H. A. (1971). *On the representation of language in the human brain.* Edmonton, Canada: Linguistic Research.

Whitaker, H. A. (1974). Is the grammar in the brain? In D. Cohen (Ed.), *Explaining linguistic phenomena.* Washington, DC: Hemisphere.

Chapter 11

A Plea for Neutral Monism from Aphasiology

Marc L. Schnitzer

University of Puerto Rico

I would like to talk about an approach to the problem of cerebral representation of language which involves a philosophical position regarding the mind–body problem, which has been called "neutral monism." Neutral monism, as many of you may know, has been rejected somewhat out of hand by Mario Bunge (Bunge, 1980).

The position may be stated thus: Mind-state descriptions and brain-state descriptions are essentially two ways of describing the same thing. What has bothered many people about this position is: What is this "same thing" that they are supposed to be two different descriptions of? There must be some *thing* of which they are two descriptions. That has been one of the major problems for neutral monism. What I'd like to suggest today is that, by adopting a position which has been called "structural realism," we can say that the thing which they are two descriptions of is something called a "structure."

Let us first consider a paradigm case of a structure—a musical composition, a tune, let's say. A tune can be represented on a piece of paper on a staff with written notes, it can be represented by being played in a certain key on a certain instrument, it can be represented in other keys on other instruments, it can be represented in various kinds of scoring, etc. And the physical properties of the various representations do not have very much in common. What they do have in common is a certain structure. In other words, if you listen to "La Borinqueña" played on a Moog synthesizer, or if you hear it played by the Boston Pops, in two different keys, in very different harmonic and rhythmic arrangements, nonetheless, what they have in common is the structure of "La Borinqueña." A structure can be more or less rigid. You can play "La Borinqueña" with a lot of mistakes and it will still be recognizable as "La Borinqueña" up to a certain point. You can write it with mistakes, and it will still be recognizable up to a point. What that point will be will depend on various factors including the structure itself, the (more or less deformed) representation, and the recognizer. "La Borinqueña" is in fact a good case in point. Originally written as a *danza* (a popular or semi-classical Puerto Rican musical form with a characteristic rhythm) in the nineteenth century, when it became the national hymn of Puerto Rico, its rhythm was changed to that of a march. Significant harmonic changes were introduced as well. Nonetheless, anyone who has heard only the danza will immediately recognize the structure in the national hymn, and vice versa.

What I would like to argue here today is that mentalistic terminology and neurophysiological terminology are two vocabularies used in two different ways of describing a single complex structure which we call language. I don't intend to try to present a model of the mind per se, just a model (or rather a proposal for the development of a model) of the mind as it functions linguistically.

I have for some time been arguing for an approach called stratificational grammar (Schnitzer, 1978, 1982). What I find interesting about stratificational grammar is that, unlike other linguistic models, it has no items and it has no processes. It has pure relationships only. And they are the kind of elementary relationships that we know the brain must be able to handle even apart from language: namely conjunction, disjunction, precedence, and direction. A stratificational representation of language consists of a network of interrelations. And all of them are interconnected by these principles. We can think of a stratificational diagram either statically or dynamically. If we think of it dynamically, we can imagine impulses going either up (in the direction of cognition) or down (in the direction of phonology or other mode of expression. It should be emphasized that these "impulses" are not to be equated in any way with neuronal impulses.). Thus (see Fig. 1), in a downward ordered AND, an impulse coming from above will result in two impulses continuing downward, one occurring before the other. An impulse reaching a downward-ordered OR from above will result in one impulse continuing downward, with preference being given to the one on the left. An impulse arriving at a downward-*un*ordered AND will result in two impulses not ordered temporally.[1]

And we can say essentially the same thing with respect to the upward direction: for example, in order for an impulse to continue downward through an *up*ward AND, both impulses would have to enter the node from

[1] Figures 1, 2, and 3 originally appeared in Schnitzer (1982) as figures 12.1, 12.2, and 12.4, on pages 247, 248, and 266, respectively. They are reproduced herein with permission of Academic Press, Inc.

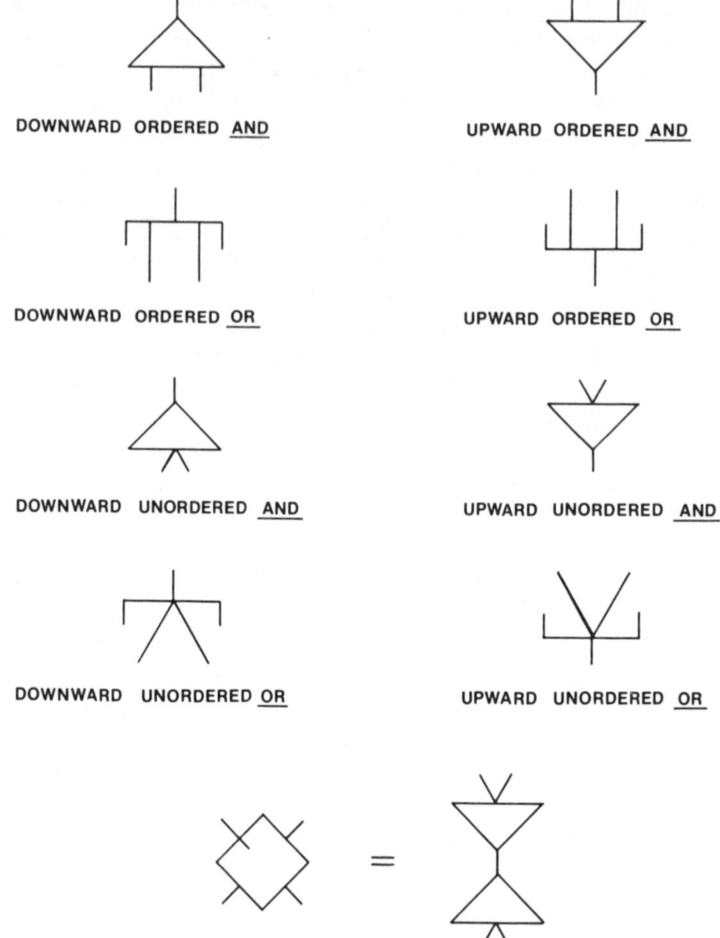

Figure 1

above (the left one first if it were an *ordered* AND). If we were looking at impulses going up, then, if an impulse entered an upward AND, two upward impulses would result (the left one first in the case of an ordered AND).

In stratificational grammar, downward impulses represent the encoding process and upward impulses represent the decoding/understanding/interpretation process.

This is just a way of looking at stratificational relationships dynamically, but the structure is there statically as well: The relationships are implicit in the structure, whether there are any impulses passing through it or not. Stratificational grammar is so called because it contains various strata which represent various aspects of language structure/processing. Various researchers in the field have defined various strata, and there is not too much agreement as to the number of strata appropriate for a description of a given language. In a typical case, we may define six strata, going from the highest to the lowest, higher being closer to cognition and lower being closer to expression.

The highest stratum, called "*hypersememic*" or "cognitive," is a level which is not strictly-speaking linguistic. It supposedly includes the cognitive structure with which the linguistic system interacts.

The next stratum is known as *sememic*. It includes basic predicational and thematic relations (or "deep cases"), logical form, focus, topic, and the like.

Then we have the *lexemic* stratum, which deals with basic word order in different types of clause structure, essentially what is normally thought of as syntax in a traditional sense.

Next comes the *morphemic* stratum: inflectional morphology and productive derivational morphology, and perhaps some morphophonemics.

The *phonemic* stratum includes syllable, cluster, and segment structures, contrast, certain alternations as well as phonological feature composition.

Finally, the *phonetic* stratum would include nondistinctive phonetic specification. Some have noted that this stratum (like the highest one) may not be strictly-speaking linguistic.

A typical array of strata would include these—perhaps more, perhaps fewer. As I mentioned, the lexemic structure deals with phenomena which have traditionally been called 'syntactic.' This latter term is not applied to the lexemic stratum by stratificationalists, however, since one of the salient features of stratificational grammar is that *each* stratum has a tactic pattern. Each stratum is thus related to the stratum above it and to the one below it by the realizational patterns; and in addition, the tactic pattern of each stratum describes the structures that are possible within that stratum.

For example, Figure 2 represents a fragment of English clause structure which generates forms such as *Why do you...?, Why do you not...?, Why don't you...?, Why can't you...?, Why can you not...?, Why will they not...?, Why won't they...?, Why don't they...?, Why don'tcha...?, Why can'tcha...?, Why won'tcha...?,* etc., and even *Why'n'cha...?*.

At the top of this diagram, we find the lexemes which participate in these forms. It is important to note that these labels (WHY, DO, WILL, CAN, etc.) are not part of the stratificational network: they are merely written there for our convenience. In other words, the stratificational network contains nothing except the nine symbols of Figure 1 plus the lines connecting them in Figure 2. So it is a representation with pen and paper of a structure of relationships only, without any items. What makes the lexeme WILL be "will" is that its realization at the phonetic stratum is [w ɪ: ɫ], and in the up-

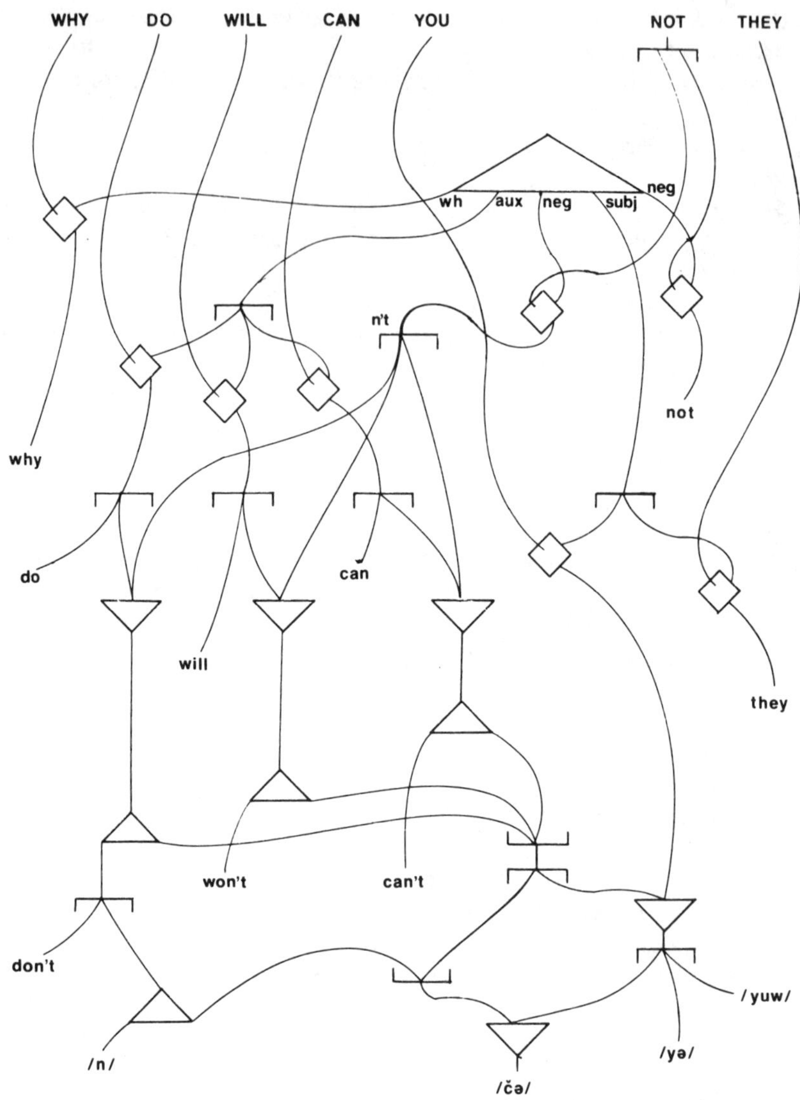

Figure 2

ward direction, this lexeme is ultimately interpreted cognitively as meaning 'will.' But there is no item 'WILL.' All we have is a system of connexions. For more detailed explanation, see Schnitzer (1982).

What I would like to claim, now that we understand something of this stratificational model, is that, if language can in some way be represented using a stratificational approach, then the model can be used as a representation of the neurophysiological description as well as the mentalistic linguistic description (at the appropriate level of analysis).

Since the only things represented in stratificational networks are precedence relationships, OR, AND, and direction, all of which we know the brain must be capable of handling anyway, it seems that there should not be too much difficulty incorporating these relations into some kind of real microlevel neurological process model, because we know the human brain to be capable of dealing with such relations. Similarly, when we talk about this in linguistic terms, we are using a mentalistic vocabulary. When we say that something is a lexeme, for example, or that it's a morpheme, or a phoneme, what we're doing is using a mentalistic vocabulary and effectively attributing to those entities a mentalistic existence. But in the structure itself, these elements do not exist as such. In the structure per se, there is nothing inherent about what is going on neurophysiologically, and there is nothing inherently mentalistic either: the neurophysiological and the mentalistic descriptions are just that—descriptions.

Nevertheless, it seems to me, neutral monism notwithstanding, that along with the approach I have been advocating, there may be some *emergent* properties. Examples of such emergent properties might be linguistic entities—forms, categories, features, and structures—considered in themselves. That is, normally we use linguistic structures for communicating and for understanding the communications of others without considering the linguistic structures qua linguistic structures. Our distinction between dynamic and static interpretations of stratificational networks deals with whether we are talking about impulses going through it, dynamically, or whether we are talking about the network itself as it stands, without considering the passage of impulses.

But when we consider linguistic entities metalinguistically, for example grammaticality judgments, what is it we do? We take a product of this linguistic system and we consider it as something outside of ourselves. So we now have in a sense created a mental entity which is no longer part of the neutral mind-body system per se, and we "reconsider" it. What is it that we do when we judge grammaticality? We try to put the form being judged through this network, in order to see if it fits. But the thing we are judging at that point has really got only a *mental* existence. So we must admit of a separate mental entity even though there is no separate mental substance as such. It is merely a product of the system whose output is being thus "reconsidered."

So linguistic forms considered in themselves constitute an example of an emergent mental property. There may be other sorts of metalinguistic tasks besides grammaticality judgment which give rise to emergent mental entities in this sense of taking outputs of the system and "reconsidering" them, i.e., putting them back into the system in a kind of external artificial way. So we can now talk about a kind of "interactionism." Certain products of the mind (e.g., sentences) interact with the unified mind-body as though they were separate entities. When a person considers the output of his own mind or of some else's mind in this way, there is an interaction between the mental entity and the unified monistic system, i.e., the person's mind-brain.

On the basis of neurolinguistic evidence, I have tried to argue that the lexemic and the morphemic strata ought to be collapsed (Schnitzer, 1982). The lexemic system deals with word order and the morphemic deals with morphology. But let us now consider two hypothetical Broca's aphasics. (Actually one is not hypothetical, but the other *is,* since I have not encountered an appropriate subject.)

A Spanish speaking Broca's aphasic, if he were speaking correctly, would say the word *irías* (you (familiar) would go) under certain conditions. Morphologically, this form consists of *ir-* (go), *-ía-* (conditional tense-aspect), plus *-s* (second person singular). In a situation in which *irías* would have been an appropriate thing to say, a Broca's aphasic produced the form *yendo,* which is the present participle (gerund) of the word for *go.* So what we have is a reduction in morphological structure—an error in morphology. Clearly, an English-speaking Broca's aphasic doesn't have a corresponding morphology there to break down, since English deals with the semantic content syntactically. So it seems that, if we are going to try to relate functionally the linguistic system with the neurophysiological system, then an English speaker with the same problem as a Spanish speaker would have to have a dissolution which we would have to call syntactic—or in stratificational jargon "lexemic." A comparable Anglophone aphasic would say something such as 'go' or 'going'—a reduction from 'I would go.'

So we would have to conclude that, if we have separate lexemic and morphemic strata in our model, then what happens in the case of the English-speaking aphasic is a problem involving the lexemic level, whereas in the case of the Hispanophone, it is to be considered a morphemic-level difficulty. This is rather peculiar. It forces us to say that the same type of neuropathology affects one aspect of language in speakers of language X and a different aspect of language in speakers of language Y. It seems to me that if one were going to, as Jason Brown (1977, p. 2) says, let the "symptoms...be the mortar of the psychology," then one would have to say that what we have here in these two cases is the same aspect of language, and that therefore, there should not be a difference between these two strata in our linguistic descriptions. In fact, stratificationalists have argued about whether there is a distinction between these strata and have not been able to decide what constitutes sufficient evidence to decide the issue. What I would like to argue is that, if we adopt a neutral monist approach in which the linguistic system and the physical system are considered to be two descriptions of the same phenomenon, then, if we encounter a linguistic dissolution due to neuropathology, we are going to have to say that it is the same dissolution regardless of the particular language involved. So I conclude that there is but one stratum involved, which I will henceforth call "morpholexemic".

At this point, I'd like to say a word or two about competence and performance. Unfortunately, the vocabulary of Western languages is such that one cannot find a neutral vocabulary in which to advocate a neutral position. We are chained to a dualistic lexicon. Be that as it may, what I wish to say is that the structure I am calling 'language' has a physical and a mentalistic description. And in both of these one can distinguish competence from performance. Under either description, what I mean by *competence* is having that structure (= having that network). So if one is a nonnative speaker who makes competence errors, it means that there is something in that structure (i.e., stratification network) which is different from a native speaker's. (By competence errors, I mean those errors which are not recognized to be errors by the speaker, upon reflection.)

Native speakers presumably (in fact, *definitionally*) do not make competence errors; but they do make performance errors of various kinds. What would constitute a performance error from a stratificational-network perspective? One example might be an upward OR node in which a downward impulse entered the node but the node did not pass the impulse on downward; or an upward AND node in which only one of the two required impulses descended upon the node, with the impulse being passed on downward anyway. So we can see that although in germs of idealized networks, everything is described in terms of EITHER-OR—BOTH-AND, in fact what is really going on is rather "squishy" (cf. Ross 1972, 1973, 1974). This squishiness could be handled by neurophysiological models which incorporated electrical interactions and/or chemical interactions, or even by certain holistic approaches in various ways (e.g., Pribram 1971). The main point is that in performance, we are going to find squishiness around these stratificational nodes, dynamically considered: We are going to find things going off when they shouldn't and things not going off when they should. And these will be realized as performance errors, as distinguished from competence errors. We can define the latter as differences between the network structure of the speaker who makes the error and the network structure of a native speaker.

I think that there is some evidence for identifying (in a loose way) Broca's area with the morpholexemic stratum, and Wernicke's area with the sememic stratum. At least there is evidence for the former. And the latter seems plausible in the context of the evidence for the former.

Various researches published over the years have shown that morpholexemic-type functions—morphology, superficial grammatical forms and relations in general—tend to be preserved in Wernicke's aphasia, whereas more basic predicational relations tend to be disturbed; and that in Broca's aphasia, basic sememic predicational relationships are preserved, and more superficial morphological and syntactic functions, tend to be disrupted in both input and output tasks.

A Spanish speaking Broca's aphasic in a 15-minute discourse produced 18 verbs, of which 11 were correct forms used correctly. Of the 7 incorrect forms, 5 were either gerunds or infinitives where a tensed verb was required.

Figure 3 is a fragment of a relational network for Spanish, which contains the relevant parts of the sememic and morpholexemic strata of the sentence *Ellas hablaron* (They (fem.) spoke (perfective)). Let us consider the patient's errors in terms of the network fragment presented in this figure. The first error (*preguntando* for *pregunta*), a gerund in place of a tensed verb would seem to leave out material from the sememic level, for example tense, aspect, mode, and number. Nonetheless, all this information was retrievable, pragmatically, from the context of the discourse. So it would not be incorrect to attribute this error to a problem at the level of morpholexemic realization. The same point can be made regarding the patient's three other errors involving substitution of gerunds or infinitives for tensed verbs (*encontrando* for *encuentra, escribiendo* for *escribe,* and *encontrar* for *encuentra*). The remaining errors (*dice* (sg.) when *dicen* (pl.) was expected, /empyese/ instead of *empieza,* and */komprer/ instead of *comprar*) shall now be considered. Although the use of the singular *dice* instead

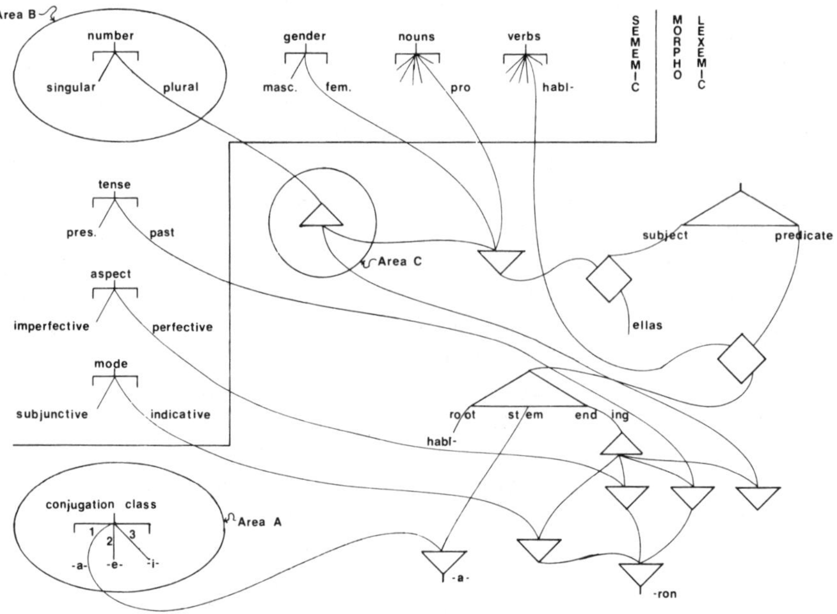

Figure 3

of the plural *dicen* may appear to be a sememic error involving the category of number (as indicated in Area B in Figure 3), in fact the sentence had a plural subject: hence, we may conclude that the patient committed an error not in number *assignment* but in number *agreement,* a morpholexotactic phenomenon (Area C). Instead of *comprar,* the patient said */komprer/, which could be attributable to the morpholexemic stratum (Area A); there seems to be no possible interpretation of this mistake in terms of any higher strata. The error of /empyese/ for *empieza* could be considered a sememic one of mode (subjunctive instead of indicative), but the error of */komprer/ for *comprar,* just noted, makes the attribution of this error to Area A of the morpholexemic stratum as well a more plausible interpretation. These last two may indeed have been mere phonemic paraphasias.

In summary, all the errors can be interpreted as morpholexemic rather than as sememic in nature. I have not intended this example to serve as any kind of conclusive evidence, but merely an illustration of the approach and of why I believe it to have some degree of plausibility.

The basic question is, of course, how the stratificational relational network may be represented in the brain. This is really an open question. But the basic elements and principles of stratificational grammar are very simple operations which we know not only that the human brain can handle, but that virtually any representational system of any degree of sophistication would be capable of handling.

This model may not be correct. The brain may deal with language in terms other than ANDs and ORs and precedence. But if the brain does deal with language in this way, it seems that we do not have to worry about micro-level neurophysiological events. Anyway, as noted above, dynamically speaking, linguistic performance is squishy, so we will find that native speakers make mistakes in speaking and have unclear judgments of acceptability.

As a final note on stratificational grammar, I should like to respond to Mario Bunge's criticism that there can be no relations without relata, as follows: It is true that stratificational grammar purports to have no items or processes, but rather relations only. That is because it represents a structure only. But if one accepts a structural realist position, the relata are mentalistic under one description and physical under another description. What these two decriptions share is not their relata, but rather their relations.

Implicit in stratificational grammar is the notion of hierarchy. The relational network is, after all, a hierarchy of strata. Many people who have discussed language, going back to Hughlings Jackson, have spoken about hierarchies. Jason Brown (1977) speaks about four levels of cognition:

1. Sensorimotor, which he ties to the subcortical level,
2. Presentational, which is limbic,

3. Representational, which is neocortical, and
4. Symbolic, which is asymmetric (=internalized) neocortical.

Alike in spirit, but on a different level, is Lamendella's work on the limbic system (1977), in which he discusses different limbic levels: appetitive, affective, and volitional. The neopallial system exercises control over these lower levels.

The two approaches, although they involve hierarchical structure, don't really come to grips with the actual data of language. One approach which does not deal directly with the neuronantomy or the neurophysiology but is related nonetheless to these approaches is that of Givón (1979), in which he talks about three different modes of communicative behavior: monopropositional, pragmatic, and syntactic.

The monopropositional mode applies typically to communication among canines, pongids, and human babies, as well as to that of normal adult speakers under various kinds of unusual circumstances.

The pragmatic mode is the mode that is found in pidgins. As pidgins develop into creoles, they develop in the direction of syntactic mode. The pragmatic mode is the mode found in early language development. When children first begin to talk, they use the pragmatic mode before developing the syntactic mode. In the pragmatic mode there is a tendency to use topic-comment structure, whereas in the syntactic mode, subject-predicate structure predominates. The pragmatic mode tends to make use of loose conjunction of linguistic elements, as compared to the tight subordination of the syntactic mode. In addition to its use in child language and pidgins (both primitive forms of language), Givón believes that the pragmatic mode represents the probable *origin* of language.

Slow rate of delivery characterizes the pragmatic mode, as does word order governed by the principle of old and new information (old first, new last)—in comparison with the syntactic mode, whose word order is governed by thematic and semantic relations. In the pragmatic mode, there is a high ratio of verbs to nouns in comparison with the syntactic mode. In the pragmatic mode there is practically no use of grammatical morphology, the latter being a salient feature of the syntactic mode. Finally, prominent intonation and stress mark focus and new information in the pragmatic mode. These are not used as much in the syntactic mode.

In addition to these basic features of these two communicative modes, Givón talks about a process of morphologicization in the syntactic mode, a tendency for syntactic elements to be cliticized into morphological ones. There is then a further tendency in the syntactic mode for the morphological elements to be gradually eroded by phonological reduction, which then necessitates the introduction of new syntactic elements—presumably to preserve intelligibility and prevent loss of information.

We can see an example of this latter phenomenon in contemporary Romance languages. More conservative Romance languages do not require subject pronouns, whereas modern French does, because a lot of the morphological endings have disappeared (in spoken French). The pronouns have thus been reintroduced in order to prevent ambiguity. So we see that this is a cyclic phenomenon, which can also be seen in progress in those dialects of modern Spanish which elide final /s/ (such as Cuban, Dominican, Puerto Rican, and coastal Venezuelan). In second person singular verb forms (which are marked by final /s/) there is a noted tendency to use an overt pronoun to avoid ambiguity in these dialects.

Draizar (1982) has recently used the Givón communicative continuum to look at the process of recovery in aphasia. In so doing, she has studied the performance of two groups of aphasics, both of which performed a picture-description task and a free-discourse "task". Both groups were subjected to Melodic Intonation Therapy (Sparks, Helm, & Albert, 1974), which is essentially a deblocking technique in which the patient begins by singing a melody along with the therapist, and then gradually has to do it himself. Words are then added. Finally, the melody is changed to a normal intonation pattern.

The difference between the two subject groups was that one used an ordered narrative structure context for the sentences used in the Melodic Intonation Therapy, whereas the other group did Melodic Intonation Therapy with arbitrary sentences.

All the patients had temporal lobe lesions. The majority also had frontal involvement. The approach I have been advocating in this talk would predict that the evolution of these aphasics from the pragmatic to the syntactic mode over time would be more pronounced among those patients with frontal lesions. Unfortunately, the performances of those patients with frontal lesions were not measured separately from those of the rest of the patients in the two groups. Nonetheless, the evolution of the communicative function of all the patients over 15 weeks of therapy was in the direction of pragmatic mode to syntactic mode, as measured in terms of the following categories:

1. Quantity of verbalization.
2. Word order (topic-comment vs. subject-verb(-object))
3. Syntactic complexity (pragmatic conjunction vs. syntactic subordination)
4. Noun-to-verb ratio (pragmatic $N \leqq V$ vs. syntactic $N > V$)
5. Use of grammatical morphemes (greater in syntactic mode)
6. Use of anaphora (greater in syntactic mode)
7. Intonation pattern (more cohesive with increased syntacticization).

Results of the comparison of the aphasics' performances before and after the 15-week therapy program showed evolution in the direction of pragmatic to syntactic mode. They were significant (ANOVA) for the factors of word order ($p = .03$), complexity ($p = .005$), and N:V ratio ($p = .025$). There were other interesting significant interactions found in this study, not directly relevant to the present discussion.

What is the significance of these results for the approach I have been advocating. We see a general trend among all the subjects in Draizar's study of evolution from the use of the pragmatic mode to greater use of the syntactic mode, which in stratificational terms can be described as evolution from the use of sememic representation without appropriate morpholexemic encoding, to the greater use of morpholexemic structure. Thus, in terms of stratificational representations, the therapy can be viewed as retraining the aphasic to make greater use of the morpholexemic stratum (which I have identified with Broca's Area). It doesn't mean that it's necessarily Broca's Area that is being retrained. Nonetheless, the retraining, in teaching the patient to use morpholexemic structures, presents evidence of movement from the pragmatic mode (sememic stratum) to the syntactic mode (morpholexemic stratum). Parallels can be seen of course, with other hierarchical approaches.

REFERENCES

Brown, J. (1977). *Mind, brain, and consciousness.* New York: Academic Press.

Bunge, M. (1980). *The mind-body problem.* Oxford: Pergamen Press.

Draizar, A. (1982). *Rapid linguistic recovery from aphasia.* Unpublished doctoral dissertation. University Park: Pennsylvania State University, Linguistics Program.

Givón, T. (1979). *On understanding grammar.* New York: Academic Press.

Lamendella, J. T. (1977). The limbic system in human communication. In H. Whitaker & H. A. Whitaker (Eds.), *Studies in neurolinguistics* (Vol. 3). New York: Academic Press.

Pribram, K. H. (1971). *Languages of the brain.* Englewood Cliffs, NJ: Prentice-Hall.

Ross, J. R. (1972). The category squish: Endstation Hauptwort. In P. M. Peranteau, J. N. Levi, & G. C. Phares (Eds.), *Papers from the eighth regional meeting, Chicago Linguistic Society.* Chicago: Chicago Linguistic Society.

Ross, J. R. (1973). A fake NP squish. In C.-J. N. Bailey & R. Shuy (Eds.), *New ways of analyzing variation in English.* Washington, DC: Georgetown University Press.

Ross, J. R. (1974). There, there, (there, (there, (there, . . .))). In M. W. La Galy, R. A. Fox, & A. Bruck (Eds.), *Papers from the tenth regional meeting, Chicago Linguistic Society.* Chicago: Chicago Linguistic Society.

Schnitzer, M. L. (1978). Toward a neurolinguistic theory of language. *Brain and Language, 6,* 342–361.

Schnitzer, M. L. (1982). The translational hierarchy of language. In M. A. Arbib, D. Caplan, & J. C. Marshall (Eds.), *Neural Models of language processes.* New York: Academic Press.

Sparks, R., Helm, N., & Albert, M. (1974). Aphasia rehabilitation resulting from melodic intonation therapy. *Cortex, 10,* 303–316.

Chapter 12

Language, the Mind, and Psychophysical Parallelism*

Hugh W. Buckingham, Jr.
Louisiana State University

INTRODUCTION

In this chapter I will treat some recurrent issues concerning the mind/body interface. My thesis is that psychological descriptions of mind are different from physiological descriptions of the brain, and that the methodology of language description and explanation is primarily a psychological one, subject to linguistic and psycholinguistic exigencies. I will also suggest that much of the present thinking on the subject reduces to at least a methodological dualism, and that this dualism takes on the flavor of the philosophical position of psychophysical parallelism. In addition I will briefly touch on some issues relating to cerebral localization of function.

METHODOLOGY AND POSITIONS ON MIND-BRAIN

Given Mario Bunge's (1977, p. 505; 1980a, p. 4; 1980b, p. 3) outline of the many views on the mind/body problem, psychophysical theory could take one of ten positions—five monistic, five dualistic. Scientists adopt this or that stand (or some combination of stands) not because they are interested so much in mind/brain theory as such, but rather because they have already adopted a certain methodology, which is not to say however that anyone necessarily believes that one can argue from a particular methodological

* I would like to thank Professor Carolyn R. Morillo of the Department of Philosophy at the University of New Orleans, New Orleans, LA, for her very kind and extremely helpful comments on an earlier version of this paper. Her remarks have helped me refine and clarify many of the nuances of the various philosophical positions on the problem of mind and brain discussed in this paper. Any ambiguities, vaguenesses, and egregious misunderstandings which may remain are entirely the responsibility of the author.

commitment to an ontological commitment or specific philosophical theory. For this reason, few if any cognitive psychologists opt for eliminative or reductive materialism, and few neuroscientists opt for phenomenalism. As an example, there is reason to believe that the 19th century British neurologist, John Hughlings Jackson, whose work had a significant impact on Sigmund Freud, developed his view of psychophysical parallelism as a personal heuristic for doing neurology and for talking about cerebral localization of function. In fact, Jackson's motivations were so clearly related to his methodologic heuristic, that he wrote that should his doctrine of concomitance turn out to be false, it should be provisionally accepted in any event as an artifice (Englehardt, 1975). The theory of "concomitance" is actually a weak form of the doctrine of psychophysical parallelism. It is a minimal empirical claim to the effect that we in fact often find some correlations between psychological states or events (defined pre-theoretically) and neurological states or events. This, in turn, is simply to say that the brain and central nervous system are the relevant underlying organs. If we had no correlations at all of this sort, there would be no more reason to study the brain than the kidney or the elbow. The strong version of psychophysical parallelism is a philosophical theory that claims that there actually are two ontologically distinct kinds of states and events—mental and physical, with no causal interaction because the two kinds are so radically distinct. In any event, it would appear that scientists whose wording on the mind-brain issue looks like psychophysical parallelism are essentially taking the weaker version.

More recently, the philosopher Ian Hacking (1982) has compared Wittgenstein and Descartes. Hacking writes that, "There is a whole domain of descriptions about how one feels thirsty, sees trees, grieves [to which I would add "knows his language"] and so forth, where one would be making some sort of conceptual error to ask for explanations of a materialistic sort" (p. 44). Hacking claims that, "This is the important sense in which Wittgenstein and Descartes are equally dualistic" (p. 44). Consequently, on Hacking's view, both of these philosphers, "hold that psychology requires forms of description and methodology quite different from those called for in natural science" (p. 42).

Still others have adopted positions that draw upon both monism and dualism. Arturo Rosenbleuth (1970), for example, is a monist who supports a double aspect theory. He writes that, "a mental process and the neurophysiological phenomena that underlie it represent two different aspects of a single event" (p. 114). For Bunge, this position would represent a psychoneural monism, where the physical and the psychological are so many aspects or manifestations of a single entity. However, Rosenbleuth claims that his philosophy is dualistic. He writes, "My philosophy is dualistic, in that I assert on the one hand the existence of our mental processes and on the other that of a material universe which determines the physical processes that develop in our brains'' (p. 114).

NEUROLINGUISTICS/LINGUISTICS

Let me now turn to the methodology of neurolinguistics and of linguistics and to the question of what it means to study language and the brain. William Orr Dingwall and Harry Whitaker (1978) and John Lamendella (1979) have outlined the many areas of neurolinguistics, most of which concern either linguistic analyses of language breakdown in aphasia or manipulative studies of brain function. To date, however, these data have had minimal impact on the methodology of constructing and verifying linguistic theories of competence, largely because models of normative function of language must be defensible according to existing criteria in linguistics and psycholinguistics (Caplan, 1981, p. 134), not neurolinguistics. Furthermore, as Hutchinson (1974) explains, ''trying to find out what a person knows in knowing a language does not necessitate doing neurophysiology. This is not to say that neurophysiology is bad, nor that it is irrelevant, but only that it is possible to go for the logic of the machine even in ignorance of its physical constitution'' (p. 48).

Noam Chomsky (1957, 1965, 1975, 1980, 1981a, 1982, forthcoming) has developed a linguistic theory of competence to explain a system of knowledge about language. It is a theory about the mind rather than the brain. It is not a theory of ''mind/brain'' in any direct sense. Chomsky's ''Generative Grammar'' (referred to nowadays as Government and Binding) models an autonomous system (modular) that is purported to have a mental reality and to be part of our biological endowment. Chomsky considers that the faculty of language is a separate and autonomous system, subject to a highly specific set of rules and representations that account exclusively for language and no other cognitive system. In this sense, Chomsky would claim that the human language system is modular and involves strict information encapsulation, a point he has argued with John Searle for many years. Since certain sentences, however, ''take some thought'' to correctly interpret binding relations, Chomsky (forthcoming) would disagree with Fodor (1983) on the requirement that modules operate extremely fast and reflex-like. In fact, Chomsky (forthcoming) claims that Fodor's (1983) view of the language module as an input system is too narrow. It would appear that Chomsky wants language to interact more with central systems in Fodor's sense, but at the same time remain informationally encapsulated and structured.

Although at first blush Chomsky would appear to be a mentalist in the extreme, he has never denied that there is a physical representation in the brain of linguistic competence. In fact his belief in some ultimate physical representation for language together with his view that the linguistic system is modular place him tantalizingly close to the 19th century phrenologist, Franz-Joseph Gall, who held that human cognition was modular and that there was something very specific in the neurophysiology that could completely explain mental phenomena. For such materialism he was thrown out of Vienna in 1802 by decree of Emperor Francis I and excommunicated by Pope Pius VII in 1817. Although Chomsky would not be affected in the slightest by excommunication, it is to be hoped that he will not be run out of Cambridge for his beliefs in a "new organology" (Marshall, 1980, pps. 23-25). His ultimate reductionism placed to one side, Chomsky insists vehemently that it is the responsibility of the linguist to specify the abstract condition that neural structures must meet. He readily admits to having nothing at all to say about what those structures must or might be.

I should point out that embracing mentalism obviously does not force one into a strict dualist position (Fodor, 1968, 1975). Chomsky has written (1965) that, "The mentalist. . .need make no assumption about the possible physiological basis for the reality that he studies. In particular, he need not deny that there is such a basis" (p. 193). He goes on to observe that, "it is the mentalistic studies that will ultimately be of greatest value for the investigation of neurophysiological mechanisms, since they (the mentalistic studies) alone are concerned with determining, abstractly, the properties that such mechanisms must exhibit and the functions they must perform" (p. 193). For all his faith in ultimate physical explanation, Chomsky is not likely to turn to neurophysiology for explaining the mysteries of human language. He has even demonstrated a certain skepticism with regard to the use of data from aphasia—one of the primary sources of neurolinguistic data. He writes (1981b) that "There is some reason to believe that a divorce between grammatical competence and conceptual systems, and between grammatical and pragmatic competence, may be observed to a degree in certain pathological contexts, though here one must be cautious, as nature's experiments are not well designed for purposes of inquiry" (p. 11). Taken to its logical conclusion, this statement would cast serious doubt on many of the findings from neuropsychology, since those findings are based on a methodology that analyzes behavioral disruptions secondary to nervous system damage in order to ultimately understand normal behavior.

Chomsky (1975) follows similar lines of reasoning, in claiming that, "the study of language is part of a more general enterprise: to map out in detail the structure of the mind" (p. 86). Concerning his own methodological niche, he goes on to say that, "we might continue to regard a grammar as a separable component of this more general system and proceed to investigate its specific properties" (p. 86). Again, the investigation of the grammarian is (Chomsky, 1975), "to specify the possible rules, their organization, and the conditions on their application" (p. 90). Chomsky is insistent in maintaining that there is simply no way to learn anything of significance about grammar except to maintain a competence-performance distinction incorporating the concept of the "ideal speaker-hearer" with the clear understanding that "idealization and abstraction are unavoidable in serious inquiry" (1975, p. 86).

Jerrold Katz (1964) used to claim (but no longer would, see Katz, 1981) that mentalistic linguistic theories are like psychological theories in that they must be, "consistent with the neurophysiologist's theories concerning the type of existing brain mechanisms" (p. 134). Furthermore, he used to believe that one could refute a linguistic theory if one found, "neurophysiological accounts which described brain structure in a way that precludes the linguistic theory from being isomorphic to any of the structures in the human brain" (p. 134). I believe that the best we can hope for in our search for isomorphism is that we will ultimately find some way to "map" clearly from mentalistic to physicalistic descriptive terminology. As John Marshall has recently written (1980), "some way surely has to be found in which results phrased in the languages of linguistics, psychology, and physiology can be made to bear upon each other" (p. 25). There are tremendous problems, however, in getting the scientific jargons of the mental and physical sciences to bear upon one another. The remainder of this chapter will treat various of these problems.

The isomorphism between linguistic models and brain structure is elusive indeed; it need not be restricted to branching neural networks, for instance. The isomorphism could relate to some possible network of new relations among protein molecules or some entities each of which consists of a number of neurons. Marc Schnitzer (1978) provided some arguments for incorporating the stratificational linguistic model as an "idealized metaphor" for relating language and the brain. The metaphor implies that the isomorphism relates stratificational trees of the model to neurons in their static structure or to neurons actively firing electrical impulses during language production —the dynamic state. It is extremely difficult, however, to conceive just how it is that stratificational isomorphism could be related to networks of protein molecules or to other biochemical processes in the nervous system. The metaphor of the "impulse" can only relate to nervous electrical activity and not to the many other biochemical processes that may very well underlie much of language behavior. The "impulse" metaphor is used extensively in stratificational theory. Accordingly, we find the following in Schnitzer (1978): "The entire system consists of connexions between upward and downward ordered and unordered 'ands' and 'ors'. Dynamically, each of these nodes determines what happens to an impulse which reaches it. Statically, the stratificational diagram represents the structure-of-the-language, independently of whether or not there are any impulses traveling along the lines representing the connexions between the nodes" (p. 355). Thus, the stratificational model offers only one type of isomorphism with the brain—

that of the neuronal impulse. Furthermore, although there are tactics at each level, the stratificational metaphor requires that the human nervous system operate essentially hierarchically, but there is growing evidence that it does not operate in that fashion (Kelso & Tuller, 1981). Rather, more of a heterarchy is involved, where the neurophysiological functioning is not serial but simultaneously cooperative and parallel. Language, therefore, does not appear to be represented in the brain in the form of a hierarchy.

FUNCTIONALISM

Jerry Fodor (1975) has devoted a complete work based on the assumption that the only plausible psychological models of cognitive processes involve computation, and that the computation presupposes a medium for the computation. This medium, for Fodor, is a representational system. To Fodor's way of thinking, the business of characterizing the internal mentalistic representation of computational systems of the human organism is certainly no triviality, since for him there is no other approach.

Two basic assumptions lead Fodor (1975) away from physiological reductionism. He feels that it is entirely conceivable that nervous systems of higher primates typically achieve given psychological states by a wide range of neurological means. He assumes, as well, that given neurological structures quite likely subserve different psychological functions at different times, depending upon the character of the activities in which the organism is engaged. If this turns out to be the case for higher organisms, then Fodor reasons that those organisms would be interestingly analogous to general purpose computers. Such computers do not exhibit a structure-to-function correspondence over time. That is, the function that is subserved by a certain structure may change from instant to instant depending on the nature of the program implemented and on the computation being performed (Fodor, 1975, p. 17). If machines and brains do not exhibit a structure-to-function correspondence over time, then the functional systems would have behaviors to which their hardware microstructure would be, to a large extent, simply irrelevant. For our purposes, then, if the linguistic system is subserved by a brain that is analogous to a general purpose computer, then there will be linguistic behaviors for which the neurophysiological microstructure will be, to a large extent, irrelevant. The explanatory irrelevance of the physiological microstructure has recently been discussed by Hilary Putnam (1973).

REDUCTIONISM

In his article entitled "Reductionism and the nature of psychology," Putnam (1973) treats what he calls explanations of explanations; I believe that his notions can be extended to language and the brain. On his view, neurophysiology could possibly explain or account for language. But, explanation in the vocabulary of linguistics directly and concisely explains language behavior. The neurophysiological is a sort of "parent" (to use Putnam's term, 1973, p. 133) of an explanation. The parent explanation generally contains information that is irrelevant to what we want to explain. So if, for example, a certain neurological structure can subserve motor speech *and* other things at other times, then there will always be something irrelevant with regard to language in the neurological account of this structure. In addition, Putnam claims that the "parent" explanation contains the information which *is* relevant, if at all, in a form that may be impossible to recognize. Surely, though, the relevant features of what is to be explained should be brought out and crystalized by an explanation and not submerged in a mass of irrelevant information and in a language of inappropriate predicates. Accordingly, Putnam reasons that a parent of an explanation, "is generally not an explanation" (1973, p. 133). As Putnam claims, all this follows from the fact that, "Explanation is not transitive" (1973, p. 132). Biological function (or some subset of those functions) may explain why human language has filters for logical form or control across elements. And, filters and control form much of the explanation of syntactic grammaticality. But, it would be wrong to claim that the biological microstructure as an assemblage of neuronal impulses and biochemical reactions will explain the fact that the sentence **John was expected would win* is ungrammatical. Only something like what linguists call the "Propositional Island Condition" will do this. That condition states that no rule can involve X, Y in the structure X. . . $[_{\alpha}$. . . Y. . .]. . ., where α is a tensed S (that is, where the embedded sentence is a non-infinitival). Accordingly, the sentence *John was expected to win* is perfectly grammatical, where John is understood as the logical subject of the verb *win.* My point, though, is that the microstructure of the neurophysiological system is irrelevant here.

In sum, there are two reasons for the irrelevancy of explanation from hardware microstructure to linguistic phenemona. First, since a single structure may subserve two distinct functions at different times, then much of its actual structure will be irrelevant with respect to one of the functions. This, of course, is the argument from Fodor's general purpose computer analogy. Putnam's argument is that a "parent" explanation of some function, if it is an explanation at all, will be replete with irrelevant information concerning that function, and what may be relevant is opaque.

PHYSIOLOGY

There is some experimental evidence from electro-cortical stimulation studies that indeed Fodor's suspicions were right and that a given neurological structure may subsume different psychological functions at different times. George Ojemann, a neurosurgeon from the University of Washington, and Cathrine Mateer, a neuropsychologist, (1979) (also see Ojemann, 1983) have demonstrated that nonverbal orofacial movements *and* phoneme identification, "share the same portion of the language cortex" (p. 1402). Phoneme identification is largely a higher order sensory decoding function whereby sounds that enter the organism are categorized into abstract phonemic groupings. The production of nonverbal orofacial movements involves the willful coordination of the vocal tract musculature in achieving the articulatory shapes required to ultimately produce language sounds. Unlike phonemic identification, it is tied directly into the motor output system. The discovery of the overlapping of cortical sites mediating these different functions has lent support for motor theories of speech perception. It has also increased support for the view of Man's brain as a general purpose computer, which in turn argues that much of the hardware will be irrelevant to software explanation. It should also be pointed out that stimulation altered sequential facial movements and phoneme identification at nine sites ranging from inferior frontal to superior temporal to parietal periSylvian cortex. At least two of these sites, the anterior portion of area 44 in Pars Opercularis in the frontal lobe and a discrete temporoparietal zone, have significant structural similarities (Galaburda, 1982). They are both on the same evolutionary scale, having similar interfaces with older cortex, primary cortex and association cortex. Both regions are often larger in volume in the dominant left hemisphere, and each has a unique system of large pyramidal cells in cortical layer III. Furthermore, both zones are discretely connected by long white fiber tracts running through the arcuate fasciculus —connecting posterior cortex with anterior cortex. These zones are also connected with the activation centers of the thalamus. Thus, both zones could be functionally driven from below simultaneously and in parallel (Fried, Ojemann & Fetz, 1981). These studies, then, show that there are single anatomical structures in various areas of language cortex that perform more than one function.

Conversely, we can find single functions distributed over more than one structure. There is an enormous literature, for example, from Luis Lichtheim (1885) to Whitaker and Ojemann (1977) that lexical retrieval function is distributed over rather large portions of temporal, parietal and frontal language cortex. Fodor was also correct in his prediction here, since he postulated that it was quite likely that higher organisms could achieve a given psychological function by a wide range of neurological means.

Concluding this section, then, there does appear to be evidence from electrocortical stimulation, histology, and cytoarchitectonics that the human brain may be analogous to the general purpose computer. If this is so, then explanation from the microstructure of the hardware (in our case, the brain) will be largely irrelevant as concerns the software of language. This finding, coupled with Putnam's edict that explanation is not transitive, provides a good way to avoid the pitfalls of reductionism.

PSYCHOPHYSICAL PARALLELISM/DOUBLE ASPECT/IDENTITY

Several other alternatives to reductionism have been proposed by various writers. I will now turn to some of them and try to provide an evaluation in terms of work in neurolinguistics. One popular alternative to reductionism holds that mental states are not *reducible to* but should be *identified with* states of the central nervous system. We must be careful here, since "identifying" two phenomena with each other is not to say that they are identical in reality or that they are in fact *the same thing.* Identity theory (Borst (ed.), 1970) as a philosophical theory of mind-brain, however postulates that those events and states, which we identify a priori as mental, are *really* neurophysiological events or states. In a strict sense then, there can be no correlations, concomitance or parallelism, because it takes *two* things to correlate, to be concomitant, or to be parallel. Psychophysical parallelism, on the other hand, in both the weak and strong versions, involves the mental and the physical. Psychophysical parallelism is seen in different ways by different researchers. Marc Schnitzer (1978) writes, "Thus, 'I see a red door' is another description for a complex neurophysiological process which the speaker is incapable of reporting in neurophysiological terms" (p. 353). That is, while in our conscious selves we are "perceiving," our nervous systems are acting concomitantly. Admittedly, the crucial question is whether the nervous action is "emerging" into or in some way causing the mental intentional system, or whether it runs in synchrony and in parallel with the mental system. To some people, emergentism gets around a strict dualism, whereas the strong version of psychophysical parallelism does not. In any event, scientists and physicians do not seem ready to claim that the nervous action *IS* the mental, but rather that the descriptions of each will correlate at points. In fact, often researchers in the social sciences will make the claim that physical and psychological descriptions are simply two ways of characterizing the same thing. They rarely, however, go on to specify what that one thing is. Although their stand may look like a "double aspect" theory, it would be very unlikely to be the double aspect theory of Spinoza, who held that the physical and the mental are two aspects of the One Substance —God. Feigl (1960) points out the ambiguities with the term "parallelism." Early philosophers used the term to allow for a mental causality to correspond to neurophysiological causality (as with strict Identity theory). Others used the term to imply a total correspondence of mental and physical attributes (Double aspect theory, the "Panpsychism" of Spinoza). The third reading of this term, as Feigl argues, is what I referred to earlier as the weak form of psychophysical parallelism, and this form is favored by most modern psychophysiology. Here, causal relationships are postulated that go in a one-way direction (physical to mental), and that only involve a small subset of neural processes that are accompanied by mental processes. The causal connection between the neural and the mental are established through laws of coexistence, co-occurrence, or concomitance.

An early proponent of weak psychophysical parallelism, Hughlings Jackson (1931), wrote, "I do not concern myself with mental states at all, except indirectly in seeking their anatomical substrata. I do not trouble myself about the mode of connection between mind and matter. It is enough to assume a parallelism. That along with excitations or discharges of nervous arrangements in the cerebrum, mental states occur..." (p. 52). Jackson's wording was somewhat ambiguous since he insisted that the mental states are manifested *during,* not *from,* physiological processes. He further emphasized that mental states arise "during energising of 'motor' as well as of 'sensory' nerve processes" (p. 55). Throughout his writings, Jackson maintained strict separation between psychology, physiology, and anatomy, at least as far as their levels of description were concerned. Since language was understood as a function of mental activity, Jackson's position was that its study was primarily a psychological one, "however much that mental activity may ultimately be linked up with the integrity of some portion of the brain substance" (Head, 1926, p. 32).

One type of modern research that bears on methodological psychophysical parallelism involves the electroencephalograph (EEG). This technology allows one to measure and locate significant brain states, once the computer has averaged out extraneous electro-cortical noise. These brain states (which are actually not states in the strict sense, but rather activities) are understood as electrochemical nervous discharges, which, according to one interpretation of Mind/Brain Theory, are to be identified with mental states. In these experiments, the mental states are the psychological functions of auditory or visual perception, speech perception, recognition and the like. In addition to perception and recognition, so-called "readiness" potentials can be measured *prior* to the production of some behavioral act, such as motor speech output (McAdam & Whitaker, 1971). Furthermore, neural action can be recorded prior to some *expected* stimulus input. Thus, in a sense, we label the physical brain state in terms of the intentional mental states of "being ready," "expecting," or "recognizing."

In their study of auditory evoked potentials during speech perception, Charles Wood and his colleagues (Wood, Goff, & Day, 1971) found that, "different neural events occur in the left hemisphere *during* analysis of linguistic versus non-linguistic parameters of the same acoustic signal" (p. 1251; emphasis added). No difference occurred in the right hemisphere, however. The nonlinguistic parameter was a change in fundamental frequency (F_0) from 104 hz to 140 hz for the consonant-vowel sequence /ba/.

The linguistic parameter was a change in the acoustic cues which are necessary to perceive the difference between syllable-initial voiced stops /ba/ and /da/. A fundamental frequency of 104 hz was held constant for both syllables, but the direction and extent of the transitions of the second and third formants was varied. (F_2 and F_3 fall to the steady state for /da/, but rise to the steady state for /ba/.)

In another study, Lenore Morrell and Joseph Salamy (1971) showed that the major left-right asymmetry of electrocortical responses to speech stimuli was over the temporo-parietal region, as opposed to the frontal or rolandic areas. Given this type of data on the localizaton of differential brain states, it is hard to see how anyone could be a nonlocalizer—at least of these recorded brain states. Event-related potentials demonstrate such significant asymmetry within and across hemispheres that there is strong reason to admit of at least some degree of localization and to question repeated claims for cortical equipotentiality. The results, however, are still in accord with the basic tenets of psychophysical parallelism, except that today our instrumentation allows us to observe and measure the brain states correlated with the various psychological behaviors.

Yet another alternative to reductionism is Epiphenomenalism, where mental events are presumed to be caused, affected, or even "secreted" (Bunge, 1980b, p. 3) by physical events. On this view, the mental events cannot cause other mental events nor can they cause physical events. The psychophysical parallelism of Jackson is in opposition to epiphenomenalism, since according to him mental states arise *during* not *from* physiological processes. Note that scientists such as Wood, Goff and Day unwittingly take a stand on this issue, since they use the modifier "during" when correlating EEG activity with psycholinguistic functioning. Arturo Rosenbleuth (1970) has also used the adverbial modifier "during" in this way. He writes that, "The electroencephalographic studies justify the conclusion that the cerebral activity. . .is present during conscious periods. . ." (p. 33). Admittedly, the dividing line is thin here, but it does seem to me that the wording in EEG research favors a psychophysical concomitance (weak parallelism) rather than epiphenomenalism.

Jerry Fodor (1968, 1975) would appear to accept at least some form of the weak version of psychophysical parallelism, where there is a contingent identity between the physical and the mental. Fodor claims that a plausible version of materialism would state that psychological theories and neurological theories both involve taxonomies defined over the same objects (brain states), but conforming to distinct principles. According to this view, the members of a set of anatomically similar brain states would have to conform to certain requirements, whereas the members of a set of functionally equivalent brain states would have to conform to rather different requirements. Therefore, this type of materialist will have to settle for, "identifications of psychological states with sets of functionally equivalent brain states'' (Fodor, 1968, p. 120). Fodor, therefore, does not look for identifications of psychological states with sets of anatomically equivalent brain states. In essence, this form of materialism still separates the psychological from the neurological, assuming at best some relation of concomitance; consequently, it shares many of the premises of the weak version of psychophysical parallelism we have been discussing. In fact, Fodor is very clear on this point. According to him, one can accept the premise that, ''mind states and brain states are contingently identical'' (Fodor, 1968, p. 57) and still maintain that, ''statements about minds and statements about behavior are logically independent'' (p. 56).

A close reading of Fodor's position will reveal that there is an element of the double aspect theory. Recall that for him psychological theories and neurological theories both involve taxonomies defined *over the same objects;* those objects are brain states (not the One Substance—God—of Spinoza). It only makes sense to identify psychological states with functionally equivalent brain states. That is to say, functionally equivalent brain states can exist in different anatomical locations for the same psychological state, and consequently the identification could not hold between psychological states and token anatomical brain states. The identity is at the level of types, not tokens. The finding of Ojemann and Mateer that there are anatomically different sites that mediate lexical retrieval provides a case where the psychological state of word finding is identified with functionally equivalent brain states. Since they are in different lobes of the brain, those brain states are not anatomically equivalent. One's methodology has much to do with how one talks about what it is he is doing, and certainly most nonreductionistic positions on the mind/body issue allow for two types of scientific vocabularies. The philospher J. H. Grundy (1970) seems to be in agreement with Fodor. Grundy writes that, ''talk of mental states and of brain states may belong to different systems and be logically irreducible to or derivable from one another, but this does not prevent them from being, as a matter of contingent fact, different ways of talking about the same events'' (p. 30).

In conclusion, suffice it to say that both double aspect theories and psychophysical parallelism allow their adherents to separate descriptive jargons into the mental and the physical. The former is monistic, while the latter is dualistic. What brings the two closer together is that there is always implied a strong concomitance with the weak version of parallelism, while the coin with two faces in double aspect theory has two natures.

LOCALIZATION / NON-LOCALIZATION / ASSOCIATIONISM

There are, nevertheless, those who would assume an even closer connection between neurology and psychology. Norman Geschwind wrote widely on the central nervous system structures that appear to be implicated in: (a) object-naming; (b) vocabulary use; (c) linguistic perception; (d) repetition of utterances; (e) motor speech production; (f) reading; (g) writing and other uses of language. Geschwind's (1974) work is in line with the studies of Paul Broca, Carl Wernicke and others in the Nineteenth Century (see Buckingham, 1978). That work is directed toward establishing neuroanatomical correlates of these *general* aspects of language behavior in Man. Geschwind's localizaton theories are based on clinicopathological reports of patients who have sustained damage to the central nervous system. Based upon aphasiological evidence, one can *predict,* by inductive reasoning, (given certain neurophysiological caveats) that damage to Broca's area in the left hemisphere at the foot of the third frontal convolution of a right handed person will cause a motor aphasia (Buckingham, 1979). That is to say, there are certain vulnerabilities of given functions or behaviors to regional lesions. Some have taken these findings and have gone a step further in claiming that those functions *are located* in these regions. This is the strong version of the localization hypothesis. The weaker, and consequently safer, position would simply state that function X is vulnerable to damage from lesions in region Y *without* extending the statement to the effect that function X in nonlesioned organisms is located exclusively in region Y.

It is noteworthy that even a strong localizer of function such as Geschwind espouses a type of dualism when appropriate. For example, he (1974) writes, "I would have to accept the view that what one might call the realization in hardware of an axiomatic system would not necessarily be, so to speak, isomorphic with that system. One would hardly expect that damage to an ideal computer, capable of deriving theorems of Euclidean geometry, would produce loss of individual axioms" (p. 505). What Geschwind is implying is that the descriptive methodology of geometrical axioms (derivable from a computer program), and the descriptive methodology of computer hardware systems, are distinct—neither derivable from nor reducible to the other.

Localization theory has had opposition from those who argue that the brain is not partitioned into functional centers. The often acrimonious disputes took their form at least as early as the first quarter of the nineteenth century, when Gall was defending his localizationist views of phrenology against the cortical "equipotential" theories of the French physiologist, Pierre Flourens (Young, 1970). With the advent of clinicopathological studies of the aphasias, the localizationist position was strengthened, although the tenets of Gall's phrenology were no longer accepted (Buckingham, 1981). The anti-localization position received further support in this century from Karl Lashley, whose research methodology and theories of cortical mass-action and equipotentiality can be traced directly to Flourens (Tizard, 1959). The nonlocalizationists were interested in "intelligent" behavior, and their feeling was that as behaviors become more complex, they require more overall intellectual function and consequently become more difficult to localize. The cortex was understood by Flourens and Lashley to mediate intellectual functioning with equipotentiality.

Lashley (1929, 1951) carefully studied "goal" oriented behavior,[1] and in 1929 he published the results of his investigations on the learning and retention of maze-walking behavior in rats. He found that once the animals had learned the maze, they could traverse it in any number of ways with vastly different (functionally equivalent) arrays of motor movements, such as swimming. Furthermore, with vast amounts of cortex ablated (different cortical regions for different rats), the animals could still, with great effort due to the damaged motor system, drag themselves through the maze. It appeared to Lashley just as it had to Flourens a century earlier, that the ability to perform these goal-oriented behaviors depended on how much (nonspecific) cortical mass was intact, rather than on the intactness of this or that specific area. In addition, Lashley hypothesized that no simple association chain theory for motor commands seemed to explain these intellectual goal-oriented behaviors with invariant targets. Lashley's well-known paper of 1951 dealt at length with the essentially non-Markovian nature of higher order intellectual behavior in man. In that paper he again reasoned from facts concerning target oriented movement, but this time he drew support from the syntax of natural language, where accordingly he claimed that serial ordering processes are nonassociative. At the conclusion of this paper, he wrote that, "the problems of the syntax of action are far removed from anything which we can study by direct physiological methods today, yet in attempting to formulate a physiology of the cerebral cortex we cannot ignore them" (Pribram (ed.), 1969, p. 538). This statement, in effect, says that the complex and abstract psychological capability of serial ordering cannot yet be explained neurophysiologically, but that this ability must somehow be the product of central nervous system function. Associationism had many adherents in psychology in the 50's and before; Lashley's remarks in 1951 largely fell on deaf ears.

There are still those who seemingly espouse associationistic views of human language. For instance, Mario Bunge (1980b) has written that "language is a system of learned signals such that. . . each signal is either simple or a concatenate of two or more simple signals" (p. 200). This represents Bunge's view of syntax, and it appears to be no more than an associative chain theory. He goes on to say that the language system "allows an animal to compose an unlimited number of distinct messages—it can grow together with the animal's experience" (p. 200).

---

[1] Peter MacNeilage's (1970) theories concerning the motor control of serial ordering of speech go back to the work of Karl Lashley. In fact, there is much literature on goal/target oriented behavior (Bain, 1859; Hebb, 1949; Sommerhoff, 1974).

I believe that the linguistic system is largely underdetermined, and consequently I adhere to the argument from "poverty of stimulus." No amount of classical learning theory will account for the representative linguistic system of adult language competence. In addition, the ordering mechanism is surely more than a simple associative concatenator of words. To be sure, an associative chain model can generate an unlimited number of concatenated items, but there is no reason to believe that that model is the correct representation of human syntactic competence, if for no other reason than that it cannot handle pushdown storage structure (Chomsky, 1963, pp. 339–345).

It often turns out that those who accept associationistic accounts of language are the most prone to believe that the "chimp" studies "...have weakened the hypothesis that language is exclusively human" (Bunge, 1980b, p. 201). If one's understanding of language is founded on the principles of classical learning, and if one's view is that the syntax is a Markov concatenator, then one will be more likely to believe that what chimps learn is simply quantitatively different from human language. This view of language also has the unfortunate consequence of leading one to focus attention on the learning of words. Lexical acquisition per se is not one of the most startling linguistic abilities of humans, although the existence of universal primitive categories is. "Raw" lexical items can be taught by simple associations of stimulus and response. This, however, is not necessarily a very illuminating feature of human language.

THE REPRESENTATION OF COMPETENCE: LOCALIZABLE?

Noam Chomsky devoted many early articles to showing that syntax in natural language cannot be explained by Markov chain models (Chomsky, 1956, 1957, 1963). Although his mathematical-logical proof is quite different in nature from the reasoning of Lashley, the idea is essentially the same, and in several places Chomsky refers to the work of Lashley (Chomsky, 1959, pp. 44, 55–57; 1968, pp. 2–3, 60–61). Chomsky is no more certain than Lashley when alluding to the neurophysiological function underlying syntactic phenomena. For instance, Chomsky (1967) addressed a conference on brain mechanisms underlying speech and language where he described ambiguity, complement structure, and the so-called "A-over-A principle." Throughout his presentation he assured the audience that the "knowledge" speakers have in order to report intuitions regarding linguistic phenomena is somehow "represented" in: (a) our "minds (p. 80);" (b) our "brain (p. 81);" and (c) our "nervous system (p. 75)." Some philosophers have criticized this kind of reasoning as inconsequential (Hutchinson, 1974), trivially true (Stich, 1975) and as presenting no more than "a tantalizingly illusive metaphor" (Stich, 1975, p. 96). Both Stephen Stich (1975) and Larry Hutchinson (1974) concur that the metaphor of internal representation is nothing more than an "innocuous little argument type" (Hutchinson, (p. 50). Nevertheless, this form of reasoning allows for a computational approach to cognition, and it allows Chomsky to make the claim about the body while holding fast to his mentalistic methodology. In fact, as we have repeatedly seen, the way he words things actually enhances the importance of his methodology because it, and only it, can help the neurologist know what to look for when exploring the neuroanatomical hardware. In reality, though, Chomsky's findings have had little effect, since what Chomsky could hand the neurologist would be in no form amenable to him. To my knowledge, no one has located any region in the nervous system for syntax,[2] much less for specific rules such as "Move α." However, I would point out that I am *not* saying that syntactic *disturbance* will never be found in aphasia, nor under conditions of electrocortical stimulation. Even though Ojemann and Mateer (1979, p. 1402) evoked the following ungrammatical response on a reading task: "If my son will getting late today he'll see the principal," I rather doubt that anyone has discovered the cortical region for Auxiliary.

It should be clear that the constructs of Chomskyan human linguistic competence (i.e., a system of knowledge) are not localizable in the physical-spatial sense which localizable implies. At least one transformational grammarian, Jerry Fodor, would not be a localizationist, and since Chomsky essentially agrees with Fodor's neurological position, he would not be a localizer either. It certainly makes sense for the transformational grammarians to adopt a position of non-localization of function, for then they could avoid having to make claims such as "this transformation is here, and that transformation is there." The real merits of generative grammar are numerous as far as linguistic explanation goes; the models, however, receive *no* additional support simply because their adherents state that the knowledge they describe is somehow represented in the brain. In fact, Chomsky (1980, p. 200) places electrophysiological correlation on an equal footing with the internal logic of linguistic argumentation when appealing to the psychological reality of his linguistic constructs.

He allows for the possibility of discovering patterns of neuroelectric activity in the cortex that are exclusively related in clear cases to the presence of WH- clauses of different sorts. In such a case, Chomsky claims that he would have a new kind of evidence for the psychological reality for WH-representations, but this evidence would not relegate informant judgments to any inferior status. Aphasiological data may support some aspect of linguistic theory, but the support is psychological and not physiological. The illusion that we are getting neurophysiological support from aphasia data is due to the fact that the aphasia is secondary to physically localizable lesions

[2] A note of caution must be inserted here. Although Ojemann and Mateer (1979) claim they have localized syntax in the language cortex, what they have really localized (in three adults) are six sites scattered in the frontal, temporal, or parietal lobes of the dominant left hemisphere which, when electrically stimulated, will evoke certain, rather mild, grammatical errors. It is inconceivable that they have localized syntactic competence in the Chomskyan sense.

in the nervous system. Nevertheless, the linguistic breakdown is clearly a psychological one and should be described at that level (see Caplan, 1981, for further discussion).

THE PSYCHOLINGUISTS

Up to now our discussion has been limited to neurolinguistics, generative linguistics, computational cognitive psychology and the various philosophical positions on the mind/body question that have been taken by different researchers in these fields. We have yet to mention the work from the field of experimental psycholinguistics and what that study has to say on the mind/body issue. There is a vast amount of literature from this area that speaks directly to the purported psychological reality of transformational grammar. The studies of Fodor, Bever, and Garrett (1974), which they refer to as "experimental mentalism" are paradigm examples. And, these studies tend to have a greater impact upon transformational theory that do studies of neurophysiology.

In a recent study investigating psychological processes as linguistic explanation, Herbert Clark and Susan Haviland (1974) treated three separate abilities: (a) getting readings for sentences; (b) giving acceptance intuitions; and (c) "computing" anaphoric island reference through the process of lexical decomposition. Clark and Haviland view linguistic behavior in terms of mental states which change from moment to moment in real time. The authors criticize Chomsky's competence model as being static, and they replace it with one which is "stated in terms of a series of mental states, each represented in some symbolic form and a collection of rules that change one mental state into the next" (p. 93). Clark and Haviland appear to be doing precisely what Paul Feyerabend (1970) once suggested when he claimed that, since micro-processes in the brain are extremely difficult to observe, one would be better off to *identify* brain processes with what can be observed by introspection. Feyerabend reasons that, since the living human organism is connected with the brain, one can obtain reliable sources of information about the latter if he observes the reactions of the former—introspections included. Feyerabend has written (1970) that "Using a suitable identification hypothesis one might even be able to say that introspection leads to a direct observation of an otherwise quite inaccessible and very complex process in the brain" (p. 147). This quotation is reminiscent of the 19th century French physiologist, Fournie, who claimed that speech is the only "window" through which the physiologist can view the cerebral life. In fact, Chomsky would certainly agree that by studying the structure of human language one is thereby gaining an increased appreciation of the human mind. Although Clark and Haviland disagree with Chomsky over whether linguistic models should be static or dynamic, they agree with him in that they have presented a, "rather general proposal for the study of natural language as part of the study of the mind'' (p. 94). Thus, Clark and Haviland, like Chomsky, seem to be carving out a methodological niche rather than constructing a theory of the mind and body.

CONCLUSION

In summary, it is safe to say that the term ''mental state'' would never have arisen if curious people had not reflected on their multifarious states of consciousness. Physical brain states, on the other hand, must be observed with the proper technique and instrumentation. The claim I am making is that the fundamental differences between psychological sciences such as linguistics and the physical sciences such as neurology, neurophysiology and the like *still* embody the basic distinctions of mind and brain, and that only some form of contingent identity need exist between mind states and brain states. In any event, descriptions of both must draw upon distinct vocabularies, which implies that there will be distinct methodologies of inquiry. To my way of thinking, this methodological dualism will always be with us, whether we opt for a double aspect theory of identity (a ''neutral monism'' according to Bunge's taxonomy) or for an ''emergentist'' materialism. The mental side of the coin in double aspect will always need its psychological idiom; Fodor's theory will always need its ''functionally equivalent brain states.'' Similarly, emergentist systems will need both levels of description as well. Even if the behavior of the language system could be deduced from its description as an emergent system of entire assemblies of interconnected cells, it does not follow that it can be explained from that description, as Putnam argues (1973, p. 131). The operations required to verify statements about language and statements about brain processes are fundamentally different as are the modes of explanation for each.

Man's present inability to completely understand himself (Stent, 1975) becomes acutely apparent at the mind/body interface. Perhaps we will be forever limited to metaphor in relating the two. Nevertheless, bold efforts will continue in the search for lawful coextensions between neurology and psychology. In fact, as Fodor (1975) remarked, ''There are departments of psychobiology or psychology and brain science in universities throughout the world whose very existence is an institutionalized gamble that such lawful coextensions can be found'' (p. 17). Only time will tell whether that gamble ultimately pays off.

REFERENCES

Bain, A. (1859). *The emotions and the will* (3rd ed., 1876). New York: Appleton.

Borst, C. V. (Ed.) (1970). *The mind-brain identity theory.* London: MacMillan.

Buckingham, H. W. (1978). A review of *Selected papers on language and the brain,* by Norman Geschwind. *Studies in Language, 2,* 417–428.

Buckingham, H. W. (1979). Language localization and induction. *Cognition and Brain Theory, 3,* 20–25.

Buckingham, H. W. (1981). A pre-history of the problem of Broca's aphasia. In R. H. Brookshire (Ed.), *Clinical aphasiology.* Minneapolis, MN: BKR.

Bunge, M. (1977). Emergence and the mind. *Neuroscience, 2,* 501–509.

Bunge, M. (1980a). Introduction: The mind-body problem. In D. Bindra (Ed.), *The brain's mind: A neuroscience perspective on the mind-body problem.* New York: Gardner.

Bunge, M. (1980b). *The mind-body problem: A psychobiological approach.* Oxford, England: Pergamon.

Caplan, D. (1981). On cerebral localization of linguistic functions: Logical and empirical issues surrounding deficit analysis and functional localization. *Brain and Language, 14,* 120–137.

Chomsky, N. (1956). Three models for the description of language. *I. R. E. Transactions on Information Theory* (Vol. IT-2), 113–124.

Chomsky, N. (1957). *Syntactic structures.* The Hague: Mouton.

Chomsky, N. (1959). Review of B. F. Skinner's *Verbal Behavior. Language, 35,* 26–58.

Chomsky, N. (1963). Formal properties of grammars. In R. D. Luce, R. R. Bush, & E. Galanter (Eds.), *Handbook of mathematical psychology* (Vol. II). New York: Wiley.

Chomsky, N. (1965). *Aspects of the theory of syntax.* Cambridge, MA: MIT Press.

Chomsky, N. (1967). The general properties of language. In C. H. Millikan & F. L. Darley (Eds.), *Brain mechanisms underlying speech and language.* New York: Grune & Stratton.

Chomsky, N. (1968). *Language and mind.* New York: Harcourt, Brace & World.

Chomsky, N. (1975). Questions of form and interpretation. *Linguistic Analysis, 1,* 75–109.

Chomsky, N. (1980). *Rules and representations.* New York: Columbia University Press.

Chomsky, N. (1981a). *Lectures on government and binding.* Dordrecht: Foris.

Chomsky, N. (1981b). A naturalistic approach to language and cognition. *Cognition and Brain Theory, 4,* 3–22.

Chomsky, N. (1982). *Some concepts and consequences of the theory of government and binding.* Cambridge, MA: MIT Press.

Chomsky, N. (Forthcoming). *Changing perspectives on knowledge and use of language.*

Clark, H. H., & Haviland, S. E. (1974). Psychological processes as linguistic explanation. In D. Cohen (Ed.), *Explaining linguistic phenomena.* Washington, DC: Hemisphere.

Dingwall, W. O., & Whitaker, H. A. (1978). Neurolinguistics. In W. O. Dingwall (Ed.), *A survey of linguistic science.* Stamford, CT: Greylock.

Engelhardt, H. T. (1975). John Hughlings Jackson and the mind-body relation. *Bulletin of the History of Medicine, 49,* 137–151.

Feigl, H. (1960). Mind-body, not a pseudoproblem. In S. Hook (Ed.), *Dimensions of mind.* New York: Collier.

Feyerabend, P. (1970). Materialism and the mind-body problem. In C. V. Borst (Ed.), *The mind-body identity theory.* London: MacMillan.

Fodor, J. A. (1968). *Psychological explanation: An introduction to the philosophy of psychology.* New York: Random House.

Fodor, J. A. (1975). *The language of thought.* New York: Crowell.

Fodor, J. A. (1983). *The modularity of mind: An essay on faculty psychology.* Cambridge, MA: Bradford Books, The MIT Press.

Fodor, J. A., Bever, T. G., & Garrett, M. F. (1974). *The psychology of language.* New York: McGraw-Hill.

Fried, I., Ojemann, G., & Fetz, E. (1981). Language-related potentials specific to human language cortex. *Science, 212,* 353–356.

Galaburda, A. M. (1982). Histology, architectonics, and asymmetry of language areas. In M. Arbib, D. Caplan, & J. C. Marshall (Eds.), *Neural models of language processes.* New York: Academic Press.

Geschwind, N. (1974). *Selected papers on language and the brain.* Dordrecht, Holland: Reidel.
Grundy, J. H. (1970). Is the brain a physical system? In R. Borger & F. Cioffi (Eds.), *Explanation in the behavioral sciences.* Cambridge, England: Cambridge University Press.
Hacking, I. (1982). Wittgenstein the psychologist. *New York Review of Books,* April 1, Pp. 42–44.
Head, H. (1926). *Aphasia and kindred disorders of speech* (Vols. I & II). Cambridge, England: Cambridge University Press.
Hebb, D. O. (1949). *The organization of behavior.* New York: Wiley.
Hutchinson, L. G. (1974). Grammar as theory. In D. Cohen (Ed.), *Explaining linguistic phenomena.* Washington, DC: Hemisphere.
Jackson, J. H. (1931). In J. Taylor (Ed.), *Selected writings of John Hughlings Jackson* (Vols. I & II). London: Hodder & Stoughton.
Katz, J. J. (1964). Mentalism in linguistics. *Language, 40,* 124–137.
Katz, J. J. (1981). *Language and other abstract objects.* Totowa, NJ: Rowman and Littlefield.
Kelso, J. A. S., & Tuller, B. (1981). Toward a theory of apractic syndromes. *Brain and Language, 12,* 224–245.
Lamendella, J. T. (1979). Neurolinguistics. *Annual Review of Anthropology, 8,* 373–391.
Lashley, K. S. (1929). *Brain mechanisms and intelligence.* Chicago: University of Chicago Press.
Lashley, K. S. (1951). The problem of serial order in behavior. In L. A. Jeffress (Ed.), *Cerebral mechanisms in behavior.* New York: Wiley.
Lichtheim, L. (1885). On aphasia. *Brain, 7,* 433–484.
MacNeilage, P. F. (1970). Motor control of serial ordering of speech. *Psychological Review, 77,* 182–196.
Marshall, J. C. (1980). The new organology. *Behavioral and Brain Sciences, 3,* 23–25.
McAdam, D. W., & Whitaker, H. A. (1971). Language production: Electroencephalographic localization in the normal human brain. *Science, 172,* 499–502.
Morrell, L. K., & Salamy, J. (1971). Hemispheric asymmetry of electrocortical responses of speech stimuli. *Science, 174,* 164–166.
Ojemann, G., & Mateer, C. (1979). Human language cortex: Localization of memory, syntax, and sequential motor-phoneme identification systems. *Science, 205,* 1401–1403.
Ojemann, G. (1983). Brain organization for language from the perspective of electrical stimulation mapping. *Behavioral and Brain Sciences, 6,* 189–230.
Pribram, K. H. (Ed.) (1969). *Perception and action.* Harmondsworth, England: Penguin.
Putnam, H. (1973). Reductionism and the nature of psychology. *Cognition, 2,* 131–146. [Reprinted in J. Haugeland (Ed.), *Mind design.* Cambridge, MA: MIT Press, 1981.]
Rosenbleuth, A. (1970). *Mind and brain: A philosophy of science.* Cambridge, MA: MIT Press.
Schnitzer, M. L. (1978). Toward a neurolinguistic theory of language. *Brain and Language, 6,* 342–361.
Sommerhoff, G. (1974). *Logic of the living brain.* New York: Wiley.
Stent, G. S. (1975). Limits to the scientific understanding of the brain. *Science, 187,* 1052–1057.
Stich, S. P. (1975). Competence and indeterminacy. In D. Cohen & J. R. Wirth (Eds.), *Testing linguistic hypotheses.* Washington, DC: Hemisphere.
Tizard, B. (1959). Theories of brain localization from Flourens to Lashley. *Medical History, 3,* 132–145.
Whitaker, H. A., & Ojemann, G. (1977). Graded localisation of naming from electrical stimulation mapping of left cerebral cortex. *Nature, 270,* 50–51.
Wood, C. C., Goff, W., & Day, R. (1971). Auditory evoked potentials during speech perception. *Science, 173,* 1248–1251.
Young, R. M. (1970). *Mind, brain and adaptation in the nineteenth century.* London: Oxford University Press.

Chapter 13

A Philosopher Looks at the Current Debate on Language Acquisition

Mario Bunge

McGill University

I take it that the production and understanding of speech is the primary linguistic fact. If this is so, then linguists should focus their attention on the production and understanding of utterances, in particular (though not exclusively), of spoken sentences. In turn, admitting that this is the central task of linguists entails that they should be centrally concerned with the speech organ (the brain), and the social matrix of this kind of social behavior. That is, the nucleus of linguistics should be composed of neurolinguistics, psycholinguistics, and sociolinguistics. Everything else should revolve around this nucleus.

However, this is not so. For historical reasons linguistics started at the other end, i.e., by investigating fully grown languages rather than the primary linguistic facts. It may have started this way because linguistics was originally a branch of the humanities, which were in turn dominated by idealistic philosophy. To be sure this trend was reversed at the turn of the century when, at least in North America, the anthropologists took charge and began studying concrete speakers and speech communities. However, their domination was short-lived: the humanistic tradition came back a quarter of a century ago with the birth of generative-transformational grammar. The empirical study of the primary linguistic facts seems to have been on the defensive ever since. The consideration of *langue* has prevailed in some quarters over that of *parole,* and the spinning of speculative hypotheses concerning immaterial "mental structures" has taken the place of serious theorizing and experimenting on the linguistic abilities and disabilities of living brains. We are back in square one.

The purpose of this paper, which is part of a larger study (Bunge, 1983c, 1984), is merely to remind ourselves that speech starts in some brain or other and ends in the same or some other brain. To be sure if we wish to attain generality, e.g., because we want to write the grammar of a particular speech community, we must discard individual idiosyncrasies and concentrate on the commonalities of the members of the community. However, if we wish to understand how we learn or unlearn to speak, we cannot skip the brain, because we happen to learn with the brain. We may certainly restrict our momentary interest to describing the main features of a language, but the explanation of the primary linguistic fact calls for a study of the brain in society. Everything else regarding language acquisition (or loss) is at best sheer description, at worst groundless speculation.

I. NATIVISM REDUX

Psycholinguists study, among other problems, that of language acquisition. They are divided into two main camps with regard to this problem: the nativists and those who hold that knowledge of language, like any other knowledge, is learned. The foremost representative of nativism nowadays is Chomsky, who holds that every person is born knowing the essential principles of universal grammar (Chomsky & Miller, 1963; Chomsky, 1972, 1975, 1980; Piattelli-Palmarini, 1979). His opponents are in turn divided into two main factions: the dwindling behaviorist school, according to which language learning is a simple matter of conditioning; and the growing neuropsychological school, according to which normal persons are born with specialized neural systems (in particular the Wernicke and Broca "areas") capable of learning a language, but won't learn it unless the brain matures normally in a suitable social environment. (We disregard the so-called dispositionalism, according to which we are born with a disposition or natural gift for learning languages, because everybody accepts this harmless thesis that explains nothing.)

Chomsky (1959) discredited effectively the behaviorist doctrine of verbal behavior and acquisition by pointing out that any of us can create sentences which he has never heard or read before. He holds that the newborn human, unlike any other primate, is equipped with a linguistic "competence" that is far more than the mere ability to learn languages: it would be no less than a knowledge of UG, or the basic structure of all languages. Furthermore, since according to Chomsky every grammar is a theory, the baby would be born knowing a theory. This "theory" is very general; new hypotheses and data, to be acquired during development, are needed for the grammar of a specific language to "grow in the mind" of the child, much as he needs nourishment for the growth of his body.

Normally the child is exposed from birth to a barrage of phrases. According to Chomsky, the child's problem is not that of understanding them but "to determine which of the (humanly) possible languages is that of the community in which he is placed'' (Chomsky, 1965, p. 27). ''The child is presented with data, and he must inspect hypotheses (grammars) of a fairly restricted class to determine compatibility with his data. Having selected a grammar of a predetermined class, he will then have command of the language generated by this grammar'' (Chomsky, 1972, p. 159; see also Chomsky & Miller, 1963, p. 277, and Chomsky, 1980, p. 134). In short, children would learn their first language much in the same way accomplished theoretical physicists choose among rival theories competing for a given set of empirical data. Never before had human babies, known to be among the poorest performers in the animal kingdom, been credited with such remarkable competence.

Chomsky's view on language acquisition makes too much room for innate wisdom and too little for experience and creativity. In fact, to Chomsky, as to Socrates and some rationalist philosophers, experience would only bring out, elicit, trigger, or hone what we already have at birth: a human animal could learn only to perfect the details of that which is already ''represented'' in his genome. Skinner had been mainly interested in learning but, being a radical empiricist, he denied that we need a *theory* of learning. Chomsky, who is mainly interested in theory, denies that we need an explicit theory of *learning,* or at any rate of language learning, because we got from birth an *implicit* theory of language learning (1962, p. 528, 1975 p. 28). Fodor (1975) takes the final step by declaring that learning theories are not just unnecessary but *impossible,* because actually we do not learn anything: all ideas are innate. (It would follow then that the historians of ideas are wasting their time.)

2. *CHOMSKY'S ARGUMENTS FOR NATIVISM*

One should think that reheating the views of Socrates and Leibniz on learning in the second half of the 20th century takes not only considerable *chutzpah* but also powerful reasons and astonishing experimental findings. In fact, Chomsky offers only two reasons, neither of which is sufficient. His first argument is from the failure of radical behaviorism: since a normal child learns to speak ''very fast,'' and since it is impossible to learn or internalize a grammar from ''the meager and degenerate data'' accessible to the child, the latter ''must'' have been born with a knowledge of universal grammar—a sort of filing cabinet where the infant can file all the data he is presented with. Chomsky's second argument is from the alleged functional rigidity of all our organs: even the brain would be totally preformed or genetically programmed (prewired), just like the heart and the eye, so that the suggestion that we can *learn* to speak is just as absurd as the idea that the heart must learn to discharge its function. These are Chomsky's sole reasons for upholding nativism, and neither of them holds water.

The argument from the failure of behaviorism to account for speech production would be valid if behaviorism were one of the horns of a dilemma, the other horn being nativism. Chomsky makes it abundantly clear that he sees no via media between behaviorism and nativism: concepts must be determined essentially in an innate manner, "since we do not know of any other way of accounting for their acquisition" (Piattelli-Palmarini, 1979, p. 257). Clearly, this is an argument from ignorance, and therefore invalid. It reminds one of the old argument that, since we do not know how life came about, it must have been created by some deity.

There is of course a tertium quid: We are inventive and learn by combining experience (perception and action) with reason. Whereas we learn some ideas from experience (or by inductive generalization from the latter), we learn others by imitation, and still others are original inventions (e.g., hypotheses) that owe little or nothing to experience. There is no mystery in this: the human brain is remarkably plastic. The failure of behaviorism is no excuse for turning the clock back to Socratic nativism. The right strategy is to acknowledge the cognitive component of learning and its creative nature, as most psychologists do nowadays. Thus, Bartlett (1958), Hebb (1949), and Bindra (1976) were constructivists, and so was Piaget: "An epistemology in agreement with the data of psychogenesis could be neither empiricist nor preformationist: it could not consist in anything other than in a constructivism, with the continual elaboration of new operations and structures" (Piaget, 1979, p. 53).

Consider, for example, the task of learning to pair stimuli of a certain kind S to responses of a kind R when the organism is in a given physiological state. Formally speaking, the task is that of constructing the suitable function F from S into R. An empiricist would say that we construct F step by step, pairing every member of S off to the appropriate element of R. But this is of course impossible when S is very large, as is the case with verbal stimuli. So, the nativist imagines that we must be born with a knowledge of F and need experience only to activate such dormant knowledge. However, this conclusion is invalid because the empiricism/nativism alternative is not exclusive. There is a way out: we may guess F on the strength of a few instances and possibly with the help of some generalizations learned earlier. We may hazard now one form of F, now another, subjecting each guess to some tests until we hit on a sufficiently close approximation to the right F—or give up. (See Bunge, 1983a, Ch. 2.)

Chomsky's second argument for nativism is the supposed functional rigidity of the brain. He claims that the work of Hubel, Wiesel, and others, on the visual cortex, supports nativism by showing that the neurons in that region are highly specialized from birth, although they degenerate unless activated by suitable experiences at the right time (Chomsky, in Piattelli-Palmarini, 1979, passim; 1980, p. 39). In my view, those remarkable neurophysiological findings lend no support to the hypothesis of innate ideas, because they concern visual *sensation,* not perception, let alone ideation or speech production (see e.g., Hubel, 1982; Wiesel, 1982.) Not surprisingly, the neurons in the primary visual cortex are specialized and are organized into systems the specific function of which is seeing. (It is unlikely, though, that all of the inter-neuronal connections are inborn, and it is certain that their strength depends upon experience.)

What happens in the sensory cortex need not happen in the associative one: in the latter, plasticity may dominate over prewiring. Thus, the fact that there is a critical period for language learning suggests that, unless the neurons in the language "areas" are organized into neuron assemblies for the production and understanding of phrases, they may be "recruited" to discharge different functions—or none, as plasticity is likely to decline with age. In short, while it may well be that the visual system and other sensory systems are to a large extent genetically determined, it is almost certain that the associative cortex is extremely plastic, to the extent that we organize it ourselves as we learn. Such plasticity has been amply demonstrated in recent years (see, e.g., Bliss, 1979; Goddard, 1980; Baranyi & Fehér, 1981; Flohr & Precht, 1981.) Yet Chomsky denies it.

The latest and most sensational discovery about neural plasticity concerns a phenomenon that scientific psycholinguists should pay attention to, namely birdsong. Nottebohm (1981) found that the size of the song control nuclei in the canary's brain changes with its song repertory. The nuclei grow during learning, and shrink as the songs are discarded during the late summer and early fall. In other words, the subsystems of the brain that "subserve" (do) the song learning change anatomically from one season to the next as the song repertory varies. This suggests that similar anatomical changes occur in the human brain as it learns and unlearns language. However, this hypothesis will not be investigated as long as human language is regarded as a mysterious gift, totally unrelated to other methods of animal communication, as well as not learnable like a song or a theorem.

Linguistic nativism is open to the following additional objections. Firstly, linguists have not yet discovered whether all languages do share a basic structure and, if so, what this is: recall Section 1. Hence, to attribute to newborns the perfect command of that which linguists ignore is bizarre, and in any case it exemplifies *explicatio obscurum per obscurium.* In other words, "explaining" language acquisition in terms of innate knowledge is like saying that "we are the way we are because that's the way we (genetically) are" (Givón, 1979, p. 22). Secondly, nativism lacks inductive empirical support. (This is no blemish for a rationalist or apriorist, but it is a serious handicap for anyone else: scientists are not supposed to defend doggedly a theory in the absence of positive evidence for it.)

More to the point, there is ample indirect (circumstantial) anatomical, behavioral, and cognitive evidence *against* nativism. The first is that the infant cerebral cortex is very poorly organized: its neurons are small and have a scant arborization, so that presumably the inter-neuronal contacts are few, whence there are probably no neuronal systems capable of minding. (See the revealing plates in Conel 1939-67.) The behavioral evidence comes from developmental psychology, which shows that the child develops his abilities (''faculties'') only gradually, though by stages, and this only provided he is subjected to the right stimuli at the right times. To be sure, children learn to speak ''fast.'' But, as Galileo would ask, how fast is ''fast''?

As for the cognitive evidence against nativism, it boils down to this. Although we still ignore the precise mechanism of language learning, we do know that it is *not* the exercise of a single isolated ''faculty,'' but only one aspect of a complex sensory-motor-ideational process; i.e., speaking and listening involve knowing and doing (see, e.g., Dale, 1976). Chomsky's rejoinder, that even idiots learn to speak, is not to the point. Some feeble-minded children learn to play chess, and others to make quick mental calculations beyond the reach of the average normal adult. Idiocy, like proficiency in language learning, is a matter of degree. In any event, the case of mental retardates who learn to speak only proves that it is abnormal for language to be dissociated from intelligence. Normally, the development of conceptual skills goes together with that of sensory motor-skills.

3. *THE BIOPSYCHOLOGICAL ANTERNATIVE*

Contemporary psychology, in particular developmental and physiological, offers a viable alternative to both linguistic nativism and empiricism (Hebb, Lambert, & Tucker, 1973; Whitaker, 1973; Bindra, 1976). Here are some of the recent findings likely to contribute to a correct solution to the problem of first language acquisition: (a) a large fraction, perhaps as many as half, of the neurons in the associative cortex are uncommitted at birth; (b) these uncommitted neurons seem to self-assemble in the course of life, part spontaneously and part under sensory stimulation; (c) the resulting neuron assemblies are of short, medium, or long duration; (d) all of the mental (perceptual and ideational) processes are processes in such modifiable (plastic) neuronal systems; (e) learning is likely to consist in the formation of new plastic neuronal systems—or, equivalently, in the reinforcement of certain interneuronal connections, in agreement with Hebb's use and disuse hypothesis; (f) the thought and speech centers, though closely interconnected, are different (some aphasics can continue to think, whereas others continue to talk but have ceased to think normally); (g) all of the plastic subsystems of the brain are interconnected, so they influence one another—whence the various mental ''faculties'' are interdependent. In other words, unlike the rest of the nervous system and unlike every other organ, the associative cortex of the human brain is largely plastic. As A. R. Luria used to say, the human brain is *the self-made organ,* i.e., its organization is not totally predetermined by the genome. Shorter: Every one of us builds up his own brain as he learns.

The consequences of the above findings for psycholinguists are or ought to be momentous. Firstly, the newborn brain is capable of learning but does not know anything: it is just as mindless as Aristotle thought. Secondly, learning and the failure to learn certain things depend not only upon sensory stimulation but also on internal factors, mainly on inter-neuronal connectivity and plasticity. (The slate is indeed blank at birth, but the inscriptions that emerge on it are not the exclusive work of the environment: they are partly self-inscribed.)

Thirdly, an animal knows only that which it has learned—and the more he knows the more new items he can get to know. (On the other hand, nativism predicts that there are drastic limits to what man can get to know. Chomsky himself has hinted that we may already be in Act V of the human comedy.) Fourthly, the language "faculty" (neural center) is not independent from the other mental "faculties" (neural centers), but is closely connected with them—hence the acquisition and use of language is just one aspect of a general cognitive (and social) activity. Fifthly, language learning does not occur in a social vacuum: severely neglected children develop poor language.

In short, we are of course genetically endowed with the organ of mind, namely the brain; moreover, different people are presumably born with different abilities. However, we must learn how to speak, just as we must learn how to do sums and even how to walk. To put it differently: we may espouse moderate or potential nativism, not radical or actual nativism. According to the former, every one of us inherits peculiar abilities, e.g., to learn manual skills or to play with abstract ideas. On the other hand, radical nativism—of the kind held by Plato, Leibniz, or Kant—asserts that we are born with certain ideas. Both moderate and radical nativism are compatible with psychophysical monism as well as with dualism. However, only moderate nativism, i.e., the doctrine that we inherit different abilities or propensities, is consistent with contemporary neuroscience and psychology.

(Yet it must not be forgotten that this kind of nativism was much "in the air" for centuries—e.g., in the old adage *Quod natura non dat, Salmantia non prestat*. Huarte (1575) explained it in a famous work that was translated into several languages and reprinted many times—as well as censored by the Inquisition. He regarded the various mental "faculties"—memory, imagination, and intelligence—as functions of subsystems of the brain, and explained the differences in inborn abilities as differences in the composition of the brain. Contemporary neuroscience and physiological psychology tend to side with him—though without accepting the primitive ideas on the composition of the brain which he took from Galen.)

In particular, aphasiology confirms the biological view of speech formation and understanding. Thus, lesions within Wernicke's "area" may destroy a person's ability to understand speech, and a damage to the left angular gyrus may destroy his ability to read, though not to speak. The case of bilingual aphasics is even more interesting. Their recovery fits into half a dozen or so different patterns: whereas in most cases the patient recovers both languages roughly at the same pace, in others the recuperation is successive; in still others the patient experiences complete loss of one of his former languages, or he alternates them or even mixes them up. What is philosophically interesting is that (a) the site of lesion determines the type of deficit, and (b) the pattern of recovery depends on both the site of lesion and the linguistic history of the patient—e.g., more often than not the second language is erased more easily than the first (Paradis, 1983).

These studies suggest that knowledge of each language is "stored" in a precise neural system—separate from, though linked with, the cognitive "store." Unfortunately, all our knowledge about these fascinating facts comes from just 150 or so aphasia cases reported in the world literature. Even so, these case studies are shedding much light on the processes of speech formation and understanding. For one thing, they have confirmed that insults to the brain (e.g., strokes, injuries, and tumors) result in mental deficits—which should be impossible if the mind were an immaterial entity.

I am not claiming that we have already obtained a satisfactory explanation of language acquisition. I am claiming instead that this is a genuine open problem but, at the same time, that we know enough so that we can adopt the correct approach to it. (On the other hand, Chomsky believes that, by postulating that we are born with a knowledge of the mysterious UG, he has solved the problem in its essentials.) I am also claiming that the correct approach to this, or to any other factual problem, is not that of armchair speculation but, instead, the observational, experimental, and (incipiently) theoretical approach adopted by developmental and physiological psychology.

This approach eschews the imprecise notion of a "mental structure," central yet nowhere defined in Chomsky's work, which remains confined to prescientific mentalistic philosophical psychology. It is not that science must ignore the mind, but that it must study it as a set of brain functions. This is in a nutshell the thesis of physiological psychology, the newest and fastest growing branch of psychology. According to it, the study of mind is ultimately an aspect of brain research. To be sure, we cannot dispense with molar or phenomenological psychology; however, such studies provide only data and regularities to be explained in neurophysiological terms.

True, occasionally Chomsky pays lip service to neuroscience, as when he admits that knowledge is ultimately "represented" in our brains (1980, pp. 5, passim). However, he does not explain what he means by 'representation' in this case—which is confusing, because he also employs the expressions 'phonological representation,' 'semantic representation,' 'mental representation,' and the like. And he never states in so many words that we think and speak with the brain (rather than with the mind). All he states is that neuroscience knows hardly anything about all this, so that we are forced to continue using "abstract" (i.e., mentalistic) formulations—which is not quite true. So, one suspects that his mentalism is not just opportunistic (methodological) but principled (ontological).

4. *FROM DESCRIPTION TO EXPLANATION*

Chomsky has rightly insisted all along on the need for going beyond mere description, into explanation. Unfortunately, his own notion of explanation —which oscillates between subsumption and insight—is not the one used in science. In science, to explain a group of facts is to describe their *mechanism* with the help of an empirically confirmed theory (Bunge, 1983b, Ch. 10). We explain the propagation of light by disclosing the mechanism of generation of the magnetic component of the field by the electric one, and conversely. We explain a chemical reaction as inelastic scattering of atoms or molecules. We explain the origin of life in terms of the self-assembly of subcellular units, which in turn would self-assemble from molecules. We explain our having ideas in terms of the activity—now spontaneous, now elicited—of plastic neural systems. And we explain the formation and dissolution of social systems in terms of social relations.

In each case, an explanation, unlike a mere account, involves resorting to some mechanism which, though not necessarily mechanical, is necessarily material. Science does not know of any mental mechanisms, because the mental is no more (and no less) than a collection of brain functions. What science is in the process of discovering is the *neural mechanisms that explain mental phenomena.* On the other hand, Chomsky's postulated "mental structures," that would "underlie" the mental "faculties," do not explain anything: they just redescribe the known facts and surround them with a thick fog that cannot be pierced by either experiment or mathematical modeling.

Let us take a look at the way physiological psychology, in particular my own view (Bunge, 1980), might explain the generation and understanding of phrases or, more realistically, "the larger events in which sentences *and* nonverbal cues occur" (Menzel & Johnson, 1976). The central hypothesis is that minding, in particular forming or understanding bits of language, is the specific function, activity, or process, of certain plastic neuron assemblies which I call *psychons.* (A neuron assembly is said to be *plastic* if its connectivity, in particular its synaptic connectivity, is variable in the course of time after birth—in contrast with the rigid or genetically programmed neuron assemblies that control genuinely innate functions such as breathing or sucking.)

According to this theory, a simple idea is the ephemeral activity of a psychon, and a complex idea that of two or more psychons activated either simultaneously or sequentially. (Each such psychon is likely to be composed of thousands of neurons, and when a psychon makes a concept it undergoes a process likely to last only a fraction of a second.) Thus, thinking up the thought expressed by the sentence *I want my mum* may consist in the successive activation of two psychons, one for the verb phrase and the other for the noun phrase.

Likewise, forming the idea of a beautiful flower may consist in the activation, either simultaneous or sequential, of psychons for the concepts "beautiful" and "flower," respectively. At a deep level, the order of these two concepts may not matter, but it will if the thought is expressed in an utterance. If you are speaking English, the psychon for "beautiful" will have to be activated before that for "flower," whereas, if you are speaking Spanish *(flor bonita),* the order will be reversed. Speech errors, in particular mispronunciations, dyslectic phenomena, and spoonerisms, can be explained as wrong connections. For example, if I utter *John Peter kicked* instead of the correct sentence, it may be because the psychon for *kicked* was delayed as a result of the inhibition by some other psychon. To be sure, these and similar neuropsychological explanations of linguistic phenomena are still coarse and tentative because the whole theory is still in the oven. But they are possible scientific explanations because they jibe with neuroscience—whereas mentalism does not.

5. *CONCLUSION*

To conclude, I suggest that psycholinguists should give up mentalism—even the cryptomentalism of cognitivism or functionalism. They should become physiological (and evolutionary and developmental and social) linguists. The reason is that we happen to produce and understand speech with the brain, not with the mythical soul, let alone with the computer. The advantages of the proposed radical reorientation of psycho-linguistics are many. First, it is forward looking—unlike mentalism, which is stuck to traditional philosophy or even to theology. Second, physiological linguistics can investigate a host of new problems that cannot even be stated within the narrow mentalistic framework—such as 'What kind of neural connections are established when the toddler learns to form his first sentence?', 'Why does bilingualism favor overall cognitive ability?', and 'How does drug or lesion X affect speech production or understanding?' Third, physiological psycholinguistics can make use of evolutionary (or comparative) and developmental psychology, shunned by mentalism. Fourth, physiological linguists try to explain speech production and understanding by revealing the brain mechanisms of these processes. Fifth, this way of conceiving of psycholinguistic research facilitates its merger or integration with other sciences, in particular neuroscience and social science.

REFERENCES

Baranyi, A., & Fehér, O. (1981). Synaptic facilitation requires paired activities of convergent pathways in the neocortex. *Nature, 290,* 413–415.

Bartlett, F. (1958). *Thinking: An experimental and social study.* New York: Basic Books.

Bindra, D. (1976). *A theory of intelligent behavior.* New York: Wiley.

Bliss, T. V. P. (1979). Synaptic plasticity in the hippocampus. *Trends in Neuroscience, 2,* 42–45.

Bunge, M. (1980). *The mind-body problem.* Oxford: Pergamon Press.

Bunge, M. (1983a). *Exploring the world.* Dordrecht: Reidel.

Bunge, M. (1983b). *Understanding the world.* Dordrecht: Reidel.

Bunge, M. (1983c). *Lingüística y filosofía.* Barcelona: Ariel.

Bunge, M. (1984). Philosophical problems in linguistics. *Erkenntnis, 21,* 107–173.

Chomsky, N. (1959). Review of Skinner's *Verbal Behavior. Language, 35,* 26–58.

Chomsky, N. (1962). Explanatory models in linguistics. In E. Nagel, P. Suppes, & A. Tarski (Eds.), *Logic, methodology and philosophy of science.* Palo Alto, CA: Stanford University Press.

Chomsky, N. (1965). *Aspects of the theory of syntax.* Cambridge, MA: MIT Press.

Chomsky, N. (1972). *Language and mind* (enlarged ed.). New York: Harcourt.

Chomsky, N. (1975). *Reflections on language.* New York: Pantheon Books.

Chomsky, N. (1980). *Rules and representations.* New York: Columbia University Press.

Chomsky, N., & Miller, G. A. (1963). introduction to the formal analysis of natural languages. In R. D. Luce, R. R. Bush, & E. Galanter (Eds.), *Handbook of mathematical psychology* (Vol. II). New York: Wiley.

Conel, J. L. (1939–67). *The postnatal development of the human cerebral cortex.* Cambridge, MA: Harvard University Press.

Dale, P. S. (1976). *Language development* (2nd ed.). New York: Rinehart & Winston.

Flohr, H., & Precht, W. (Eds.). (1981). *Lesion-induced neuronal plasticity in sensorimotor systems.* New York: Springer.

Fodor, J. (1975). *The language of thought.* New York: Crowell.

Givón, T. (1979). *On understanding grammar.* New York: Academic Press.

Goddard, G. V. (1980). Component properties of the memory machine: Hebb revisited. In P. W. Juscyk & R. M. Klein (Eds.), *The nature of thought. Essays in honor of D. O. Hebb.* Hillsdale, NJ: Erlbaum.

Hebb, D. O. (1949). *The organization of behavior.* New York: Wiley.

Hebb, D. O., Lambert, W. E., & Tucker, G. R. (1973). A DMZ in the language war. *Psychology Today, 6,* (11), 55–62.

Huarte de San Juan, J. (1575). *Examen de ingenios para las ciencias.* (Reprinted 1976). Madrid: Editora Nacional.

Hubel, D. H. (1982). Exploration of the primary visual cortex, 1955–1978. *Nature, 299,* 515–524.

Menzel, E. W., & Johnson, M. K. (1976). Communication and cognitive organization in humans and other animals. *Annals of the New York Academy of Sciences, 280,* 131–142.

Nottebohm, F. (1981). A brain for all seasons: cyclical anatomical changes in song control nuclei of the canary brain. *Science, 214,* 1368–1370.

Paradis, M. (Ed.) (1983). *Readings on aphasia in bilinguals and polyglots.* Montreal: Didier.

Piaget, J. (1979). La psychogenèse des connaissances et sa signification épistémologique. In M. Piattelli-Palmarini (Ed.), Théories du language, théories de l'apprentissage (pp. 51–64). Paris: Ed. du Seuil.

Piattelli-Palmarini, M. (Ed.) (1979). *Théories du langage, théories de l'apprentissage.* Paris: Ed. du Seuil.

Whitaker, H. A. (1973). Comments on the innateness of langage. In R. W. Shuy (Ed.), *Some New Directions in Linguistics.* Washington, DC: Georgetown University Press.

Wiesel, T. (1982). Postnatal development of the visual cortex and the influence of environment. *Nature, 299,* 583–591.

Chapter 14

From Schema Theory to Computational (Neuro-)Linguistics*

Michael A. Arbib

University of Massachusetts, Amherst

We shall analyze three different computational models of language that we have developed, only one of which is neurological, both to report progress and to explore the challenges to future research posed by the different approaches that they take.

An influential approach to linguistics is that espoused by Noam Chomsky, which holds that language is a faculty unique to man, and poses for linguistics the challenge of seeking the innate rules of the 'language organ' which both characterize the uniqueness of its organization and explain the acquisition of language. For Chomsky, the important datum is whether or not a string of words constitutes a well-formed sentence of a given language. By contrast, the approach to language that we shall espouse here seeks mechanisms of perception and production. While noting that language behavior is highly developed in man, we stress that it is a system of communication and that it involves both action and perception. We see it as mediated by a brain that has evolved from other brains, and thus we seek to understand the brain mechanisms of language within a wider analysis of brain mechanisms subserving action and perception.

Even though we are concerned with both language and brain, it will not be the case that all our linguistic models will be in terms of neural nets. Even

* A preliminary version of this paper was presented to the Cognitive Science Group at McGill University, Montreal, January 29, 1983. My thanks to Myrna Gopnik for her kind hospitality on that occasion. The research reported herein was supported in part by grant no. 80-6-13 from the Alfred P. Sloan Foundation, and by grant no. IST-8104984 from the National Science Foundation. The ideas outlined here will be developed at far greater length in the forthcoming book *From Schema Theory to Language* by Michael A. Arbib, E. Jeffrey Conklin, and Jane C. Hill, to be published by Oxford University Press.

in our models of visuomotor coordination (Arbib, 1981), we use higher-level constructs like motor schemas or depth-computing systems, in addition to the explicit modelling of certain subsystems as neural networks. This is a particular case of the general distinction, in artificial intelligence and brain theory, between top-down and bottom-up modelling. One may either work 'top-down,' starting from some overall function, and breaking it into 'pieces,' seeing how the overall function can be subserved by the interaction of these different sub-functions; or one can work 'bottom-up,' starting from basic units such as LISP instructions or the function of individual neurons, and putting these together to yield subroutines, or neural networks, that can subserve certain functions. Of course, these two approaches may not 'meet in the middle''—the pieces obtained by top-down analysis may not meet the constraints of bottom-up modelling. Thus, after the initial cycle of top-down or bottom-up modelling, a process of refinement is required which might best be described as 'middle-out.' We shall use the term *schema* to characterize the 'middle unit' which serves as the unit for a top-down analysis, and the entity to be explained by a bottom-up analysis. Schema theory is the bridge, high-level enough to provide a graspable language in which we can analyze functions of interest to us, yet low-level enough that we can hope, in principle, to reduce each schema to a computer program or a neural network.

Arbib and Caplan (1979) started their analysis of computational neurolinguistics by studying the faculty approach to neurology, which held there to be one brain region subserving each overall mental faculty. Neurological deficits were then to be seen as either the removal of such a faculty, or the severing of a pathway which connected the 'mental organs' subserving two such faculties. We then observed that a more sophisticated view of localization was offered by Luria, building on the Russian work of Bernstein and Anokhin, of 'functional subsystems,' in which each overall function was subserved by the interaction of a number of subsystems, and each subsystem could play a role in several different overall functions. We thus view localization in terms of the localization of different schemas whose cooperative computation yields some performance, rather than proceeding directly from an overall faculty to a region in which it is localized. Thus, the effect of a lesion is now to be seen not in terms of the removal of a function, but rather in terms of the interactions of the remaining portions of brain. However, one must stress that even this more refined, cooperative computation, approach to neurolinguistics is still at the level of interacting regions of the brain, far removed from the synapse-cell-circuit level of much of modern neuroscience. Certainly, from this point of view, one can see why I am somewhat uncomfortable with Chomsky's talk of language as a faculty, and the suggestion that we should seek the innate rules of the 'language organ.' Instead, one is led to explore the hypothesis that, when one analyzes the cooperatively computing regions of the brain subserving a language performance, at least some of them are also implicated in nonlinguistic perception and control of movement.

In our approach to an 'action-oriented' linguistics, we shall certainly be much influenced by the constructivist theory of cognitive development offered by Jean Piaget, which runs from sensory-motor schemas to adult cognition, including language. Certainly, Chomsky is right when he criticizes Piaget for not providing a sufficiently articulated theory of grammar. However, we believe that it is even more important for us to learn from Piaget's tracing of cognitive structures to their sensory-motor roots. Again, our approach will tend to be computational, where Piaget's was descriptive. Where he described overall stages of mental development, we would seek to understand mechanisms of schema change that could provide the explanation of such stages. We see the schema as an active process. How is it that schemas in interaction with each other subserve cognitive behavior; how is it that, while undergoing these interactions, the schemas change in a fashion that coheres into the stage-by-stage development of cognition? We shall seek, then, to provide computational models of schemas and, where appropriate, their neural instantiations.

To put the following models in perspective, it will be useful to distinguish three levels: at the first level, we have the almost unimaginable complexity of the 'neural reality' of the billions of dynamically interacting neurons that link the activity of our receptors with the activity of our muscles in an ongoing action/perception cycle; then, at the next level, we have a rich but somewhat intuitive account using schemas in an informal sense; and, finally, there is a particular formal model of schemas—perhaps using neural nets or a formal grammar or a semantic net—which gives us increased rigor but at the cost of throwing away many of the intuitions that were captured within our informal descriptions. I believe that, in a subject like linguistics, it is absolutely vital to maintain a tension between the informal intuitions that one has (whether from one's everyday experience, or from work in the laboratory) and the current formal models that one is exploring. I do not find it helpful when certain authors tell us that their current theory is in fact the reality. At our present stage of development, there are many models, and it is by comparing and contrasting them that we can resolve the differences between them to evolve new and more comprehensive models. I believe that this is a process that must continue for a long time to come before we can reach a set of models which it even begins to be safe to confuse with reality.

The core of our argument will be based on the analysis of three models developed within my group. Helen Gigley [1983] has developed a model of sentence understanding which is constrained to explain the effects of lesion data on the brain. It is structured in terms of interacting subsystems, so that the effect of a 'lesion' to one of these subsystems is not to terminate the model's performance, but to degrade it in a way that can be compared with data from the aphasiological clinic. Unfortunately, the state of the art is such that we cannot yet correlate the performance of the model at all well with asphasiological data. This is not only because of the preliminary stage of modelling in neurolinguistics, but also because asphasiological data has been gathered for clinical diagnosis in a way that pays little attention to the issues of performance modelling. The questions we ask in science are always to some extent model-driven.

Jane Hill has offered a 'computational neo-Piagetian' model of repetition and response [Hill and Arbib, 1984]. She explains the way in which a 2-year-old child responds to, or repeats in a transformed way, the sentences of an adult, and she does so in such a way that the internal mechanisms of the model change over time in a fashion which can explain data on language acquisition.

Jeffrey Conklin [1984] has a model of language production which is based on data he has gathered on people describing a visual scene. He seeks to understand how it is that people chunk the information about the scene into packages that can be grouped together and then used to generate a sentence at a time.

These models address very interesting questions in language, but the questions are rather different, and so it is not surprising that, on this first round of modelling, the models themselves are somewhat disparate in nature. Yet, it would seem that in the long run any adequate model of language performance must address the issues raised in these models. Thus, we must see them as stages in the evolution of more comprehensive, and more coherent, linguistic models in the future.

In trying to place these three models in a common perspective, we shall see that, not surprisingly, each involves the interaction of data encoded at different levels (or, in different spaces) of representation. These data are acted upon by processes (knowledge sources, in the jargon of artificial intelligence), or the data themselves may be embodied in the dynamic processes which change them.

Before we analyze our own models in these terms, let us look at two other models from the AI literature: the HEARSAY model of speech understanding, and the VISIONS model of vision.

The job of HEARSAY (Erman & Lesser, 1980) was to take the spectrograph of an utterance and process it to yield the interpretation of the utterance according to some syntactic-semantic grammar. What was important was that the data were inherently noisy—a local sample of the speech stream might be interpreted, with varying levels of confidence, as any one of several distinct phonemes (to get some idea of this, just recall the problem of listening to a song on the radio for the first time). Not only were the phonemes ambiguous, but there was no clear segmentation of the speech stream into the individual words. The data space, called the blackboard, of the HEARSAY system was stratified into different levels for phonemes, syllables, words, phrases, and semantics. The system would at any time have a number of hypotheses, with different confidence ratings, at each level for certain portions of the utterance. It is worth stressing how far we are here from the binary character of much of linguistics. There is no unequivocal parsing at any time; rather, there is a family of differently weighted hypotheses. In fact, AI itself has only recently made the transition from a set of binary constructs to the shifting of confidence levels on a set of alternate hypotheses—as is very marked in such successful 'expert systems' as MYCIN. Returning to HEARSAY, one example of a knowledge source (KS) would be one for the lexicon, which could take a sequence of phoneme hypotheses and return an appropriately weighted word hypothesis; an appropriate syntactic KS could take a sequence of words and not only come up with a phrasal interpretation, but also a prediction of what type of word would have to be present to round out the phrase—a hypothesis that could then be checked at the lower levels. By a sequence of such interactions, proceeding both up and down the levels, HEARSAY finally converges on an overall interpretation of the utterance.

One disappointing feature of HEARSAY is that, although the logic of the system is inherently distributed, with the suggestion that many KSs are simultaneously active, providing the continual changes in data which allow them to cooperate to yield the overall interpretation, the actual implementation of HEARSAY was a serial one, with a single scheduler serving to rate the probability of different KS activations, and then selecting only one KS to be activated at a given time. Arbib and Caplan [1979] offer an analysis of what might be called a 'virtual HEARSAY,' in which we speculate on how one might obtain a distributed HEARSAY in which different subsystems are concurrently active, in a manner that might more closely approximate the function of the brain in linguistic processing.

The job of the VISIONS system (Hanson & Riseman, 1978) is to go from a color photograph to an interpretation of it in terms of a labelling of objects present within the photographed scene. Starting from pixels (picture elements), it extracts local features, and then seeks to aggregate these into edges or regions. These regions can then be aggregated or subdivided to provide meaningful surfaces which can then be used to activate object schemas. Finally, the schema interpretation of the various objects in the scene can be aggregated into a semantic net which shows what objects are present, and what are the basic relationships between them. Low-level processes for edge-finding and region-growing in terms of coherence of local texture can cooperate to come up with confident estimates of regions. However, one region may 'bleed' into another because of highlights, while another region might be subdivided because of shadows or random variations in texture.

At this stage, then, high-level knowledge could be invoked, as in completing a side of a parallelogram to split off the roof of a house from the sky, or in aggregating several regions beneath the roof to form a rectangle, using the knowledge that this is the shape of doors, windows, and shutters.

We present these models not to suggest that they are modules that can be plugged into those models that we are about to describe, but rather to show that there is an evolving methodology of competition and cooperation of which our own models provide three further examples.

One word of caution: in a cooperative system, the notion of levels may be somewhat misleading. For example, House [1982] offers a competitive/cooperative model of depth perception. There are two subsystems involved, one of which forms an initial depth map on the basis of accommodation cues, while the other forms an initial depth map on the basis of stereopsis cues. However, these two subsystems are in constant interaction, and finally converge upon a common depth representation. At that time, it would seem somewhat misleading to refer to either of these two equal maps as being purely at the 'accommodation' level or 'stereopsis' level, although those level labels are indeed appropriate to a functional analysis of what is really involved here. Yet, during the behavior of the model, there is only a small period of time at which one can easily correlate the activity in that subsystem with its 'external' label.

With this background, we now turn to a brief analysis of each of our three models, and we will then close with a brief assessment of the challenge that these models provide to further research.

A NEUROLINGUISTIC MODEL OF SENTENCE UNDERSTANDING

The input to the Gigley model consists of a sequence of words, already segmented, but coded in some convenient phonetic alphabet. This poses the system the challenge of the ambiguity of homonyms. The problem is to take a sentence which contains several possible homonyms and not only come up with a parsing but also a choice of one 'meaning' for each homonym. In the present model, the 'meanings' are impoverished, with minimal cues, such as word type, which are just enough to let us see how cues about meaning can resolve certain ambiguities. As each word is entered into the phonetic space, it triggers all the corresponding meanings in a 'meaning space.' The problem is to end up with a semantic net that represents the overall interpretation of the sentence, in a high-level 'pragmatic space.' The intermediary between the meaning space and the pragmatic space is a grammar space, in which the rules of a categorial grammar are encoded as prediction nodes. For example, the grammatical rule that a sentence is obtained by a noun followed by a verb would be encoded by having a sentence node which would be activated by the presence of a noun at the meaning level, and which would predict the presence of a verb in the following time period of the utterance. Again, as in HEARSAY, each node will have certain activation levels associated with it, so that at any time in each space there will be several, differently weighted, active hypotheses. However, as distinct from the current implementation of HEARSAY, this model is completely distributed. At each time step, every node in every space is an active process which changes its level of activation while affecting the activity of other nodes at the same time. Through these parallel interactions, the system will, following the sequential introduction of one phonetic word after another, converge upon an interpretation of the sentence in the pragmatic space.

As we have emphasized before, what is crucial to the model is that it is programmed in such a way that we can not only simulate the overall function of the system, but can also simulate its functions after various 'lesions' have removed certain subsystems or certain specific capabilities. In some cases, the model will predict that, after a lesion, no overall pragmatic interpretation is formed—a convincing model of an aphasic who could understand nothing. This is, of course, one of the easier phenomena to model! Clearly, it is more interesting when the model yields a truncated representation which can be correlated, via comprehension tests, with the representations formed by aphasics. Unfortunately, there are relatively few aphasic tests which provide just the sort of data needed to help us develop a model of this kind. One series of tests that Gigley [1982] conducted as part of her thesis was to show patients a series of pictures such that several of the pictures could be referred to by homonyms—such as a man rowing a boat followed by a picture of a row of beans. With these tests, she was able to show that aphasics still had some access to multiple meanings—though, of course, this does not show that they access them all simultaneously. However, there are psycholinguistic data on simultaneous multiple access, and the presence of models such as Gigley's encourages the extension of these psycholinguistic tests to aphasic populations.

LANGUAGE ACQUISITION IN THE 2-YEAR-OLD

We now turn to the Hill model (1983) of language performance and acquisition in the 2-year-old child. Central to the model is the interaction between cognitive and linguistic representations. What the child says, and how the child changes, is based upon her appreciation of the context. A cognitive grouping can lead to a linguistic regrouping, which can form an important part of the process of language acquisition. We do not ascribe to the child adult linguistic groupings, such as noun or verb, or the language universals inferred from the study of adult language. Words start as separate units, and it is only through the pattern of usage that they become grouped into various classes. The grammar that we have chosen for the 2-year-old is a template grammar. Initially, at the two-word phase, there are almost as many types of grammar as there are authors in the field. We feel that a template, consisting of a relation followed by an object slot, makes the minimal assumptions. Over time, these two-word templates get 'pushed together' to form three- or four-word templates. And that is as far as the model goes. Hill observed the performance of a 2-year-old child named Claire over a 10-week period, and the model represents the week by week change in her performance over that time. It is worth stressing that the child's performance was different every week. We do not believe that any model can truly represent what is going on in the child if it is based on lumped data from a group of children over any extended period of time.

Such data do not accord well with a Chomskian view that what the child is doing is learning criteria for well-formed (in the adult sense) sentences. A child goes, day by day, week by week, through different stages as its language comes closer and closer to the adult norm—though it must be emphasized that almost every adult has his own distinctive idiolect. In fact, Chomsky would not claim that the child has at any time an adult grammar, but rather that every grammar that a child has obeys the same set of language universals as the adult's. He would suggest that, if you have an adult model, it is more parsimonious to argue backward from it to the model of child grammar than to create a child grammar de novo. Why not build a model which it is easy to have develop into the adult model? Now, given our talk of seeing a number of alternate models which are then to be resolved, we certainly believe it is worthwhile for some linguists to follow this Chomskian program. However, we feel it is also worthwhile to follow a different, more Piagetian, approach, in which what one takes as basic is not a set of adult descriptors, but rather a growth process. We ask whether it is possible to avoid building in the rules of adult language, but rather to have them constructed through experience within a particular type of environment. Until we have well-articulated acquisition models of both kinds, which we can then compare in some depth, we shall not understand language acquisition at all well.

Given an adult sentence, the job of the Hill model is either to 'repeat it,' but in an abridged form, or to respond to it. The nature of the response will, of course, depend upon some representation of the context.

In the grammar for the child at this age, we only use flat templates. This is based on the psycholinguistic observation of Ed Matthei (1979) that when told to look for the 'second green ball' the child will look at the second ball and be surprised if it is not green—he uses a flat structure in which he expects 'second' and 'green' to modify ball equally, rather than seeing the word 'second' as modifying the construct 'green ball.' We see that the model explains not only how the child processes each adult's sentence as it is heard, but also how the child's language mechanisms change as each sentence is processed. We disagree with the 'tadpole and frog' view of Gleitman and Wanner (1982) that the child's early language is in fact not language at all but a different 'tadpole,' namely prelanguage, which does not grow into, but is quite different from, the 'frog' of adult language. Of course, we cannot prove our thesis that the child's language matures into adult language, for the model only follows the child through a few months of its third year. However, we feel that the surprisingly rich phenomena that we have exhibited suggests that it would be premature to capitulate to the 'tadpole and frog' theme, and so we see the need for further studies to show whether a basic repertoire of mechanisms can indeed subserve the development from the 2-year-old's language to that of the adult. What is to be stressed is that our model does not look at acquisition based on criteria of adult well-formedness, but rather analyzes how a process of continual and dynamic change could yield language structures which come closer and closer to these adult criteria—but without having these adult criteria built into them as part of the acquisition mechanism. It is also important that, in this model, the changes that take place depend importantly on the interaction between language and cognition.

We would also stress the nonbinary nature of the model. It is not that at any time there is a set of rules which currently belong to the grammar, so that a sentence is well-formed if and only if it can be generated by these rules. Rather, there is a set of differentially weighted rules for perception and production which do not classify any sentence as being either well-formed or not, but rather determine which behavior is more likely to occur within a given context. Once a template is formed, its weighting may continually decline so that it no longer plays any important role in behavior, or it may have its weight maintained or increased, so that it may in time come to be seen as part of the adult grammar.

GENERATING DESCRIPTIONS OF VISUAL SCENES

The third model that we shall discuss, due to Jeffrey Conklin [1984], grew out of a concern for charting possible interactions between computational linguistics and machine vision. The task was, given a photograph of an outdoor scene, to generate a verbal description of the scene. In fact, the scenes that we have studied people describing are more complex than those that can currently be analyzed by a machine vision system. Nonetheless, we prepare for each such scene a representation of the kind that we expect in due course to be obtainable by computer analysis: a semantic network in which each node represents an object in the scene, while an edge joining two nodes represents some relationship between the corresponding objects. Again, continuing our emphasis on weights rather than all-or-none determinations, we add to the nodes of the network a salience measure. To gain more insight into salience, Conklin, Ehrlich, and McDonald [1984] asked people to take a photograph and (a) write down a description of the photograph; or (b) given a list of objects which might or might not appear in the photograph, rank order them in terms of the importance of their appearance in the photograph. On this basis, they were able to come up with a salience ordering for objects in the scene. Interestingly, the ordering from the list and from the description was similar, but not quite the same, and it was part of Conklin's thesis to explain this discrepancy. An object could be salient either because it was large and central (low-level salience) or because of its intrinsic interest, such as a person (high-level salience). Moreover, an object could be increased in salience by being near a salient object: for example, if one showed a person a scene and then a new scene changed by the addition of a human figure, then objects near the human in the second scene would have a higher salience than they had in the first. Such considerations led to an informal theory of salience, rather than a computational model which could go from a scene to the salience ordering. The second part of the thesis starts with a semantic network with salience labelling, generated by the experimenter. The challenge was to design a computer program which can go from this weighted network to a sequence of sentences of the kind that a person might generate in describing the scene. Conklin's system is called GENARO, and it creates structures that can serve an input to MUMBLE, a system designed by David McDonald [1981] which can use rhetorical cues to restructure a formalism into the form of English language output. GENARO inspects the semantic network and places objects on a stack in order of decreasing salience. In each subcycle, it takes the most salient element off the stack, and then inspects the network to find its most salient relationships. A number of rhetorical rules compete, and the one that 'wins' provides one package of rhetorical specification. GENARO repeats this subcycle until it has enough packages to constitute a rhetorical unit, and this unit is then sent to MUMBLE for translation into a sentence. The process then continues as long as desired to give a more and more elaborate description of the scene, until some time limit is reached, or the semantic network is exhausted.

MUMBLE is a metasystem—to work in any domain, it must be given a dictionary which provides the rhetorical rules appropriate to the current domain of discourse. Thus the design of the scene description system not only involves the design of the way GENARO will process a weighted semantic network, but also requires the provision of an appropriate dictionary to MUMBLE.

UNITIES AND DIVERSITIES

These, then, are our three models. They address quite different data: lesion data, acquisition data, and scene description data. They also use quite different grammars: a categorial grammar in prediction-node form; a template grammar; and, in the case of MUMBLE, a production grammar based on Chomsky's transformational grammar. These models of grammar are rather disparate. However, once we go from the static description of the rules to the dynamic processes which implement them, it is not clear how great the difference is, or, more to the point, whether the differences are essential. In any case, we do need process grammars for both parsing and production, and ways in which to refine them on the basis of both the performance issues addressed here, and on the basis of syntactic and semantic data.

In our analysis of visuomotor coordination, we have come up with a rich, though still somewhat informal, notion of a schema subserving action or perception, which can tune many parameters as it comes to embody the recognition of complex objects in the environment and provide the parameters necessary for interaction with that object. By contrast, the semantic representation in the above models has been greatly impoverished, corresponding, essentially, to a fragment of a semantic net, perhaps tagged with numbers for salience—providing a sort of minimal conceptual dependency. There is no conceptual problem here. We know that in this first pass in making these three language models, we have deliberately left out most of the richness of language. We did not allow any pragmatic cues in determining meaning in the Gigley model; we artificially introduced a concept space in the Hill model, without explaining how it is that the child knew that a particular object was present; and, in the Conklin model, we explicitly separated the processes of visual perception from the processes of language production. Once we move beyond these simplifications, then we shall have to move beyond the simple semantic nets to incorporate more and more of the features of the full schema theory. In fact, in a fully developed scene-description model, one would expect there to be a continual interaction between description and perception—as the rhetorical need to add certain information to a sentence would drive eye movements which would modify the ongoing process of perception.

In conclusion, then, we see that, far from being discouraging, the somewhat disparate character of these three models provides a stimulus for the further development of a framework in which we can study language in interaction with action and perception. This theme is further developed in the forthcoming book *From Schema Theory to Language* by Michael A. Arbib, Jeffrey E. Conklin, and Jane C. Hill.

DISCUSSION

The Claire model is obtained by observing carefully the psycholinguistic data and extracting a few generalizations, and then showing that a simple mechanism of language acquisition employing these few generalizations can explain a larger body of data. The big question, then, is how far the model can be extended—can it explain the 3-year-old, the 4-year-old...? At the moment, there seems no simple way to get the transition to recursive rules without augmenting the mechanism in some way. Perhaps, eventually, we shall be able to see how a general learning mechanism could go from the child's repeated use of intensifiers, such as 'big big big...' to the spontaneous occurrence of nesting, which can then be used to generate other recursive rules as well. Or are we really going to have to postulate that there is an actual maturational mechanism corresponding to Piaget's stages, so that new types of process or learning rule become available as the child matures, to drive the transition from one stage of language behavior to the next? I hypothesize that this is not necessary, but do not yet see how to eliminate it.

It is also worth noting that none of these models has a rich enough concept space to represent the use of language itself. In AI terminology, the system does not have 'knowledge about knowledge'. It is clear, then, that any acquisition model must have more built into it than was built into the Hill model. The exciting question is whether what has to be added can be seen as fleshing out a set of general learning processes, or whether in fact one must actually build in adult linguistic universals, as Chomsky has postulated. No one who studies the aphasiological data can doubt that there are specific brain structures which are specially adapted for human language performance. What we would quarrel with is the postulation that these can and should be studied in isolation from 'non-linguistic' brain regions (or even the claim that such a dichotomy is indeed supportable). We also doubt that the specialization of regions of the brain to support language processing implies that they must be specialized to encode ab initio certain linguistic universals.

In the book "Language and Learning: The Debate between Jean Piaget and Noam Chomsky" (Piatelli-Palmarini, 1980), it is interesting to note that biologists seemed more sympathetic to the work of Chomsky than Piaget, even though I would claim that Piaget's concern for the development of logic and language from a sensory-motor basis is in fact more biological. I think we can understand this by noting that the major biological model for development is that of embryology, and in embryology we normally think of the genes as specifying the form of the adult organism, with environmental effects seen as disturbances which are to be regulated against. However, I would claim that the formation of the adult language is very different from the formation of the adult body. It would perhaps be better to compare the process of language acquisition to the biological process of evolution, which we all accept to be very much open to environmental influence, no matter how much it must rest upon built-in biological mechanisms of variation. No one would claim that the form of a man was preprogrammed in the genes of an amoeba from which he evolved. I claim that when Chomsky appeals to biology, he is not in fact offering a biological theory of language. He is using analogies to biological systems, which are unconstrained by data; he is not looking, for example, at the data of aphasiology to explain the mechanisms which underlie language.

I also suspect that Chomsky's emphasis on innateness—the idea that the basic universals of syntax are already programmed in, so only a small amount of triggering is required to provide the adult language competence—is fostered in no small part by his emphasis on a rather abstract level of syntactic description, rather than a rich analysis of the particularities of language constructs, let alone the immense culturally determined diversity of the lexicon. I also think it is somewhat misleading to claim, without further evidence, that the acquisition of language over a period of nine years or so is inexplicable. We have already seen that Claire's language changes week by week, and that with a relatively simple learning mechanism, and a few hundred sentences of input, we can explain a nontrivial part of her language development. It is thus not unreasonable to expect that general learning mechanisms can indeed explain a great deal of the data provided by half a million sentences heard over a 9-year period.

REFERENCES

Arbib, M. A. (1981). Perceptual structures and distributed motor control. In: V. B. Brooks, (Ed.), *Handbook of physiology—The nervous system II. Motor control* (pp. 1449–1480). Bethesda, MD: American Physiological Society.

Arbib, M. A., & Caplan, D. (1979). Neurolinguistics must be computational. *Behavioral and Brain Sciences, 2,* 449–483.

Conklin, J. C. (1984). *Salience as a heuristic in planning text generation.* Ph.D. dissertation, Department of Computer and Information Science, University of Massachusetts/Amherst.

Conklin, J. C., Ehrlich, K., & McDonald, D. (1983). An empirical investigation of visual salience and its role in text generation. *Cognition and Brain Theory, 6,* (2).

Erman, L., & Lesser, V. R. (1980). The HEARSAY II system: A tutorial. In W. A. Lea (Ed.), *Trends in speech recognition* (pp. 361–381). Englewood Cliffs, NJ: Prentice Hall.

Gigley, H. M. (1983). HOPE—AI and the dynamic process of language behavior. *Cognition and Brain Theory 6,* 39–88.

Gigley, H. M. (1982). *A processing model of English language comprehension.* Ph.D. Thesis, Department of Computer and Information Science, University of Massachusetts/Amherst.

Gleitman, L., & Wanner, E. (1982). *Language learning: The state of the art.* Cambridge: Cambridge University Press.

Hanson, A. R., & Riseman, E. M. (1978). VISIONS: A computer system for interpreting scenes. In: A. R. Hanson & E. M. Riseman, (Eds.), *Computer Vision Systems* (pp. 129–163). New York: Academic Press.

Hill, J. C. (1983). A computational model of language acquisition in the two-year-old. *Cognition and Brain Theory 6,* 287–317.

Hill, J. C., & Arbib, M. A. (1984). Schemas, computation, and language acquisition. *Human Development, 27,* 282–296.

House, D. H. (1982). The frog/toad depth perception system—A cooperative/competitive model. In *Proceedings of the Workshop on Visuomotor Coordination in Frog and Toad:*

Models and Experiments (Tech. Report 82-16). Department of Computer and Information Science, University of Massachusetts/Amherst.

Matthei, E. (1979). *The acquisition of prenominal modifier sequences: Stalking the second green ball.* Ph.D. Dissertation, Department of Linguistics, University of Massachusetts/Amherst.

McDonald, D. D. (1981). MUMBLE: A flexible system for language production. In *Proceedings of the 7th IJCAI* (Vol. II), Vancouver, Canada.

Piattelli-Palmarini, M. (Ed.) (1980). *Language and learning: The debate between Jean Piaget and Noam Chomsky.* Cambridge, MA: Howard University Press.

PART VI

SEMANTICS

Chapter 15

Approaches to the Semantics of Questions in Natural Language: Part I

N. D. Belnap, Jr.
University of Pittsburgh

The intent of Belnap (1982), building on Bennett (1979), was to contribute some detailed proposals concerning the semantics of natural language questions in a Montague framework (Montague, 1974). In this paper, I survey the work of a variety of researchers in the field in order to consider some fundamental issues which must be faced in giving a semantic account of natural language questions in the "possible worlds" style of Montague. Naturally, what I say presupposes the usefulness of the Montague style and does not envisage its wholesale abandonment, but let me say first that I shall also deal with the work of others, so long as it is at least formal, and second that I certainly expect significant enrichments from sources such as the theory of "situations" of Barwise (1981) and Barwise and Perry (1981, 1983).

In this first part of a two-part paper, I take up the relation between direct and indirect questions, and the relation of each to answers. I define the Equivalence thesis (that direct and indirect questions are semantically equivalent) and the Independent meaning thesis (that indirect questions are categorematic), I complain about the Reduction thesis (that questions are "reducible" to commands or assertions), I defend the Answerhood thesis (that the answers to a question are at least part of its meaning), and I test a number of semantic proposals for their ability to generate a theory of answers (the Answerhood test).

My tentative plan for Part II is as follows. I will move to a more detailed discussion of a variety of approaches to the semantics of questions, touching especially on the distribution test for answerhood, the unique answer fallacy, completeness claims as parts of answers, and quantification into questions. I will reach the surprising conclusion that some approaches to the semantics of questions are better than others.

1. DIRECT AND INDIRECT QUESTIONS

Consider the following exhibit:

Direct question	*Indirect question*
John: Did Mary come?	John asked whether Mary came.
John: What did Mary eat?	John asked what Mary ate.

I have labeled the items on the left *direct questions* and those on the right *indirect questions,* but there is enormous terminological blithering in this area. Some people don't like the rubric "indirect questions" for the items on the right, since these clauses don't ask or put questions and perhaps don't have answers (what is the answer to what Mary ate?). Some people don't like the term "question" for any of these, and prefer "interrogative", thinking of the proportion "sentence:statement::interrogative:question." Some don't like the direct/indirect terminology (what on earth is indirect about what Mary ate?), others use it doubtless because of its connections with direct vs. indirect speech reports, as exhibited above. Some syntacticians emphasize features of the right hand elements by labeling them "wh-complements", while others worry that such terminology might lead to confusion with relative clauses. If I were legislating with some hope of success, I might forget that the left hand elements as well as the right can find themselves in larger contexts, and call the left items "stand-alone interrogatives" and the right items "embeddable interrogatives"; but I have no such hope and so adopt "direct question/indirect question" as (a) usual and (b) memorable, with the understanding that the terminology is doing no work at all other than to mark the distinction exhibited.

There are a number of different theories about the relations between direct and indirect questions; before looking at them, I want to clarify what forms are being distinguished by drawing analogies with declaratives and imperatives. A direct question is a *stand-alone form,* which can be followed by a full stop (question mark). It is analogous to a stand-alone declarative sentence, followed by a full stop (period), and to the stand-alone imperative sentence followed by a full stop (period, or, sometimes, an exclamation point). Each of these stand-alone forms has one or more nominalized *embeddable forms,* most easily discerned in an indirect speech report (tensed for comfort):

Stand-alone	*Embeddable*
Did Mary come?	J asked P *whether Mary came.*
Mary came.	J told P *that Mary came.*
Come!	J ordered Mary *to come.*

I think we can already conclude this: the nominalized embeddable forms *are* (by their nature) embeddable forms; their point or function is to permit us to embed in larger contexts, contexts which can take only a noun, a form of the stand-alone sentences.

Why are new forms needed for embedding? For English, the answer seems to be to be this: English loves its nouns above all else, especially the noun-verb construction, and vastly prefers this method of embedding to any other. It is for this reason that the embeddable forms are all nominal in character. Hiz (1962) once called that-clauses "nominalized sentences"; and I wish to adopt his point of view though not quite his terminology: that-clauses are nominalized declaratives, indirect questions are nominalized interrogatives (or questions—in this paper I have no good reason to enforce a terminological distinction), and infinitive clauses are some of them nominalized imperatives. And the reason they are nominalized is to make embedding easy.[1] ("Deliberative questions" in the sense of Wheatley (1955) such as "what shall I wear?" or "shall I come?" take nominalized embeddable forms involving both question-words and infinitives such as "what to wear" or "whether to come." This fits with the suggestion of Mayo (1956) that their answers are imperatives. I know of no published accounts of the semantics of these, nor of "skill-questions" such as "how do you (does one) tie a square knot," which embeds as "how to tie a square knot.")[2]

2. *EQUIVALENCE THESIS*

What about the semantic relation between the two forms? I think everyone agrees that, in the case of embeddings such as coordination that do not (like the above) require linguistic tinkering, embedded sentences should receive the same semantic treatment as stand-alone sentences (let's forget about indexicality):

Stand-alone	*Embedded*
Mary came.	Mary came, and Peter was with her.
Did Mary come?	Did Mary come, and was Peter with her?
Come!	Come, and bring Peter!

Logicians are most familiar with arguments for the first case: unless "Mary came" has the same (or an equivalent) semantic value both standing alone

[1] Three notes: the declarative background for this view of the function of indirect questions is to be found in the "prosentential theory of truth" of Grover, Camp, and Belnap (1975); Thomason has repeatedly suggested in conversation a relation between imperatives and infinite clauses; and an extended and persuasive argument that indirect questions really are properly so-called is given by Baker (1968, 1970).

[2] With regard to the former, Thomason tells me that conversations he had with R. Cooper and E. Engdahl suggested that the matter was straightforward. With regard to the latter, Alan Ross Anderson was fond of observing that there was at least one abstract entity which you could show people, maybe even *homo javanensis:* how to tie a square knot.

and embedded as a conjunct, then "simplification" would be mysterious. But it seems to me noncontentious that the semantics of "did Mary come" and "Come" are also independent of whether they are embedded (coordinated) or not.

I want now to go a step further and assert the *Equivalence thesis,* that even if linguistic tinkering such as nominalization intervenes, the stand-alone and embeddable forms should be semantically equivalent. I say "equivalent" and not "identical" for at least this reason: a typical possible-worlds treatment of the sentence "Mary came" might give it the type of truth-values, so that its sense is a mapping from indexes into truth-values; and simultaneously give "that Mary came" the type of a proposition, so that its sense is a (constant) mapping from indexes into propositions—the same proposition at every index. That's all right with me, for even in this case, the semantic value of the stand-alone sentences is recoverable from the semantic value of the that-clause, and vice versa. Thus, "propositions" may be reified as functions from indexes into truth-values, the very sort of sense-value given to the stand-alone sentence, so that we have the following recipe: the sense of the that-clause is a function which carries every index into the sense of the stand-alone sentence; and the sense of the stand-alone sentence is obtained by applying the sense of the that-clause to any index you like.

Differences like these amount to differences in what I call "semantic style": it is true that sentences and that-clauses are given different types of semantic values; *but* the values are equivalent, so that the difference is only stylistic. (Which is not to say that it is not for some purposes important.)

The conclusion is this: the semantic values of stand-alone questions and their embeddable forms should be equivalent if not identical. (Also imperatives vis-a-vis infinite clauses.) I repeat the key premise: the only reason for the embeddable forms is to make the embedding run more smoothly; but there is no profound semantic increment, decrement, or change from the stand-alone form.

The hypothesis of the Equivalence thesis is that we have in hand one direct question and one indirect question which can be recognized as paired, perhaps as "paraphrases" of each other (I am unsure of the best terminology). The thesis would be uninteresting, if it were not by and large true that in fact direct questions and indirect questions come in such pairs, and if it were not also true that the pairing is by and large easily recognizable; but it is not part of the thesis that recognizable pairing is universal. A possible counter example is due to Bolinger (1978). There he considers direct yes/no questions such as "did Mary come?" and *two* indirect forms, "whether Mary came" as noted above, but also "if Mary came" as in "John asked (wondered, did not know) if Mary came." The data Bolinger presents might be taken as suggesting that "whether" and "if" yield two indirect forms of the same direct question, but I think instead that he is saying that it is "if" rather than "whether" that functions to yield "the" embeddable form of yes/no questions. Certainly, Bolinger argues that the indirect forms do not mean the same: "*whether* always implies contrasted propositions" (p. 99), whereas "*if* only reports a question" (p. 99), and "a question advances a hypothesis for confirmation, in any degree, not just in terms of polar opposites" (p. 104).[3] And, certainly Bolinger argues that adding an "or not" to a direct yes/no question makes a difference: "did you like Hawaii?" cannot be replaced by "did you like Hawaii or not?" The former seems to permit answers of intermediate strength such as "only a little," whereas the latter tends to ask for "polar opposites." The parallelism between Bolinger's two claims, one about indirect and one about direct questions, appears to indicate that Bolinger is suggesting that "if Mary came" is the embeddable form of "did Mary come?" while "whether Mary came" is the embeddable form of "did Mary come or not?"

Even if the suggestion I impute to Bolinger is right, we might or might not wish to represent the differences he argues for at the semantic level;[4] and if we do, we might or might not wish to take Bolinger's own suggestion as a hint for developing the divergent semantic analyses.[5] But these matters do not touch on any foundational issue, and, indeed, in my subsequent remarks I shall continue to suppose that "whether" gives us the embeddable form of direct yes/no questions. What *is* foundational is this: *if* Bolinger is right that "if Mary came" is the embeddable form of "did Mary come?", *then* the semantic analyses given to these two forms should be equivalent (and similarly for the semantic analyses of "did Mary come or not?" and "whether Mary came").

One thing the Equivalence thesis predicts is that ambiguity of direct questions and their indirect cousins go hand in hand. I don't suppose this is strictly true (nothing in linguistics ever is), but there certainly are some interesting cases where this happens. For example, "where can I find a couple of screwdrivers?" is ambiguous, as between asking for a single place for the

---

[3] I think by "question" Bolinger here means "direct so-called yes/no questions such as 'did you like Hawaii?'"

[4] For example, we might take the difference to concern only implicatures and not literal content and by this means avoid a challenge to the Equivalence thesis.

[5] What I have in mind is this: "whether Mary came" would have as its possible direct answers just "Mary came" and "Mary didn't come," while "if Mary came" would (on the suggestion I impute to Bolinger) have these together with other sentences expressing degrees of confirmation: "Mary probably came," "it's not likely that Mary came," "it's doubtful that Mary came," and the like. (The form (q?A) of Stahl, 1969, is superficially similar in asking for some function *f* of A; Stahl, however, restricts *f* to truth functions.) But it does seem to me unlikely that there is a *theory* here. I worry for example about "did you like Hawaii?" The possibility of having "only a little" as an answer seems to depend on details of the syntax of the question that no semantic theory on the scene is likely to pay attention to—for good (I should say) reason.

two screwdrivers, or as allowing the two screwdrivers to be in different places; and the indirect form has exactly the same ambiguity: "where I can find a couple of screwdrivers" as in "I wonder where I can find a couple of screwdrivers." (It is beside the point that the "I wonder" declarative has, as a whole, a third reading, according to which I am wondering, for each of a couple of screwdrivers, where it can be found.)

3. *OBJECTIONS TO THE EQUIVALENCE THESIS*

To the Equivalence thesis one might object that though the direct and indirect forms may well have something in common, they are surely not "equivalent" since they do such different jobs. For example, stand-alone interrogatives are used to ask questions, whereas the nominalized embeddable forms cannot be used for this purpose: one can ask a question by uttering "did Mary come?" but not "whether Mary came."

The remark is true, the argument fallacious. "Equivalent" does not mean "identical in all respects," but only in certain important respects that it is the duty of semantics to highlight. With regard to the example, of course indirect questions cannot be used to ask questions, since (and only since) they are nouns. So much is a fact of nonphilosophical English grammar. I am not at all inclined to urge that indirect questions are in some deep sense names as well as nouns, since I think the principal reason they are nouns is (merely) to permit embedding in the preferred English manner—noun/verb—but let us for a moment suppose that they name in some serious sense. Then I want to say: what the embedded forms name is questions—the very same questions that are asked or put by the stand-alone forms. According to this recipe, for example, "whether Mary came" names the same question that "did Mary come?" can be used to ask. Analogously, although I think that the principal function of "that" is to permit English embedding of declaratives,[6] to the extent that that-clauses are taken as names, I want to say that "that Mary came" names the same statement that "Mary came" can be used to make; and "to come" names the same order that "come!" can be used to give (as in "John gave Mary the order to come," "John told Mary to come," "Mary refused to come.").

I know of only one thoroughly explicit extended argument against the Equivalence thesis, that of Hausser (1976). In fact, Hausser, has five arguments. (a) Direct and indirect questions "have different denotations" (p. 20). Perhaps, but as explained above, I am using "equivalence" in a sense which evades the complaint (p. 11) that "expressions which are of different categories (and correspond to different types) can hardly be semantically equivalent." (b) They have different intonations and (c) different word-

[6] See Grover, Camp, and Belnap (1975).

orders (p. 20; only English is spoken of). True, and certainly relevant, but surely *slim* hypotheses from which to deduce a semantic difference. (d) I agree that the possibility of using direct and indirect questions in equivalent locutionary acts "is of no semantic significance" (p. 21), and my argument does not rely on such a premise. (e) Hausser says that he fails "to see in what intuitive sense ['Bill knows who arrived'] should have anything to do with the question ['who arrived?']," though he can see the point for "Bill asked who arrived" (p. 21). But if Hausser is right about the first example, then we are left with a mystery between the "Bill knows who arrived" example and "Bill knows the answer to the question as to who arrived," and in general it is left totally mysterious why virtually every indirect question can be embedded after "the question as to."

Hausser's argument occurs as part of a proposal which in fact distinguishes direct and indirect questions semantically: the direct are realized via translation into fully closed lambda expressions, whereas indirect questions get translated into sentences, but open sentences (see, e.g., p. 26). This is convenient for the treatment of question-embedding verbs, since now they can *all* be construed as taking sentential (or open-sentential) complements. But, at least without a lot of extra tinkering, the suggestion won't work. That sentences which are clearly closed in English are translated into sentences which are open in the target language which provides the semantics, should already make one nervous: those free variables in the open sentences translating indirect questions are going to have to get closed somewhere, somehow. But apart from this, the proposal, as it stands, does not allow us to distinguish between indirect questions which are translated into open sentences because they are indirect questions, and indirect questions which are translated into open sentences because they are open (e.g., "whether she came"). It therefore appears that it would be difficult for the apparatus (without modification) to represent the ambiguity of "John wondered whether someone came," which depends on the two possible scopes of the quantifier.

If all this is true, it seems to count as a somewhat indirect reason in favor of the Equivalence thesis. And the strength of the reason is increased by observing that the problems I mention for the Hausser approach to indirect questions are all solved by giving his indirect questions exactly the same representation as his direct questions—namely, via lambda abstracts, binding those and only those variables which need to be bound. The price-tag on the theory that results might to him seem high: one then has to treat question-embedding verbs as infinitely or anyhow multiply ambiguous as to type, because of the plethora of types of lambda abstracts. But I must say that since Hausser has already decided to treat *direct* questions as having the same ambiguity, this does not seem to weigh against the modification. Or to turn the point around: if the price is too high for verbs embedding indirect questions, then one should not in the first place have allowed direct questions to be of many types.[7]

Another objection against the Equivalence thesis is this: direct questions have an imperatival element but indirect questions do not. One might of course not wish to include this imperatival element in semantic representations, which in fact is the most common choice,[8] and one I make myself; in this case the Equivalence thesis is not threatened. Even, however, if the choice is made to include the imperatival element in the semantic representation of direct questions, but not in that of indirect questions, there might still be a residue of the Equivalence thesis which would suffice for such purposes as I can think of: namely, that the semantic representaton of paired direct and indirect questions might be each recoverable from the other (perhaps simply by a mindless adding of subtracting of a semantic marker of the imperatival element). Furthermore, since it would seem that a precisely analogous remark is in order for the "assertoric" element of stand-alone declaratives, I find this objection largely undisturbing.

Closely related to it is the Katz and Postal (1964) observation, endorsed in Wachowicz (1978),[9] that certain adverbs such as "probably' can be used with indirect questions but not with either direct questions or imperatives. "Who probably stole the Picasso?" sounds bad, but "I know who probably stole the Picasso" sounds fine. I am not sure the data are accurate (surround those occurrences of "probably" with commas and everything sounds better), but if the conclusion is to be that direct and indirect questions must be distinguished semantically, then, by parity of reasoning, we shall also have to conclude that stand-alone declaratives and embedded declaratives must be treated differently; for "you probably stole the Picasso" is fine, but "if you probably stole the Picasso, you won't get away with it" gets an asterisk from me. So, by a kind of reductio ad absurdum, the Equivalence thesis survives, at least to the following extent (which is all I want): there is as close an equivalence between the meanings of direct and indirect questions as there is between the meanings of stand-alone and embedded declaratives.

4. *INDEPENDENT MEANING THESIS*

If the semantic content of direct and indirect questions is equivalent, it follows, I take it, that indirect questions are categorematic: each is an independently meaningful constituent of the larger structures in which it finds

[7] Wesley Salmon: "One man's *modus ponens* is another man's *modus tollens.*"

[8] Even Åqvist and Hintikka note that the imperatival element in their representations play no interesting role.

[9] Wachowicz also says that "there is a semantic difference between indirect questions which are statements and direct questions which are requests" (p. 158). There is not enough context to make plain what is intended here; surely not that "whether Mary came" is a statement.

itself, contributing its meaning as a unit. I do wish to draw this conclusion, which I shall label the *Independent meaning thesis.*

It is part of the thesis that a sentence such as "John knew whether Mary came" can receive a sensible semantic treatment by taking its form to be "John knew IQ," where "IQ" holds the place of an arbitrary indirect question. It is also part of the thesis that those who treat it as having some form like "John knew-whether S" will give us only spotty results and insights. There are perhaps only finitely many question-embedding verbs and perhaps only finitely many so-called wh-words; but the numbers of each are large, so that the multiplication caused by the hyphenation-treatment makes dizzy those who think much about the matter. And there is an additional multiplicative factor to be considered in view of questions with more than one wh-particle ("John knows who ate which apples").

It is also part of the thesis, presumably the most interesting because the easiest to try to falsify, that indirect questions have the same meaning regardless of how embedded:

Did Mary come?
John knew *whether Mary came.*
Peter guessed *whether Mary came.*
Whether Mary came didn't matter.
Whether Mary came depended on where she wished to be.
Rebecca wondered *whether Mary came.*

It is hard to make the case directly in ordinary English, since these indirect questions are what Baker (1968) happily calls "sentential nominals" instead of "object nominals," which means in part that they don't pronominalize very well with "it" or the like: in the absence of substantial context, it would be a joke for someone to say "Rebecca wondered whether Mary came, whereas Peter guessed it."[10] It would be an equal travesty to try to relate the thesis to something like "What mattered to Paul is the very same thing that depended upon where Mary preferred to be," for this recipe, too, treats indirect questions as if they were serious names of objects instead of devices to ease the embedding of interrogatives.[11] No, the Independent meaning thesis only urges that the contribution of the indirect question to each of the above examples should be the same: one has not understood the meaning of "whether Mary came" unless one has understood, not what object it names, but what meaning it provides to every one of those sentences.

As others have pointed out, Hintikka's approach trips over the Independent meaning thesis. On that approach, "John knows whether Mary came"

---

[10] Analysis titters.

[11] It seems to me that Vendler (1972), for example, relies too much on the fact that English itself can be pressed to forget that sentential nominals are not object nominals, so as to cause us to worry about "objects" of knowledge or belief.

is equivalent to "If Mary came then John knows that Mary came, and if Mary did not come then John knows that Mary did not come," where one notices, and this is the point, that the indirect question has been totally eliminated. Hintikka does not discuss indirect questions embedded with such verbs as "wonder" or "depend," saying only that "such questions will not be discussed here" (Hintikka, 1978, p. 285). But as others, such as Karttunen (1977, p. 9), have said, it seems extremely unlikely that the approach is sufficiently generalizable so as to give us a way of treating all embeddings of the same indirect questions alike.

Note in particular that we are not successful enough if we give an imperative-epistemic treatment of direct questions which does not also solve the problem of how they behave when embedded in non-epistemic ways, for the following conversation makes perfectly good sense.

John: *Did Mary come?*
Peter: I couldn't care less *whether Mary came.*
Rebecca: But who cooks depends on *whether Mary came.*

We shall not have succeeded in our treatment of questions unless we can give an account of this conversation which is based on assuming identical or equivalent meanings for the direct and the two indirect questions. Even Wachowicz (1978), in the midst of a spirited defense of the Aqvist-Hintikka reduction (Section 5 below), appears to agree, for she says that "it is unclear how it could follow from the epistemic operator that verbs such as *matter* can take indirect questions" (p. 158). Wachowicz goes on to label "not obvious" which property of indirect questions makes them compatible with "matter," "depend," and the like; my candidate is clear: all verbs which take indirect questions, whether epistemic or nonepistemic—or even nonpsychological—recognize a more or less clearly envisioned range of alternatives. And *that* is what is semantically associated with indirect questions (see Section 6), with the following qualification: sometimes alternatives are a lot less clear than they are more clear, as when we are bewildered. Baier (1976), who has properly drawn attention to such cases, points out we may well use "ever" as a suffix to signal such a state, as in "wherever can Mary be?" In these cases, however, it seems to me we signal our concern with alternatives even when we are not in a position to bring a single one to mind.

The case for the thesis that indirect questions are one and all associated with alternatives is strengthened by considering indirect deliberative questions ("What to wear") and indirect how-to questions of skill ("how to tie a square knot"); these, too, invariably have at the very least a flavor of alternatives—in these cases, presumably not propositions—up for consideration.

5. *REDUCTION THESIS*

It is well clearly to note that the *Reduction thesis* is not the same as the Equivalence thesis. According to the latter, direct and indirect questions have equivalent meaning, while according to the Reduction thesis, a direct question has a meaning equivalent to some declarative or perhaps imperative which contains an indirect question as a part. The following are the candidates which I have seen proposed as "reductions" of the direct question, "did Mary come?"

(a) I ask you whether Mary came.
(b) Tell me whether Mary came.
(c) Bring it about that I know whether Mary came.

Karttunen (1977) and Harris (1978) prefer the reduction (a), perhaps because—unlike (b) and (c)—(a) is a declarative. Bennett (1979) offers an argument against this reduction, which I rehearsed in Belnap (1982) and so will not repeat here. But is seems crucial to notice that reduction (a) is by no means aptly characterized as a reduction of questions to declaratives, for the indirect question "whether Mary came" is explicitly left behind. In fact, there is an interplay here between the Equivalence thesis and the Reduction thesis. A conclusion of Harris (1978) is that "the question turns out to be not a primitive major category of language or grammar" (p. 33), his argument being that he has succeeded in making good on reduction (a): "interrogative forms [are] transformationally derivable from non-interrogative *ask whether* forms" (p. 33). The mistake, as indicated by the Equivalence thesis, is to suppose that "ask whether" declaratives do not contain questions. Let me note in addition that, as Karttunen (1977) writes, (a) really comes to "I ask you *to tell me* whether Mary came," and so contains not only an embedded interrogative, but one which is embedded in an (embeddable form of an) imperative which itself is embedded in the declarative. (Conclusion left to reader; see Hausser, 1976, p. 9, for help.)

The reduction (b) is mentioned in passing in Wachowicz (1978—see also Belnap, 1969, and Lewis & Lewis, 1975). I have not been able to find any strong arguments against the proposed reduction (b), and, indeed, recommend using it as a heuristic when thinking about direct questions; but I think we ought not be in a hurry to give it a flat-out endorsement, if only because of examples in which the direct question is embedded under a verb like "wonder": "John wondered, did Mary come?" For even if *perhaps* wondering can be unpacked as "asking oneself," it does seem extravagant to take wondering as "requesting oneself to tell oneself"—it's just too much. (Lewis & Lewis, 1975, p. 51, make the same or a similar point.)

The matter can stand a little more discussion. One motive for the reduction (a) is very likely a hope that its success would allow "truth-conditional semantics" to solve more of the problems of semantic theory than it otherwise appears able to do. I believe such a hope is frustrated by the facts, at least if one agrees with me that the principal problem which truth-conditional semantics has solved in the case of declaratives is precisely the embedding problem. That is, in the case of declaratives one can see how their truth conditions play a role in explaining their contribution to the wholes formed by embedding them in larger contexts. But consider Lewis (1972), according to which "did Mary come?" is said to have the same meaning—though not the same effects in use—as (a), taken as a straight self-description;[12] and in particular the two are said to have the same truth conditions (pp. 209–210). Apart from the qualification of the last paragraph, I am not interested in arguing whether or not this claim holds; suppose it does. The point that needs making is that as far as I can see, quite unlike the case of declaratives, the truth-conditions laid on interrogatives give no explanatory help whatsoever when it comes to embedding them in larger contexts, so that the analogy with the declaratives is nil. For example, it seems to me a datum that the truth conditions of (a) have no explanatory role at all in determining the contribution of "whether Mary came" to "whether Mary came depends on where she prefers to be." In fact, it even seems to be possible that, explanations aside, the truth value of "whether Mary came depends on where she prefers to be" is wholly independent of the truth conditions of (a); but one would need a fully articulated semantics to judge whether or not some trick is possible, since one can at least distantly imagine a semantical account which would permit extracting the propositions corresponding to "Mary came" and "Mary didn't come" from the set of worlds in which you are supposed to tell me whether Mary came. For this reason, I stop the dialectic with the conjecture that such a trick would have no explanatory point or force.

Lewis (1972) himself does not offer a fully truth-conditional account, since his "meanings" are intensionally decorated trees (pp. 182–186). What then of *his* proposal to identify the meaning of "did Mary come?" with that of (a) (p. 208)? In the first place, this plan obviously conflicts with the Equivalence thesis, for (a) would have the same tree (meaning) as "whether Mary came," so that the tree for "whether Mary came" would have itself as a proper part—impossible.[13] But, even apart from this formalistic point, it seems worth observing that the only part of the Lewis tree for "did Mary come?" (namely, the tree for (a)) that is useful for any embedding is the tree for the contained indirect question, "whether Mary came" itself. You might just as well throw away the rest. For example, given "John knows *whether Mary came,*" it would not do at all to consider instead "John knows (that) *I ask you whether Mary came.*"

The dialectic might proceed one more step. Lewis might say, "I only want to give *direct* questions the 'I ask you' treatment; I'd be happy to give

[12] Lewis and Lewis (1975) propose the variant "you are supposed to tell me whether Mary came."

[13] Lewis avoids this trap by departing from the independent meaning thesis: the indirect question in the reductum does not appear at any node, "tell whether" being gobbled up into a single verb (p. 209). The difficulties of departing from the Independent meaning thesis in this particular way will be evident to anyone who has condidered the number of complexity of forms of indirect questions which will have (I suppose) to be individually tied to "tell"—and separately (?) to the various other embedding verbs.

indirect questions any tree you like. Then I can have my truth conditions for direct questions while still buying your Independent meaning thesis and even your Equivalence thesis, since you can easily see that I can recover the meaning (tree) of direct questions from indirect, and vice versa, just by adding or deleting 'I ask you' from a tree." I think all that is true; but I must say it seems to be to be so easy as to cast doubt on the fruitfulness of the Lewis account of "meaning." It seems to me to come to little more than noticing that direct and indirect questions come in grammatically recognizable pairs; in particular, the strategy is totally independent of the *particular* proposal to tack on "I ask you." Any words would have done.

The reduction (c), which was recommended by Aqvist (1965) and endorsed by Hintikka (1976 and elsewhere), can be seen to be flatly wrong.[14] It may be that an unembedded direct question is always a request, and it may also be that it has an epistemic flavor about it, but it is nevertheless obvious that the suggestion fails. The case of test- or schoolroom-questions and rhetorical questions is often mentioned, but there are endless others. The prosecutor, in putting a question to the witness, is not making a request that the witness see to it that the prosecutor knows the answer to some question. In fact, the prosecutor may well be aware that the witness is a liar, totally untrustworthy. The suitor with "will you marry me?" is not asking to be put in some epistemic state (but note that the reduction to "tell me if you will marry me" survives handsomely, as does the similar reduction—perhaps to "tell the jury"—in the case of the prosecutor's question). But an even deeper trouble with the reduction (c) is this: there are many ways to bring it about that someone is in the epistemic state of knowing the answer to a certain question which are not at the same time ways of satisfying the request which that question makes. If James says to Bill, "did Mary come?" and Bill gets Sally to answer James's question, then he has brought it about that James is in the right epistemic state all right, but without answering his question, without telling him whether Mary came, and without satisfying the request made by James's question.

Furthermore, as the case of the prosecutor shows, things can go the other way: your direct question put to somebody believed to be untrustworthy can be satisfied without satisfaction of the request to bring it about that you are in a certain knowledge state. So the requests made by "did Mary come?" and (c) are simply not the same; the reduction fails.[15]

---

[14] The richest critique of which I know is that of Harrah (1980, 1981b); there is no point I make here not implicit or explicit there. See also Harrah (1981a) for some general considerations regarding the Reduction thesis, including some interesting symmetries. The failure of the reduction (c) was ably argued somewhat earlier by Lewis and Lewis (1975, pp. 48-50). An incisive criticism of the entire performatory program is to be found in Gazdar (1977).

[15] The entire point will have been missed by one whose mind wanders to the task of laying out an epistemic account of the scene in the courtroom. That is of course an interesting thing to do; but it is not to be confused with the provision of an account of the semantics of the interrogatives the prosecutor employed in asking his questions.

Though Lang (1978) does not explicitly endorse the reduction (c), he does explicitly argue that to ask a question is to make an epistemic request. His principal argument seems to be this: considering "when was Churchill born, or don't you know?", Lang argues that since the "don't you know" tag has point here, the questioner must be "interested in the answer epistemically." I think that's probably true, even though I am not sure exactly what it means. It certainly does *not* mean that the questioner does not want an answer unless the respondent knows the answer: it makes perfectly good sense to follow up with "if you don't know, then use what you do know to answer the question to the best of your ability; and if nothing you know is relevant to the question, then guess." All of this is consistent with "epistemic interest" conceived vaguely.

Lang also says that the "only consequences [hearing the true answer] can have in the context of the question-answer relationship are epistemic ones" (p. 308). Even to the extent that this is true, however, it is clear that the epistemic consequences are seldom "knowledge." When I ask which way to a restaurant in a foreign city, I expect and get sincere help, the best that is available, but seldom "knowledge." When I ask my doctor what is wrong with me, there is indeed an epistemic transaction, but neither before nor after the transaction does either of us "know." Furthermore, there are quite other sorts of "consequences" of answers to questions, such as to the answers to "will you marry me?" (hardly an epistemic fishing expedition) or "how many beans in the jar?" (the true answer to which wins the bicycle). But, in a way, these are red herrings; my chief point is that, even when in fact the questioner is asking with an eye to improving his epistemic state, it remains unlikely that he is requesting "knowledge."[16]

In Belnap (1969), I suggested that although questions might sometimes be taken as epistemic requests, they might also be taken as "linguistic requests," having in mind the "tell me whether Mary came" version of "did Mary come?", and thinking of the former as unpacking into "either tell me that Mary came or tell me that Mary did not come." Lang (p. 308) replies that it is "something akin to an empty exercise to set up an elaborate and magnificent system of various kinds of questions and answers, the former of which have no other function but to elicit a linguistic response and the latter of which have no other purpose but to satisfy that linguistic request." I did not speak with sufficient clarity, for I did not intend a suggestion as silly as all that. I should have mentioned my silent assumption that at least the standard considerations apply, so that for me to ask you to "tell" me

[16] It would be wrong to conclude that there is no further point in pursuing the Åqvist-Hintikka "reduction" of questions (whether direct or indirect) to imperative-epistemic form. It may well be that the style of "reduction" they propose can shed light on questions; and indeed, given the Distribution thesis (Part II), that, for any indirect question IQ, to know IQ is to know some answer to the question as to IQ, this *must* be so.

something is normally for me to ask you to "tell" it to me *sincerely* rather than at random. A similar point has been made about all kinds of imperatives: for me to ask you to shut the door is not to ask you to do it in any random way you like, but in accordance with background rules and procedures which govern such things (you are not—normally—to shut it by throwing a leopard at it). Lewis and Lewis (1975, p. 50), and Aqvist (1980) want you to tell me *truly* (as opposed to my candidate, "sincerely"), but our suggestions are not quite parallel. For them the truth is part of succeeding in the task assigned, where I intended the "sincerity"-rider (like the "don't throw a leopard at it"-rider) to be a background constraint which goes without saying.

6. ANSWERHOOD THESIS

Having established as I think the Equivalence thesis and the Independent meaning thesis, I should next like to argue for the *Answerhood thesis:* the semantic representation of a question, whether direct or indirect, should give us enough information so as to determine which propositions count as possible answers to it. (By "possible answer"I mean a proposition such as might be expressed by what Belnap and Steel (1976) call a "direct answer," an answer with neither too much nor too little information; in particular, not just any helpful "response" counts as an answer. A "possible answer" is *precisely* the sort of thing the question calls for.)

I do not say that the representation should *be* the set of its possible answers as in Hamblin (1973—see also Stahl, 1969, and Belnap & Steel, 1976). I do not even wish to insist that the semantic representations of questions be *equivalent* to the set of their possible answers, which would presumably be the technical counterpart of the dictum of Hamblin (1958) that to understand a question is to understand what counts as an answer thereto. The thesis only states that possible answerhood must be recoverable from the semantic representation, without forbidding that the representation contain extra information as well. (For example, there might be in the representation enough type information to allow Tichy (1978) or Hausser and Zaefferer (1978—see Sections 8.9 and 8.10 below) to recover their short answers.)

But, it might be objected, indirect questions don't have answers. The answerhood thesis could bypass such a superficial objection, based on uninteresting niceties of English grammar, by asking instead that the theory supply answers for the direct question which is invariably paired with the given indirect question. But there is another device which may persuade those who rely on grammatical niceties. Baker (1968) points out that (almost) any indirect question can follow "the question as to," a feature of English which allows theoreticians to say some of the things they would like to say in ordinary if awkward English. I want to suggest the appositeness of answers to indirect questions by exhibiting that one can, in at least a wide variety of contexts, substitute "what the answer is to the question as to IQ" in place of an indirect question IQ. Three examples:

- John learned *whether Mary came;* John learned *what the answer was to the question as to whether Mary came.*
- *Whether Mary came* depended on where she preferred to be; *what the answer was to the question as to whether Mary came* depended on where she preferred to be.
- John wondered *whether Mary came;* John wondered *what the answer was to the question as to whether Mary came.*

Even though I offer only three cases, I think that, if you will try various other constructions which take indirect questions, you will generally find that the substitution works.[17]

Support for the Answerhood thesis comes from observing that thinking of indirect questions in terms of their answers sheds at least some light on every single verb which embeds indirect questions. I work from the list in Karttunen (1977—there is an even larger list in Baker, 1968), taking one example of each of Karttunen's nine types.[18]

(a) To recall whether Mary came is surely to recall the answer to that question. (b) To learn whether Mary came is to learn the answer to that question. (c) To inform Jack whether Mary came is to inform Jack of the answer to that question. (d) To have decided whether Mary came, not in the sense to have judged, but in the sense to have been the one who decided, is to have been the one who decided (in the sense of having made the case rather than in the sense of having judged) which answer to the question was to be the true one. (e) To guess whether Mary came is to guess which possible answer is the true one. (f) To be certain whether Mary came is to be certain which possible answer is the true one. (g) To wonder whether Mary came is to wander among the possible answers to that question. (h) To care whether Mary came is to care which possible answer is the true one. (i) For

---

[17] But not always; for example, Bolinger (1978, p. 94) notes that English does not like "if" after prepositions, so that "the question as to if Mary came" won't wash. Furthermore, one would hardly want to *repeat* the substitution having done it once; but much more important, the particular substitution suggested above depends on there being a *unique* true answer to support the "the" in "the answer," a presupposition which sometimes fails, as I have often urged; see e.g. Belnap (1982, p. 172). Still, I wonder if the possibility of the substitution might not be a limited test for the indirect question/relative clause distinction.

[18] Both Karttunen and Baker omit any verbs of *change;* what time Mary arrived varied from day to day; changing where the thermostat points changes how hot the room is; what the temperature is is rising (?); whether Mary came never altered. Perhaps these go with the *depend* group. (I remark that the examples are somewhat awkward inasmuch as an only limited consideration suggests that change verbs prefer "concealed questions" in the sense of Baker (1968). In this case, the questioned example above would be just "the temperature is rising.")

whether Mary came to depend on where she prefers to be is for which possible answer is the true one to depend on where she prefers to be.[19]

I conclude that we cannot have an adequate theory of how indirect questions embed unless (Answerhood thesis) their semantic representations determine for each indirect question the set of its possible answers.

7. *OBJECTIONS TO THE ANSWERHOOD THESIS*

There is an objection to the Answerhood thesis which I would like to state, though I am far from satisfied that I know how to persuade you that the objection is misguided. The objection arises, I think, from concentration on direct questions to the exclusion (in violation of the Equivalence thesis) of their indirect cousins. If, in these circumstances, one thinks about the role of direct questions in actual discourse, it is easy to persuade oneself that there is not much to say about which responses are "helpful" and which not "helpful"—especially if one takes "who"-questions as paradigmatic (see Belnap, 1982, pp. 193–97). One can easily conclude on this basis that the concept of answerhood is entirely too unstable to admit of a useful theory. The road now forks: one can accordingly despair of an interesting and tidy theory of questions at the semantic—rather than speech-act—level. Or one can, like Groenendijk and Stokhof (1981) give a careful semantics while explicitly abstaining from giving a theory of answers.

There seems little point in arguing with those who take the first fork.[20] The best argument I know is the long one, namely, that studies presupposing that the question-answerhood relation is in fact reasonably definite and reasonably stable have led to useful and insightful research, much of it cited in the course of this paper. Perhaps it is worth noting that the presupposition involves distinguishing answers in some not very technical sense from other responses—in about the sense, say, in which we can allow that the witness, in saying "ask your old lady," *responded* to the prosecutor's question but did not *answer* it. (The judge might of course well say that the witness's "answer"—rather than "response"—was unresponsive, because although as I think the distinction is there in English to be marked, it is certainly not true that English consistently marks it with the terminology I have recommended.)

---

[19] Perhaps the "worst case" is that of verbs strongly connoting attention, such as "consider"; but even then to say that "to consider whether Mary came" comes to "to consider what the answer is to the question as to whether Mary came" seems (not wholly accurate but) helpful.

[20] In a pioneering paper, Prior and Prior (1955) conclude in a somewhat different context that "erotetic logic would seem to be antisymbolic," a remark turned into an irony by the substantial and wholesome influence of this wonderful paper on later symbolic developments.

With regard to the second fork, I also haven't much to say. I do believe that those who have addressed themselves explicitly to the matter of answerhood have by so much provided better theories; but I am hardly interested in laying down a commandment to the effect that everyone should get involved in answerhood. I do believe this: every interesting extant semantic theory of questions implicitly contains a theory of answerhood; it is there to find, even when the author of the theory has not provided it; for if it does not provide a theory of answers, it isn't sufficiently interesting.[21]

It is not clear to me whether or not Åqvist (1972) is prepared to object to the Answerhood thesis. He does say that it is of "utmost importance" that "logical relations among questions such as implication, equivalence, and the like can be studied without our having to specify *in advance* the so-called question-answer relationship" (p. 29; emphasis mine), but the Answerhood thesis as framed above does not say the specification has to be "in advance," so that this in itself is not an objection. Åqvist says further, though, that the *reason* it is so important to take an approach not based on the question-answer relation is that "it turns out that in quite a few cases this relationship simply lacks the clarity and determinacy so often attributed to it." My reply on behalf of the Answerhood thesis is this: if a case does not permit a reasonably clear and determinate account of answerhood, then that very case will not permit a reasonably clear and determinate and *interesting* account of (say) equivalence between questions via their semantics.[22]

8. *ANSWERHOOD TEST*

Not every theoretician of natural language questions attempts to give a semantic representation of questions in terms of "possible worlds" semantics. But let us concentrate on those who do; a consequence of the Answerhood thesis is that their task is not complete unless they give us a way of teasing out of their representation the possible propositional answers to the questions they analyze. I shall put to this *Answerhood test* every treatment of which I know that smacks of enough formality so as to permit the possibility of a definite verdict.

8.1 *Cohen*

Though Prior and Prior (1955) cite some antecedents, the first formal account of questions of which I know is that of Cohen (1929); and even though this work was done long before the advent of rich intensional logics, still, I want to say that Cohen passes the Answerhood test: for him "a question... is simply a propositional function," and "an answer to a question must be

---

[21] See footnote 7.

[22] Of course two hopelessly confused questions could be seen to be syntactic variants of each other—but then the semantic theory would not come into play in an interesting way.

simply a proposition which is a value of the given propositional function" (pp. 353–54). Cohen was doubtless confused about use and mention and all that jazz, but this early piece is still worth reading. It is in each case of a contemporary intensional apparatus easy to see how to cater to Cohen's proposal; for example, in Montague's IL, it would amount to translating "who kissed Mary?" into *"Lx(x* kissed *m),"* or perhaps the semantically equivalent *"Lx(^ (x* kissed *m))";* and its answers would be propositions of the sort expressed by sentences such as "(*j* kissed *m*)." More fully, with *Q = Lx(x* kissed *m)* for instance, and with *"p"* ranging over propositions, the family answers is *Lp*V*x[p = ^ (Q(x))].*

The construction in the language of Tichy (1978—see Section 8.9 below) would be *"Lx(Lw(x* kissed *m)w),"* with answers *"Lx((j* kissed *m)w)."* The family of answers would therefore be *Lp* V *x[p = Lw((x* kissed *m)w)].* All is clear.

8.2 *Harrah and the Erotetic Logicians: Stahl, Kubinski, Belnap and Steel*

It was Harrah (1961, 1963) who first caused me to believe in the Answerhood thesis; Harrah gives explicit definitions of "direct answer" for the types of interrogatives he treats. So of course do Belnap and Steel (1976); and Stahl (1969), last in an interesting series of essays, flat out defines a question as a set of sentences (its answers). Kubinski (1960, 1968) is equally careful to tell us what counts as an answer to his various interrogative forms. But the Answerhood test is not appropriate in any of these cases, for they deal with the *logic* of questions, a normative matter, whereas what we are now involved in is the descriptive task of getting the semantics of English right. Nevertheless, this general line of development, pushed further in important ways by Harrah (1969, 1975, 1978—he calls it the "abstract interrogative" approach)—must be kept firmly in mind by anyone who cares to describe the semantics of English questions; surely that is the lesson of the history of trying to get straight on the semantics of declaratives (no man broke with logic but what he ain't smart).[23]

8.3 *Åqvist and Hintikka*

Åqvist (1972) does not discuss answers, but Åqvist (1965) has an extended discussion of the matter. The treatment, however, only relates answerhood

---

[23] This is doubtless the appropriate point at which to draw a comparison and a contrast: in the *normative* theory of questions (their logic) I have urged that we devise systems of questions and answers that render effective the property of being a sentence that is a (direct) answer to a given interrogative (another sentence). I have urged the normative importance of this requirement, although I have been persuaded by Harrah that not *all* questions need satisfy it. And I also think the effectivity requirement should be kept in mind when considering natural language questions; but effectively is *not* part of the Answerhood thesis, which speaks not of sentences but of propositions. The reason is topic: I am in this paper considering semantics, not grammar, so that effectivity is simply out of place.

to the syntactic form of the representation of an interrogative in imperative-epistemic logic; we are given no way to go from the *semantic* representation to a notion of answerhood.

Hintikka (1978) though titled "Answers to Questions," suffers from the same defect, nor is it removed in his longer treatment (1976).[24] There is also a certain lack of generality about the Hintikka account of answerhood (and of Åqvist's as well): at the technical level, we are given only a question-by-question account. On the informal side, we are indeed given a general account: by a "potential conclusive (or full) answers...I mean an answer which would satisfy the questioner *if* it were true and *if* he were in a position to trust the answer...". Since one had almost been expecting that an answer would be something such that, if the questioner knew it, then he would be in the epistemic state which Hintikka calls the "desideratum" of the question, this sounds suspiciously as if it relys on a "justified true belief" account of knowledge, and is therefore open to the usual Gettier counterexamples. In any event, because of having to have a questioner, the Hintikka recipe is unable to help us with indirect questions embedded in non-epistemic contexts. Or indeed even nonstandard epistemic ones; on the Hintikka approach, to guess in what year Columbus discovered America appears to constitute a different act depending on whether the guess is made in response to a standard question on the one hand or a "test" question on the other hand or a "test" question on the other (or, just for the hell of it, on yet the other). Still, and this is important, for particular cases we can sometimes tell what Hintikka would count as an answer with sufficient accuracy so as to permit comparisons with other treatments.

8.4 Lewis

The brief proposal of Lewis (1972), as is stands, fails the test. There is doubtless enough information in his trees to permit *us* to generate any number of theories of answers; but the trees themselves do not tell us how to pick among them. In other words, we cannot extract Lewis's theory of answers from Lewis's theory of questions.

8.5 Hamblin

In 1958, Hamblin proposed that "knowing what counts as an answer is equivalent to knowing the question," so that it is hardly surprising that his 1973 formal development in a Montague context should pass the Answerhood test with flying colors: questions are represented as denoting sets of

[24] Hintikka himself might not take this as a criticism, because he has a principled practice of intertwining semantics with syntactic forms; for instance, the range of his variables depends contextually on the sequence of intensional operators in the scope of which they lie. My own view is that it is much too early to abandon the hope of keeping syntax and semantics clear of each other.

propositions, and we are told that those propositions are its possible answers (p. 48, p. 52).

8.6 *Hull*

Another example of a researcher not working with intensional languages is Hull (1975).[25] Hull limits himself to considering singular questions such as "which student left early?", which are reconstructed as "(WH, $student_x$, x left early)," and which request "the identification of the unique member of the extension of ['student'] for which the sentence ['x left early'] is true."[26] Short answers can be proper nouns, free pronouns, or definite descriptions ("the"-phrases), and a question plus a short answer is what is given a truth value, including the "zero" value if the short answer does not denote an entity that (in the example at hand) is a student.

I am not sure that Hull gives us enough information to tell what his theory of propositional answers is; it depends on what the "zero" value comes to. I am nevertheless going to go ahead and impute to him what anyhow I think is an interesting theory. The basis of the imputation is that the avowed purpose of the "zero" value is to distinguish the status of the response "Fred" to "Which student left early?" in the two cases when (a) Fred is, and when (b) Fred isn't a student. I want to impute to Hull the view that, in both cases, the response "Fred" is code for "Fred is the student who left early," but that in the second case, when Fred isn't a student, *the response is not an answer.* If this is correct, then it will not do to saddle Hull with the task of telling me outright which propositions he counts as possible answers to "which students left early?", for these will vary with the circumstances. That is, I am imputing to Hull, *not* a theory of propositions which sometimes take a third "zero" value, but instead a theory of normal two-valued propositions which are sometimes possible answers and sometimes not: the "zero" value of a question-answer pair is a signal not of absence of truth value, but of absence of answerhood. Hull therefore has on my account a world-relative instead of world-independent notion of possible answer.[27]

If this imputation is correct, then I claim that Hull, near enough, passes the Answerhood test. From the semantic representation of a question as a pair of intensions (one for the noun phrase such as "student," one for the body of the question such as "left early") I can recover at each world which

---

[25] This builds on Keenan and Hull (1973), which it reviews, but which I have not myself consulted.

[26] The limitation is said to be "for the purposes of exposition," but I suspect the formal apparatus would need much development were it not for this limitation.

[27] The *normative* utility of such a concept is explored in Belnap (1972) and in Belnap and Steel (1976). Let me note here Thomason's conviction (and indeed mine) that the concept is *descriptively* useful as well. Belnap (1982), pp. 173-74), has a few words on the topic.

entities fall among the students, and for each of these I can form the (Rusellian) proposition that that entity is the student who left early; such are the possible answers to the question *at that world*—some of them true, some false, as is appropriate for a set of *possible* answers.[28]

8.7 *Karttunen*

The seminal 1977 paper of Karttunen, conceived in the Montague framework, almost explicitly passes the test. For him, questions "denote sets that only contain the propositions that jointly constitute a true and complete answer" (p. 11). Evidently from such a set we can construct their generalized conjunction, each of which (as the possible world varies) is a possible answer in the sense at issue. Karttunen and Peters (1980) does not deviate from this framework principle.

8.8 *Bennett and Belnap and Thomason*

Bennett (1977) (which does not pass the test) was later abandoned by Bennett (1979), which explicitly passes the test. There, the denotation of question at an index is explicitly represented as a set of "open" propositions,[29] each of which is to count as a true and complete answer to the question at that index. We recover all possible answers by letting the indexes vary. Belnap (1982) employs precisely the same format, as does Thomason (1977), so that the same applies.

8.9 *Tichy*

Like Hausser (Section 8.10 below), Tichy (1978) takes short answers as fundamental (pp. 278–279), but instead of permitting Montague "terms" such as "the neighbor's son," he permits only what others call "rigid designators" in the construction of which there is no room for variation with indexes.[30] And, like Groenendijk and Stokhof (Section 8.12 below)—and of course antedating them—he represents questions as functions having indexes as their arguments, but instead of mapping the indexes into propositions, Tichy maps them into the type of what he takes to be their short answers.

---

[28] I have omitted the further complexities of Hull's answer involving definite descriptions for expository reasons; for from a Montague point of view it is just a matter of struggling with a few lambdas to generate for a world all propositions having the form (so to speak) of "the so and so is the student who left early," where "the so and so is a student" is true at that world.

[29] Open propositions are mappings from sequences of individuals into propositions—constant mappings when the translation of the question has no free variables. They were introduced for technical (and important) reasons concerned with quantification into indirect questions; the same reasons, I think, which led Groenendijk and Stockhof (1981), section 3.8, to introduce all those abstracts.

[30] This is accurate only for the usual questions of lowest type; higher type questions could doubtless inquire after what Tichy calls "offices."

Thus, "each question. . .is an intension, a function from possible worlds to objects of a certain type," and to answer such a question "is simply to cite a definite object of [that type]" (p. 278). Tichy himself does not seem to care about answers qua full statements, and pokes some fun at those that do (pp. 278–79), but there is nevertheless no difficulty teasing out of his representation of a question the family of propositions which count as its possible answers, for Tichy tells us that "the answer is *right* if the cited object is the value of (the question) at the actual world." Taking the second "is" seriously, we can see that, for Tichy, (propositional) answers are identity propositions. Let Q be a function on possible worlds representing a question, let A represent a short answer, let w range over possible worlds, and permit me to use L for lambda. Then a possible answer to Q would be a proposition $Lw(Qw = A)$. (The connections with Groenendijk and Stockhof are striking.)

8.10 Hausser and Zaefferer

Hausser and Zaefferer (1978—see also Hausser, 1976) pass the test. In their work, the emphasis is on "minimal" or "nonredundant" answers such as "Bill" as an answer to "who dates Mary?", rather than "redundant" answers such as "Bill dates Mary." Belnap (1982), noting that Hamblin (1958) calls "Bill" a "coded" answer, proposed to mark the distinction by the terminology "short/long" so as not to prejudice the issue of which answers are fundamental. In these terms, the Answerhood thesis is concerning itself with long answers, or rather with the propositions they express. Now Hausser and Zaefferer advance a notion which, so far as I know, was first put forth by Cohen (1929); a question is, or is something like, a "propositional function." There is, however, an important difference: the arguments for their "propositional functions" are not individuals, but instead the intentions of "terms" in the Montague sense such as not only "Bill" but also "everyone at the party," "nobody," and "someone."[31] Adverbial questions such as "where was John going?" would be "propositional functions" defined with arguments having the type of the sense of the appropriate adverbs such as "to the store." The representation clearly passes the Answerhood test, since the propositions which count as answers to a given question can easily be recovered from its semantic representation as just those propositions which result from applying the representing propositional function to any argument (e.g., term-sense) in its range. (Hausser and Zaefferer don't quite say this explicitly, but it seems to be the only possible reading derivable from their discussion around p. 347. For example, "a fish" is counted as an answer, even though contradictory, to "whom does Mary kiss?", since it is of the right type.)

---

[31] Egli (1973) earlier advances the same thought—and in addition considers a substitutional account (pp. 368-369). It is also present in Halvorsen (1978).

8.11 Boer

I think Boer (1978) passes the Answerhood test, but I have not been able wholly to see through his particular forest of lambdas and brackets.[32] I begin by observing that Boer himself, in spite of offering a fully formal account of 'who' and 'whether' in the style of Cresswell (1973), says not a single technical word about answers, so that this is a case in which it is left to the reader to judge for himself if the Answerhood test is passed. Boer tells us the kind of meaning indirect questions have: they are properties of properties of propositions (pp. 318-319—just as all nominals in the Cresswell scheme intend properties of properties), but he does not tell us at the intuitive level just what properties of properties of propositions we are dealing with. He does appear to say that indirect questions always arise from matrices, and I think it is pretty clear from his rules (p. 317) and his examples (p. 319) that he wants to say that to know (tell, etc.) the answer to an indirect question based on a certain matrix is to know (tell, etc.) the conjunction of all its true instances.[33] If what I've said so far is true, then it would appear that Boer would agree with Karttunen (1977): in any world, the true answer to an indirect question based on a certain matrix would be the conjunction of its true instances; and the possible answers would be obtained by letting the world vary. This imputation is made more likely by Boer's comment that the result of working through one of his examples "is basically the same as that yielded by Karttunen" (p. 319).

8.12 Groenendijk and Stokhof

Groenendijk and Stokhof (1980, 1981) are reluctant to claim for their theory that it passes the Answerhood test. The representation they give to indirect questions is clear: a function from indexes into propositions; and they do say that "it seems to make a good deal of sense to say that the proposition denoted by a question at a given index, is the proposition expressed by a true answer to that question at that index" (1981, p. 59)—similar remarks are made in the 1980 paper (p. 13, p. 32). But at the same time, they seem to worry that the concept of answerhood requires relativization to "situations" (1980, p. 10) or "cases" (1981, p. 59). Groenendijk and Stokhof do not explicitly consider the possibility that a theory of questions

---

[32] This is a complaint about the finitude of time rather than a complaint about Boer: all of us who present theories of questions that can handle more than the most trivial cases and that do not arm-wave the technical aspects are bound to enmesh the reader in a symbolic briar patch.

[33] This recipe "ignores use/mention niceties," as Boer says, it ignores the special features of "who" that Boer claims, including "teleological relativity," it ignores questions about whether "know" ("tell," etc.) distributes over conjunction, and it ignores a clause requiring that the matrix has a true instance; but do let all that go in the interest of getting through the forest unharmed.

and answers must leave room for *both* a situation-relativized *and* an unrelativized notion of answerhood; such is indeed my view, and in fact I further believe that one cannot make much sense out of the relativized versions without making reference to the unrelativized concepts. Belnap and Steel (1976, sec. 3) following in the path of Harrah (1961), elaborate a number of these concepts. Furthermore, I do not know how to interpret much of what Groenendijk and Stokhof do in their substantial and interesting papers without interpreting the proposition that a question denotes (at an index) as the proposition which (at that index) is a complete and true answer to the question. Given this interpretation, and in spite of their reluctance to make the claim themselves, I say that Groenendijk and Stokhof pass the Answerhood test, because we can clearly recover the full set of possible answers to one of their questions by letting the index vary. (There has just appeared a splendid book, Groenenedijk and Stokhof 1984, that includes the aforementioned papers and much more besides—including some reflections on issues raised by [the preprint of] this paper.)

8.13 Summary

The Answerhood test must be easy, because everyone who has done extended work on questions in natural language in a possible worlds framework passes the test—even those who to some extent or other reject the Answerhood thesis.

This is a matter of considerable importance for at least the following reasons.

- Given a framework for representing questions semantically, we can use its theory of answers to evaluate the framework itself in more or less independence of its treatment of particular questions forms in natural language. For example, Karttunen's style of representation forbids questions with inconsistent answers, while Hamblin's allows them.
- Given two or more different representations of questions, we can compare how they treat the same natural language question form by comparing, not directly their semantic representation of the question, but what they count as answers to the question. If they agree on answerhood, we might not wish to pause overlong to choose between them (but of course we might). If they do not agree on answerhood, we might be able to clarify the nature of the disagreement while staying away from meaty questions as to which is "the best" representation.
- We may find that what a researcher takes as an answer to a certain natural language question is influenced by what sorts of answers his framework permits. To run the same example again, it might be interesting to hear from Hamblin the empirical conjecture that no natural language questions can have inconsistent answers, since his framework

allows the reverse position; but it would be much less interesting to hear the view from Karttunen, since his framework permits him to take no other position.

I shall take up such matters in Part II.[34]

REFERENCES

Åqvist, L. (1965). *A new approach to the logical theory of interrogatives.* Uppsala: Almqvist & Wiksell. Republished as *A new approach to the logical theory of interrogatives: analysis and formalization.* Tuebingen: Tuebinger Beitrage zur Linguistik 65, Verlag Gunter Narr, 1975.

Åqvist, L. (1974). On the analysis and logic of questions. In R. E. Olson & A. M. Paul (Eds.) *Contemporary philosophy in Scandinavia* (pp. 27–39). Baltimore and London: Johns Hopkins University Press.

Åqvist, L. (1980). *On the 'tell me truly' approach to the analysis of interrogatives.* Preprint.

Baier, A. (1976). Realizing what's what. *Philosophical Quarterly, 26.*

Baker, C. L. (1969). Indirect questions in English. (Doctoral dissertation, University of Illinois, Urbana, 1968). Ann Arbor, MI: University Microfilms.

Baker, C. L. (1970). Notes on the description of English questions: The role of an abstract question morpheme. *Foundations of Language, 6,* 197–217.

Barwise, J. (1981). Scenes and other situations. *The Journal of Philosophy, 78,* 369–397.

Barwise, J., & Perry, J. (1981). Situation and attitude. *The Journal of Philosophy, 78.*

Barwise, J., & Perry, J. (1983). *Situation semantics.* Cambridge, MA: MIT Press.

Belnap, N. D., Jr. (1969). Åqvist's corrections-accumulating question-sequences. In J. W. Davis & D. J. Hockney (Eds.), *Philosophical logic* (pp. 122–134). Dordrecht: Reidel.

Belnap, N. D., Jr. (1972). S-P interrogatives. *Journal of Philosophical Logic, 1,* 331–346.

Belnap, N. D., Jr. (1982). Questions and answers in Montague grammar. In S. Peters & E. Saarinen (Eds.), *Processes, beliefs, and questions* (pp. 165–198). Dordrecht: Reidel.

Belnap, N. D., Jr., & Steel, T. B., Jr. (1976). *The logic of questions and answers.* New Haven & London: Yale University Press.

Bennett, M. (1977). A response to Karttunen on questions. *Linguistics and Philosophy, 1,* 279–300.

Bennett, M. (1979). *Questions in Montague grammar.* Bloomington, IN: Indiana Linguistics Club.

Boer, S. E. (1978). 'Who' and 'whether': Towards a theory of indirect question clauses. *Linguistics and Philosophy, 2,* 397–345.

Bolinger, D. (1978). Yes-no questions are not alternative questions. In H. Hiz (Ed.), *Questions* (pp. 87–105). Dordrecht: Reidel. Synthese Language Library, volume 1.

Cohen, F. S. (1929). What is a question. *Monist, 39,* 350–364.

Cresswell, M. (1973). *Logics and languages.* London: Methuen.

Egli, U. (1973). Semantische repraesentation der Frage. *Dialectica, 27,* 363–370.

Gazdar, G. (1977). *Implicature, presupposition, and logical form.* Unpublished manuscript, Indiana University Linguistics Club [mimeographed].

Groenendijk, J., & Stokhof, M. (1980). *On the semantic analysis of wh-complements.* Unpublished manuscript, University of Amsterdam.

Groenendijk, J., & Stokhof, M. (1981). *Semantic analysis of wh-complements.* Unpublished manuscript, University of Amsterdam.

[34] I am thoroughly indebted to R. Thomason.

Groenendijk, J., & Stokhof, M. (1984). *Studies on the semantics of questions and the pragmatics of answers.* Doctoral dissertation, University of Amsterdam.

Grover, D. L., Camp, J. L., Jr., & Belnap, N. D., Jr. (1975). *A prosentential theory of truth. Philosophical Studies, 27,* 73–125.

Halvorsen, P.-K. (1978). *The syntax and semantics of cleft constructions.* Unpublished doctoral dissertation, University of Texas at Austin.

Hamblin, C. L. (1958). Questions. *Australasian Journal of Philosophy, 36,* 159–168.

Hamblin, C. L. (1973). Questions in Montague English. *Foundations of Language, 10,* 41–53. Also in B. Partee (Ed.) *Montague Grammar,* New York, 1976,

Harrah, D. (1961). A logic of questions and answers. *Philosophy of Science, 28,* 40–46.

Harrah, D. (1963). *Communication: A logical model.* Cambridge, MA: MIT Press.

Harrah, D. (1969). On completeness in the logic of questions. *American Philosophical Quarterly, 6,* 158–164.

Harrah, D. (1975). A system for erotetic sentences. In A. R. Anderson et al (Eds.), *The logical enterprise* (pp. 235–245). New Haven: Yale University Press.

Harrah, D. (1978). Hintikka's theory of questions. In R. J. Bogdan (Ed.) *Jaakko Hintikka,* Profiles series). Dordrecht & Boston: Reidel.

Harrah, D. (1980). *On reducing questions to commands.* Preprint, University of California at Riverside.

Harrah, D. (1981a). The semantics of question sets. In D. Krallmann & G. Stickel (Eds.), *Zur Theorie der Frage.* Tubingen: Gunter Narr Verlag.

Harrah, D. (1981b). A logic for all questions? *Philosophia, 10.*

Harrah, D. (1984). The logic of questions. In D. Gabby & F. Guenthner (Eds.), *Handbook of philosophical logic* (pp. 715–764). Dordrecht: Reidel.

Harris, Z. (1978). The interrogative in a syntactic framework. In H. Hiz (Ed.), *Questions* (pp. 1–35). Dordrecht: Reidel. Synthese Language Library, volume 1.

Hausser, R. R. (1976). *The logic of questions and answers.* Preprint.

Hausser, R. R., & Zaefferer, D. (1978). Questions and answers in a context-dependent Montague grammar. In F. Guenthner & S. J. Schmidt (Eds.), *Formal semantics and programmatics for natural languages.* Dordrecht: Reidel.

Hintikka, J. (1976). The semantics of questions and the questions of semantics. [Special issue]. *Acta Philosophica Fennica, 28.* Amsterdam: North-Holland.

Hintikka, J. (1978). Answers to questions. In H. Hiz (Ed.), *Questions* (pp. 279–300). Dordrecht: Reidel: Synthese Language Library, volume 1.

Hiz, H. (1962). Questions and answers. *Journal of Philosophy, 59,* 253–265.

Hull, R. D. (1975). A semantics for superficial and embedded questions in natural language. In E. Keenan (Ed.), *Formal semantics of natural language.* Cambridge, MA: Cambridge University Press.

Karttunen, L. (1977). Syntax and semantics of questions. *Linguistics and philosophy.* Reprinted in H. Hiz (Ed.), *Questions* (pp. 165–210). Dordrecht: D. Reidel, 1978.

Karttunen, L., & Peters, S. (1980). Interrogative quantifiers. In C. Rohrer (Ed.), *Time, tense and quantifiers.* Tubingen.

Katz, J. J., & Postal, P. (1964). *An integrated theory of linguistic descriptions.* Cambridge, MA: MIT Press.

Keenan, E. L., & Hull, R. D. (1973). The logical presuppositions of questions and answers. In D. Franck & J. Petoefi (Eds.), *Praesuppositionen in philosophie und linguistics* (pp. 441–466). Frankfurt: Athenaeum.

Kubinski, T. (1960). An essay in the logic of questions. *Atti del XII. Congr. Intern. di Filosofia, 5,* 315. Firenze.

Kubinski, T. (1968). The logic of questions. In Raymond Klibansky (Ed.), *Contemporary philosophy-La philosophie contemporaine 1* (pp. 185–189). Florence: La Nuova Italia Editrice.

Lang, R. (1978). Questions as epistemic requests. In H. Hiz (Ed.), *Questions* (pp. 301–318). Dordrecht: Reidel. Synthese Language Library, volume 1.

Lewis, D. (1972). General semantics. In D. Davidson & G. Harman (Eds.), *Semantics of natural language* (pp. 169–218). Dordrecht: Reidel.

Lewis, D., & Lewis, S. R. (1975). Review of *Contemporary philosophy in Scandinavia,* R. Olson & A. Paul (Eds.). *Theoria, 61,* 39–60.

Mayo, B. (1956). Deliberative questions: A criticism. *Analysis, 16,* 58–63.

Montague, R. (1974). *Formal philosophy* (Edited by R. Thomason.) New Haven & London: Yale University Press.

Prior, A., & Prior, M. (1955). Erotetic logic. *Philosophical review, 64,* 43–59.

Stahl, G. (1969). The effectivity of questions. *Nous, 3,* 211–218.

Thomason, R. (1977). *Multiple quantification, questions, and Bach-Peters sentences; some preliminary notes.* Unpublished manuscript [Xeroxed holograph].

Tichy, P. (1978). Questions, answers and logic. *American Philosophical Quarterly, 15,* 275–284.

Vendler, Z. (1972). On what one knows. In *Res cogitans* (Chapter 5). Ithaca, NY: Cornell University Press.

Wachowicz, K. (1978). Q-morpheme hypothesis. In H. Hiz (Ed.), *Questions* (pp. 151–163). Dordrecht: Reidel. Synthese Language Library, volume 1.

Wheatley, J. (1955) Deliberative questions. *Analysis, 15,* 49–60.

Author Index

Italics indicate bibliographic citations.

Subject Index

R

S

T

V

W